Stories Fr

Newfoundland & Labrador,
and The Isles of Notre Dame

Perched on Canada's eastern shores, and battered by the relentless North Atlantic, Newfoundland & Labrador was known as "Britain's Oldest Colony, and is now Canada's newest Province. Shaped by the sea, and centuries of wresting a living from its uncertain bounty, its people have developed a culture at once unique and enduring.

One of Newfoundland's most storeyed and historic locales is The Isles of Notre Dame District (The Isles). Located off the Island's rocky northeast coast, the Isles are home to many historic settlements such as Twillingate, Moreton's Harbour, Herring Neck, Fogo, Joe Batt's Arm, Tilting and Change Islands.

This work takes a look at the Isles' rich past, along with that of the larger entity of which it is part, through an overview history and geography of the Province, along with historical vignettes culled from the *Twillingate Sun* newspaper and a variety of other sources.

DAVID J. CLARKE is a graduate of Memorial University of Newfoundland's Doctoral programme in history. Dr. Clarke has taught students at Memorial and the University of Liverpool, and has worked on historical projects at both Fogo and Twillingate. Dr. Clarke is the author of a number of works of local history. He currently makes his home in Twillingate.

Cover image: Twilight at Back Harbour, Twillingate (Author's photo)

Author's portrait : Ms. Brenda Shand

Stories From These Shores

Newfoundland & Labrador and The Isles of Notre Dame

David J. Clarke

2014

For Brenda,
who loves the Isles

Contents

PREFACE & ACKNOWLEDGEMENTS i

Section 1 ~ Newfoundland & Labrador

1 Newfoundland & Labrador ~ Geography 1
2 Prehistory and Beyond ~ Native Peoples 13
3 Britain's Oldest Colony ~ Newfoundland 26
4 The Big Land ~ Labrador 52

Section 2 ~ On This Day

5 On This Day... 67

Section 3 ~ A Few More Sunspots

6 Poetry Corner 169
7 Royalty 202
8 "Local & General" 233
9 "High Spirits" ~ Alcohol and Temperance 355
10 "Memorials of the Past" ~ Early Religion on the Isles 399

Section 4 ~ An Isles Miscellany

11 Stories From These Shores 419

ENDNOTES 445

PHOTO AND ILLUSTRATION CREDITS 460

BIBLIOGRAPHY 471

By the Same Author

A History of the Isles – Twillingate, New World Island, Fogo Island and Change Islands

St. Peter's Anglican Church, Twillingate. From the Nineteenth to the Twenty-First Centuries (Prepared for the St. Peter's Anglican Church Women)

Sunspots. Best of the Twillingate Sun, 1880-1953, Vol. I

Sunspots. Best of the Twillingate Sun, 1880-1953, Vol. II

An Historical Directory of the Isles – Twillingate, New World Island, Fogo Island and Change Islands

The Isles Historical Dictionary. Featuring Twillingate, New World Island, Fogo Island and Change Islands, Newfoundland & Labrador

All titles available at: www.amazon.ca and www.amazon.com

Preface and Acknowledgements

Unfinished business. That should probably be a theme of this book, since it was unfinished business that got me to thinking about the work you now see before you. When I produced the first edition of my *History of the Isles* in 2011 I intended to introduce it with an overview history and geography of Newfoundland & Labrador. In the end, the work was weighty enough that I had to trim some material, including this general look at the Province. Since then, I've always hoped it would see the light of day, and felt now was as good a time as any.

By the same token, my research into the *Twillingate Sun* newspaper produced two volumes of the book *Sunspots*, a retrospective on the best articles appearing in its pages over some seventy years from 1880 to 1953. With the publication of *Sunspots II*, I thought that I was done with the old paper, except as a general reference; I had already produced some 900 pages of material relating to it! Still, to keep the volumes down to a manageable size I had cut a few topic areas, much as I'd done with my overview history of the Province. That got me wondering if there might be enough interesting material remaining in those pages to merit another look. To my surprise, I found that there was more than enough, if not for a stand-alone book, at least to merit inclusion as a major section of a larger work.

A third element of "unfinished business" was an idea that had been on my mind for some time; a "this day in history" type of look at the old Isles of Notre Dame District ("The Isles," as I refer to the area), starting with 1 January and running through 31 December.

These three elements form the bulk of the book you see before you. As is the case with my previous works, it mainly deals with the Isles, found on Newfoundland's northeast coast, and comprised of Change Islands, Fogo, New World Island and Twillingate. This area was home to aboriginal peoples for thousands of years, and saw the arrival of its first permanent European settlers some time in the first half of the eighteenth century. Towns like Fogo, Twillingate and Moreton's Harbour have long been a storeyed part of Newfoundland history, most famously through their inclusion in the song *All Around the Circle*. A century ago, Twillingate and Fogo were considered some of the most important of Newfoundland's fishing outports, with the former town often referred to as "The Capital of the North." In this era other towns of the region, such as Change Islands, were themselves home to important merchant house branches, and busy centres of the codfish export trade that sustained all Isles communities.

This book is divided into four distinct sections, starting with the overview geography/history of the Province of Newfoundland & Labrador, mentioned above. Were I to produce such an overview today I might change a few things, giving more space to some items and less to others, or even revise my thoughts on certain matters altogether. However, I've decided to present what is essentially the same work as would have appeared at the beginning of *A History of the Isles* in 2011, had there been room to include it.[1] I hope that it will serve as a brief, if interesting, introduction to what was once known as "Britain's Oldest Colony," and now "Canada's Newest Province" (At this point I must once again extend my thanks to retired Senator Hon. William Rompkey, who reviewed my chapter on Labrador. Senator Rompkey has had a longstanding connection to Labrador, and I could have found few people better qualified to give me their thoughts on this vignette).

Section Two, titled "On This Day...," was also detailed previously. It briefly recounts events in the history of Newfoundland & Labrador, and on the Isles, from John Cabot's arrival in 1497, through to Confederation in 1949, arranged according to the day of the year on which each happened (Events relative to the entire Province, or which happened outside the Isles, are given in bold). I should note that, especially in our early history, certain events may have only been recorded in retrospect, leading to discrepancies. In some cases different chroniclers have given more than one date for the same occurrence, and

---

[1]

My sections on the modern Innu, Inuit and Mi'Kmaq people, for example, may have been superceded, to some extent, by developments since 2011.

In the modern context I use the name Newfoundland & Labrador for the Province, but normally refer to the place simply as "Newfoundland" when discussing past events, as this was the official name by which the Colony/Dominion was always known.

the reader will note some instances where I have recorded a different date for the same event. I have tried, where possible, to find multiple references for the various events in this section, but it is still possible that some incorrect dates have slipped through.

Section Three is essentially a third volume featuring the best of the *Twillingate Sun*. Three Chapters that I was unable to include in my earlier *Sunspots* books, featuring local poetry, items relating to the British Royal family, and the temperance movement, form a major portion of the section. Its longest part is a Chapter derived from the paper's "Local and General" column.[2] In producing my earlier books, I mostly stayed away from these items, as they are normally short pieces, rather than the longer articles I was focussed on. In reviewing them, I found a plethora of interesting and informative material which, while not lengthy, offers some genuine insight into how our ancestors lived in the late nineteenth and early twentieth centuries. The Chapter titled "Memorials of the Past" is an interesting serial on early religion at Twillingate, which had escaped my attention on the first go around.

Four of the five Chapters in this section follow the format I used for the *Sunspots* volumes, usually preceded by my own commentary (given in italics), and referenced through Chapter Notes at the end of the book. The "Local and General" Chapter is a little different. Since most articles are short, I have preceded each one with the issue in which it appeared in square brackets. All pieces are arranged by subject area, according to the year in which such were published. The subject areas are quite varied, but generally reflect those matters of most importance to readers of the day – hopefully their descendants as well – nautical matters, churches and religion, education, law and healthcare, to name but a few. All of these short articles have been allowed to "tell the tale" entirely on their own, without any introduction from the author or explanatory end notes.

As was the case in both volumes of *Sunspots*, I have made some adjustments in spelling and punctuation, plus corrected obvious typos,

---

[2] I have mostly used material from the early years of the Sun in this Chapter, particularly the tenure of its first Editor, Jabez P. Thompson (1857-1938).

for the sake of clarity. Other than that, I have been careful to leave the words of the editors and contributors just as they were written so that we can have a better idea of just what concerned the people of the Isles all those decades ago.

Section Four consists of a number of historical vignettes, or "Stories From These Shores," which I thought would appeal to modern readers, offering insight into our collective past, colourful characters, or a good historical mystery. The final selection in this Chapter is very special to me, it being a piece written by my Great-Uncle, Ernest George Clarke (1917-67), some fifty years ago. Uncle Ern was the last Editor of the *Twillingate Sun*, and anyone who has had the pleasure of reading his editorials from 1947-53 cannot but be impressed with his writing style. He was often encouraged by family members to produce his memoirs, and might well have done so, had he not passed away at the age of fifty. Very little of his writing remains, outside of what can be found in the Sun, so I take great pleasure in being able to introduce another work of his to the reading public.

....

In addition to Senator Rompkey, there are a number of persons whom I would like to thank for their assistance (It goes without saying that any mistakes in this work must be charged to my account, not theirs).

Mr. John Nelson, of the State of Alaska, whose Maternal ancestry extends back to Change Islands, was good enough to provide me with a copy of an old manuscript recounting the construction and development of the Methodist (United) Church on Change Islands. Collected by his Mother during a visit to Change Islands in the 1960s, it forms the basis for one of the vignettes in Section Four. Many thanks for sharing this, and agreeing that I might use it, John!

I also wish to send out kudos to my friend Jim Troke of Twillingate, who served alongside me on a local heritage committee, for letting me use his photograph of, and insights into, the "Wheelbarrow Man," Joey Strickland, featured in Chapter Eleven. He also drew my attention to the *Twillingate Sun* stories featuring Richard Wrey (See, Chapter Nine). Much appreciated, Jim!

Likewise, Alfred Manuel, another historical committee colleague and friend, was good enough to recite from memory a verse about Mr. Strickland, as well as sharing other anecdotes about the Wheelbarrow Man. Thanks a million, Alf!

During the preparation of my most recent book, *The Isles Historical Dictionary*, Cottlesville native Milt Anstey provided me with extensive commentary and information, as well as some corrections. Like Jim, Milt is a prodigious and conscientious collector of local genealogy & history. His input made the Dictionary a much stronger book than it might have been otherwise, and his influence extends to this work as well. I am grateful for your generosity and thoroughness, Milt!

I thank Ms. Jenny Oliver of the Poole Museum Society for granting me permission to adapt her blog story on the schooner *Mountaineer* for this book, and to David Watkins of the Poole History Centre for his permission to use their image of the vessel to accompany the piece. I am also grateful to Ms. Oliver for passing along links to additional source material on the subject.

My Cousin Peter Clarke has my gratitude as well, for agreeing that I might use his Father's short story, "Be it Ever So Humble...," as one of the articles in Section Four.

A big thank you goes out to Mr. Donald Linfield of Durrell for sharing his experiences as Captain and crewman on-board the schooner *Grace Boehner*, and to his Daughter Peggy for her help in passing along additional information on the vessel.

Stories From These Shores follows in the tradition of most of my other books in being illustrated throughout (Many readers will have seen some of the pictures previously, though a goodly number have never appeared in any of my books). I would like to express my appreciation to all persons who have consented to let me use their photographs in this or previous works. I once again send special thanks to Mr. Don Loveridge, formerly of Twillingate, who has provided access to his large collection of family photographs (Most taken by his Uncle, John "Jack" Loveridge) for all of my books. Without the inclusion of this large and invaluable set of photographs, it is doubtful I could have presented my histories as illustrated editions (Don, and all those who have provided photographs, are credited at the end of the book).

As always, there are many people who have not assisted me directly in preparing this book, but who have nevertheless been a source of inspiration. My Mother and Father, Margaret and John Clarke, have believed in me since I was a toddler, and continue to do so today. I could not have asked for better Parents or greater supporters. The same is true of my Grandmother, Barbara (Fifield) Burton. Though they did not live to see any of my books in print, my other Grandparents, Leonard and Dulcie Clarke, and Stewart Burton, are never far from my thoughts; they always inspire me with their memory. I send my love to you all!

My other relatives and friends, though too many to list individually, have also been firm supporters of my writing, whether through their encouragement and belief in me, and/or supporting my efforts by buying my books. It is humbling to have such a loyal "fan base," and I thank each and every one of you from the bottom of my heart!

Last, but certainly not least, I send along love and thanks to my Girlfriend, Brenda Shand, to whom this book is dedicated. Brenda has supported me unconditionally since the day we met. She is a daily inspiration in all my endeavours.

Section 1 ~
Newfoundland & Labrador.
A Brief History and Geography

1
Newfoundland & Labrador ~ Geography

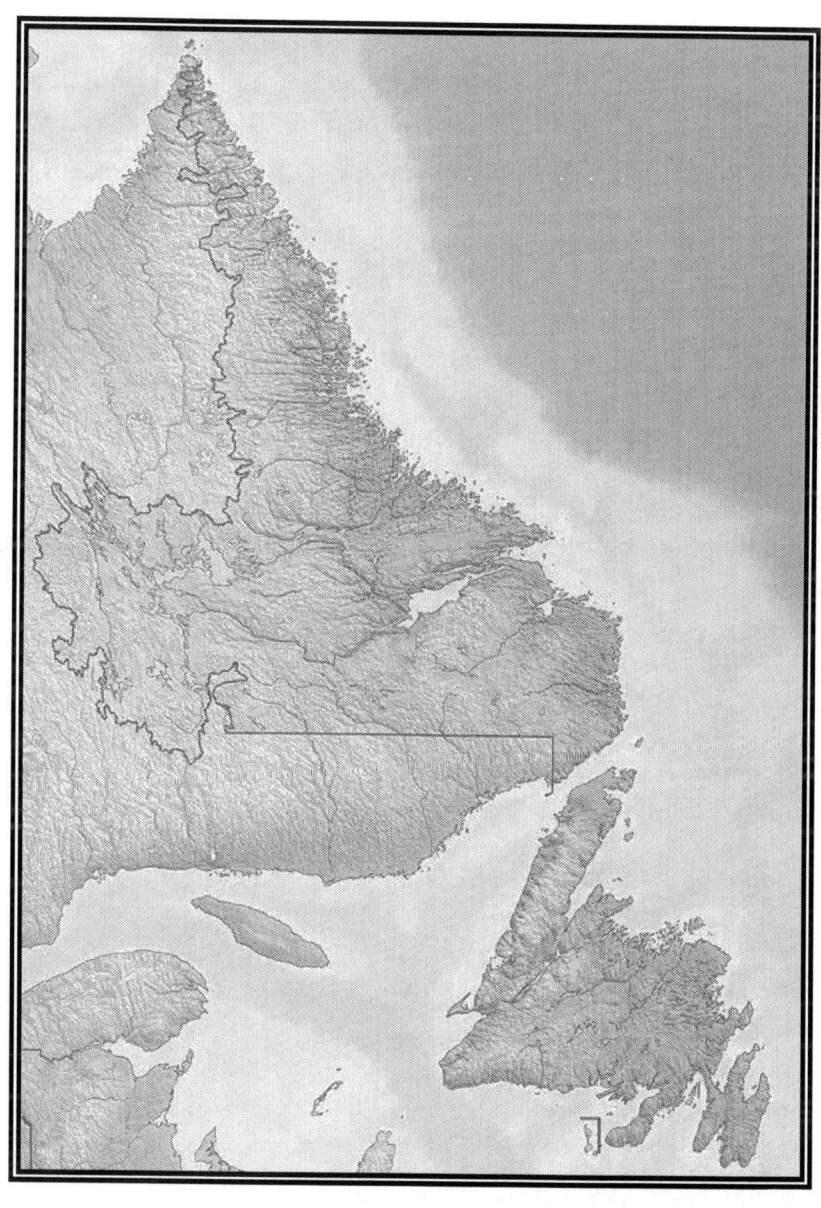

Newfoundland & Labrador

DAVID J. CLARKE

Newfoundland sits off the east coast of North America and the Gulf of St. Lawrence. It is located from about forty-six to sixty degrees north latitude, and fifty-two to sixty-eight degrees west longitude. Newfoundland is about the size of the American State of New York and, together with its larger mainland Sister Labrador, make up the Canadian Province of Newfoundland & Labrador. The Island of Newfoundland is North America's most easterly point, and is closer to much of western Europe than western Canada. Labrador is part of the North American landmass, and forms the east coast of the Ungava Peninsula. Labrador is bounded by the Labrador Sea, the Atlantic Ocean, and the Province of Quebec. To the west of Labrador's northern extremity, Cape Chidley, lies the large Ungava Bay, with Gray Strait due north. With less than 600,000 inhabitants, Newfoundland & Labrador is Canada's next to least populous Province – only Prince Edward Island has less people. Even with its low population, the Province has a larger land area than the other three Atlantic Canadian Provinces put together. Its total area is approximately 405,000 square kilometres – about 111,000 for Newfoundland and 294,000 for Labrador. With their jagged coastlines of bays, inlets and fjords, Newfoundland & Labrador combined have almost 18,000 kilometres of coastline. The two portions of the Province are separated by the Strait of Belle Isle, just twenty kilometres wide in some places. Visitors to Newfoundland – who don't arrive by air – cross over the Cabot Strait from Nova Scotia, which is about 145 kilometres wide.

....

The Grand Banks

Both portions of the Province present an amazing spectacle for residents and tourists alike, but one of its most important geographic features cannot even be seen. Although not open to direct observation, this feature still greatly affects Newfoundland & Labrador. In fact, it has done so for all of our recorded history. Europeans were first attracted to the Island of Newfoundland, and later to Labrador, by its incredibly rich marine resources. Most who wrote the first accounts of the region's history were here either to prosecute, protect, or control, the fishery. All of Newfoundland's waters teem (or teemed) with fish, but no region was more productive than the Grand Banks.

Dorymen fishing the Grand Banks, late-nineteenth century

Lying off Newfoundland's southeast coast, the Banks are a marine feature not just of national, but world, significance. The banks run approximately 800 km east to west and are about 320 km wide. During the last glaciation much of the Grand Banks were covered in ice, and shallower portions to the southeast were dry land – the average depth today is only ninety-one metres. Once the ice melted the Banks were acted upon by the meeting of the cold, southbound Labrador Current and its opposite number, the warm Gulf Stream. Plankton was concentrated in the area, feeding a variety of prey species including capelin, which fed larger fauna like cod, haddock, seals and whales. Some of these last giants bypassed the intermediate species altogether, feeding directly on plankton. Over thousands of years the Grand Banks developed into one of the most abundant zones of marine life on the globe. Until about 1500 AD the Banks' fish, crustaceans and mammals lived out their life cycles in peace, undisturbed by human fishers. It is true that by 1500 Native peoples had long inhabited the Island of Newfoundland, but their fishery was mainly inshore and not on a scale to alter the delicate natural balance. For the last 500 years the undersea ecosystems of all Newfoundland & Labrador's Banks have been under assault by increasingly sophisticated fishing techniques. As of 1977 Canada extended its fishery jurisdiction from three to 200 miles, although two areas, the "Nose" and "Tail" of the Grand Banks, are still in international waters. With proper management this renewable but precarious resource will remain for many future generations, although the failure of the stocks to fully rebuild to pre-1990s levels after a 1992 fishing moratorium continues to worry scientists and others.[1]

As bountiful as the seas have been with fish, this is not the Banks' only treasure. The top layers of sediment on the Grand Banks are recent, and scoured by the action of south-bound icebergs. Farther down in the Earth are ancient layers of rock filled with decayed plant life left by rising and falling ocean levels over millions of years. This residue left another resource, potentially more valuable to the people of Newfoundland & Labrador, if not so long-lasting, than the fishery – oil and natural gas. Projects to develop these fossil fuels, like the most well known, Hibernia, have great potential for the Province, and Canada in general. Sub-sea oil and gas usage occurs over a number of stages, each involving a potential threat to marine life on the Grand Banks. Like the fishery, hydrocarbons offer great promise, but must be managed with care if future residents of the region are to enjoy both the economic and natural advantages of Newfoundland & Labrador.

Of course, oil and gas were of no concern to the first inhabitants of Newfoundland & Labrador, but many features of their geography, flora, and fauna, proved attractive lures. Although not always inviting weather-wise, Newfoundland & Labrador have their advantages, both on land and at sea.

....

Stories From These Shores

Mountains, Rivers & More...

The largely triangular island of Newfoundland has no really lofty mountain ranges. The highest are the Long-Range Mountains, running along the island's west coast, which reach heights of 800 metres. Labrador's Torngat Mountain Range – from the Inuktituk word *torngak* or "spirit" – is more impressive. Stretching along the coast from Port Manvers to Cape Chidley, the range reaches heights of over 1,600 metres above sea level, perhaps fitting for a region known as "The Big Land." Equally impressive are the Torngat's age. Dated at about 3.7 billion years old, the rocks there are among the oldest known on the planet. The same applies to Labrador generally, which forms the eastern edge of the Canadian Shield.

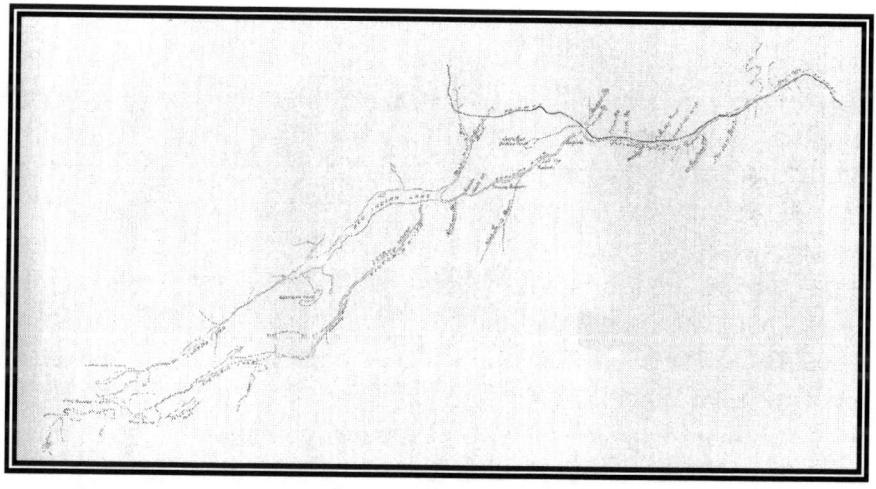

The Exploits River and its connected lakes and streams

Newfoundland & Labrador have many thousands of lakes, rivers and streams, although they are generally small. Newfoundland's longest river is the Exploits which begins in the southeast, flowing into Red Indian Lake and finally out to the coast at Notre Dame Bay. This entire watershed became an important refuge for Newfoundland's Native Beothuk people from the late-1700s. The Gander, Terra Nova and Humber are other important Newfoundland rivers. Today such bodies of water aid in utilizing the land's other natural resources. The Corner Brook paper mill in western Newfoundland used hydroelectric power channelled from Grand and Deer Lakes. The rivers were also used to carry timber to the mill. In Labrador, the Churchill River and Falls are the site of one of North America's most important hydroelectric developments. The Churchill, along with rivers such as the Naskaupi and the Goose, flow into Lake Melville. At 3,069 square kilometres Lake Melville, actually an extension of Hamilton Inlet, is the largest natural lake in the Province.

....

A World of Ice

Both the Island of Newfoundland, and Labrador, are beautiful but harsh places to live. Almost every year the northeast coast of Newfoundland is surrounded by a great sheet of pack ice that drifts south from the Arctic in Spring as the far north heats up. In the early Summer the ice pack melts away, but it is usually followed by much larger chunks of ice that break off the polar ice caps, also drifting south until they melt. These chunks are the famous icebergs that many tourists flock to the Island to see each year – Twillingate is one of the best locations to view them. The icebergs are pieces of the great northern glaciers, and retain the features of such. Glaciers form over thousands of years as ice and snow gradually accumulate in mostly frozen regions of the globe. Some icebergs have blue streaks which form when portions of glaciers melt and re-freeze. They may also contain dust, dirt and volcanic ash from their original surroundings. Up to 40,000 bergs may break away from Arctic glaciers each year, spending from three months to two years in Baffin Bay before drifting south. Newfoundland's icebergs are less than ten percent of all the bergs produced, and are carried south by the East Greenland Current. By the time they reach Newfoundland waters only about ten percent of the original iceberg is left – the rest having melted away or broken off. Many vessels have been damaged or sunk over the years by collisions with icebergs. The most famous case is that of RMS *Titanic* in April, 1912. The icebergs also pose a potential threat to the

Grand Banks' oil and gas infrastructure. To deal with this hazzard the International Ice Patrol was formed. So, although a great draw for tourists, icebergs are in the negative column as far as marine navigation is concerned.

....

Living in the Fog – Weather

Channel, c.1900

The Province's weather has often been problematic for its inhabitants. Even though most of Newfoundland is farther south than Great Britain, and on about the same latitude as the French wine growing regions, the island has a less hospitable climate than either Country, especially from October to April. The harsh nature of Newfoundland's environment is due in part to the effects of the cold Labrador Current running past its shores, and the Spring ice flows which the current brings. The southeast corner of Newfoundland, the Avalon Peninsula, is renowned for its fogs, and popular tradition says that on the Island you can experience all four seasons in a single day. One portion of western Newfoundland, near Channel Port aux Basques, is called Wreckhouse, as its winds of up to 180 kilometres per hour have blown trains off the tracks. Labrador is even more unforgiving. Its climate is probably the coldest for its latitude of any area of the globe! In the north temperatures can fall to minus sixty degrees Celsius in Winter. Ice blocks many of its bays from December to May, while snow covers the land even longer, from September to June.

....

Shaped by the Past

Newfoundland & Labrador isn't just affected by the ice of today. Our modern geography is, at least partially, a result of an ice age about 25,000 years ago. Glacial episodes such as this didn't just affect the Grand Banks, but the very land itself. During this time the Earth's climate cooled and a giant glacier of ice started moving southward from the polar regions, covering first Labrador, then Newfoundland (except the Codroy Valley region). For the next 10,000 years northeastern North America was covered by an ice field up to a kilometre thick. As the glacier grew it scraped and tore up the land, filling in lakes and killing all the life in them. Then, around 14,000 years ago, the Earth's climate changed again and the huge glacier started melting away. 4,000 years later the Island was finally ice-free. By then the great ice mass had profoundly changed the face of the land. Most of the soil was already scraped away by the glacier, and the runoff when it melted took away even more. The thin soil ensured that Newfoundland would never be a very productive farming region, apart from a few areas like the Codroy Valley, with about 148 growing days a year. Any people who wanted to settle the Island would have to look for other ways to survive. Fortunately for them, Newfoundland did make up for its lack of good farming soil with other resources, especially prolific fisheries.

Codroy Valley, pre-1936

....

Flora

As the Earth warmed following the ice age, vegetation like grass and evergreen trees started returning to Newfoundland & Labrador. The decaying plants then added to the soil, making it a little more fertile. The Island was once home to stands of white pine, mostly cut down by early settlers. Newfoundland is still about forty percent forest, common species being spruce, fir, birch, aspen, poplar and ash. The Island also has many flowering plants. One interesting plant is the Province's emblem, the Pitcher Plant, a carnivorous species that feeds on the insects it catches in its specialized leaves. This is a very useful adaptation, as the pitcher plant lives in the acid bogs that cover fifteen percent of Newfoundland's surface, and these bogs are generally lacking in nutrients. Other common plant varieties include saprophytes like Indian pipe and coralroot that feed off decaying food matter, plus daisies, the late-blooming goldenrods, fireweed, and many others. A number of berry types are also at home in Newfoundland, including blueberries, raspberries, blackberries (crowberries) and bakeapples (or cloudberries, which prefer boggy environments). Much of Labrador's north and its coast are treeless, with only small Arctic plant varieties like mosses and lichens. There are a few hardy flowering plant species, and the south and west are forested, mainly with black spruce and balsam fir.

The pitcher plant (Sarracenia purpurea)

....

...And Fauna

After the return of its flora, ancient Newfoundland & Labrador saw the return of fauna – first insects, then birds, fish, and finally larger creatures that (on the Island) probably crossed over the Strait of Belle Isle on Winter ice. Newfoundland's forests teem with wildlife, but there are only about half the species found in mainland Canada. Wolves were once numerous, but are now extinct on the Island.[2] There are beaver, red fox and lynx, along with caribou and black bear, Newfoundland's largest native animals. Even larger, and thriving on the Island, are moose, introduced around the turn of the twentieth century. Coyotes are another recent, and not especially welcome, arrival. Marine mammals include seals and several whale species such as humpbacks. On rare occasions walrus have even been known to stray south from their usual far northern refuges. Sea life is generally abundant, with many varieties of shellfish, crustaceans and fish. One of Newfoundland's most interesting marine visitors is the mysterious giant squid, which grows to over eighteen metres long, including its tentacles. The late Dr. Fred Aldrich, of Newfoundland's Memorial University, spent many years studying the elusive invertebrate, dissecting eleven giant squid from 1964 to 1982. A number of the creatures have been found washed ashore in Newfoundland, including two in 2004. Well-known Notre Dame Bay native George Earle even composed a poem recounting how in the late-1920s a Fogo Island man made such a find! Among the fish found off Newfoundland are sharks. The world's second-largest species, the harmless, plankton-feeding Basking Shark, is known to frequent our waters. Other common fish species include herring, flounder, and most important for the fishing industry, cod.

The Atlantic cod, scientific name *Gadus morhua*, has been prized by fishers for centuries. Of the ten modern families and over 200 species of codfish, almost all are native to cold waters in the Northern Hemisphere. The cod belongs to the order Gadiforms, known for their white flesh; the cod's is the whitest of all. The Atlantic cod is the largest species and has the whitest meat. The meat has virtually no fat and is almost one-fifth protein. When dried the meat's protein content is as much as four-fifths. Practically all of the codfish can be eaten, from the head to the gut to the roe (eggs). Its skin can even be cured as leather. Cod will eat almost anything, making them an easy prey to jigging, a baitless type of fishing. They are also not well equipped to outrun trawler nets. Even with Canada's east coast cod moratorium, over six million tons of gadiforms are caught each year across the globe – half of this harvest is made up of the Atlantic cod. It was the great concentration of codfish on the Grand Banks that first attracted Europeans to the area. Today cod and species such as snow crab are threatened by overfishing.

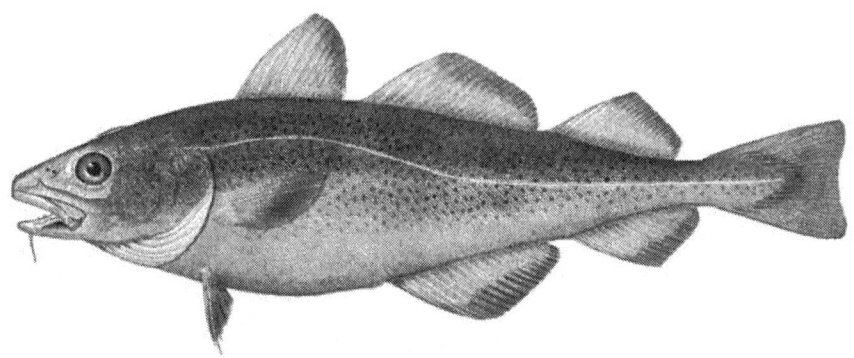

Atlantic cod (Gadus Morhua)

Like the land and the sea, Newfoundland's air is also full of life. More than 200 bird species nest in Newfoundland, including puffins, crows, murres (turres to Newfoundlanders) and gulls. Birds of prey such as eagles and owls also visit. There are no native reptiles or amphibians, save a few introduced species of frogs and toads, and the occasional leatherback turtles that cruise offshore. Labrador is home to many of the same species of birds and mammals as the Island, and its caribou herd is the world's largest. One of Labrador's most spectacular species is the great polar bear, once called water bears by residents of Newfoundland, where they occasionally strayed. For millennia these species enjoyed Newfoundland & Labrador by themselves. Then, about 9,000 years ago, another important piece of the region's faunal puzzle fell into place when the first humans settled in Labrador.

2
Prehistory and Beyond ~
Native Peoples

Europeans often talked about "discovering" North America, but they were very recent arrivals compared to the ancestors of today's First Nations peoples. Anthropologists and archaeologists are still debating exactly when, from where, and how, the first people reached the Americas. Linguistic and biological evidence points to a place of origin in northeast Asia. These travellers may have crossed over from Asia into modern Alaska across the Bering Strait anywhere from 17,950-13,350 calendar years ago. The earlier date was around the end of the last ice age, the Late Wisconsin, when the Bering Strait was dry land. A huge ice sheet covered most of Canada, and seas were lower due to the large amount of water frozen into the glaciers. It has been theorized that an ice-free corridor existed through which early humans made their way into North America. Other recent evidence suggests that there was no ice-free passage at this time. This begs the question, how did the first people reach North America? In fact, they may have been skilled coastal mariners, making their way around the northern Pacific rim by raft or small boats.

....

The First Arrivals – The Maritime Archaic
Settlement in Newfoundland & Labrador is much more recent than for North America in general. The oldest known human habitations in the Province are found on the Labrador side of the Strait of Belle Isle. Most of these peoples' remains have been lost over time, but archaeologists have found many stone tools like spear points, knives and scrapers. A child's burial from L'Anse-Amour, Labrador is one of the oldest found in North America, dated at 7,500 years ago. Because most of this culture's sites have been found near the coast it is thought they relied heavily on marine resources such as seals, walrus, sea birds and fish, along with inland species like the caribou. We will never know what these early settlers called themselves. Originally their culture, which was spread throughout New England, Atlantic Canada and the Lower South Shore of the St. Lawrence River, was called the "Red Paint"

tradition from their use of red ochre. More recently they have been named the Maritime Archaic after their dependence on the sea's resources.

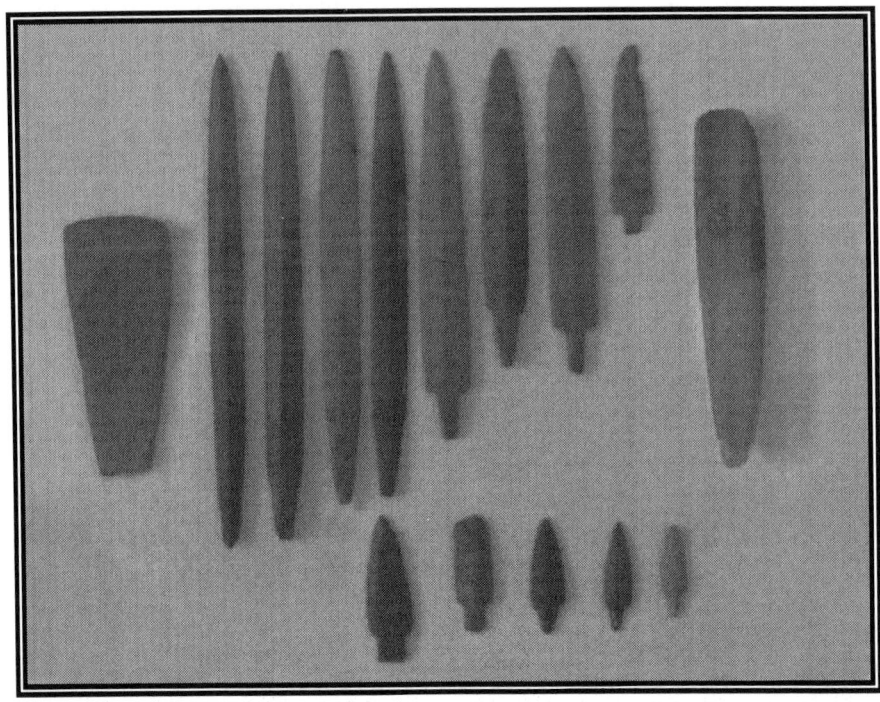

Maritime Archaic Implements (Author's photo)

The Maritime Archaic people spread out from southern Labrador about 6,000 years ago, and then to Newfoundland a thousand years later. One of the most impressive Maritime Archaic sites on the Island is a cemetery at Port au Choix on the Great Northern Peninsula. The area contains the remains of at least 100 persons buried from about 4,000 to 3,500 years ago. One notable feature of the Maritime Archaic burials is their extensive use of red ochre (Mentioned above), a tradition practised by the later Beothuk people. The numerous artifacts found with the skeletons include not only weapons and tools, but what are likely religious and magical objects. At Port au Choix the objects found weren't just made of stone, but from bone, ivory and antler as well. The use of marine creatures like whales, seals, fish and birds is clearly shown by remains found at the site. One of the most interesting Port au Choix objects is an effigy thought to represent a killer whale. We don't know exactly why it was carved, but perhaps it was used to harness the strength and power of the animal by magic. Although their numbers were probably never very large, the Maritime Archaic lived in Labrador and Newfoundland for thousands of years. Around 3,000 years ago, for reasons unknown, they either emigrated from, or became extinct, on the Island, but may have survived longer in southern Labrador. There is some evidence that the Maritime Archaic Indians could be ancestors of both the Beothuk and Innu peoples.[1]

....

Palaeo-Eskimos

Around the time the Maritime Archaic declined on the island a new race of people appeared. No one is sure what role, if any, they played in their predecessors' disappearance. The two groups might have openly made war on one another, or may have tried to avoid each other whenever possible. The people now called Palaeo-Eskimos were of a different race and spoke a different language from the Maritime Archaic. Palaeo-Eskimo culture seems to have originated in Alaska around 4,000 years Before Present (BP). In the Newfoundland & Labrador context Palaeo-Eskimo culture is generally divided into early (3,800-2,200 BP) and late (2,500-500 BP) phases. As archaeologist Ralph Pastore notes, the first phase overlaps with the second, but there is disagreement as to whether one derived from the other.

According to archaeologist James Tuck, the very first of Labrador's early Palaeo-Eskimo peoples bear a strong resemblance to Greenland's Independence I culture, while those in the period from 3,500-3,000 BP are often referred to as "Pre-Dorset." A common feature of the Palaeo-Eskimo peoples were their tool forms. They used many of the same materials to make tools for similar purposes as the Maritime Archaic, but apart from their uses, early Palaeo-Eskimo tools were very different from those of the people they replaced. Most of their remaining material is stone, as many other substances decay in Newfoundland's acidic soil. Made from a fine-grained, colourful stone, these objects are noted for their fine workmanship and small size, the second feature giving rise to the descriptive term "microblades." The two groups may have shared some of their technology, with the Eskimos giving the Indians the bow and arrow, and the toggling harpoon being passed along in the other direction.

Evidence shows that around 3,000 BP Newfoundland & Labrador experienced rapid population growth. This trend heralded the emergence of another early Palaeo-Eskimo culture, the Groswater people, named for Groswater Bay, Labrador. Pastore asserts that the Groswater tool tradition is similar enough to that of the Province's earliest Palaeo-Eskimos to assume that the new arrivals derived from the older group. In their various incarnations the early Palaeo-Eskimos inhabited the Province for about 1,600 years. Although these Palaeo-Eskimo groups occupied most of the coastline of Newfoundland & Labrador, like the Maritime Archaic before them, they eventually vanished from the archaeological record, a result, Pastore speculates, of extended periods of poor hunting.

Around the time the early Palaeo-Eskimos disappeared from Newfoundland-Labrador a new group arrived, who were possibly related to the Groswater people. This group is known to us as the Dorset, and they are considered the "late" phase of the Palaeo-Eskimo tradition. The Dorset first settled in northern Labrador around 2,500 BP, and about 500 years later in Newfoundland. They are still remembered by the modern Inuit as the *Tunit* people, making them the earliest inhabitants of the Province for whom a contemporary name survives. The Dorset occupied many parts of the Province and may have been the most widespread of all our prehistoric-peoples. The Dorset people had a variety of tools and weapons similar in usage to their predecessors, although their form was quite different. Unlike the Palaeo-Eskimos, the Dorset don't seem to have used bows and arrows, or domesticated dogs. Their hunting was also more focussed on ice-edge species like seals and walrus. The Dorset were great artists, and their soapstone carvings representing animals and humans are still admired. The Dorset people inhabited Newfoundland for around 1,000 years and then were gone, although they lived on for several hundred years more in northern Labrador.²

For part of the time Eskimo groups lived on the Island traces of Indian peoples are missing from Newfoundland's archaeological record. The Maritime Archaic may have lived on in Labrador, but no traces of them have been found from 3,500-2,000 years ago. Then, about the beginning of the Common Era, new evidence of Indian habitation can be found. It is unclear if these were totally new peoples, or if they were actually descended from the Maritime Archaic. For almost a thousand years these new Indian groups and the Dorset both inhabited the Island, and the two cultures probably had contacts with one another. Once the Dorset were gone the Indians spread more widely and were most likely ancestors of the Beothuk tribe.

....

The Beothuk

Ancestors of the Beothuk are believed to have inhabited the island of Newfoundland since at least 400 AD. A group known today as the "Little Passage" people are thought to have been the prehistoric phase of Beothuk culture. While their language is only known from a small number of word lists, some experts consider their tongue to have been part of the Algonkian family.

The Beothuk lived in small bands of fifty or less, and the total population of the group in Newfoundland may never have amounted to more than 2,000 individuals at any one time. These bands spent their Summers on the Newfoundland coast hunting species such as salmon and seals, and moving inland during the Winters. Birds and caribou also made up an important part of the Beothuk diet, with caribou skins put to a wide variety of uses.

We know very little about the Beothuk religion or belief system, although it is known that the colour red was very important to the group, with red ochre used to coat their bodies and implements.

No one is certain when Europeans first encountered the Beothuk, though it may have been when the Vikings arrived, around 1000 AD (See below). One of the first well-documented meetings between the two groups was engineered by English adventurer/colonizer, John Guy (d. circa 1629), whom we'll meet again in Chapter Three. Guy travelled to Newfoundland in 1610 with the intention of establishing a colony, and remained until 1613. During his time on the Island he located a group of Beothuk in Trinity Bay, establishing a good rapport with them.

A fanciful depiction of John Guy's meeting with the Beothuk in 1612

Sadly, this state of affairs didn't last. Many of the Europeans who followed Guy to Newfoundland weren't nearly as humane in their treatment of the Beothuk, who struck back at the invaders when they could. For the next 200 years the two groups were mutually antagonistic, with the natives refusing to trade or interact with White settlers. Over time, the band's territory became more and more restricted, first to the northeast coast, and finally the area around Red

Stories From These Shores

Indian Lake.

By the early nineteenth century Beothuk numbers appear to have dwindled considerably. It has been a truism that this was a result of their being massacred by Europeans. However, the real cause was likely more complex, a result of disease and the inability of the group to access the coastal resources on which they had depended. As of 1829 only one individual was known to be living, a woman named Shanawdithit. When she died of tuberculosis at St. John's in June of that year, many considered the group to be extinct.[3]

....

The Inuit

The most recent prehistoric arrivals in Labrador were the Thule, a people whose descendants call themselves *Inuit*. They first came from the western Arctic in the wake of a warming trend about 1,000 years ago, reaching Labrador in the thirteenth century. Unlike earlier Eskimo cultures, however, the prehistoric Inuit never colonized Newfoundland. The Thule lived off a variety of resources like whale, seal, fish, birds and land mammals. In traditional Inuit spirituality these animals were believed to have souls much like humans. The Thule Inuit practised rituals which demonstrated respect toward game species and gave thanks for the land's bounty. Without these a hunt was unlikely to be successful and the people would starve. Marine resources are still closely associated with the modern Inuit, although a number of inland groups are more dependant on caribou. Both caribou and marine mammals were hunted with harpoons, bows and arrows, and spears. The Inuit also practised the art of trapping. Although there are some women hunters in Inuit society, a division of labour has normally been practised. Men hunt and fish while women process and distribute catches among kin groups. The Thule Inuit were, and are, supremely adapted to a northern existence, aided by inventions like their boats – the *kayak* and *umiak* – plus dogsleds and snow knives.

In modern times such innovations have largely been replaced by European technology including speed-boats, snowmobiles and firearms. Still, these have all been ingeniously adapted to the Inuit way of life.

DAVID J. CLARKE

Despite living in the orbit of Europeans for over 200 years, and often being educated by Moravian Missionaries, much traditional Inuit culture is still intact. Today the Inuit, through groups like the Labrador Inuit Association (LIA) are politically active, taking an interest in issues such as environmental pollution and securing control of local natural resources for the benefit of members. In January, 2005 the LIA signed a historic land claims settlement with the Provincial and Federal governments. As part of the deal the Labrador Inuit have been granted a degree of self government. Their representatives can now legislate on matters like language, culture, health and education in the territory now called *Nunatsiavut Kavamanga*. The agreement also saw the creation of the Province's third national park – the first in Labrador – the Torngat Mountains National Park Reserve, to be administered by Parks Canada and the Inuit. Another step forward at the meeting was then-Premier Danny Williams' formal apology on behalf of all citizens of the Province for the forced resettlement of two Inuit communities in the 1950s. Today about seven percent of all Canada's Inuit, some 5,000 people, live in Labrador, mainly in the communities of Hopedale, Makkovik and Nain.

Inuit women and sod house

Stories From These Shores

....

Metis

Modern Labrador is home to another group partially descended from the Inuit, although by their very nature they are not prehistoric arrivals. Known as *Metis* since the 1970s, they are mainly the descendants of British men, Inuit women, and their children, who themselves often intermarried. Their traditional society was largely based on fishing, trapping and hunting. Changing little through the nineteenth century, it was centred on the coast of southern Labrador. Life for the Metis underwent great changes in the twentieth century. *Inuktitut* (the Inuit language) has declined markedly among the Metis, and they now rely not only on traditional subsistence activities, but also commercial activities and some Government transfers. For many years the Metis had no organised voice, but since 1985 have been represented by the Labrador Metis Association (now Nation). In recent years the Labrador Metis have had their share of obstacles to overcome. They continue to fight for official recognition, but their partially mixed ancestry appears to be a stumbling block. As Inuit descendants the Labrador Metis are concerned that the recent LIA treaty is supposedly the last Canadian settlement based on Inuit ancestry. As Michael Johansen has reported in *Downhome* magazine, even the name Metis is regretted by some, as it gives emphasis to their European ancestry and links them with Canada's other Metis, a totally different group. Labrador's Metis are unlikely to give up their efforts at recognition. They are very politicized and committed to cultural preservation, a trait they share with the Inuit and another Labrador Native group, the *Innu*.

....

Innu

Called *Montagnais-Naskapi* or "Mountaineers" by the first European arrivals, the Innu, who speak a language known as *Innu-aimun*, inhabited Labrador's interior and south coast by at least 1500 AD. They are likely direct descendants of the earlier Point Revenge culture that was established in Labrador by about 200 AD, and there is speculation that the Innu may be related to the Beothuk. The Innu people were mainly dependant on the resources found in Labrador's interior, especially caribou, moose, bear and lake fish. These species were pursued in the Winter and Spring while the Summer months were devoted to hunting coastal mammals like whales and seals, along with various bird species. Polygamy was practised by the Innu, although women could leave Husbands who did not provide well for them, and they generally had more influence than European women of the day. The Innu, like the Inuit, still inhabit Labrador. Though most are Christian, the Innu continue to practice traditional religious ceremonies. One of the more important ceremonies, still remembered by some Innu, involved the Shaking Tent or *kushapatshikan*. During this ritual skilled shamans entered the tent to speak to various spirits. A particularly important matter on which to consult the spirit world was the finding of game animals, although the tent could be used for other purposes like contacting Innu groups living far away.

Innu making canoes near Sheshatshui, c.1920

Although they maintained a largely independent lifestyle, the Innu were negatively impacted by European diseases, and incursions by the settler-allied Iroquois. Population numbers, in decline for many years, began to rise again in the mid-1900s. Although in the past the Canadian government has encouraged the Innu to take up agriculture, hunting and trapping remain important elements of their society. The Innu continued fur trading with non-aboriginals into the twentieth century. Today about 1,600 Innu reside in Labrador. When not hunting in the interior, most Innu now live in the settlements of *Natuashish* (to which they relocated from Davis Inlet, sixteen kilometres away) and *Sheshatshui*. In recent years the Innu have been plagued by problems such as substance abuse. It is hoped that new initiatives like the move to Natuashish spell a brighter chapter in the history of this proud and hardy people. Joining the First Nations' trend toward political activism, in recent years the Innu have made active efforts to limit low-level flying by NATO jets over their Labrador hunting territory.

....

Mi'kmaq

In Newfoundland the most numerous Native group today are the *Mi'kmaq* (once spelled Micmac). These people call the Island *Taqamkuk* – Newfoundland Mi'Kmaq being *Taqamkukewa'q*, or "people of the land across the water." With over 2,500 persons resident on the Island, this group is concentrated in the southwest. About 780 persons call the community of *Miawpukek* home. Settled in the 1870s, Miawpukek is commonly known as Conne River, since 1987 Newfoundland's only recognized Native reserve. There are also numbers of Mi'Kmaq living in the area surrounding Miawpukek, plus the Port aux Port Peninsula and in the Gander Bay region.

There is some uncertainty as to how long the Mi'Kmaq have inhabited Newfoundland, although they were certainly permanently established by the early contact period, around 1500. Evidence suggests they visited the Island much earlier. Being master canoe builders and handlers, the Mi'Kmaq were certainly capable of making short sea voyages, and even fitted sails to their canoes by the early historic period. In 1999 Conne River Chief Mi'sel Joe and seven companions recreated a voyage from Newfoundland to Nova Scotia by birch bark canoe, their journey forming the basis of a television documentary.

The Mi'kmaq originated in Atlantic Canada, which, along with the northeastern tip of the US, they call *Mi'Kma'ki*. They were the most numerous people in the region when the first Europeans arrived. Mi'kmaq society was based around extended families headed by *Sagamores* or *Saqamaws* (Chiefs). The Mi'Kmaq lived in small bands during the Winter, but came together in larger groups for the Summer months. This was also a time when the Saqamaws could meet to discuss matters of importance to their communities. The moose was a basic staple of the Mi'Kmaq diet. All parts of the animal were used for clothing and leather items, plus the bone and antlers for weapons, tools and even gaming pieces. In addition to moose, these prodigious hunters also took fish and birds.

Nineteenth century Mi'Kmaq village

Unlike many Native groups, the Mi'Kmaq were unsurprised by their first meetings with Europeans; their spiritual beliefs included the idea that blue-eyes strangers from the east would arrive and greatly change their lives. There was even one story of a woman who had a vision of floating islands with tall trees on which there were people – much like European ships. Following the conversion of Grand Chief Membertou in 1610 the Mi'Kmaq gradually adopted the Roman Catholic faith, becoming French allies and trade partners. As military allies of France the Mi'Kmaq participated in raids on Newfoundland

Stories From These Shores

English settlements in 1696, 1705 and 1708. Following the British capture of Canada in 1760 times were difficult for the Nation, now under the suzerainty of their traditional enemies. Still, the hardy people persevered, and at this time the largest Mi'Kmaq migration to Taqamkuk occurred. On the Island there were reports of enmity between Mi'Kmaq and the Beothuk, but the true nature of their relationship may never be known for certain. It seems the two groups normally avoided each other, but on at least some occasions may have been on friendly terms.

Despite their early interaction with Whites, elements of traditional Mi'Kmaq beliefs survived, and their culture remains strong in Atlantic Canada. A Grand Council is still in operation. The total Mi'Kmaq population now stands at about 20,000, of whom around a third can speak and/or write in their native tongue, a part of the Algonquian language family. Nova Scotia has designated October Micmac History Month. In Newfoundland Conne River's annual drug and alcohol-free Powwow has become an important event for both Natives and interested tourists, attracting 6,000 visitors in 2004. With a strong spiritual element, the Powwow celebrates not only the culture of the Mi'Kmaq, but also of the Province's previous Aboriginal inhabitants. The three-day celebration includes various traditional events such as a sunrise ceremony, sweat lodge and dancing. Conne River, a community of 860, is home to a number of successful enterprises including Micmic Air, the Glen John Arts Centre, and a fish hatchery. In addition, Saqamaw Joe and the Band Council are pioneers in organizing a programme whereby band members work for fourteen weeks a year to qualify for assistance under the Federal Indian Act, an idea being examined by other Canadian Native reserves. The local school, St. Anne's (*Se'tA'newey*), plays its own role in Mi'Kmaq culture by promoting the Native language, spirituality and traditional values.

Currently, many of Newfoundland's 10,500 Mi'Kmaq are represented by the Federation of Newfoundland Indians (FNI). In June, 2008, Federal Government and FNI representatives signed a historic agreement-in-principle to create the Qalipu Mi'Kmaq First Nation Band. In 2011 an Order in Council provided the legal basis for the Band's formal establishment.

3
Britain's Oldest Colony ~ Newfoundland

The Norse

Even before the Thule arrived in Labrador, and possibly before the Mi'Kmaq reached the Island, Newfoundland was visited by people who later committed their story to writing. For many years, though, scholars weren't sure if Newfoundland was the place being written about, or even if the stories were based on real events. These tales – the *Sagas* – were very much real. They tell of the first verified contact between people of the Old and New Worlds, as voyagers from Europe made an appearance in North America. These voyagers were the Scandinavian warriors and explorers popularly called Vikings. Their open boats (knarr), propelled by oars or a simple square sail, were among the most efficient sea-going craft of the Dark Ages, and the Vikings used them to great advantage. After raiding and then settling in the British Isles and France from the late 700s AD, the Vikings turned their attention further afield. Swedish Vikings reached Russia, others visited the Byzantine Empire, now modern Turkey, and fought the Arabs. Locals were shocked by the Vikings' behaviour before they (the Vikings) embraced Christianity, especially their occasional human sacrifices.

The Vikings always seemed to like a challenge and were possessed of a restless spirit. By the late-800s they settled the island of Iceland. One colonist was Thorwald, exiled from Norway after committing murder. He was accompanied by his Son Eric the Red, exiled in turn from Iceland after his own killings. Sailing west Eric discovered a large Arctic island which he named Greenland to encourage settlers. Eric established two settlements there which survived for 500 years before failing due to worsening climate conditions. One of Greenland's new colonists was Eric's son Lief, or Leifr (*fl.* 1000). Young Lief Ericsson and his mother were converts to Christianity, but Eric followed the old pagan religion until he died. Lief heard tales of the traveller Bjarni Herjolfsson, possibly the first European to see mainland North America, although Herjolfsson never landed. Buying Herjolfsson's boat, Lief Ericsson sailed off around the year 1000 to find the new land. Lief and his crew first spotted an island they named *Helluland,* or Flat Stone Land, believed to be Baffin Island. They next came to a place whose trees led to the name *Markland* – Forest Land, probably Labrador. Finally, the explorers came to a place they named *Vinland* after the grapes they found growing there. (Another Saga gives most of the credit for exploring these areas to Þorfinnr, or Thorfinn, Karlsefni). It is now thought that Vinland has some connection to Newfoundland. If not actually Vinland itself, the Island may have been used as a base camp for exploring a larger area of that name. Over the next few years other Vikings tried to establish a colony at Vinland. This lasted for a time, but it was abandoned after hostilities with the Natives, whom the Vikings called *Skraelings,* and violent quarrels amongst the settlers themselves. The settlement was abandoned, but remained in the Viking tradition through their oral tales, later written down as the Sagas. As the years passed people forgot the reality behind the Sagas, and most assumed they were nothing more than legends.

Lief Eiriksson discovers North America,
by Christian Krohg (1893)

One person who believed the Sagas recounted real events was Norwegian adventurer Helge Ingstad (1899-2001). He noticed similarities between physical descriptions of the land in the Sagas and Newfoundland. Along with his wife, professional archaeologist Anne Stine (1918-97), Ingstad explored Newfoundland's Northern Peninsula in the 1960s, and noticed how well a place called L'Anse aux Meadows fit with the characteristics of Vinland. With the help of local residents the Ingstads were able to find a Viking settlement which could indeed be Vinland. The name of the place was a stumbling block for many years, as grapes do not grow in Newfoundland. Possibly the Vinlanders discovered some of the Island's many berry varieties that can be used to grow wine, and named the settlement from there. Scholar Magnús Stefánsson has argued that beer was the Norse beverage of the era. Wine drinking was quite rare. According to Stefánsson, the problem may also stem from confusion over the terms *vín* and *vin*. The name could actually derive from abundant grasslands, rather than having anything to do with wine. Other academics like Alan Crozier favour the "Wineland" interpretation. Whatever the truth behind the name Vinland, L'Anse aux Meadows is still the only authenticated Viking settlement in North America.

....

Cabot's Voyages

Once the Vikings left Newfoundland's Natives had the Island to themselves for 500 years. In his work on Britain's Royal Navy, Arthur Herman argues that the earliest English presence in Newfoundland may have been that of Bristol fishers as early as the 1480s. If true, their voyages and discoveries would predate even that of Columbus. The evidence for this is circumstantial at best. The first confirmed European landing in eastern North America, after the Vikings, occurred in 1497. That year a Venetian sailor in the employ of England's King Henry VII (1457-1509), re-discovered the Island.

This mariner is remembered as John Cabot (c. 1450-c. 1499), the anglicized form of the name Zuan, or Giovanni, Caboto. Following a failed voyage the previous year Cabot, with a crew of about eighteen, set sail in May 1497, in a vessel that may have been called the *Matthew* after his wife Mattea. After five weeks at sea Cabot made landfall at what he thought was China. He really landed in part of North America, traditionally Bonavista, Newfoundland, or Cape Breton Island, Nova Scotia. Some scholars think Cabot just sailed west along the nearest latitude line to the port of Bristol, England, or Dursey Head in Ireland. He would thus have landed on Newfoundland's Great Northern Peninsula, perhaps at the community of Griquet. Historian Peter Pope notes that merchant John Day, who reported Cabot's voyage (possibly to Colombus), had the mariner sailing before an east-northeasterly wind while outward bound. In May this could have taken him along the path of the Vikings, around sixty-one degrees north, at least as far west as Greenland. The old Norse route would have been known in Bristol, so this itinerary is possible for Cabot as well.

Newfoundland postage stamp depicting John Cabot's vessel, the Matthew

Wherever he started from, and wherever he landed, it seems

Cabot found something worthwhile. According to the few known accounts of the voyage, Cabot and his men discovered a bountiful fishery with cod so thick they could be taken aboard in baskets! Henry VII must have been impressed with Cabot's results. The explorer was given a reward of £10 and an annual pension of £20; this in an era when one could rent a house for £2 a year! In 1498 Henry sent Cabot out on another mission paid for by Bristol and London merchants. Some of Cabot's ships might have returned from this voyage, but what exactly happened to Cabot was never recorded, and he disappeared from the pages of history. It is usually thought Cabot went down on one of his ships, but that isn't certain.

For a long while John Cabot's role in exploring this part of the world went unappreciated, as his Son, Sebastian (c. 1470-c. 1557), later took credit for some of his Father's work. The belief that Sebastian was the real discoverer of Newfoundland was current for many years. Writing in 1612, John Guy observed in his journal that Newfoundland "...was discovered by <u>Sebastian Cabot,</u> in the name and at proper charges of <u>Henry</u> the seventh king of <u>England</u>, in the year 1496..."[1] To whichever Cabot we give the laurels, it is certain that the English took their time in following up on his discovery. For the next hundred years or more the exploration of Newfoundland was mainly carried out by adventurers from other countries.

....

The Early European Presence

Just a few years before Cabot sailed the Pope divided up lands in the New World between Spain and Portugal. The Portuguese share included Newfoundland, and they soon took an interest in this promising fishing station. Between 1500 and 1502 two Brothers, Gaspar and Miguel Corte-Real, set out on voyages to the Island, but both disappeared – Miguel while trying to find his sibling. Another Brother returned home in 1503 after failing to locate either Gaspar or Miguel. The Portuguese were thus among the first explorers of Newfoundland, although their fishery here at the time was small (Another important group of visitors in this era were the Basques, whom we will discuss further as part of Labrador history. The Basque people visited Labrador from the sixteenth to the seventeenth centuries).

Sir Humphrey Gilbert

By the time the Basques left, France and Spain had been fishing off Newfoundland for decades. Around the same time England first took a serious look at colonizing the Island. During the reign of Queen Elizabeth I (1533-1603) Sir Humphrey Gilbert (c. 1539-1583), half-Brother of the great Sir Walter Raleigh (c. 1554-1618), sailed for Newfoundland to establish an English presence. He arrived in Newfoundland with a motley fleet of three vessels in August 1583; another ship had deserted Gilbert and taken to piracy. After summoning leading mariners and masters together on the fifth of the month, Sir Humphrey took possession of St. John's Harbour– Newfoundland's principal port – and the surrounding territory in the name of Elizabeth. The act gave the English a symbolic claim to Newfoundland, but for many years it was little more. Gilbert's expedition was a disaster for the Captain. Returning to England in his fleet's smallest vessel, the

Squirrel, Gilbert went down with her during a storm off the Azores.

Queen Elizabeth never backed Gilbert's claims to Newfoundland, and didn't promote settlements there. Still, an English migratory fishery gradually emerged, but the English were by no means the most important Newfoundland fishers in the period – that honour went to the French. In fact, their presence was so well established from an early date that France held fishing rights in much of northwestern Newfoundland through the early twentieth century – this was their French Shore. In later years the French took less interest in Newfoundland as a colony, concentrating their efforts on the Caribbean, New France (Quebec), and Louisiana. In the seventeenth century this was not the case, and a settlement was founded as the stepping-stone to conquering and colonizing the Island. *Plaisance,* or modern Placentia, was located on the western side of the Avalon Peninsula. The settlement was founded in 1662, and its protected harbour fortified with cannon. Plaisance became the centre of, and supply depot for, the prosperous French Newfoundland fishery. Although Anglo-French relations in Newfoundland were at first peaceful, raids and counter-raids became common from the 1690s on. Finally, with the Treaty of Utrecht ending Queen Anne's War in 1713, Placentia and all other French territory on the Island was relinquished, and French fishing rights recognized in the form of the French Shore.

....

England's Sponsored Colonies

Although he reigned before the establishment of Plaisance, the French fishing presence persuaded Elizabeth's successor, King James I (1566-1625), to promote English settlements in the "New Founde Land." The first colony was founded at Cuper's Cove (Cupids) by John Guy, who was enthusiastic about Newfoundland's prospects, noting in his journal that "...the Newfoundland fish, being so acceptable in France, Spain and Italy, may...yearly return great quantities of money."[2] The bounty was real, but the Cuper's Cove colony was not a long-term beneficiary – it failed. Part of Guy's land grant was sold off to William Vaughan (1575-1641), who started his own settlement at Aquaforte in 1617. Like Guy before him, Vaughan returned to England. Another venture was

Bristol's Hope, under Robert Hayman (c.1575-1629). Unlike Vaughan's venture, Bristol's Hope was something of a success and was supported by Bristol fishing merchants. Another colonization scheme by Lord Vaughan also failed, but was followed in 1627 by a more ambitious attempt.

Sir George Calvert, First Lord Baltimore

The spirit behind this venture was Sir George Calvert, later Lord Baltimore (c. 1580-1632). His "Colony of Avalon" – originally called "Avalonia" – was founded at Ferryland on Newfoundland's Avalon Peninsula. Calvert was a Roman Catholic convert, and although his settlement was a commercial venture, he also saw it as a place of religious toleration – an unusual principle in that era. By 1628 Ferryland seemed well on its way to becoming Newfoundland's first successful English colony. Avalon had its own blacksmith, cobblestone streets, some stone buildings, a quay complex, and a sewage system. Before long though Calvert gave up on the Colony of Avalon. His experiment in religious toleration was opposed by the settlement's Protestant clergy, and he found himself forced to defend the colony against French incursions. Newfoundland dealt Sir George his heaviest blow when the

Winter of 1628-9 proved especially severe. The preceding Winters had been mild, and Calvert believed his first Newfoundland colonists had deceived him with glowing reports of the climate. The future Lord Baltimore left Newfoundland with his Catholic followers in the Summer of 1629 to found a settlement in the new American colonies. He never returned to Newfoundland.

In 1637 David Kirke (c.1597-1654) was given control of Ferryland by James' Son, King Charles I (1600-1649). Kirke was French-born, but spent his life in service to the English Crown. Before starting his career as a Newfoundland planter, Kirke and his Brothers raided French commerce in the name of their English sovereign. David Kirke managed the colony ably, although in a very high-handed way, for a number of years. He might have continued to do so except for the English Civil Wars which broke out in 1642. Kirke loyally backed his sponsor, King Charles, who ended up losing the wars and finally his head. Having offered to aid Charles, Kirke was viewed with suspicion by the new English Republic (later the Protectorate) under Oliver Cromwell (1599-1658), and Ferryland was disarmed. Kirke died with his claims to Ferryland disputed by the Calvert family. The town suffered raids at the hands of Holland and France in the late seventeenth century, and its demise as a sponsored settlement marked the end of English attempts to found official colonies in Newfoundland. For the next hundred years or so the Island was considered little more than an overseas fishing station, although a small permanent settler population never left.

....

Fishing Station

Generally, the eighteenth century was a time of growth for both the British fishery and settlement in Newfoundland, even if colonization was not encouraged. A 1699 Act of Parliament, known as King William's Act, was the first to deal specifically with Newfoundland. It didn't forbid settlement exactly, but it was clear the English Government then thought of Newfoundland in terms of its fishery, not as a settlement colony. Settlers were forbidden from establishing plantations or cutting wood closer than ten kilometres from the shoreline. This effectively reserved the coast and adjoining timber for the migratory fishery. This has given rise to the idea that West Country merchants, along with willing Governments, spent most of the 1700s trying to root out all permanent habitation on the Island. This is only partly true, and even the fish merchants recognized the value of settlers, not least when there was a war on. It was in the 1700s that the English began moving out of their original territory in eastern Newfoundland – the Avalon Peninsula – into former French preserves like Placentia and Fortune Bays. By the early eighteenth century they moved into Notre Dame Bay, where the two most important settlements were Fogo and Twillingate. At about the same time a number of important developments took place as the settler fishery expanded, moving to new grounds such as the Grand Banks, and exploiting new species like salmon. One of the most important parts of Newfoundland's later outport economy was also founded at this time – the seal hunt. These fisheries attracted additional settlers to Newfoundland. For the most part these were no longer West Country English, as nearly all the original settlers had been.

Many of the servants and labourers needed in the new fisheries were Irish, mainly recruited from the ports of Cork and Waterford, and their hinterlands. This pre-famine immigration was so important that today about half the Province's European-descended population has Irish roots. Their presence and culture is particularly strong on the Avalon Peninsula's Southern Shore, although the people and their heritage can be found Island-wide. The first Irish fishery servants were often unskilled and poorly educated. As a result of this, not to mention English prejudices, most Irish in early Newfoundland were at the lowest rung of the social ladder; Irish women were even sold on the Island as wives and servants. In the eighteenth century a number of spectacular crimes, like the murder of Magistrate William Keene by a former Irish servant and her compatriots, further soured Anglo-Irish relations in Newfoundland. The Catholic Church (the faith of almost all the Irish) was officially repressed, and the authorities made a concerted effort to reduce Irish settlement. Religious discrimination was finally ended in 1784, and political reforms of the 1800s gradually gave Catholics a voice. Still, until the mid-nineteenth century sectarian bigotry and bloodshed continued.

DAVID J. CLARKE

Pirate Captain Bartholomew Roberts

Throughout the eighteenth century Newfoundland soldiered on as an English fishing station, being raided by pirates like Bartholomew Roberts (1682-1722). From 1763-7 southwestern Newfoundland was the subject of extensive surveying and mapping by James Cook (1728-79). Just prior to Cook's visits the Island suffered through the last North American engagements in the Seven Year's War (1756-63). French troops had taken St. John's, and were supposedly aided by disaffected Irish who manned a patrol vessel for the invaders.

Despite its role in the English fishery, Newfoundland was seriously lacking in law, order and government. A symptom of this lawless state, according to reformers, was the amount of alcohol consumed by settlers and migratory fishers. One of Newfoundland's most important imports was rum. With its seafaring tradition, the daily rum ration was ingrained in early Newfoundland culture. Following practices of the time, rum was also consumed by children. Amazingly, St. John's, with only forty-two permanent dwellings in 1726, also had sixteen taverns. Almost one seventh of the families then living on the

Island kept public houses. In those rare moments when the early fishers were not working there was little to do. Rum, selling at twenty-five cents a gallon, offered the best solution. In the next century, with the arrival of Church infrastructure and stricter morality, the rum culture changed but did not entirely disappear (See, Chapter Nine). "Newfie Screech" is still a celebrated rum in the Province, and forms part of the "Screeching-in" ceremony welcoming arrivals from away.

....

Rule of Law

At least drink did offer *some* compensations. Early justice on the Island left even more to be desired. For many years Newfoundland was ruled by the "Fishing Admirals." Under this system the first ship master into a harbour each season took charge of the area until the vessels left in the Fall. The next arrival became his second-in command, and so on. The traditional view of the "justice" administered by the Fishing Admirals – a view challenged by historian Jerry Bannister – was that it was usually arbitrary and often cruel. The only supplement to their authority were occasional patrols by the Royal Navy. Commanders of naval convoys sent out to protect the fishery could act as a court of appeal against the Fishing Admirals, but they were not always present. In the Winter there was no system of government at all. The settlers themselves pressed for a better form of government, although they were opposed by the West Country merchants, hoping to keep the migratory fishery intact. In 1729 the first positive step was taken when the British Government formalized the role of naval commanders. It was decided that the ranking naval officer in Newfoundland would become its Governor. Under the new system Justices of the Peace were appointed, and court houses and prisons built. The first Naval Governor, Henry Osborn (1694-1771), saw that justice was dispensed throughout the year, both for criminal and civil matters.

....

DAVID J. CLARKE

Becoming a Colony

The eighteenth century was also a time of growth for religion in Newfoundland. After the failure of the sponsored settlements, there was little in the way of religious instruction on the Island. The initial Anglican missionaries arrived in the early 1700s. Methodism was established by mid-century, with other Protestant denominations soon following. At the very end of the century, following repeal of the most harsh measures against their religion, Roman Catholics in Newfoundland saw their first Bishop appointed – James Louis O'Donel (1737-1811).

The appointment of a Naval Governor, and the growth of religion on the Island, were only the first steps in Newfoundland's road toward full colonial status. By 1820 the British authorities, heeding the calls of Newfoundland reformers like the Scot Dr. William Carson (c.1777-1843), and Irishman Patrick Morris (c.1789-1849), recognized the need for true colonial government on the Island. Newfoundland was officially declared a Crown Colony in 1824, and its first circuit courts were inaugurated about the same time. Along with colonial status Newfoundland got its first civil Governor, Sir Thomas Cochrane (1789-1872). Seven years later the Colony's first true internal government, consisting of an assembly and council, marked the start of "Representative Government." This reform did not solve all of Newfoundland's problems, and occasional violence sparked by ethnic and religious differences still marred the political scene. In an effort to smooth the waters, the British Government merged the Assembly with the Council in 1842.

Even this step did not go far enough for many Newfoundland political reformers. By the 1840s they began to clamour for "Responsible Government," where executive power would be exercised by the Assembly's majority party, duly elected by the people. In those days "the people" didn't mean the same as it does today. A full half of the adult population – women – had no vote. Also, Newfoundland's Assembly was not an independent government in those days – its decisions generally had to be ratified in Britain. Nonetheless, Responsible Government was an important step forward. It became a reality for Newfoundland in 1855. Newfoundland's first Premier, Philip Francis Little (c. 1822-1897), a lawyer born on Prince Edward Island, had been one of the primary spokespersons for the new form of government. Like all governments, this one had its flaws, and Districts like Fogo-Twillingate were at first considered under-represented, as were Roman Catholics.

P. F. Little

....

Modernization
Another milestone of the period was the laying of the first transatlantic telegraph cable, completed and landed at Heart's Content Bay in 1866. There were also new economic developments about this time. In the last quarter of the century the administration of Sir William V. Whiteway (1828-1908) initiated a "Policy of Progress" for the Colony. One plank

of the policy was to try and win back some of the French Shore fishing rights for the people of Newfoundland. A few small concessions were gained, but the British Government didn't want to risk problems with France. It was almost thirty years before any real progress was made. The main part of Whiteway's plan called for a national railway like that in Canada. Newfoundland railway construction had its up and downs but was supported by both Whiteway's and Robert Thorburn's administrations. Sir William formed a new administration in 1889 and soon put out tenders to complete a line to Hall's Bay. In 1890 railway construction was taken over by Robert Gillespie Reid (1842-1908), who became one of the Colony's largest landholders. He was also associated with the Bank of Montreal, which became an important financial institution on the Island after the great bank crash of 1894 (See below). In the end the project did little to reinvigorate the Island's economy, although it created some wage employment – a dollar a day for navvies – always rare in Newfoundland before 1949.

....

Growing Pains

Despite the general progress, there were also hardships and setbacks facing the Colony as it entered the twentieth century. Many residents of the towns and villages outside St. John's (and some in the City as well) lived with grinding poverty, despite hard work in the fishery, seal hunt and the lumber woods. Over eighty percent of the population were fishers, or fishery workers, and suffered accordingly during downturns in the fish and seal markets.

These problems were only aggravated by a pair of disasters that hit the Island in the 1890s. In the nineteenth century St. John's was a growing centre, but one largely constructed of wooden buildings, often clustered close together, and with inadequate firefighting services. Fire ravaged the city in 1817, 1846, and again in 1855. In 1892 the most devastating fire of all hit Newfoundland's capital. It started at Timothy Brine's barn, Long's Hill, allegedly by a drayman's pipe dropped into a pile of hay. When attempts were made to put the blaze out it was discovered that the water had been shut off to install new mains (It was turned back on by this time, but the flow hadn't reached that part of town). A nearby reservoir tank was drained for a fire drill and not refilled. Circumstances could not have been worse. It was July and the city hadn't seen rain for a month. To add to the problems, a strong northwest wind was blowing, fanning the flames through St. John's tightly-packed buildings. The fire did not end until the next morning. By that time much of the city, including businesses, churches, schools, and residences were destroyed. Amazingly, only two people died, but thirteen million dollars in property damage was done and 11,000 people were homeless. The city soon rebuilt from the ashes, but two years later another blow struck.

View of St. John's after the Great Fire of 1892

On 10 December, 1894 Newfoundland's two main banking institutions collapsed. The process was like a set of dominoes falling. A British bank called in loans owing it by Newfoundland's Commercial Bank, but the institution was unable to pay. To meet its obligations the Commercial Bank also called in client loans. Merchants couldn't make repayment as most of their funds were advanced to fishers preparing for the Spring fishery. Unable to meet its British debts, the Commercial Bank closed. Its action caused a run on Newfoundland's other major bank, the Union, which had to follow suit and shut its doors. These events were remembered in Newfoundland as "Black Monday." Financial chaos threatened the Colony, paper money was worthless, firms went bankrupt and bread riots erupted in the streets. Two Premiers resigned in succession after failure to solve the crisis, and Whiteway returned to office in February, 1895. For a time it appeared the only solution would be Confederation with Canada. The crisis ended almost as quickly as it began. One of Whiteway's ministers – future *Prime Minister* – Robert Bond (1857-1927), jumped into the breach. Offering his entire personal fortune of $100,000.00 as a guarantee, Bond was granted a three million dollar loan in London. The crisis ended and the economy rebounded; talk of union with Canada went out the door for the next few decades.

....

The Whirlwind Years

With these crises behind it Newfoundland seemed to be in good shape; the colony would even assume "Dominion" status in 1907, the smallest unit of the British Empire to acquire the designation. Still, the fifty years after 1900 were among the most trying in the Colony's history, as they were for much of the world. The year 1914 opened in tragedy for the new Dominion, when on 31 March, 132 sealers from the vessel S.S. *Newfoundland* were trapped on the ice during a fierce blizzard – seventy-eight men perished. The sealing fleet's Commodore, Abram Kean (1855-1945), was widely blamed for the disaster but went on to twenty more years at the hunt, becoming Newfoundland's most successful sealing skipper of all time. In the same storm that claimed the *Newfoundland*'s crew another vessel, the *Southern Cross*, was lost with all hands, 174 men, while returning from the hunt.

Only four months after the twin disasters at the ice fields, Newfoundland, as part of the British Empire, was drawn into hostilities with Germany and its allies in World War I (1914-18). The "Great War," as it was then called, produced one if the most enduring national memories of Newfoundland & Labrador. On 1 July, 1916 the Newfoundland Regiment charged German trenches in a part of the Battle of the Somme known as Beaumont-Hamel. 272 of the nation's soldiers died that day. Compared to the overall costs of the Somme this was minimal, but still a national tragedy to a small Colony. Although later celebrated in the Province as Canada Day, 1 July is still a day of remembrance in Newfoundland & Labrador. For its actions in 1916 the Newfoundland Regiment was awarded the honour of a "Royal" prefix, only the third time the distinction was conferred in wartime. A Beaumont-Hamel Newfoundland Memorial was opened at the battle site by Field Marshal Lord Haig (1861-1928) in 1925.

During these years misfortune seemed to hound the Island, as a hurricane in 1925 claimed the lives of thirty fishers. Then, in 1929, an undersea earthquake caused a tidal wave that killed twenty-eight people on the Burin Peninsula. The tsunami also destroyed the local seabed, ruining the inshore fishery for the next ten years; this at a time when the world was already slipping into economic chaos. Luckily, the Grand Banks offshore fishery was already becoming more important in the area.

If the loss of nearly three hundred men in one day at Beaumont-Hamel was not enough, the First World War had a generally negative impact on the Colony. Barring natural disasters like the south coast tsunami, the 1920s were a fairly prosperous time for Newfoundland, especially the first part of the decade. However, the war had left Newfoundland's Government with massive debts. The situation grew worse when the Great Depression of the 1930s hit. People lost confidence in their leaders' abilities, and the situation came to a head. Elected Prime Minister for the third time in 1928, Richard Squires (1880-1940) was accused of corruption in 1932. He was already blamed for the Island's low wages, and had reduced veterans' pensions. On 5 April rioters stormed the Colonial Building, seat of the House of Assembly, forcing Squires to flee. An election in June 1932 saw Squires lose his seat and the Government.

Amid all the turbulence, some good did arise in this era. In the mid-1920s Newfoundland remained one of the few places in the British Empire (along with South Africa) where women still couldn't vote. Squires was strongly opposed to women's suffrage, but an organized campaign, including numerous petitions, gained the vote for women in 1925, while Sir Richard was out of office. Campaigners included reformer/activist Julia Salter Earle (1878-1945) and the Women's

Franchise League, composed of many prominent St. John's ladies. As early as 1930 Lewisporte District elected the first female member of the House of Assembly. Ironically, she was Sir Richard's own wife Helena (nee Strong, 1879-1959), and the Prime Minister supported her election. A further irony was that Squires herself was one of the few well-placed women in the Capital not active in the Franchise League. Newfoundland women's new freedom didn't last long. Soon politics and crisis combined, taking the right to vote away from women and men alike.

Sir Richard Squires

Stories From These Shores

....

Commission of Government

After Squire's Liberals were defeated in the 1932 general election, Frederick Alderdice (1872-1936) and his United Newfoundland Party came to power. A major problem for the new administration was the massive debt Newfoundland had incurred in the war and through failed development schemes. Alderdice believed that politics had grown corrupt, suggesting that the Dominion needed a "Commission of Government" to manage its affairs for a number of years. In the end Britain and Canada agreed to aid the struggling Colony. In return Newfoundland accepted a commission, headed by Lord Amulree (1860-1941), that would try and find long-term answers to the Island's problems. The main finding of the Commission, presented in 1933, was that Newfoundland's problems stemmed not from the Depression, but from government corruption and waste. The Colony's debt would be taken on by Britain, but in return Newfoundland was to surrender the Responsible Government it won less than a century before. Until Newfoundland was back on its feet a Commission appointed in Great Britain – similar to that suggested by Alderdice – would govern the Country. Frederick Alderdice thus became the Dominion of Newfoundland's last Prime Minister.

During its sixteen year tenure as Newfoundland's Government the Commission attempted, as best it could, to implement the recommendations of the Amulree report, not to mention spending six years on a wartime footing. Not the least of its accomplishments was the creation of the Newfoundland Ranger Force in 1935. By the end of its tenure the Commission of Government was one of Newfoundland's few administrations to leave a budget surplus. Still, many people thought the surplus was built by being overly parsimonious and ignoring the sufferings of poor Newfoundlanders.

....

The War Years, 1939-45

The fortunes of ordinary Newfoundlanders took a turn for the better, ironically, when war was declared against Nazi Germany in 1939. Just as in 1914, thousands of Newfoundlanders volunteered to fight in the armed services or enlisted with the Overseas Forestry Unit to cut wood in Britain. Unlike the First World War, the Second was financially beneficial for the Nation. Canada was placed in charge of Newfoundland's defence during the war and built air force facilities at Goose Bay, Labrador, Gander and Torbay (Then just outside St. John's, now part of the city). Newfoundland, as North America's most eastern point, was vital in the Battle of the Atlantic against German submarines or "U-Boats."

S.S. Caribou *in dry dock, c.1926*

There was a down side to this position. In 1942 U-boats sunk four iron-ore vessels at the mining centre of Bell Island. In the second of two raids a torpedo hit and partially destroyed a pier on the island. This action earned Bell Island the dubious distinction of being the only place in North America to suffer a direct German attack during the war. There were also numerous ships sunk in the waters off Newfoundland. The most famous of these was the passenger steamer *Caribou*, sunk on 14 October, 1942 by a torpedo from U-69. Captain Benjamin Tavernor and most of his crew perished in the sinking, along with many passengers and military personnel; in total 136 of 237 persons onboard. The Americans arrived at Newfoundland in 1940, perhaps anticipating joining the war. They became a belligerent the next year after the Japanese attack on Pearl Harbor. The US built three bases on the Island, at Argentia, St. John's and Stephenville. All told, thousands of Canadian and American service personnel were stationed in Newfoundland & Labrador during the War, contributing greatly to the local economy. Many Newfoundlanders not serving overseas found employment on the American and Canadian bases, making a cash wage for the first time in their lives. The newcomers were generally welcomed by Islanders and there were a number of marriages between local women and foreign servicemen. Overall, the financial situation of the Colony had never been better, nor its people more prosperous.

....

Confederation

During the War a new question emerged for the British Government concerning its Colony; when and how would the people of Newfoundland return to self-government? The Commission was an interim measure, not meant to last forever. The American presence was welcomed by many Newfoundlanders. It was feared the Colony might develop closer ties with its republican neighbour, perhaps leaving the Commonwealth, as the Empire was now called, for good. An old solution was proposed that involved merging Newfoundland with its sister Dominion, Canada. The idea was welcomed by Britain as it meant the Mother Country would no longer have to financially support Newfoundland, but it would remain part of the Commonwealth. Canada, under Prime Minister William Lyon Mackenzie King (1874-1950), was attracted by Newfoundland & Labrador's resource wealth, not to mention the fact that Newfoundland's financial situation was much better than had been thought. A final "benefit" for Canada was Newfoundland's homogenous population. Sadly, both Governments had racist tendencies in the 1940s, and Canada gladly welcomed a population almost entirely White.

The understanding between Britain and Canada on the issue

didn't mean Newfoundlanders would willingly give up their nationhood. Since Canada became a country in 1867 Newfoundland had rejected Confederation more than once. St. John's businessman and Newfoundland Premier, Charles Fox Bennett (1793-1883), is still remembered for leading the anti-Confederate fight in the late-1860s. After Commission of Government and the Depression, Newfoundland's situation in the 1940s was much different. With Canada's support Britain set up a National Convention to decide the future of Newfoundland. This was less of an outright conspiracy than is often suggested, but it is clear Britain wanted Confederation. There is no need to go into all the details of the Confederation debate here, but in the end the "yea" forces won the day, following two referendums in 1948. The vote was very narrow, but Confederation edged out a return to Responsible Government. Newfoundland & Labrador officially became a Canadian Province in 1949. 1 April was the original date of union, but this was changed to midnight, 31 March to avoid having Confederation marked on April Fools' Day.

Joseph R. Smallwood signs Newfoundland into Confederation

Stories From These Shores

The Confederation issue was very bitter, with pro-Confederation strength mainly drawn from the small outports, and Responsible Government favoured by a majority in St. John's and on the Avalon Peninsula. Many outport residents thought the Responsible Government forces were led by a merchant class wishing to return common Newfoundlanders to their pre-war poverty and dependence. Anti-Confederates believed joining Canada meant selling our birthright, and that Confederation advocates were traitors to their Country. Neither side was really correct in assessing the other's motives, but this does show the bitterness of the issue, which isn't completely gone today.

....

The Smallwood Era

The Confederate cause gained invaluable support in the person of native-born Newfoundlander, Joseph R. "Joey" Smallwood (1900-1991). Born at Gambo, but raised mainly in St. John's, Smallwood had been a newspaper reporter at home, in Canada, and in the United States. He was a prolific author, and for a number of years hosted the popular Barrelman radio show. Smallwood always took an interest in farming, and retired as the Barrelman in 1943 to run a pig farm at Gander. In 1946 Smallwood's career turned toward politics when he was elected to the National Convention as member for Bonavista Centre. Over the course of the debate Smallwood's oratory skills propelled him to leadership of the Confederate forces. Following union with Canada Smallwood, leading the Liberal Party, became the first Premier of the Province of Newfoundland. He remained in power until 1972. In some ways the Smallwood era (and that of his Progressive Conservative successors, Frank Moores and Brian Peckford) was the most prosperous period Newfoundland has ever known. Throughout his long tenure in office there were many Newfoundlanders who believed their Government benefits came directly from Joey himself, and it was not unheard of for persons to be buried with his picture.

Opinions on Smallwood have always been sharply divided. He has often been blamed for development deals that didn't favour the Province, like the Lower Churchill Falls project in Labrador. There were also a succession of badly-planned industrialization schemes, proposed by men like Dr. Alfred Valdmanis (1908-70) and John C. Doyle (1915-2000), that went sour (The ill-fated rubber products plant and chocolate factory are infamous examples). Outport resettlement in the 1950s and 1960s generated its own resentments. This Government project saw many small Newfoundland communities abandoned so services could be concentrated in larger areas. A bitter loggers' strike in 1959 also recalls an oppressive image of Smallwood for some. On the other hand, he oversaw a number of important developments like the creation of Newfoundland & Labrador's first degree-granting institution, Memorial University. Economically, the Province was turned completely around in the decades after Confederation. Hospitals, schools and highways appeared at a rapid pace. Fewer children died, and the rate of tuberculosis dropped dramatically. In these respects, Joey's vision had been right after all. The former Premier suffered a stroke in 1984 that robbed him of his great speaking and writing abilities. He died on 17 December, 1991, and his legacy still generates controversy. What cannot be denied about Joseph R. Smallwood is his place among the great Newfoundlanders.

....

Looking to the Future
Since the 1990s, and probably earlier, Newfoundland's economic situation has been precarious. The Island's main fishery – cod – had been over-exploited for years. Even Canada's extension of fisheries management jurisdiction to 200 miles (322 km) offshore on 1 January, 1977 did not alleviate pressure on the resource. Things came to a head fifteen years later. In 1992 a cod moratorium was announced by then-Federal Fisheries Minister John Crosbie (b. 1931), Son of Responsible Government proponent and businessman Chesley Crosbie (1905-62). It was hoped the fishery closure would give the stocks time to rebuild, but they have not yet fully recovered. The Province has tried numerous ways of rebuilding its economy as young people flock elsewhere to look for employment. Nothing has yet replaced "king cod" as the backbone of Newfoundland's economy, but ventures in alternative fisheries, offshore oil and gas, information technology, mining, plus tourism, have given some relief. Despite setbacks, Newfoundlanders & Labradorians

have always been survivors and have rebounded in the past. Smart money says they will do so again.

4
The Big Land ~ Labrador

The history of Labrador does not parallel that of the Island, and should be treated separately. We have noted the long presence of First Nations peoples in the Big Land. They were the original settlers of both portions of the modern Province; European knowledge of Labrador came much later. According to the Viking Sagas, on the voyage which eventually took them to Vinland, Lief Ericsson and his crew landed at a flat, wooded area with white sandy beaches. This was the place they named Markland. It very closely matches Cape Porcupine, just south of Hamilton Inlet on the Labrador coast. Called the Wonderstrand today, it may have been the first European landing site in continental North America. Possibly the first Europeans to set foot in Labrador, the Vikings were not the last.

....

The First Europeans – Basques and Others

Sebastian Cabot. An early explorer of Labrador?

Stories From These Shores

An old tradition alleges that the Basque people arrived in 1470, years before Colombus' voyage. There is no firm proof of this. The term *Baccalao* was applied to Labrador and taken as evidence of a Basque discovery, but the word was a widespread fishing term in the era; its use is not definitive. The true European discoverer of Labrador remains unknown. There is some justification in supposing that John Cabot's explorations actually took him to the coast of Labrador. If so, this would make Cabot and his English patrons the discoverers of Labrador, rather than Newfoundland or Cape Breton. There is better evidence that John's Son Sebastian commanded a voyage to Labrador in 1508. The younger Cabot claimed to have explored as far north as 67½ degrees, which would have taken him to Cape Chidley, and the voyage may have been a quest for the Northwest Passage. Discovery claims have also been made for the Breton French. The Dutch (who visited with the Innu), and the Portuguese, were other early arrivals.

Whoever first discovered Labrador, the Basques were among the most important European users of its resources in the sixteenth and seventeenth centuries. The Basques speak *Euskera*, a language not closely related to any other, which may be the oldest living tongue in Europe. Their homeland straddles northwestern Spain and southwestern France, a region they call *Euskadi*. Aside from being known as shepherds, the Basques were great mariners and pioneers of whaling. Starting in the mid-1500s they came every Summer to parts of southern Labrador, especially Red Bay, to hunt whales and process their blubber into oil. The whalers set out each Spring from Basque ports, spending part of the year on the Labrador coast chasing their quarry from small boats called *chalupas*. Once a whale was caught its blubber was removed and the oil boiled out in large copper cauldrons. Unlike the famous "Yankee" whalers of the nineteenth century, the Basques didn't boil out the oil on their ships; they had shore-based stations for this. At the height of the fishery as many as 800 workers (all male) may have lived at Red Bay. One of the most famous relics of this industry is the wreck of a 300 tonne galleon, believed to be the *San Juan*, which sank at Red Bay during a storm in 1565. Basque whaling in Labrador ended in the early 1600s due to a shortage of whales, a loss of vessels during the Spanish Armada's attack on England, and the growth of piracy.

DAVID J. CLARKE

Basque Chalupa, preserved at Red Bay (Author's photo)

Although contenders as the first Europeans in Labrador, it doesn't appear as though the Basques gave the Big Land its modern name. The derivation of "Labrador" is uncertain, though one explanation is that early Portuguese expeditions brought home Native slaves whom the King declared the best labourers, or *"labradores,"* he had ever seen. A map of 1534 described Labrador as being discovered by an English vessel out of Bristol. The crewman who first sighted land was a farmer from the Azores, and the sailors called it "Labrador." *Lavrador* means husbandman – farmer or landowner – in Portuguese. Another version of this story ascribes the name to João Fernandes, also a farmer/landowner of the Azores. He was given permission by Portuguese King Manuel I (1469-1521) to search for new lands in the western Atlantic in 1499. Fernandes supposedly found a land he called *Tierra del Lavrador* in 1500. This may have been Greenland, but within a century the name was shifted westward to modern Labrador.

....

The French and English

Apart from the Basques, most Europeans who sighted Labrador in the sixteenth century were explorers. Frenchman Jacques Cartier (c. 1491-

1557) sailed the coast, landing in June 1534. He gave Labrador the unfortunate and inaccurate label, "...the land that God gave to Cain." Several English explorers also cruised the Labrador coast in this era. John Rut (*fl.* 1512-28) arrived in 1527 at the behest of Henry VIII (1491-1547), and may have explored St. Lewis Inlet. Rut soon tired of his northern expedition and set sail for the West Indies, stopping over in Newfoundland. Martin Frobisher (c. 1539-1594) followed Rut to Labrador in 1576, '77 and '78. John Davis (c. 1550-1605) arrived in 1586, leaving the first known reference to English fishing off Labrador. All three were searching for the Northwest Passage, a fabled route to the Orient overtop the American Continent.

Exploration continued in the 1600s. Henry Hudson (*fl.* 1607-11) passed by in 1610, and a number of French explorers also visited, including the engineer/surveyor Jean Bourdon (1601-68), who in 1657 made the first overland journey from Canada to Labrador. Bourdon suffered an attack from the Inuit, although at least one of his countrymen had better luck in his dealings with them. The Canadian-born Louis Jolliet (1645-1700) was one of the most famous French adventurers to visit Labrador's shores. Having originally trained for a career in the priesthood, Jolliet was celebrated for his expeditions to the Mississippi River and Hudson's Bay in the 1670s. Although the evidence is slim, a contemporary document alleges that Jolliet made an initial voyage to Labrador in 1689, and had hopes of returning. He was not to be disappointed. Departing Quebec in April, 1694, the explorer arrived off the Labrador coast that Summer. Jolliet and his crew of eighteen sailed off the coast, which he charted, while engaging in trade with local Inuit. Arriving back in Quebec around mid-October, Jolliet published the journal of his voyage, at that time the most detailed account of the Big Land and its people. Containing sixteen cartographic sketches, this journal provided the first map of the Labrador coast between Cap Charles and Zoar.

Jolliet's friendly interaction with the Inuit was an exception. The French were fishing off Labrador from the early 1500s, allying themselves with the Innu in battle against the Inuit. Far more important to the Innu was French assistance against the powerful Five Nations Iroquois Confederacy to the south. In the end disease and Iroquois incursions marginalised the Innu, forcing them into traditional Inuit territory. For a time the relationship went better for the French, who controlled Labrador's Native trade until the Treaty of Paris in 1763. One French subject, Pierre Constantin, was actually granted title to all western Labrador in 1713.

....

The Moravians Arrive

Moravian Mission at Hopedale, pre-1902

Despite French success at establishing a friendship with the Innu, relations between Europeans and the Inuit remained turbulent for quite some time. For about a century such relations were marked by open hostility. This changed with the arrival of missionaries from the Moravian Brethren (*Unitas Fratrum*). Believing much of the trouble with the Inuit had been started by White fishers, Governor Sir Hugh Palliser (1722/3-96) invited the Moravians into Labrador to convert the Inuit. Hopefully the missionaries could keep the Natives apart from the English fishers, protecting both groups. The first attempt to establish a mission in 1752 ended with the Europeans being slain by the Inuit. The Moravians were finally able to convert many of their number after the arrival of Jens Haven (1724-96) and a new party of missionaries in

1764. Over the next century missions were established at such places as Nain, Hopedale and Ramah, the furthest station north. For the next two centuries the Moravians generally acted on behalf of their flock, not only in the field of religion, but in education as well. Their presence filled a gap left by an absentee Government. Although this was a positive relationship in many respects, there is no doubt Inuit culture has undergone significant changes as a result of the missionary presence.

....

Fishers, Furriers, Merchants and Mariners
From about 1763, with the end of the Seven Year's War, there are records of an organized English fishery off Labrador. Previously there seem to have been only a few English furriers, fishers and traders active on the Labrador coast. Governor Palliser soon asserted British sovereignty over Labrador. He also structured the Labrador fishery as a ship-based operation, building a Fort in Chateau Bay to guard English interests; one source gives the fort's name as Fort Pitt, another as Fort York. In 1774 Labrador, which had been under the jurisdiction of Newfoundland, was placed under Canadian authority by the Quebec Act (In 1809 Labrador was placed under Newfoundland's jurisdiction once more). By the 1770s merchants like the Slades of Twillingate and Fogo were already sending fishing vessels to Labrador. The first British commercial establishments on the coast were set up at Cape Charles by Nicholas Darby in 1767, and by Noble & Pinson at Temple Bay circa 1768. These merchants did not venture too far north as the Innu, former French allies, and the Inuit, were still hostile in this period.

Despite such activity, it was a number of years before much was known about Labrador, perhaps a major reason why some still considered it worthless. One of the first and best records of the coast was by Captain George Cartwright (1739-1819). Cartwright spent many years in Labrador, penning a lengthy journal of his travels in 1770. Cartwright first came to Newfoundland with his brother John, who had been sent to make peace with the Beothuk Indians. Captain Cartwright took an enlightened view of the Labrador Natives and is credited, along with the Moravians, with establishing friendly relations among the First Nations and Whites in Labrador. Though a kind ambassador to the

Aboriginal peoples, Cartwright was a failure in his efforts at trade, especially in the wake of deprivations by the privateer *Minerva* out of Boston.

George Cartwright

Regrettably, not everyone shared Cartwright's appreciation of Labrador. Jacques Cartier's short-sighted assessment of the region, although by then 200 years old, was still taken as fact. In 1794 Aaron Thomas travelled to Newfoundland as a crewman on HMS *Boston*. Thomas left behind a remarkable journal of his experiences on the Island, and in it made some comments on Labrador as well. Thomas proclaimed that Labrador, which he never even visited, was valueless, unless one could find a market for ice, stone and flint – iron ore, nickle, and hydro-power were many years in the future at that stage.

Despite assessments like Thomas,' Europeans and their

descendants were still interested in Labrador. The Americans were active Labrador fishers. It is likely that they were present prior to 1794, and their trade was of a considerable size before the War of 1812. As of 1820 it was estimated that more than 500 American vessels were fishing the Labrador coast, bringing in about five times the catch of their British counterparts. Besides the fishers, American whalers and traders were also active, and were said to have been especially lawless and troublesome for the authorities. In the same era the French harassed the British in Labrador. By 1780 Spear Harbour was fortified against French incursions, and in 1794 Temple Bay had no less than four forts. The need for defence on the Labrador coast was demonstrated in 1795. That year Revolutionary French vessels arrived, attacking British fishers, and capturing a number of ships. Palliser's original fort was bombarded. Its inhabitants fired their buildings and hid in the woods until the French were gone.

After 1783, when the English and French began more vigorous enforcement of French Shore treaty provisions, many Newfoundland ship fishers moved operations to the Labrador coast. Following in the wake of Noble & Pinson, a number of West Country merchant houses set up establishments there, and in 1813 the first Justices of the Peace were appointed for Labrador. In 1824 a Court of Civil Jurisdiction was set up for the coast. Over the course of the nineteenth century Newfoundland fishers extended their presence off the shores of Labrador. In the early years this was done exclusively by small sail vessels, but in the late-1800s a regular steamer service to Labrador was started. The annual Labrador fishery became firmly established, and some persons chose to settle permanently on the coast.

....

The "Bay"

Despite such interest in its coastal resources, first the British and then the Newfoundland authorities took little interest in Labrador Generally. They preferred leaving the administration of Labrador, such as it was, to others. For most of the nineteenth century the famous fur traders, the Hudson's Bay Company (HBC), played a dominant role in the region. This process began in 1821 when the HBC amalgamated with its main rival, the North West Company. Posts were established at Lake Melville, *Aillik*, *Saglek*, and North West River, to name just a few. Company employees were often the first Whites to view portions of the interior. The HBC also aided the growth of Labrador's Metis population. European men immigrated to areas such as Lake Melville to trap furs, and married Native women. "The Bay" remained a force in Labrador until the twentieth century when a new cash economy spelled an end to its fur trading business. The company gravitated more and more toward retailing. By this time, though, society in central Labrador was greatly altered. As natural resources declined and settlers moved in, the Innu came to depend increasingly on the HBC.

....

The Grenfell Mission

As the twentieth century approached many more changes were in the air. For years Labrador's only medical services were provided by a doctor sent annually by the Newfoundland Government, supplemented by visits from surgeons on British warships. By this time the Labrador fishery was expanding. The Newfoundland authorities finally felt compelled to take some action for the provision of medical services. Calls were put out for doctors to serve in the North. With the arrival of Doctor Wilfred T. Grenfell (1865-1940) and the Royal National Mission to Deep Sea Fishermen, the first real interest was taken in the health of Labradorians. Grenfell arrived in Newfoundland from England the day after the Great Fire of 1892. That Summer the young doctor spent three months visiting the Labrador coast in the hospital vessel *Albert*. He soon made the well-being of Labradorians and northern Newfoundlanders his life's mission. Following their tour of the coast, Grenfell and his compatriots reported back on conditions.

*Grenfell Mission Hospital
at Battle Harbour, 1920s*

It was decided to build two cottage hospitals in Labrador, at Battle Harbour and Indian Harbour. Another hospital was soon opened at St. Anthony, on Newfoundland's Northern Peninsula, which later became Grenfell's main headquarters. From these humble beginnings the Grenfell Mission's work began. Aside from hospitals, the Mission's accomplishments included the construction of schools, orphanages, and successful lobbying for coastal lighthouses. Much of what the Mission achieved was carried out on its own account, as the Government in St. John's was often parsimonious and neglectful where Labrador was concerned. Grenfell, and doctors like Harry Paddon (1881-1939), spent decades working on behalf of Labradorians – not just in medical matters – when few others would even listen.

....

Neglect
This state of affairs was brought home by the treatment of certain Labrador veterans at the end of World War I. Although Labradorians weren't even allowed to vote, many volunteered for military service. Among their number was Native recruit John Shiwak (1889-1917), a

celebrated sniper who later lost his life in battle.[1] At the War's end returning soldiers were dropped off in Battle Harbour, some over 480 kilometres away from home. The veterans were forced to pay for board until they could find transport to their communities, and were then responsible for their own travel costs. When the soldiers of North West River walked into their community in January, 1919 it was the first anyone there knew of the War being over. Dr. Paddon was outraged and agreed to speak on the veterans' behalf. Even so, it took five years for the men to be compensated. For such efforts Paddon and his family – Wife Mina and Son Anthony – are fondly remembered in Labrador. Mina was made an Officer of the Order of the British Empire for her work.

Okak, Labrador, pre-1919

Neglect of Labrador continued when the war was followed by a devastating epidemic in 1918. "Spanish Influenza," as it was called, actually originated in China. It first appeared in Newfoundland when three sailors carrying the virus were brought ashore on 30 September. A few days later three more infected sailors arrived at Burin. The outbreak spread on the Island like wildfire. It was soon carried to Labrador on the mail vessel *Sagona*. Putting in at every port, the *Sagona* left behind not only supplies but the deadly Spanish Flu as well. Many settlers fell ill that Fall and were too weak to cut their Winter's wood. Besides dying of the flu, many succumbed to cold. The hardest hit communities were the Inuit settlements of Okak and Hebron, where most residents perished. The Hudson's Bay Company begged for Government assistance, but this was refused since coal for the trip was lacking. Some aid, including a doctor and medicine, was dispatched. Unfortunately, this was June, 1919 and about a third of Labrador's Inuit – over 350 people – were already dead!

Ironically, Newfoundland's treatment of Labrador was much like its own early experience under British rule. It was suggested that Labrador residents should have representation in the House of Assembly as early as 1863. Premier Hugh Hoyles (1814-88) felt Labrador was no more than a fishing station, and vetoed the suggestion. There was no real justification for this act, but it meant Labradorians had no political voice for over eight decades. Successive Newfoundland Governments failed to provide funding for even the basics like education or health care; Churches, the HBC, and the Grenfell Mission were left to fill the breach.

....

Twentieth Century Affairs

Despite such neglect, the Newfoundland Government soon found itself master of an even larger portion of the Big Land. As we have seen, the 1774 Quebec Act placed Labrador under the jurisdiction of Canada. In 1809, however, control over a portion of Labrador was passed back to the Newfoundland authorities. Quebec strongly opposed the move, but the real wrangling began when both the Quebec and Newfoundland Governments realized the value of interior resources, like timber, that might be exploited. In 1927 the boundary question was ruled on by the Judicial Committee of the Privy Council at London. Canada, principally representing Quebec, argued that Newfoundland should control a narrow strip of coastal territory, reflecting traditional usage of Labrador as only a fishing station. The Newfoundland case alleged its control should extend far inland, along the course of rivers, past the Grand Falls, to areas used by White and Aboriginal trappers. Much of

Newfoundland's case was based on archival research by native-born P.T. McGrath, and secured a decision in the Island's favour. Ironically, discussions almost became a moot point three years earlier when the cash-strapped Newfoundland Government attempted to sell its Labrador rights to Quebec for $30,000,000.00. In the end the deal fell through, and Quebec opted to wait for the Privy Council decision, to its detriment. Labradorians don't appear to have been consulted about the matter in any case.

The Grand Falls, Labrador, c.1895

As on the Island, the twentieth century and Confederation have seen many further changes in Labrador. Under the Commission Labrador had its first Government which took an active interest in the region. For example, Commissioner John Hope Simpson (1868-1961) initiated the development of western Labrador's iron ore potential. The Newfoundland Ranger Force, set up by the Commission, were also Labrador's first permanent Government officials. Besides performing the duties of a police force, the Rangers also acted as game, fishery and forest wardens, as well as intermediaries between the people and Government. In 1942 the Commission took over HBC operations, marking the first direct Governmental role in Labrador's economic well-being.

The outbreak of World War II further transformed Labrador. Goose Bay was opened as an airport for Allied air transport of war materiel and anti-submarine patrols. Goose Airport provided the first large-scale experience of wage labour for many Labradorians. For the first time also the Big Land's settlers, Inuit, and Innu, were drawn together into a single community. By the 1950s medical facilities, postal services, telephones and an HBC store had all come to the area. At the end of the decade radio broadcasting began, and a firehall was constructed in the 1960s.

After the war the next big change was Confederation. Here the ramifications were even more profound than on the Island. Not only did Labrador become part of Canada, but the process itself was a political revolution. When British Prime Minister Clement Atlee (1883-1967) convened the National Convention to decide the future of Newfoundland & Labrador in 1946, United Church Minister Lester Burry (1898-1977) was elected as the representative for Labrador. For the first time the Big Land's people participated in the democratic process and had their own official representative. Burry was not impressed with the treatment of Labrador by Newfoundland, and felt Confederation might offer a way out. The people responded positively, voting more than eighty percent in favour of joining Canada. They soon elected their first member of the House of Assembly, Harold Horwood (1923-2006).

....

Problems and Potential

Despite the decision to join Canada, there are many problems remaining. The social and cultural dislocation of the land's Native peoples remains a critical issue, as do calls for clarification of their status since the Terms of Union (The Innu and Inuit were treated almost as if they didn't exist during the Confederation debates, though the recent land claims settlement with the Inuit is a major step forward). NATO training flights from Goose Bay have also generated controversy. Native groups have rallied against low-level flying, although many in Labrador favour the economic boost provided by foreign air-forces. The threatened pull-out of many of these air forces is itself worrisome to some Labradorians. Labradorians have seen massive developments take place on their home soil, including Churchill Falls, the development of western Labrador and its iron ore reserves, and the Voisey's Bay nickle project. Still, just as some Newfoundlanders feel they are not getting the full benefits of Confederation, so do many Labradorians believe they are cheated as part of the Province of Newfoundland & Labrador. Nationalist movements like the New Labrador Party (NLP. Founded, 1971) have surfaced. In 1974 the region unveiled its own flag, created by members of the NLP. Such developments not only reflect the proud spirit of Labradorians, but the feeling that – as the Royal Commission on Labrador reported in the 1970s – Labrador was not getting its fair share of benefits from recent industrial developments. In the twenty-first century such problems remain. Likewise, Labradorians are affected by issues facing the Province as a whole, like the decline of fish stocks. The solutions remain to be seen.

Section 2 ~
On This Day.
Newfoundland & Labrador
and Isles History by Date

5
On This Day...

January

1

1809. Fogo Island entrepreneur William Cull is engaged by Newfoundland Governor Holloway to lead an expedition into the Beothuk Winter territory at Red Indian Lake. Two Beothuk are sighted but no contact is made.

1833. Newfoundland's House of Assembly opens, and elects its first Speaker, J.B. Garland.

1842. The *Petrol*, a vessel belonging to the firm of Slade & Cox, is lost with all hands on a run from Fogo to Twillingate when a vicious storm blows up suddenly.

1845. James Spearman Winter, later Newfoundland Premier, and a Supreme Court Justice, is born at Lamaline.

1864. Merchant Robert Slade dies at the age of sixty-eight.

1917. Following a plebiscite in 1915, Newfoundland enacts a total prohibition of alcohol, except for medicinal use.

1934. Doctor Albert Wood of Twillingate officially joins the staff of the Notre Dame Bay Memorial Hospital, an institution he had long supported.

2

1886. The Salvation Army holds its first services in Newfoundland, at St. John's Victoria Hall. It is reported that one man and three girls were present.

3
1885. Barr'd Island merchant James Rolls, Sr., formerly of Sturminster Newton, Dorset, dies.

1930. George Pardy, aged sixty-two, is killed at Little Harbour when a telegraph pole, snapped by a house being hauled to a new property, falls on him. Harry Gedge of Durrell is seriously injured in the same incident.

4
1920. A serious fire breaks out at Fogo's new St. Andrew's Church, the result of an overheating furnace. Through the efforts of locals the building is saved.

St. Andrew's, Fogo (Author's photo)

5
1855. Death of Henry D. Winton, Sr., publisher of the *Public Ledger* newspaper.

6
1850. Roman Catholic Bishop Michael Fleming celebrates the first Mass in St. John's Catholic Cathedral (Later the Basilica).

1914. The Fogo wireless station's mast is toppled during a wind and glitter storm.

7
1897. The Ashbourne merchant family acquire a dwelling at Twillingate, later known as the "Ashbourne Longhouse," from Edwin John Duder.

8
1892. Peter Palmer Rogerson, Brother of Newfoundland politician Hon. James J. Rogerson, is drowned at New York.

9
1847. Fogo and Twillingate District's Member of the House of Assembly (MHA), John Slade, dies at Thames Street, Poole.

1947. *Twillingate Sun* Editor, Stewart Roberts, dies in his home on North Side, Twillingate, aged fifty-nine.

10
1918. The schooner *Ada D. Bishop* departs Twillingate with a cargo of codfish and disappears.

1945. Airman Neil W. Harnett of Twillingate is killed in an plane crash.

11
1938. An Imperial Airways Fox Moth flown by Captain Douglas Fraser becomes the first aircraft to land at the newly-created Newfoundland (Gander) Airport.

1940. Some of Twillingate's first recruits depart for Lewisporte onboard the S.S. *Sagona* as part of the Newfoundland Overseas Forestry Unit.

12
1860. The Harbour Grace Gas Works are lost to fire.

1894. Captain W. Taylor, commanding Munn & Company's brigantine *Kestrel*, is presented with a binocular glass by the Danish Government following his rescue of two seamen in mid-ocean.

13
1915. The armed merchant cruiser HMS *Viknor* sinks with all hands off Ireland's north coast. Among the dead are Seaman George Coates of Fogo and Seaman Enos Barnes of Change Islands.

14
1859. The "Merchant's Block" of St. John's Water Street suffers a fire, one of several to hit the area in the nineteenth century.

1926. Edward J. Linfield of Twillingate tries out a new radio, one of the first in the area, for the first time.

Edward J. Linfield

15
1944. Samuel C. Maley, a native of the Isle of Man, former deputy sheriff and veterinarian, dies in his adopted hometown of Twillingate.

16

1947. Following the death of owner/Editor Stewart Roberts, the *Twillingate Sun* newspaper suspends publication for the only time in its history. It resumes on 15 February under new owner Ernest G. Clarke.

17

1891. James Fitzgerald, a native of Tintern, Wexford, Irleand, and the longtime Stipendiary Magistrate at Fogo, dies at the age of seventy-nine.

1926. Churches across Notre Dame Bay hold a "Hospital Sunday," to raise money for the local medical facility, based at Twillingate.

18

1880. Richard Squires, a future Newfoundland Prime Minister, is born at Harbour Grace.

1890. A public meeting is convened at Twillingate's Court House to enact measures for preventing the spread of diphtheria. A Vigilance Committee is also established.

1932. Businessman Arthur G. Ashbourne dies suddenly at his residence in Durrell, aged fifty-seven.

19

1944. At 3:00 pm Magistrate Beaton J. Abbott officially opens the Twillingate Regional Library.

Beaton J. Abbbott

20
1876. Newfoundland's first Christian Brothers arrive at St. John's aboard the SS *Moravian*.

1918. Summerford's first United (Methodist) Church is opened and dedicated by Rev. S. S. Milley.

21
1930. Messages from King George V and British Prime Minister J. Ramsay MacDonald are received at Twillingate via short wave radio.

1933. Dr. Charles Parsons makes a radio broadcast from the Newfoundland Hotel detailing the important work done by the Notre Dame Bay Memorial Hospital at Twillingate, and noting a financial crisis caused by Government cutbacks to the institution.

22
1928. The second St. John the Evangelist Anglican Church, serving Barr'd Islands and Joe Batt's Arm, is lost to fire.

23
1917. The troop carrier HMS *Laurentic* sinks after striking a mine laid by U-80 off Malin Head, Northern Ireland. Seamen Ephraim Freake and Frederick Randell of Fogo are lost.

24
1884. Sergeant Fennessy is killed in a snow slide at Bett's Cove.

25
1907. The brigantine *Robin* sinks off Fogo harbour after hitting ice while being towed by the coastal steamer *Portia*.

26
1926. Crosby Lodge, Loyal Orange Association (LOA), Twillingate, surrenders its charter and joins with the Loyalty Lodge. Martin Phillips is elected first Worshipful Master of the combined Lodge.

27
1847. Tim Ryan is found dead in Signal Hill Prison, St. John's, shortly after being acquitted by the Newfoundland Supreme Court of the murder of Michael Morrissey.

1915. St. Peter's Anglican Rectory, Twillingate, built only a few years earlier, burns to the ground.

1917. The Ashbourne merchant premises on South Island, Twillingate, are seriously damaged by fire.

28
1850. Newfoundland's pre-Confederation seat of Government, the Colonial Building, opens for the first time.

29
1832. Politician Michael T. Knight, who goes on to serve as Representative for Twillingate District in the 1890s, is born.

30
1866. William Valence Whiteway is elected Speaker of Newfoundland's House of Assembly.

31
1860. Ambrose Shea is elected Speaker of the Colonial House of Assembly.

1864. The St. John's premises of Muir and Duder, which has branches on the Isles, is burnt at St. John's.

February

1
1888. Death of Sir Hugh Hoyles, former Premier, and Newfoundland's first native-born Chief Justice.

2
1833. A committee of merchants and leading citizens is formed at Twillingate to alleviate some of the distress caused by a poor fishery and a potato crop failure the previous year.

1915. The armed merchant cruiser HMS *Clan McNaughton* is lost in the North Sea with all of her compliment, including Jonas Watkins of Farmer's Arm (Summerford).

1945. Andrew Lunnen, longtime printer with the *Twillingate Sun*, dies near his home on North Side, Twillingate, while on his way home from work.

3
1870. Governor Sir Stephen John Hill opens the Newfoundland House of Assembly, speaking in favour of Confederation with Canada, contrary to the wishes of the Colonial Government.

4
1924. Rev. William Seeley Mercer perishes in a snowstorm while returning to Fogo from parish duties at Seldom-Come-By. A highway and Church are later dedicated in his honour.

5
1853. Edwin John Duder is born at St. John's.

6
1879. A.J.W. McNeily is elected Speaker of the House of Assembly.

1890. Judge Daniel W. Prowse, later the author of *A History of Newfoundland*, alleges that he lost the chance of obtaining a knighthood due to his stand on the French Shore question.

7

1865. The Market House, St. John's, is the site of a large anti-Confederation rally.

1890. The Hotel Glover, Topsail, is lost to fire.

8

1881. William Pride, aged nineteen, of David Button's Cove, Twillingate, is fined one dollar for driving his sled dogs in a reckless manner.

9

1889. A chapter of the Masonic Order is established at Twillingate at a meeting held in the town's Court House.

1931. The residence of John Andrews, North Side, Twillingate, catches fire, but is saved through the quick action of locals.

1943. Albert Edgar Hickman, who served the shortest ever term as Newfoundland Prime Minister (May-June, 1924), dies.

10

1926. Noted fishing skipper, Edward "Ned" White of Durrell, dies at the age of seventy-two.

11

1894. The Newfoundland Brewing Company's premises in St. John's are destroyed by fire.

1927. The cooper shop at Ashborne's "Upper Trade," Twillingate, is destroyed by fire.

12
1819. Birth of Frederick B.T. Carter. He would go on to serve as Newfoundland's Premier and its Chief Justice. For part of his political career, Carter served as the representative for Twillingate and Fogo District.

1872. Former Twillingate and Fogo District MHA, and Speaker of the House of Assembly, Thomas Bennett, dies in England.

13
1868. The Methodist parsonage and chapel on Twillingate's South Side are lost to fire.

1933. Thieves break into G.J. Carter's business at South Side, Twillingate, stealing a considerable amount of tobacco and other goods.

G.J. Carter premises, South Side, Twillingate

14
1823. The St. John's Library, later known as the Athenaeum, is established.

1922. The Twillingate Telephone & Electric Company warns locals that damage to the Company's poles and wires caused by house hauling will not be tolerated in future.

1942. The catapult-armed merchant ship *Empire Spring* is hit by a torpedo from U-576. The vessel sinks, taking about fifty crewmen to the bottom, including Third-Officer Arthur William Gillett of Twillingate.

1947. Former Newfoundland Ranger Ernest G. Clarke assumes the reigns as the last owner/Editor of the *Twillingate Sun*.

15
1928. Renowned shipbuilder and businessman, Thomas French of Tizzard's Harbour, dies at the age of eighty-five.

The schooner Champion, *built by Thomas French*

16
1920. Former Premier and Twillingate District Representative, Augustus Goodridge, dies at St. John's.

1928. Janet Stirling, Sister of famed opera soprano Georgina, dies in England.

1934. With the Dominion suffering from financial turmoil and years of mismanagement, Newfoundland gives up its system of Responsible Government, as an unelected Commission of seven men is sworn in to govern the Country.

17
1881. James Jones and Eli Atkinson of Herring Neck are lost while sealing when their boat overturns during a sudden storm.

1883. Twillingate's Court House burns to the ground.

1927. Men begin hauling a home, formerly owned by the Howlett family, from Durrell to another part of Twillingate's South Island, where it will be used as the Harbour View Hotel.

1930. A gale of near hurricane force hits the Twillingate area, putting telegraph lines out of commission and damaging property.

1942. Three men, including William Young and George Pippy of Twillingate, die while working onboard Ashbourne's auxiliary schooner *Bessie Marie* at St. John's.

1943. Ben Churchill of North Side, Twillingate, is trapped overnight on Burnt Island while duck hunting, but is found safe the following morning.

18
1918. The crew of the vessel *Cecil L Shave*, including Charles Hart of Fogo, are lost when she is torpedoed by the German submarine, U-155 west of Gibralter.

1933. Future Newfoundland Premier Frank Duff Moores is born at Carbonear.

1942. The American naval vessels *Truxton* and *Pollux* run aground on Newfoundland's Burin Peninsula. 186 men survive, aided by residents of the nearby towns of Lawn and St. Lawrence.

19
1934. Men break into the premises of French Brothers, Summerford, taking foodstuffs such as flour, molasses and sugar.

1940. A Moreton's Harbour chapter of the Women's Patriotic Association (WPA) is formed during a meeting held at the local school hall. Mrs. F.J. Osmond is elected President.

20
1881. Merchant Edwin Duder dies, aged fifty-eight years.

1926. Death of renowned mariner, Captain A. James Gillett, of Durrell.

1940. Summerford residents form a chapter of the WPA. The meeting is held in the local school hall, and Mrs. F. Wheeler becomes President.

21
1881. Doctor William Stirling amputates the right hand of John White, Twillingate, after White's gun bursts while birding, mangling the digit.

22
1933. A house jointly owned by Darrell and Edward Anstey of Back Harbour, Twillingate, burns to the ground, the flames fanned by a strong wind.

23
1891. 200 distressed women and children are fed at St. John's Fishermen's Home by Lady O'Brien and other local philanthropists.

24
1818. Death of Newfoundland Governor, Admiral Sir Francis Pickmore, at St. John's.

1872. The Newfoundland Temperance League is organized at St. John's.

Death of Aubrey George Spencer, former Anglican Bishop of Newfoundland.

1918. The steamer S.S. *Florizel* of Bowring's Red Cross Line, runs aground at Horn Head Point, Cappahayden, during a storm. Of the 137 persons on board, only seventeen passengers and twenty-seven crew survive.

1921. The first annual meeting of the Notre Dame Memorial Hospital Association is held, with William B. Temple, George Blandford, A.J. Gillett, Arthur Manuel, Jacob Moors, Benjamin Roberts, Charles White, W.J. Minty and Arthur H. Hodge elected as Directors.

25

1857. Robert Bond is born at St. John's. He would go on to become one of Newfoundland's most successful Prime Ministers, representing Twillingate District for much of his political career.

1935. Businessman George J. Carter, whose firm maintained branches at Herring Neck and Twillingate, dies at St. John's.

1939. The Notre Dame Bay Memorial Hospital's cottage is burned to the ground. Dr. John M. Olds and his family lose all their belongings.

Loss of the Hospital Cottage, 1939

26

1936. Frederick Charles Alderdice, who served as Newfoundland's last Prime Minister, dies at St. John's.

1945. Members of St. Peter's Lodge, Society of United Fishermen (SUF), Twillingate, petition the Commission of Government to determine the feasibility of constructing a ship canal from Bridgeport to Chanceport, New World Island.

27

1861. Newfoundland Governor Sir Alexander Bannerman dismisses the Government of Premier John Kent.

1892. The "Trinity Bay Disaster," in which twenty-four men are driven off to sea and lost.

1904. Annie Violet Wheeler (nee Payne), author of the book, *Cherished Memories*, is born at Fogo.

28
1856. Frederick I.R. Stafford is born at Montreal. He will go on to become a medical doctor, practising at Twillingate from 1882 to 1906.

1931. William Murcell of Herring Neck drowns crossing the ice while returning home from Twillingate.

1943. The Notre Dame Bay Memorial Hospital is seriously damaged by fire, though no one is hurt. Rebuilding takes three years, due to wartime shortages.

29
1875. Thirteen men are lost while attempting to board the French vessel *Violetta* from the ice in St. Mary's Bay.

March

1

1900. Death of former Twillingate and Fogo District Representative, and Premier, Sir Frederick B.T. Carter.

1927. The Judicial Committee of the Privy Council, London, rules in Newfoundland's favour in its dispute with Canada over the boundary of Labrador.

2

1898. The *Ada*, under Captain Barnes, departs for the seal fishery, the last sailing vessel to prosecute the hunt from Harbour Grace.

3

1898. The rules of Newfoundland's House of Assembly are suspended, allowing the Reid Railway Bill to be rushed through its various stages.

1899. Henry Edward McCallum arrives in Newfoundland to take up his post as Governor.

4

1863. Newfoundland's first sealing steamer, the *Bloodhound*, clears from the port of St. John's under Captain A. Graham.

1898. Sir Robert Bond protests the Governor's assent to the Railway Bill, on behalf of the Opposition.

1908. An elderly native of England, aged eighty, and a young girl, are burnt to death in a tragic fire at Cobb's Arm.

5

1819. A Beothuk woman named Demasduit (Mary March) is captured by a party led by John Peyton, Jr. Demasduit's Husband, Nonosabasut, is killed during the affair.

1920. Doctor Frederick I.R. Stafford, formerly resident at Twillingate, dies.

6
1886. The *Colonist* newspaper is started at St. John's.

1899. The *Lottie*, Newfoundland's last sail-powered sealing vessel, clears port at St. John's.

1900. The Winter Government resigns.

7
1861. The House of Assembly is dissolved following the forced resignation of the Kent Administration.

1881. Dundee sealing crews haul stone for the construction of St. John's Church of England Cathedral.

8
1834. Doctor William Carson introduces a Bill to establish a town council at St. John's.

1888. The *Twillingate Sun* reports that a Father and Son at Fogo had killed a bird in the harbour, believed to have been a Great Auk, a species declared extinct decades earlier.

Great Auk (Pinguinus impennis)

1899. Governor McCallum visits sealing steamers, and later addresses the men at the Prince of Wales Rink.

9
1879. Francis Lind is born to parents Henry and Elizabeth Lind at Bett's Cove. In 1914 Lind would enlist with the Newfoundland Regiment at Fogo and go on to fame as Newfoundland's unofficial war correspondent, "Mayo" Lind.

1934. Men from New World Island cause a disturbance at the Twillingate Court House, in the wake of a trial for stealing food from the French Brothers' store in Summerford. Several prisoners escape, but are later taken into custody, along with some of those who helped free them.

1939. Twillingate's South Side United Church is saved through the work of a bucket brigade after a fire lit by a sexton for a wedding ignites the roof.

10
1862. The first herds of seals strike near Twillingate, sparking what would be remembered as the "Great Seal Haul." A church bell is later cast to commemorate the event.

1874. The Sealing Bill comes into effect, fixing this date (10 March) as that on which steamers may head to the ice.

1884. A proclamation prohibiting the sale of "intoxicating liquors" is enacted, covering Fogo Harbour, Eastern Tickle, Locke's Cove, L'Argent's Cove, Seal Cove and Little-Seldom-Come-By.

11
1915. HMS *Bayano* of the British Tenth Cruiser Squadron is sunk by the German submarine U-27 off Carswell Point in the Firth of Clyde. Edmond Brown and Joseph Farewell of Fogo are among the dead, while Stephen Keates of Barr'd Islands is rescued.

1929. Bridgeport residents hold a public meeting in the United Church School to petition the Government to construct a public building for postal and telephone service.

1949. Dr. J.M. Olds, aided by Captain Ned Clarke and others, sets out by snowmobile, horse and dog teams to reach a patient undergoing a difficult labour at Joe Batt's Arm. He arrives late the following day, in time to save the life of Mother and baby.

12
1900. Absalom Sheppard, one of the earliest settlers of Indian Islands (Born, Harbour Grace), dies, aged eighty-six. He is buried at Eastern Cove.

1918. J. Sheppard and his Wife are found frozen to death on the ice near Twillingate.

1928. A fire destroys the home of John Curtis of Virgin Arm.

13
1833. Notice of a Bill to incorporate St. John's is given in the House of Assembly by Newman W. Hoyles.

14
1764. Merchant George Davis pens a letter to Captain James Cook. The letter notes the story of Thomas Fizzard (Tizzard), formerly of Bonavista, who claimed to be the first person who ever "drove a nail" at Twillingate.

1874. The House of Assembly adjourns after sitting continually for thirty-two hours.

1926. A retail store, formerly belonging to the Howlett business at Durrell, is hauled to nearby Farmer's Arm, and used as a retail store, as part of Ashbourne's "Lower Trade."

1928. St. Peter's Anglican Church, Twillingate, holds a sacred concert to raise funds for the Notre Dame Bay Memorial Hospital. More than sixty-eight dollars are collected.

1938. Death of well-known carpenter, Alfred Manuel of Twillingate, aged seventy-two.

15
1931. The sealing vessel S.S. *Viking* suffers an explosion and sinks off Newfoundland's Horse Islands while under charter by an American crew filming scenes for a Hollywood movie. Filmmakers Varrick Frissell and Alexander Gustavus Penrod are killed, along with twenty-five others.

Taking supplies over the ice to Viking *survivors from S.S.* Sagona

1937. Five men from Durrell – Edward Clarke and crew – are trapped on the ice while sealing. Ashbourne's vessel, *Lone Flyer*, is readied to rescue the men, but they are able to make it to shore after receiving food from another boat.

16
1858. W.B. Jennings, who will go on to represent Twillingate District and serve as Minister of Public Works, is born.

1927. Former Newfoundland Prime Minister and Twillingate District MHA, Sir Robert Bond, dies.

17
1938. Master mariner and coasting skipper, Robert Young, of North Side, Twillingate, dies at the age of eighty-six.

1941. Nathaniel Jenkins, for many years a successful fishing skipper in the employ of Ashbournes, Ltd., passes away at Durrell, aged eighty-one.

18
1889. Reuben Elliott and James Barnes of Ragged Point are stranded on the ice while seal hunting. They are rescued by Captain Knee in the steamer *Falcon* after having been given up for dead.

1900. The steamer S.S. *Clyde* arrives in Newfoundland. The vessel goes on to serve Notre Dame Bay for half a century.

19
1881. Death of Joseph J. Pearce, a native of Fogo, and for many years Twillingate's Sub-Collector of Customs, in his seventy-first year.

1896. A new Methodist Church is opened at Moreton's Harbour, with Twillingate incumbent, Rev. Levi Curtis preaching the dedicatory sermon.

20
1878. Newfoundland's first telephone is installed, connecting the residences of John Delaney and John Higgins.

1938. The Salvation Army commemorates the fiftieth anniversary of Salvationism at Twillingate with a special service. Adjutant and Mrs. Rideout preside over the occasion, which is highlighted by a letter from Twillingate's first Salvation Army Officer, Thomas H. Collier.

1943. Harvey Bulgin and his passenger, Ted Wheeler, both of Summerford, go through the ice near Lewisporte in Mr. Bulgin's truck. The vehicle is lost but both men are saved.

21
1898. *Greenland* Disaster. Forty-eight men perish at the ice during a storm.

1944. A meeting is held at the Memorial Hospital, Twillingate, under Chief Harry Randell, to organize a South Side Fire Brigade.

22
1935. A large polar bear comes ashore at Durrell, and is killed by Kenneth Legge and Ted Moody.

23
1861. St. John's Athenaeum is established.

1886. Newfoundland journalist/lawyer/Politician Alfred Bishop Morine, born in Nova Scotia, attempts to seize the *Mercury* press.

24
1867. Writing from Fogo, merchant agent Charles Edmonds notes that conditions in the community are "frightfully bad," with many locals bordering on starvation.

25
1834. A petition is received in the House of Assembly, signed by Robert Slade and others in Twillingate, along with certain residents of Torbay and Pouch Cove, asking for statute labour on the roads.

1856. Newfoundland's House of Assembly passes a Bill increasing the number of Representatives to twenty-eight (From fifteen), this provision to take effect at the next general election.

26
1883. Twillingate adopts the "local option" prohibiting the sale of "intoxicating liquors."

1912. Fogo's wireless relay station, operated by the Canadian Marconi company, is officially announced as open for business.

1940. Sir Richard Squires, former Prime Minister of the Dominion of Newfoundland, dies at the age of sixty.

27
1943. While in the Firth of Clyde the aircraft carrier HMS *Dasher* is rocked by a tremendous explosion. 379 crewmen die, including Able Seaman William Stephen Lloyd (Harbin) Linfield of Twillingate.

28
1836. Robert Thorburn, future Premier of Newfoundland, is born in Scotland.

1929. Heavy seas cause extensive damage in the Twillingate area, destroying a breakwater at Crow Head, the wharves of John Gillett at Durrell, and stages in Wild Cove. A number of schooners at Durrell are also nearly driven ashore.

29
1928. *Twillingate Sun* Editor Stewart Roberts has a shed, formerly belonging to Edward Roberts, hauled up Path End, Twillingate, to serve as the newspaper's new office, replacing that which had been used since 1880.

1898. A public funeral is held for victims of the *Greenland* Disaster.

30
1826. Captain Rudkin and Ensign Philpot fight the last duel in Newfoundland. Philpot is killed.

1886. Men demanding food or work riot in front of the Colonial Building.

1914. "*Newfoundland* Disaster." 132 men depart the steamer S.S. *Newfoundland* to hunt seals on the ice flows, only to be caught in a vicious blizzard. By the time they are rescued only fifty-five men remain alive.

31
1857. Alfred Bishop Morine, later an influential Newfoundland politician, is born at Port Medway, Nova Scotia.

1862. As of this date 30,000 seals are landed at Twillingate in what comes to be known as the "Great Seal haul."

1914. The 520 gross ton sealing steamer *Southern Cross* is lost in a blizzard off the Newfoundland coast with her entire crew of 174 men.

S.S. Southern Cross

April

1
1828. William Valence Whiteway, later Newfoundland's longest-serving Premier, and a Representative of Twillingate and Fogo District, is born in Devonshire, England.

1854. The merchant firm of Steer & Ayre opens for business at St. John's.

2
1876. The Society of United Fishermen hold their first parade, at the funeral of Thomas Wilkie.

1879. The *Evening Telegram* newspaper is registered at St. John's by proprietor W.J. Herder.

1928. Sailmaker John Colbourne Cook of Twillingate, dies at his home on North Side, aged sixty.

3
1867. Georgina Stirling is born at Twillingate to Dr. William Stirling and Wife Ann (nee Peyton). She will go on to become one of the late-Victorian era's greatest sopranos – the "Nightingale of the North."

1884. The *Neptune*, under Captain S. Blandford, arrives at St. John's with what was then the largest ever number of seals taken in one voyage, 41,983.

1908. Merchant Richard Dorman Hodge, a native of Crewkerne, Somerset, England, dies at Twillingate.

4
1942. Merchant/politician, William E. Waterman, whose family once carried on an extensive trade in places such as Twillingate and Fogo, dies at Broadstone, Dorset, aged eighty-six.

5

1852. "Spring of the Wadhams." A great gale results in the loss of twelve vessels, with several others abandoned.

1914. St. Peter's Church, Twillingate, holds a special memorial service to remember the more than seventy sealers who perished in a blizzard during the *Newfoundland* Disaster.

1927. Medical Superintendent Dr. Charles Parsons, and Henry Rideout, set off on a fundraising tour of Notre Dame Bay in support of the Memorial Hospital at Twillingate.

1932. Rioters protesting Government mismanagement storm the Colonial Building in St. John's, forcing Prime Minister Sir Richard Squires to flee.

6

1815. Merchant John Slade officially transfers his Twillingate business interests to his Nephews, Robert Slade and John Slade, Jr.

1864. Twenty-six ships are lost and another 140 jammed in the ice when a major storm hits Notre Dame Bay. No vessels arrive in St. John's with seals until 23 April.

1918. The Directors of the Twillingate Telephone and Electric Company vote to award the sum of $10.00 to telegraph operator Miss S. Foley "...for her valuable services in reading out the war news..." to customers.

1926. Members of Twillingate's Society of United Fishermen hold a parade and celebratory dinner to mark fifty years of the organization's presence in the community.

7

1917. A number of sealers from the community of Joe Batt's Arm are driven off on the ice flows. Though a search is organized, the only trace ever found of the men is a gaff belonging to one of their party.

1941. George Hamlyn, a former resident of Crow Head, drowns at La Scie.

8
1889. Moreton's Harbour, Tizzard's Harbour, Western Head, Whale's Gulch... Carter's Cove and "all other settlements north of Virgin [Arm] on New World Island" adopt the "local option," prohibiting the sale of alcohol.

Western Head, New World Island, c.1946

1904. The *Entente Cordiale* is signed between France and Great Britain. The agreement sees France give up its treaty rights on Newfoundland's so-called "French Shore, rights it had held since the eighteenth century.

9
1859. The brig *Petrel*, Master George Clough, is found in a sinking condition. The crew are rescued and brought into St. John's by the S.S. *Osprey*, under Captain Gulliford.

10
1835. The Legislative Council passes Newfoundland's first Game Law.

1852. Future Premier William Whiteway is admitted to the Newfoundland Bar.

1890. Twillingate physician, Dr. William M. C. Stirling, Father of soprano Georgina Stirling, dies at Twillingate.

11
1942. The Hillgrade Women's Patriotic Association holds its first meeting and organizes a working committee.

12
1912. The Fogo wireless station reportedly receives the RMS *Titanic*'s distress signal, passed along from Cape Race, the only land-based facility to receive the message directly.

13
1822. William Wells, Thomas Drake, Samuel Lacey, Henry Blackmore, James Warr and Geoffrey Tizzard of Back Harbour, and John Stuckless of Cat Cove, make their way back home after having been stranded on pack ice for nearly two weeks (Drake later burns to death in a house fire at Back Harbour, with nearly all of his family).

1858. The town of Harbour Grace is devastated by fire.

1894. The administration of William V. Whiteway resigns.

1925. The administration of Walter Monroe grants Newfoundland women the right to vote following a spirited campaign by the League of Women Voters.

14
1894. Augustus Goodridge, a Representative for Twillingate District, becomes Premier, and promptly prorogues the Legislature.

15
1811. James Louis O'Donel, Newfoundland's first Roman Catholic Bishop dies in Waterford, Ireland.

1831. Captain William Dwyer of Tilting rescues two stranded men from the Wadhams Islands.

Tilting, pre-1930

16
1850. Birth at St. John's of Thomas C. Duder, who will go on to serve as Fogo District's MHA, and as a Cabinet Minister under Augustus Goodridge and Jonathan Winter.

17
1871. Police Inspector Foley arrives from Ireland to take charge of the Newfoundland Constabulary.

18
1886. Louisa Journeaux of Jersey in the Channel Islands drifts out to sea in an open boat. She is rescued by a passing ship, taken to Newfoundland, and eventually returns home.

19
1871. Six houses are burnt at Cochrane Street, St. John's, in the "Tilman's Fire."

20
1887. Newfoundland Governor George William (later *Sir* William) Des Vœux departs the Colony to take up the Governorship of Hong Kong.

21
1865. Sir Hugh Hoyles is sworn in as Newfoundland's first native-born Chief Justice.
      Sir F.B.T. Carter is sworn in as Newfoundland's Attorney General.

1914. The body of Maggie Power, a servant at Purcell's Harbour, and formerly of Triton, is found near Little Harbour Hill. The exact cause of her death is never determined.

1925. A banquet is given at Twillingate's Masonic Temple in honour of Mr. Henry Rideout and his Son, Alfred, who oversaw construction of the Notre Dame Bay Memorial Hospital.

1928. W.A. "Artie" Scott, Son of former Twillingate Magistrate, W.J. Scott, joins the Seventy-Two Car Club, in recognition of his sales record with his Chevrolet dealership in Washington State. Scott is a veteran of the Canadian Mounted Rifles and a former POW.

1935. One-time opera singer Georgina Stirling dies of cancer at Twillingate, aged sixty-eight years.

22
1847. Governor Sir Gaspard LeMarchant arrives in Newfoundland.

1886. Governor George William De Vœux arrives in Newfoundland.

1928. The residence of George Roberts, Wild Cove, is destroyed by fire while he and his Wife are attending church services on North Side, Twillingate. Volunteers manage to save nearby buildings.

23
1799. Rev. John Hillyard leaves London on his way to take up missionary duties at Twillingate. While there he will become the first Minister to preach the Gospel on Fogo and New World Islands.

24
1859. John Cox and five Sons are lost with their schooner near Harbour Breton.

25
1889. Hon. Robert Bond presents a bell to the Episcopal Church at Whitbourne.

26
1866. James Stephens, a co-founder of the Irish Republican Brotherhood – the Fenians – arrives at St. John's on his way to New York. He escapes the authorities' net, though there is a $5,000.00 reward offered for his capture.

27
1863. The steamer *Anglo-Saxon* goes down near Cape Race with the loss of 307 persons. 137 are rescued.

1880. Sir F.B.T. Carter is appointed Chief Justice of Newfoundland (Another source gives the date as 28 May).
       Henry Waterman, lighthouse keeper at the Wadham Islands, drowns.

F.B.T. Carter

1898. Former *Twillingate Sun* Editor, Jabez P. Thompson, founds a second newspaper, *The Vindicator*, at Brigus.

28
1862. Numbers are painted on houses in St. John's for the first time.

1894. The Block House on Signal Hill is burnt.

29
1868. Newfoundland's House of Assembly passes resolutions of condolences to the Widow of Thomas D'Arcy McGee, the slain Father of Canadian Confederation.

1881. While preparing to depart Twillingate for St. John's the schooner *Vivid* accidentally collides with another vessel, *Lucy*, causing some damage to the latter ship.

30
1868. The bodies of eleven members of Dr. Felix Dowsley's party are found at Gull Island by Captain Rowsell and his crew. The unfortunate souls had survived the wreck of their vessel, the *Queen of Swansea*, only to perish of exposure and starvation on the barren island.

May

1

1868. The bodies of eleven persons, who died on Gull Island after being wrecked in the *Queen of Swansea* disaster, are removed to Tilt Cove.

2

1497. John Cabot departs Europe in his vessel, the *Matthew*.

1861. General election. Conservatives William Whiteway, a future (Liberal) Premier, and Thomas Knight, are chosen to represent Twillingate and Fogo District

1867. The St. John's Medical Society is formed with Dr. H.H. Stabb as its first President.

3

1923. General election. Kenneth M. Brown, Arthur Barnes and George Jones become Twillingate District's MHAs under Richard Squires' Liberal Reform banner. George F. A. Grimes, another Liberal Reformer, is Fogo District's new Representative.

Captain George Jones, MHA

DAVID J. CLARKE

4
1847. Garland C. Gaden is appointed Sheriff of Newfoundland's "Northern District" (which includes the Isles).

1882. Newfoundland railway labourers go on strike for higher wages. Their ringleaders are arrested.

5
1796. William Epps Cormack, the first European to cross Newfoundland, is born at St. John's.

1880. The Bett's Cove mine founders, but with no fatalities.

1943. The Notre Dame Bay Memorial Hospital holds a "General Labour Day," in which volunteers help in clearing away debris left over from a disastrous fire earlier in the year.

Volunteers cleaning up after the Twillingate Hospital fire

6
1834. Newfoundland's Chamber of Commerce petitions the House of Assembly to send a naval squadron to protect fishers from French and American "outrages."

1848. John Thomas Mullock, the future Roman Catholic Bishop of Newfoundland, arrives in the Colony.

7

1855. General election, the first under "Responsible Government." Twillingate and Fogo District returns Conservatives W.H. Ellis and T. Knight.

8

1859. Future Newfoundland Prime Minister, Edward P. Morris, later the First Baron Morris, is born at St. John's.

1909. General election. Outgoing Prime Minister Robert Bond retains his seat in Twillingate District, as do James A. Clift and George Roberts. Henry J. Earle likewise continues as Fogo District's MHA.

9

1876. St. John's Phoenix and Cathedral Fire Brigades give notice of disbanding, to take effect 1 July.

10

1869. A Newfoundland Delegation including Premier Carter heads to Canada to discuss Confederation.

1885. Little Harbour's Methodist Church opens, with Rev. H. Hatcher, incumbent of Moreton's Harbour, presiding.

11

1898. John Kent's former homestead, Quidi Vidi, is destroyed by fire.

12

1822. Newfoundland's first fire brigade, the Phoenix Fire Company, is formed at St. John's, with N.W. Hoyle as its Captain.

1884. The first trial of men implicated in the Harbour Grace Orange riots commences.

1937. All of Twillingate's fraternal societies turn out for a parade from the local Court House, to Yate's Hill (South Side) and back, in celebration of King George VI's coronation. Magistrate Abbott reads an address to His Majesty, which is signed by himself, the clergy, and the heads of the societies. That night fireworks are launched from "Harbour Rock."

1948. The coasting freighter *Bertha E. Way* is burnt to the waterline off Twillingate after a fire erupts in its engine room. No injuries are suffered by the seven man crew.

13
1861. Soldiers fire on a mob at St. John's during election riots, killing two men and wounding several others.

1937. Races are held at Twillingate's Tickle Bridge in honour of King George VI's coronation. In one such race, Dr. Olds' horse bests that belonging to Reverend Burden. Bunting flies all over the town, and the Court House hosts a dance.

14
1871. Walter Stanley Monroe, Newfoundland's Prime Minister from 1924 to 1928, is born in Ireland.

15
1916. The Twillingate Telephone & Electric Company, Ltd. reports to District Representative James A. Clift that it has thirty-four telephones in operation.

1922. Work begins on the site of the Notre Dame Bay Memorial Hospital, under Benjamin Roberts.

16
1838. A meeting of subscribers is held at Twillingate's original St. Peter's Church to undertake the construction of a new house of worship.

1942. Albert Sellars, bosun on the S.S. *Glenco*, rescues two women – a Mother and Daughter – who had gone into the water while the vessel was docked at Change Islands.

17
1877. The coastal steamer *Plover* arrives in Newfoundland for the first time.

1891. St. Mary's Anglican Church, Herring Neck, still under construction, is first used for a worship service.

1930. Lady Helena Squires (nee Strong) is elected the first female Member of Newfoundland's House of Assembly, in a by-election in Lewisporte District, receiving eighty-one percent of the vote (Ironically, Lady Helena had earlier supported her Husband, Prime Minister Sir Richard Squires,' stand against granting women the right to vote).

18
1816. Sir Francis Pickmore is appointed Governor of Newfoundland.

1861. 250 men of the Sixty-Second Regiment arrive in St. John's via the steamer *Delta*, to help keep order in the wake of recent election riots.

19
1835. Journalist Henry D. Winton is attacked and mutilated by masked men while riding from Harbour Grace to Carbonear. He is treated by Dr. William Stirling, Sr. Although a large reward is offered, the assailants are never caught.

20
1841. Bishop Michael Anthony Fleming lays the foundation stone for St. John's Roman Catholic Cathedral (Later the Basilica).

1865. Sir Hugh Hoyles is sworn in as Chief Justice of Newfoundland.

1870. Darkness spreads over the Island of Newfoundland, a result of massive forest fires in Quebec.

21
1863. Newfoundland's first coastal steamer, the *Ariel*, arrives on the Island.

22
1855. The Newfoundland Legislature opens for the first time under Responsible Government, with Philip F. Little as Premier.

1887. The coastal steamer *Plover* collides with the schooner *Trixie H.*, resulting in the death of five persons.

1944. Beaton Tulk is born at Ladle Cove, Newfoundland. He will go on to serve as the Province's seventh Premier.

23
1855. MHA John Kent introduces the first Bill (Revenue) under Newfoundland's new system of Responsible Government.

24
1895. All of the Duder Company holdings on Newfoundland's northeast coast are sold in the aftermath of a serious bank crash.

1921. A mortar is placed outside Twillingate's Customs House under the direction of Magistrate Isaac J. Mifflin. It serves as the town's first Great War memorial.

25
1853. Newfoundland Magistrate Peter W. Carter is wounded after being shot by a man named Long.

26
1893. James Spearman Winter is sworn in as a Supreme Court Justice.

27
1802. Vice-Admiral James Gambier (Later Lord Gambier), is appointed Governor of Newfoundland.

Governor James Gambier

1885. A Redistribution Bill divides the District of Twillingate and Fogo into two parts. Twillingate District consists of the territory between Cape John and Farewell Point, and to the westward of a line drawn due north from Farewell Point. Fogo District lies between Farewell Point and Cape Freels, and the islands to the eastward of a line drawn due north from Farewell Point. Twillingate retains three representatives, while Fogo has one.

28
1891. Twillingate's Temperance Hall is host to a "bear show," featuring "extraordinary feats" performed by the animals, under the direction of their trainers. The act is later staged at Moreton's Harbour.

1931. Jacob Butler and his Wife, Mary Ann (Primmer. Formerly of Twillingate), die of natural causes at Sansom's Island on the same day.

29
1852. Merchants Edwin Duder and Robert Muir purchase the residence later known as the "Ashbourne Longhouse" from its original owner, planter/trader William Menchinton of Somerset.

1877. James Wilson arrives at Twillingate to establish a Congregational Church in the community.

30
1728. Newfoundland's first resident Justice of the Peace is appointed.

1928. Professor N.M. Guy lectures at Twillingate's Alexandra Hall on "Building a Great Society."

31
1833. The Governor adjourns Newfoundland's House of Assembly.

1858. 300 French fishermen are lost during a gale on the Grand Banks.

June

1
1854. The Union Bank opens for business at St. John's.

1866. W.D. Pearce, S. White and P. Connors are drowned in Twillingate harbour when their sailing craft capsizes (Another source gives the date as 27 May).

1927. Six year old Norah Cull of Shoal Bay, Fogo Island, is accidentally shot by her older Brother, who had been going hunting. She is taken by boat to the Hospital at Twillingate and successfully treated.

2
1924. General election. Kenneth M. Brown, George F. Grimes and Thomas G.W. Ashbourne get the nod to represent Twillingate District. R. Hibbs is Fogo District MHA. All represent the Liberal-Progressive Party, which goes down to defeat.

R. Hibbs, MHA

1932. Andrew Lunnen, typesetter with the *Twillingate Sun* newspaper, has his arm broken when it becomes entangled on a printing press belt. The break is set by Dr. Blackwell at the Notre Dame Bay Memorial Hospital.

3
1872. P. Geehan and Johanna Hamilton are sentenced to hang by Newfoundland Chief Justice Hoyles for the murders of his Wife and Brother-in-law. Hamilton's sentence is later commuted to transportation.

1875. St. Peter's Lodge No. Twelve, Society of United Fishermen (Twillingate), is granted its Charter.

1897. A Newfoundland delegation, including Premier Whiteway and Edward Morris, departs for England to attend Queen Victoria's Diamond Jubilee.

1908. A serious operation is performed at Change Islands by Doctors Campbell (Change Islands), Wood (Fogo) and Anderson (Joe Batt's Arm), one of the first recorded instances of local Doctors working in tandem.

1948. A referendum is held to decide the political future of Newfoundland. Of the three choices offered – Commission of Government for five more years, Confederation with Canada, or Responsible Government – none wins a majority of the vote, leading to another referendum later in the year.

4
1798. Irish patriot Lord Edward Fitzgerald, Husband of Lady Pamela (formerly of Fogo), dies of wounds received while being arrested by British authorities.

5
1849. Bishop Feild consecrates the Church of England Cemetery at Petty Harbour.

1866. The brig *Selina* sinks in the Narrows off St. John's after colliding with an American warship. One man named Pomeroy is drowned.

Stories From These Shores

6
1865. Robert Muir, of the firm of Muir & Duder, dies.

1887. The Town of Fogo is connected to the outside world by telegraph.

1890. The art journal *R Trovafore* prints one of the first international accounts of a rising new opera star, Twillingate native, Georgina Stirling.

1907. Longtime Fogo physician and Magistrate, Thomas Malcolm, born in Scotland, passes away.

1917. John Colbourne, Josiah Colbourne, Titus Stuckey and Doyle Whitt are drowned at Purcell's Harbour.

7
1885. A tremendous gale causes extensive damage to vessels and other property at Twillingate, Herring Neck, Change Islands and Fogo Island.

8
1863. Rev. Charles Pedley's work, *History of Newfoundland From the Earliest Times to the Year 1860*, is published.

1876. Anglican Bishop Edward Feild, who consecrated Twillingate's St. Peter's Church in 1845, dies in Bermuda.

9
1809. Tilting settler Michael Turpin, formerly of Ireland, is captured and killed by a group of Beothuk men near Sandy Cove (Other dates have been given for this event, including 13 June).

1846. The "Glue Pot Fire," which started in the premises of a cabinet maker named Hamlin, causes some $4,000,000.00 in damage at St. John's, destroying most of the city's merchant premises.

10

1718. John Slade – later known as "Slade the Elder" – is baptised at Winfrith Newburgh, Dorset, England.

1856. Former Sub-collector of Customs at Twillingate, Samuel Prowse, dies at Okehampton, Devonshire, England, aged sixty-four.

1881. Carpenters from the visiting Royal Navy warship, HMS *Druid*, go ashore at Twillingate to help rebuild houses destroyed in a fire.

11

1793. Charles Fox Bennett, who will go on to serve as Newfoundland's fifth Premier, is born at Shaftesbury, England.

1809. Fogo residents William Newbury and J. Wagg write English merchants John and William Fryer, indicating their weariness with the Napoleonic Wars then raging in Europe.

1917. James Adey of Twillingate finds a gaff floating in the water off Western Head. Writing on the item, unnoticed at the time, indicates that it was owned by one of the Joe Batt's Arm sealers who were lost earlier that Spring. Adey later arranges for the gaff to be returned to the sealer's relatives.

1919. The Military Medal earned by Augustus Bulgin of Durrell is presented posthumously to his family at Twillingate's Alexandra Hall.

1932. General election. Twillingate District elects Conservative, N. Gray over Liberal challenger Lady Helena Squires, Newfoundland's first woman MHA. Fogo's new MHA is Conservative Harold J. Earle.
  The same election sees Lady Helena's Husband, Prime Minister Sir Richard Squires, fall from power. This vote also marks the final time that Newfoundlanders go to the polls under Responsible Government.

12

1892. St. Margaret's Anglican Church, Change Islands, is officially opened, replacing the earlier St. James the Apostle Church. The service is attended by Reverends White, Temple and Chamberlain (The date has also been given as 16 June).

1900. A massive strike involving 1,500 miners begins at Bell Island.

13

1937. Former Newfoundland Prime Minister Sir William Frederick Lloyd dies at St. John's.

1943. Death of John Hodder, blacksmith, of Twillingate South Side.

14

1919. British aviators John Alcock and Arthur Brown lift off from a St. John's field in their modified Vickers Vimy bomber, landing in Ireland. It is the first nonstop transatlantic flight.

Alcock and Brown depart

1929. The *Bessie Marie*, Newfoundland's last three-masted schooner, is launched at Burlington, Green Bay, on order from Ashbourne's Ltd. of Twillingate.

15
1853. Philip F. Little, George H. Emerson and Robert J. Parsons are appointed delegates to the British Colonial Office to press Newfoundland's case for Responsible Government.

1899. Newfoundland Governor McCallum hosts his first public ball.

16
1927. The schooner *Earl Grey* is towed ashore at Seldom-Come-By after striking School Room Rock and becoming partly waterlogged.

17
1894. Twelve persons are lost when the schooner *Rose*, under Captain H. Goss, strikes ice and sinks near LaScie.

18
1878. The cornerstone of St. Andrew's Church, St. John's, is laid by Dr. Muir of Edinburgh.

19
1764. Governor Palliser issues rules to guide the "Fishing Admirals" in their dealings with French fishers and authorities on the French Shore.

1873. The topsail schooner *Memento*, owned by Edward Duder, is lost with all her crew on Renews Rock.

1898. The Society of United Fishermen celebrates its silver jubilee.

20
1863. James Cantwell of Tizzard's Harbour, drowns.

1900. Cabot Tower officially opens at St. John's.

1941. A public meeting is convened at Twillingate's Court House to make plans in case of a German air raid.

21
1762. A French force captures St. John's during the Seven Years War.

1884. A chapter of the Loyal Orange Association is inaugurated at Moreton's Harbour, with the proceedings Chaired by Titus Manuel of Twillingate. Joseph B. Osmond is named the first Worthy Master.

1890. A late season snowstorm hits Twillingate.

1946. Forty-five Members are elected to form a "National Convention," to recommend potential forms of Government for Newfoundland & Labrador, after more than a decade of unelected Commission of Government.
    Twillingate District selects Thomas G.W. Ashbourne as its representative, with Alfred Watton, Jr. attending on Fogo District's behalf.

22
1897. Bishop Michael Francis Howley lays the cornerstone of Cabot Tower as Newfoundland marks Queen Victoria's Diamond Jubilee and the 400th Anniversary of John Cabot's voyage.

23
1822. HMS *Drake*, bound to St. John's from Halifax under Captain Baker, sinks off St. Shott's. All sixty crew are lost.

1920. Dr. Wilfred Grenfell and eight Twillingate residents sign the articles of association for the Notre Dame Bay Memorial Hospital Association.

24
1497. John Cabot arrives in North America, most likely at Newfoundland or Labrador.

1880. The first issue of the *Twillingate Sun and Weekly Northern Advertiser* appears under owner/Editor Jabez P. Thompson.

1883. Sir Ambrose Shea is knighted.

1892. Bishop Howley is consecrated by Bishop Power.

1908. Death of former Newfoundland Premier, and MHA for Twillingate and Fogo District, William Whiteway.

Sir William Whiteway

1921. Merchant Frederick Linfield dies at Twillingate.

1927. Nurse Elsie B. Wood of Boston is married to merchant Arthur H. Hodge of Twillingate, by Dr. Wilfred T. Grenfell.

25
1873. The Anglo-American Telegraph Company is created through the amalgamation of the Anglo-American and French Telegraph Company, and the New York, Newfoundland & London Telegraph Company.

1878. Sir John Glover becomes Governor of Newfoundland for the second time.

1948. Thomas Gerald Rideout, who went on to serve (briefly) as Newfoundland's fourth post-Confederation Premier, is born at Fleur de Lys.

26

1873. The steamer *Great Eastern* lands one of a series of Atlantic telegraph cables at Heart's Content.

1892. Bishop Michael Howley delivers his first sermon following his consecration.

1897. An antimony mine at Moreton's Harbour goes up for public auction, and is purchased for only $500.00.

27

1884. The accused in the Harbour Grace "Orange" riots are found not guilty.

28

1859. The steamship *Argo*, of the Galway line, is lost off Trepassey but its crew and passengers are saved. One of its officers is Timothy Cummins, reportedly Newfoundland's first British-certified Master Mariner.

29

1916. Francis "Mayo" Lind, who enlisted at Fogo, pens his last letter from the front to the St. John's *Daily News*. He is killed in action two days later at Beaumont Hamel.

30

1827. Anglican Bishop John Inglis arrives at Twillingate on an episcopal visit.

1864. The Weights and Measures Act comes into force in Newfoundland.

1880. The schooner *Challenge*, bound from Bristol on behalf of the firm of Owen & Earle, strikes an iceberg off Little Fogo Island in dense fog. While considerable damage is sustained, the vessel makes it safely to Twillingate two days later.

1897. Georgina Stirling gives a concert at St. John's St. Patrick Hall.

July

1
1827. Twillingate's original St. Peter's Anglican Church is consecrated, and ninety-three people are confirmed.

1872. P. Geehan is hanged for the murder of his Wife and Brother-in-law.

1916. The Battle of Beaumont Hamel, part of the opening day of the Somme Campaign, sees more than 700 of the Newfoundland Regiment's 801 men killed or wounded.

Beaumont Hamel commemorative stamp

1924. Field Marshall Douglas Haig unveils Newfoundland's National War Memorial on Water Street, St. John's.

2
1869. Brothers Philip and William Perry are officially granted a parcel of land at Indian Islands that will later be known as Perry's Garden.

1940. Twillingate men meet at the local Court House under Chair, Magistrate Abbott, to form a branch of the Newfoundland Patriotic Association.

3
1845. Bishop Feild consecrates St. Peter's Anglican Church, Twillingate.

1889. Justice Hon. G.H. Emerson, a former Twillingate and Fogo District Representative, and one of the delegates sent to England in 1854 to urge the granting of Responsible Government to Newfoundland, dies at the age of ninety-one.

1940. The *Grimsby*, A small Norwegian steamer escaping the Nazi invasion of its homeland, makes a stop-over at Twillingate en route to New York.

4
1844. Anglican Bishop Edward Feild arrives in Newfoundland for the first time.

1845. No less than forty-five icebergs are reported off Long Point, Crow Head.

5
1898. Newfoundland's first teachers' convention kicks off at St. John's St. Patrick's Hall. 400 attend.

6
1846. The City of Halifax sends $6,000.00 for those affected by St. John's "Glue Pot" Fire. The British Government sends a further $5,000.00.

1880. HMS *Druid* arrives at Twillingate under Captain Kennedy, and entertains many local visitors. The vessel is charged with destroying unauthorized saw mills, thought to be detrimental to the salmon fishery.

7
1847. James P. Howley is born at St. John's. He will go on to become the Director of Newfoundland's Geological Survey, and makes a lasting contribution to the Colony's Aboriginal history with his 1915 book, *The Beothucks or Red Indians*.

8
1892. The Great Fire erupts in St. John's., destroying a major portion of the City's downtown.

1930. Magistrate Jabez P. Thompson, former editor of the *Twillingate Sun*, pens his first article for the paper – an anniversary tribute – since selling it to George Roberts in the 1890s (It appears in the Sun a few days later).

1945. Magistrate Beaton J. Abbott leaves Twillingate after serving in the community for nearly a decade, to take up a new posting at Grand Bank.

9
1833. Newfoundland's first Assembly is prorogued.

10
1860. The Prince of Wales, later Edward VII, departs England for a Royal visit to Newfoundland.

11
1892. HMS *Blake* arrives from Halifax with relief supplies for sufferers of St. John's Great Fire.

12
1888. The schooner *Star of the West*, owned by William Waterman & Co., of Twillingate is wrecked at St. Peter's Island. Her crew, under Master Thomas Wells of Back Harbour, is saved.

1907. The Grand Master of Newfoundland's Orange Order, Donald Morrison, lays the cornerstone for the Twillingate Chapter's new Lodge building, the Alexandra Hall.

1920. Death of Magistrate, and former *Twillingate Sun* owner, George Roberts.

13
1859. Lawyer (Later Judge) Daniel Woodley Prowse marries Sarah Anne Edlestone Farrar. He is best remembered for his *History of Newfoundland*.

14
1850. Bishop Michael Fleming dies at St. John's.

15
1888. The firm of Frederick Linfield – later E.J. Linfield – opens for business on Twillingate's North Side.

Frederick Linfield

1907. Twillingate Masons hold the official opening ceremony for their new Lodge building. The organization's acting Deputy Grand Master for Newfoundland, Hon. J.A. Clift, is present for the occasion.

16

1813. St. John's merchants report to Governor Richard Keats that provisions are running dangerously low, resulting in a large importation of food and supplies.

17

1839. Newfoundland is granted its own Church of England Bishopric.

1846. In an effort headed by the Lord Mayor, more than £13,000 is subscribed in London towards St. John's fire relief.

1891. Dr. Philip Hubert, head of Newfoundland's Health Department, dies at St. John's after contracting diphtheria during his professional rounds.

18

1867. The Belfast *News Letter* reports that a group of four Newfoundland buyers have been arrested at Moville, Ireland, on the suspicion that one of them might be James Stevens, head of the Fenian Brotherhood. The men are soon released.

19

1869. Governor Stephen John Hill arrives in Newfoundland.

1880. The schooner *Bismark*, owned by Edwin Duder, is wrecked at the Wadhams on its way to Fogo from St. John's.

1881. Intruders enter the shop of Thomas Conners at Herring Neck, stealing some £31 in cash and goods.

1899. The Royal Navy holds a review on St. John's Parade Ground, with some 1,000 men participating.

20

1818. Governor Charles Hamilton lands at St. John's to take up his new duties.

1940. Captain William Roberts, of the schooner *Bessie Marie*, is slightly injured after falling into her hold while at Twillingate.

21
1834. Catherine Snow is hanged from the window of St. John's old Court House for her part in the murder of her Husband the previous year.

22
1880. The "Battle of Foxtrap." Locals, fearing their property will be expropriated, attack railway surveyors. Order is only restored through the despatch of mounted police from St. John's, with Judge Prowse at their head.

1948. A second referendum on Newfoundland & Labrador's political future results in a narrow victory for Confederation with Canada over Responsible Government.

23
1860. The Prince of Wales' vessel arrives in Newfoundland waters.

24
1860. Albert Edward, the Prince of Wales, lands in St. John's at noon.

25
1844. Engineer William Thomas Wells is dismissed from his duties overseeing the construction of Twillingate's first "Tickle Bridge."

1879. Twillingate Magistrate John Peyton, Jr. dies, and is buried alongside his Father in a graveyard on Burnt Island, near Exploits.

1899. Richard Penton and a man surnamed Pierce drown at Joe Batt's Arm.

1938. A large forest fire near Carter's Cove on New World Island causes extensive damage.

1943. A visiting Member of the British House of Parliament, Mr. Hammond, preaches at Twillingate's South Side United Church.

26
1898. The *Greenland* Disaster relief fund closes after raising some $17,000.00.

27
1778. An American privateer captures and destroys twelve fishing vessels off Renews.

1866. The steamer *Medway* steams into Heart's Content, Newfoundland, with the western end of the Atlantic telegraph cable, laid on the ocean floor from Europe by the *Great Eastern*.

1895. Governor John O'Brien departs Newfoundland following a six year tenure.

28
1766. Governor Palliser issues an injunction against enclosing land in Newfoundland for agriculture.

1889. Rev. William Temple presides over the first Flower Service held at Twillingate.

29
1863. Thomas D. Scanlon, of the Anglo-American Telegraph Company, who reportedly found a written account of Twillingate's first settlers, marries Miss Nowlan.

1875. The first meeting of the Twillingate-area's Methodist Board of Education is held at the local parsonage. Rev. John Reay is elected Chairman and Secretary.

Rev. John Reay

30
1916. St. Peter's Anglican Church and the North Side Methodist Church hold special services to remember those Twillingate residents who were killed at the Battle of Beaumont Hamel, about four weeks earlier.

1926. Sir Michael Patrick Cashin, who served as Newfoundland's Prime Minister for a few months in 1919, dies.

1937. Teacher Fred Lacey, originally of Carbonear, drowns while returning to Summerford from Dildo with a load of grass for hay.

31
1874. Tenders are accepted for a building that will become the St. John's Athenaeum.

August

1

1855. Birth at St. John's of Alfred Henry Seymour, who would become a Newfoundland judge, magistrate and politician.

2

1822. Rev. John Leigh, Twillingate's first resident Anglican priest, returns to his old parish aboard the brig *Snap* for a six week visit.

1875. Albert Edgar Hickman, a future Newfoundland Prime Minister, is born in Grand Bank.

3

1797. The crew of HMS *Latona* mutiny at St. John's, but are thwarted by their officers and marines.

1845. A.J.W. McNeilly is born at Armagh, Ireland. He will go on to serve as Newfoundland's Solicitor General and Registrar of the Supreme Court, and represent several electoral Districts, including Twillingate and Fogo.

1868. John Breen and J. Fitzgerald of Fogo, along with two other men, drown while hauling a seine at Sleigh Harbour, Labrador.

1871. The St. John's Regatta is revived after an absence of ten years.

1892. The New World Island Mining Syndicate is formed in Britain, and buys an antimony claim at Moreton's Harbour.

4

1855. The Newfoundland House of Assembly closes its first session under Responsible Government.

5
1583. Sir Humphrey Gilbert claims Newfoundland as England's first overseas Colony.

1858. The original Atlantic cable, which operated for only four weeks, is landed at Trinity Bay from the USS *Niagara*.

6
1812. An eighteen gun American privateer attacks the *Royal Bounty* off St. John's, killing one man and wounding several others. The vessel strikes her colours but the crew are set free in an open boat, safely making their way to Placentia.

American privateer engaging a British vessel, War of 1812

1883. Three boys from Torbay, rowing in the St. John's Regatta's juvenile race, are drowned when their boat capsizes.

7
1946. Newfoundland Ranger Michael Collins (# 166) is killed in a motorcycle crash at Stephenville, one of only three members of the Force to lose their lives in the line of duty.

8
1869. The steamers *Germanic* and *Cleopatra* are lost off Cape Race, but all crew and passengers are saved.

9
1839. Augustus F. Goodridge, who will go on to serve as Newfoundland's Premier while sitting as an MHA for Twillingate District, is born at Paignton, Devonshire, England.

1864. A copper mine opens at Tilt Cove, Notre Dame Bay.

10
1858. A ball is held at the Colonial building in St. John's to celebrate the laying of the first trans-Atlantic cable. Promoter Cyrus Field is present.

1880. HMS *Flamingo*, assigned to protect fishers on the Newfoundland coast, makes a stopover in Twillingate before heading to Seldom-Come-By two days later.

11
1918. St. Andrew's Anglican Church, Fogo, completed two years earlier, is consecrated by Bishop White.

12
1858. Dr. William A. Stirling dies at Twillingate, aged seventy-two years.

13
1855. Engineers remove the upper portion of Merlin Rock, in the St. John's Narrows, to allow large steamers to enter the port.

1916. A new St. Andrew's Anglican Church is completed and opened at Fogo, replacing an earlier St. Andrews, consecrated by Bishop Feild in 1845.

14
1842. An official congregation of the Presbyterian Church is first organized at St. John's. Their first clergyman is Rev. Donald A. Fraser.

The Presbyterian Kirk (L), St. John's, pre-1892

15
1880. The second St. John the Evangelist Anglican Church opens, serving Barr'd Islands and Joe Batt's Arm.

1896. Berry pickers start a fire which, not being properly extinguished, leads to a massive forest fire, destroying a considerable amount of timber and property at Wild Cove, near Moreton's Harbour and Tizzard's Harbour.

16
1917. Private John Henry Simms of Fogo earns the Military Medal for his bravery commanding a Lewis Gun Section at the Battle of Langemarck. The following day he dies from wounds received.

17
1823. Rev. John Leigh, former incumbent at Twillingate's St. Peter's Church, who complied a Beothuk vocabulary with the aid of the Native woman Demasduit, dies.

1841. Andrew Pearce, former merchant agent and collector of customs for the port of Twillingate, dies in the seventieth year of his age.

18
1896. The steamer *Ingraham* arrives at Moreton's Harbour, at the request of Colonial Secretary, Hon. Robert Bond, to render assistance to locals who are dealing with the aftermath of a destructive forest fire.

19
1894. Death of Thomas D. Scanlon of the Anglo-American telegraph Company.

20
1825. Former Newfoundland Governor, William Waldegrave, First Baron Radstock, dies in London.

1881. Merchant Edwin John Duder marries Margaret E. Stead.

1914. A precursor to the Women's Patriotic Association is formed at a meeting held in Twillingate's Court House. Mrs. L. Earle is elected the group's first President.

21
1821. Rev. Thomas G. Laugharne becomes the first Church of England clergyman to visit Barr'd Islands.

1891. The steamer *Hiram Perry* arrives at Twillingate, carrying members of Notre Dame Masonic Lodge, Little Bay, and guests, on a visit to their brethren of Twillingate Lodge.

22
1883. Sir Ambrose Shea hosts a grand ball in honour of Prince George, second Son of the Prince of Wales, on the occasion of His Royal Highness' visit to Newfoundland.

Sir Ambrose Shea

23
1888. Nominations are held for St. John's first ever municipal election.

24
1845. New chandeliers, purchased from St. James' Church, Poole, are first lit at St. Peter's Anglican Church, Twillingate.

1894. The cornerstones of St. John's Presbyterian Church and Masonic Temple are laid.

1939. The engine house of Frank Roberts' motor boat explodes while on collar at Twillingate. His assistant Sidney Boyde suffers minor burns.

Stories From These Shores

25
1846. Outgoing Governor John Harvey departs Newfoundland.

1914. At the outset of the Great War a meeting is held at Twillingate, under Magistrate Scott, to form a local Patriotic Committee.

26
1621. Edward Winne writes to Sir George Calvert (Later Lord Baltimore), detailing the progress of their settlement at Ferryland.

27
1939. Reporter Joseph R. Smallwood, the "Barrelman," who will go on to play a major role in Newfoundland politic, visits Twillingate.

1940. Harry Hyde of Change Islands is one of only seven men rescued after the double sinking of their sloop, HMS *Penzance*, and a rescue ship, the S.S. *Blairmore*, by the German submarine, U-37. Change Islander Francis C.R. Peckford is lost.

1942. A. Brian Peckford, who will go on to serve as Newfoundland's third post-Confederation Premier, is born at Whitbourne.

28
1935. Tinsmith and businessman Silas Facey dies at his home on Twillingate's North Side at the age of sixty-nine.

29
1864. Michael Patrick Cashin, later Newfoundland's Prime Minister, is born at Cape Broyle.

1896. At the request of Robert French, about 100 Twillingate residents stock up supplies and prepare to sail for Tizzard's Harbour to help deal with a major forest fire. The expedition is called off when it is learned that conditions have already improved.

30
1888. Polling day in St. John's first municipal election.

31
1882. A young boy is attacked by dogs at Twillingate near the residence of Dr. William Stirling, but is rescued by the Doctor's Daughters and then treated by the physician.

September

1

1872. Former Newfoundland Premier John Kent dies at St. John's.

John Kent

1876. The light is first lit at the Long Point lighthouse, Crow Head.

1881. The Methodist "Church on the Hill" opens for services on Twillingate's North Side.

1885. The first dynamo for electric lighting arrives at St. John's.

2

1796. St. John's is placed under marital law by the Governor when a fleet of French ships appears off the narrows; the vessels do not attack.

1893. A Mrs. Primmer and her three children drown at Twillingate.

1927. Robert Samuel "Bob Sam" Roberts, longtime light keeper at Long Point (Crow Head, Twillingate), passes away at the age of sixty-one.

3
1917. Seamen Andrew Ginn of Fogo and Albert Cluett of Cape Cove, Fogo Island, are among 136 fatalities following a raid on their barracks at Chatham by German Gotha bombers.

1939. With the British declaration of war, Newfoundland becomes a combatant against Nazi Germany.

4
1833. The Colony's first nuns, members of the Presentation Order, arrive in Newfoundland.

1881. A new Methodist church is dedicated at Church Hill, Twillingate, with Rev. W.W. Percival, Superintendent of the Methodist Church's St. John's Circuit, officiating.

1883. Fishing boats belonging to William Dove and John Mutford are driven ashore at Crow Head during a late Summer gale.

5
1921. The schooner *Douglas Adams* departs Lisbon, Portugal for Twillingate, and is never heard from again.

1942. A German U-Boat attacks vessels anchored at Lance Cove, Bell Island, destroying the *Saganaga* and *Lord Strathcona*.

6
1883. The steamer *Canima* goes down off Gull Island in St. Mary's Bay.

7
1810. Newfoundland Governor, Admiral John Thomas Duckworth, departs St. John's on a tour of inspection to northern parts of the Island.

8
1942. Death of Reverend Levi Curtis, a one-time incumbent of Twillingate's Methodist (United) Church, and a founder of Memorial College, later Memorial University.

9
1855. St. John's Roman Catholic Cathedral (Basilica) is consecrated by Bishop John Thomas Mullock.

1870. Michael Francis (Later Bishop) Howley, returns to Newfoundland for the first time since his ordination.

10
1883. Newfoundland Governor, Henry Berkeley Fitzhardinge Maxse, a Crimean War veteran, dies at Government House, St. John's.

1947. The Newfoundland Tuberculosis Association purchases an old PT Boat from the American Government. It will go on to fame as the floating TB clinic, *Christmas Seal*, Captained by Twillingate master mariner, Peter Troake.

11
1937. Newfoundland Governor Humphrey Walwyn visits Twillingate.

1939. The Bay steamer S.S. *Clyde* is used to tow the German freighter *Cristoph V. Dornum* into Botwood harbour as a war prize.

1946. Newfoundland's National Convention meets for the first time at the Colonial Building, St. John's.

12
1805. Newfoundland Governor Erasmus Gower orders merchants to post all prices in a conspicuous place in their stores.

1876. Twenty-five vessels are lost during a gale on the Labrador coast.

1883. The remains of late Governor Henry Maxse are repatriated on board the steamer *Caspian*.

13
1880. The steamship *Flavian* is towed into St. John's after it ran ashore near Ferryland.

14
1844. Builder William J. Murphy completes the spire on the tower of St. Peter's Anglican Church, Twillingate.

1876. Governor John Hawley Glover sets off on a tour of the Newfoundland coast aboard HMS *Eclipse*.

15
1891. Joseph Ings of Purcell's Harbour is the sole survivor of the wreck of the schooner *Blossom* off Gull Island Cove, Bay of Exploits.

1925. Memorial University College officially opens at St. John's.

16
1895. Robert Bond is acclaimed as the Member for Twillingate District after J.P. Thompson steps down in his favour. Bond would represent the District for the remainder of his political career, including his time as Prime Minister.

17
1803. William Cull of Barr'd Islands is paid £50 reward for capturing a Beothuk woman, whom the authorities hoped might become an ambassador to her people.

1876. Edward Francis of Twillingate drowns after being knocked overboard from a schooner at the Narrows in St. John's.

1889. The Twillingate chapter of the Masonic Order receives its official warrant as a constituted Lodge, No. 2,364.

18
1880. A vessel belonging to Mrs. Brien of Tilting is lost at Flower Island, near Barr'd Islands, while bound for St. John's with a cargo of salt cod. Her crew is saved.

1883. Two young men from Indian Islands, Albert Wainwright and Samuel Cobb, are drowned when they fall off the deck of a vessel beating into Oliver's Cove, near Tilting.

1894. General William Booth, worldwide head of the Salvation Army, visits St. John's.

1907. A ferocious gale hits Newfoundland's northeast coast, causing damage to fishing infrastructure and other property, in towns such as Twillingate, Moreton's Harbour, Fogo and Change Islands. Twenty-nine schooners are wrecked at Twillingate, four at Eastern Tickle and four at Fogo, with dozens meeting the same fate in other locales.

1920. The schooner *Luetta* is driven ashore at Herring Neck in a gale and becomes a total wreck.

Schooner Luetta

19
1846. Newfoundland experiences its worst gale in thirty years, causing extensive damage and some loss of life.

20
1779. Newfoundland Governor, Admiral Richard Edwards, orders Justices of the Peace to carry out a census of the Island.

21
1864. Sir Ambrose Shea and Sir Frederick B.T. Carter travel to Canada as Confederation delegates.

1915. Newfoundland Governor Sir Walter Edward Davidson and his Wife, Lady Davidson, arrive at Twillingate for an official visit.

22
1882. David and Elijah Compton are drowned while squid jigging near French Beach (Durrell), when their boat is capsized by a large wave. A companion, Eli Cooper, makes it safely to shore.

23
1899. Fire erupts at St. John's Holy Cross Schools, St. Patrick Street.

24
1895. Former *Twillingate Sun* editor Jabez P. Thompson is appointed Stipendiary Magistrate at Brigus.

25
1832. Nomination day for Newfoundland's first general election. Polling starts the same day.

1895. Georgina Stirling participates in the opening concert for St. John's new Methodist Hall.

26
1871. George Hodder becomes the first member of the Loyal Orange Association to be initiated at Twillingate.

Stories From These Shores

1907. Newfoundland's status within the British Empire is officially changed from "Colony" to "Dominion," giving the Country theoretical equality of status with Australia, Canada and New Zealand. The title of Newfoundland's head of Government is now "Prime Minister," rather than "Premier."

27
1915. Governor and Lady Davidson visit Moreton's Harbour.

1942. A plane arrives at Twillingate bringing diphtheria anti-toxin to combat an outbreak of the disease in the community and on New World Island.

1946. Governor Gordon MacDonald visits Twillingate, presiding over the opening of a new bridge across Shoal Tickle.

Governor MacDonald opens Twillingate's new Tickle Bridge

28
1892. A vocal and instrumental concert featuring renowned soprano Georgina Stirling, then on a visit home, is staged at Twillingate, raising some forty dollars for a Back Harbour native who lost her St. John's home in the City's Great Fire.

29
1764. Newfoundland's first customs house is established at St. John's.

1847. The cornerstone of St. John's Anglican Cathedral is laid.

30
1880. A resident of Tizzard's Harbour named Edward Cantwell accidentally shoots and kills his Brother, thinking him to be one of the dogs that had been stealing fish off the family flakes (Another source gives the date for this incident as 13 October).

1924. Newfoundland Governor William Lamond Allardyce and his Wife, Lady Elsie Elizabeth, arrive at Twillingate to officially open the Notre Dame Bay Memorial Hospital.

October

1

1842. Robert Tremblett, who served as a physician at Twillingate for more than twenty years, dies at age forty-eight.

1885. The brigantine *St. Joseph* arrives at Twillingate from Montreal, with its Captain and Mate infected with smallpox.

1924. The newly-opened Notre Dame Bay Memorial Hospital, Twillingate, receives its first patients.

1942. An floatplane lands at Twillingate harbour, bringing extra diphtheria serum to supplement a batch delivered a few days before.

2

1827. The first meeting of the "Boeothuck" Institution is held at Twillingate's Court House.

1946. The Barr'd Islands Iceflow Cooperative Society is formed at the residence of Nehemiah Combden. Israel Godwin is its first President.

3

1816. Rev. John Leigh, Twillingate's first resident Anglican clergyman, arrives at Twillingate following a petition from citizens to the Society for the Propagation of the Gospel (SPG).

1864. Newly-appointed Governor Anthony Musgrave arrives in Newfoundland to begin his term of office.

4

1897. Sir William Whiteway issues a "Manifesto to Electors."

1914. The first members of the Newfoundland Regiment, the famed "Blue Puttees," set sail for Europe. Among their number are recruits from Change Islands, Fogo, Indian Islands, Moreton's Harbour, Seldom-Come-By and Twillingate.

S.S. Florizel *preparing to depart St. John's with Newfoundland's first recruits, October, 1914*

5

1885. Twillingate's telegraph office, located in the local court building, sends and receives its first messages. Board of Works Chair Smith McKay, and Magistrate Francis Berteau, are on hand for the occasion.

1911. A.J.W. McNeilly, a one-time MHA for Twillingate and Fogo District, and Solicitor General, dies aged sixty-six.

1943. Long-time Collector of Customs and Magistrate, Andrew Cook, formerly of Scotland, passes away in his adopted hometown of Fogo.

6

1881. Newfoundland Governor Henry Maxse is sworn in.

1897. Newfoundland Liberals meet in the British Hall, St. John's, to kick off their election campaign.

1911. Former Newfoundland Premier Sir James S. Winter dies at Toronto.

7
1899. Newly-appointed Governor, Henry Edward McCallum, and his Wife, arrive in Newfoundland.

8
1881. The steamer *Standard* arrives at St. John's carrying the first consignment of iron for the Newfoundland Railway.

9
1842. Rev. William Marshall performs the first Methodist marriage at Change Islands.

1857. Jabez P. Thompson is born. He will go on to found the *Twillingate Sun* newspaper, and represent Twillingate District as an MHA, before accepting a post as Stipendiary Magistrate at Brigus.

1867. Thirty-seven lives are lost during a severe gale off the Labrador coast. Captain William Jackman saves twenty-seven people from drowning at Spotted Islands by bringing them to shore, one by one, on his back.

1879. William Robertson Warren is born at St. John's. He will go on to serve as Newfoundland Prime Minister for a few months in 1923-4, following the downfall of Richard Squires' first Ministry.

1888. Former Newfoundland Governor Anthony Musgrave dies at Brisbane, Australia.

1909. The Anglo-Newfoundland Development Company's paper mill opens at Grand Falls.

1917. Augustus Bulgin of Durrell earns the Military Medal for his role as a company runner during the Battle of the Brombeek. He is killed in action the following year.

1933. Twillingate's first Girl Guide Company is inaugurated, with Mrs. (Rev.) Hollands as its first Captain.

1940. Death of missionary doctor, Sir Wilfred Grenfell, who was a major supporter of the Notre Dame Bay Memorial Hospital project.

10
1877. Shea & Company's St. John's office is burglarized, the thief making off with $400.00.

11
1885. Eighty-nine fishing craft, along with seventy lives, are lost during a massive gale off Labrador.

12
1754. Newfoundland Justices of the Peace are ordered to erect gallows on their Districts' public wharves to execute anyone found guilty of robbery or felony.

13
1876. St. John's Free St. Andrew's Presbyterian Church, Duckworth street, is destroyed by fire.

14
1885. More than 100 locals petition MHA Jabez P. Thompson to seek reelection to Twillingate District as a supporter of William Whiteway. He is unsuccessful, but reclaims the District again in 1889.

1890. The steamer *Bonavista* departs St. John's with Newfoundland's first shipment of boneless codfish.

1942. The passenger ferry S.S. *Caribou*, is attacked and sunk by the German submarine U-69 on her regular run between Port aux Basques and North Sydney, Nova Scotia. 137 souls are lost, including Captain Benjamin Taverner.

15
1881. Sailors ashore at Twillingate from HMS *Fantome* cause a disturbance. Some of their number are injured when Sergeant Wells attempts an arrest.

16
1869. W.W. Halfyard, later the Representative for Fogo District, and a Cabinet Minister, is born at Ochre Pit Cove, Bay de Verde District.

1884. A meeting is held at Little Harbour, under Rev. Jeremiah Embree, to finalize plans for a new Methodist Church in the community.

1894. A by-election in Twillingate District sees incumbent Michael T. Knight defeated by Giles J. Foote.

17
1872. The Allan Line steamship *Hibernian* arrives in Newfoundland. She is the first steamer contracted by the Newfoundland Government to carry mail.

1885. St. John's first electric lights are lit at the stores of Edwin Duder, Ayre & Sons, and several other merchants.

1888. Future Newfoundland Premier Hugh Hoyles is born in St. John's.

18
1897. A new Methodist (United) Church, featuring interior work by Joey John Taylor, opens on Change Islands.
The original, 1,100 ton S.S. *Bruce* arrives at Sydney, Nova Scotia on its maiden run between Newfoundland & Canada.

19
1850. The vessel *Canopus* discovers the eighty-seven ton schooner, *Mountaineer*, owned by John Slade and Company, drifting abandoned off the Newfoundland coast. Though its cargo is intact, there is no sign of the ship's boats, the crew, or their personal possessions. No trace of them is ever found (See, Chapter Eleven).

1871. William Ford Coaker, who would go on to found the Fisherman's Protective Union at Herring Neck, and serve as Twillingate District's MHA, is born at St. John's to William and Elizabeth (Ford) Coaker.

William Coaker's birthplace

20
1940. Rev. D.C. Noel, Anglican incumbent at Herring Neck, narrowly escapes death when his boat and clothes catch fire while he is trying to start a marine engine. Noel is saved by local Austin Hurley.

21
1897. Philip Francis Little, Newfoundland's first Premier under Responsible Government, dies in Ireland.

22
1888. First railway passenger service from Harbour Grace Junction to Placentia.

23
1922. A Summerford resident, Mrs. Small, is party to the community's first telephone conversation with a caller from Moreton's Harbour.

1927. Former Twillingate Magistrate, William John Scott, J.P., dies suddenly while leading the congregation in prayer at the North Side United Church.

24

1794. Lieutenant Lawny of the Royal Navy is killed at St. John's while attempting to impress men to join the ship *Boston*.

1935. Edward Patrick Morris, Lord Morris, former Prime Minister of Newfoundland, dies in London.

25

1864. Corporal Downey of the Royal Artillery is accidentally blown up at the Fort Amherst (St. John's) Battery.

26

1885. The mate of the vessel *St. Joseph* dies from smallpox at Twillingate, and is buried the next day on Burnt Island at the harbour's mouth.

1946. Thomas Wendell "Tom" Marshall is born at Glace Bay, Nova Scotia. Starting his career in law, he will move into politics, and become Newfoundland & Labrador's eleventh post-Confederation Premier.

27

1779. One Cornelius Newking is killed during an altercation at St. John's, run through with a cutlass by a Royal Navy sailor.

28

1829. Michael Anthony Fleming is consecrated "Bishop of Carpathia" by Bishop Thomas Scallon, the first time the Roman Catholic Church consecrated one of its officials in Newfoundland.

1897. General election. Twillingate District returns Liberals Robert Bond and Donald Browning, plus Conservative Alan Goodridge. Conservative Thomas C. Duder gets the nod in Fogo District.

1921. The Ashbourne schooners *Ariceen* and *M.P. Cashin* are driven ashore at Twillingate during a violent storm. Ashbourne's and other merchant premises also experience damage.

Schooner Ariceen

29

1794. Two men are hanged for their role in the death of Lt. Lawny, RN.

1832. Edward Burt is instructed to keep watch at the mouth of Twillingate harbour from daylight until a half hour after sunset to ensure that any vessels entering the harbour are not infected with cholera, then raging in North America and the United Kingdom.

1836. Henry D. Winton registers the *Public Ledger* newspaper at St. John's.

1841. Henry John Earle, who will go on to a successful career as a merchant and politician at Fogo, is born at St. John's to Henry and Catherine Earle.

1928. Twillingate and Fogo Districts elect their first members of the House of Assembly – Kenneth M. Brown and Richard H. Hibbs, respectively – under the Re-distribution Act of 1925. Both are members of Richard Squires' Liberal Party. Previously, Twillingate District was much larger, and returned three members to the House.

Newfoundland women vote for the first time in a general election, with a turnout rate of ninety percent.

30
1865. Constables Sage and McKay of the Newfoundland Constabulary, along with another man, are stabbed and seriously wounded in Hoylestown, St. John's, while trying to arrest a party of drunken seamen.

1913. General election. Opposition Leader Sir Robert Bond, and fellow Liberal-Unionists James A. Clift and Walter Jennings are re-elected to Twillingate District.

31
1885. General election. Reform Party candidates Smith McKay, Augustus Goodridge and Michael T. Knight are returned for Twillingate District. James Rolls, Jr. becomes the MHA for Fogo District.

1887. Fogo Island and Change Islands are linked to the world by telegraph for the first time via a cable laid by the steamer *Favourite*.

1904. General election. Prime Minister Robert Bond is Twillingate District's representative, along with James A. Clift and George Roberts. Liberal Henry J. Earle is reelected as Fogo District MHA.

November

1
1858. Former Newfoundland Premier Philip Francis Little is appointed to the Supreme Court.

1886. The Electric Light Co. provides St. John's city streets with their first electric lighting.

2
1844. Builder William Murphy completes the final carpentry work on Twillingate's new Anglican Church, St. Peter's.

1942. A German U-Boat hits targets at Lance Cove, Bell Island. The vessels *Rose Castle*, and the Free French *PLM 27* are sunk, in the second submarine attack of the year.

1908. General election. Prime Minister Robert Bond, James A. Clift, and George Roberts are all reelected as the Liberal Members for Twillingate District, with Henry J. Earle securing another term as MHA for Fogo District.

In a two-hour speech at Herring Neck's Orange Lodge, William Ford Coaker launches the Fisherman's Protective Union (FPU), and signs up its first nineteen members.

LOA Lodge, Herring Neck

3
1919. General election. Liberals Walter B. Jennings, George Jones and Solomon Samson are the new Representatives for Twillingate District. Another Liberal, Richard Hibbs, is chosen to represent Fogo District.

4
1878. General election. William Whiteway supporters Alexander J.W. McNeilly, Stanley B. Carter, and Richard P. Rice get the nod for Twillingate and Fogo District.

4-5
1915. Private Richard Edward Hynes of Indian Islands helps fend off an attack by superior numbers of Turkish troops at Gallipoli. For his actions Hynes is presented with the Distinguished Conduct Medal.

6
1839. Andrew Pearce and others lay the foundations for the new St. Peter's Anglican Church at Twillingate. Rev. Chapman officiates.

1882. General election. Smith McKay, Richard P. Rice and Jabez P. Thompson are chosen to represent Twillingate and Fogo District. All are supporters of incumbent Premier, William Whiteway.

1889. General election, returning Whiteway Liberals Edward R. Burgess, Jabez P. Thompson and T. Peyton to Twillingate District, and Reform Party candidate James Rolls, Jr. for Fogo.

1893. General election. Liberal Jabez. P. Thompson, along with Conservatives Augustus Goodridge and Michael T. Knight are elected Twillingate District MHAs, with Conservative Thomas C. Duder returned for Fogo District. Knight loses his seat to Liberal Giles Foote in a by-election the following year.

7
1817. A major fire erupts on Water Street, St. John's, burning for hours. 130 houses, businesses, warehouses and wharves are all lost to the flames. Some $2,500,000.00 in damage is done but no lives are lost.

1865. General election. Conservatives William Whiteway and Thomas Knight are re-elected to Twillingate and Fogo District.

1874. General election. Conservative Premier Frederick Carter and his colleague Charles Duder are elected MHAs for Twillingate and Fogo District.

8
1900. General election. Liberal Premier Robert Bond, along with followers James A. Clift and George Roberts, are elected MHAs in Twillingate District. Local merchant Henry J. Earle represents Fogo District for the Liberals.

1908. Former Twillingate Magistrate Francis Berteau, a native of the Channel Island of Jersey, dies at the age of eighty-five.

9
1831. Fogo expatriate, Lady Pamela Fitzgerald, who had retired to a French convent, dies in poverty. Her remains are later re-interred in England.

1937. Clyde Kirby Wells, who will become Newfoundland's fifth post-Confederation Premier, is born at Buchans Junction.

10
1872. Birth of Frederick Charles Alderdice, Newfoundland's last Prime Minister, at Belfast, Ireland.

1940. The cold storage vessel *Senef* arrives at Twillingate to load the first ever fresh codfish fillets shipped out of the port (Prior to this date, all the product exported was in salted form).

11
1850. Thomas Martin of Twillingate is sentenced to fourteen years banishment for stealing from the firm of Slade & Cox.

1887. The coastal steamer *Plover* is nearly lost trying to enter Twillingate harbour after striking Cockles Rock. To prevent it from sinking, the vessel is beached near the Tobin and Waterman premises, North Side.

12
1859. The schooner *Marian* is lost with all fifteen of her crew en route from Change Islands to St. John's.

13
1869. General election. In Twillingate and Fogo District anti-Confederate candidates Smith McKay and Charles Duder defeat incumbents William Whiteway and Thomas Knight.

1880. Twillingate's Constable Lacey arrests a sailor belonging to the brig *Constance* on suspicion of robbing six dollars from a man named Ward.

1922. The vessel *Arkansas* is wrecked at Flint Rock Cove, near Bridgeport, having departed Twillingate the previous day after selling its catch of fish. Its owner, Captain David Glavine, and his four man crew survive and are aided by locals.

14
1942. Merchant Arthur Manuel dies at Twillingate, aged seventy.

15
1940. St. Peter's Anglican Church, Twillingate, holds a sacred concert in support of London's air raid victims.

1942. Daniel Jennings of Moreton's Harbour, Edward Combden of Barr'd Islands and Herbert Stuckey of Herring Neck are among the casualties when the aircraft carrier HMS *Avenger* is sunk by the U-155.

16
1897. William Whiteway resigns as Premier (his last time in office), after losing a general election.

1928. Dr. Charles Parsons and Mr. Henry Rideout set out on their second tour of Notre Dame Bay, fundraising for the Memorial Hospital at Twillingate.

Dr. Parsons (Front-left) and Hospital staff, 1925

17
1897. The Government of James Spearman Winter, Newfoundland's first "outport" Premier, is sworn in.

18
1929. Twillingate diarist Stephen Loveridge records a "[s]light tremor of the earth at 5 p.m."
    On Newfoundland's Burin Peninsula the effect is much more severe, causing a tsunami, resulting in a number of deaths and extensive destruction to property.

Burin Relief Trucks at St. John's, 1929

19-20
1894. A storm of nearly hurricane force rages along Newfoundland's northeast coast, causing extensive damage.

20
1939. The Twillingate branch of the Women's Patriotic Association is reestablished following the outbreak of World War II. Mrs. A.J. Wood is elected President.

21
1817. A major fire, the second that month, erupts at St. John's, consuming a number of Water Street businesses. Together, the pair of blazes are known as the "Great Fire of 1817."

1918. Seven cases of Spanish Influenza are reported in the Twillingate, New World Island area.

22
1886. Residents of Herring Neck present a thank you to Samuel Peach, following his successful deepening of a canal across Charles Cove Neck and other public works.

1940. The South Side United Church, Twillingate, holds a sacred concert in support of London's air raid victims.

23
1876. Fireworks and a torchlight parade mark the arrival of Governor John Glover and his Wife in St. John's.

24
1884. Barr'd Islands, Joe Batt's Arm and Shoal Bay adopt the "local option," prohibiting the sale of alcohol.

25
1855. Four new streets – Victoria, Cathedral, Darling and Chapel – are named at St. John's.

26
1914. By-election. Union leader William Ford Coaker is returned unopposed to Twillingate District, following the resignation of Sir Robert Bond.

27
1891. John Brown of Bluff Head Cove and Reuben Elliott of Ragged Point are drowned when their boat overturns in heavy seas while the pair return from Trump Island, Friday's Bay.

28
1859. William O'Donnell becomes the first Irish lawyer admitted to the Newfoundland Bar.

29
1933. Doctor Charles Parsons makes a plea in the *Twillingate Sun* newspaper for the mixture of brown flour with white to prevent beri-beri, a condition caused by a lack of vitamins.

30
1913. General election. Opposition Leader Sir Robert Bond retains his seat in Twillingate District, as does James A. Clift, and the pair are joined by R. Jennings. W.W. Halfyard becomes the new MHA for Fogo District.

DAVID J. CLARKE

December

1
1887. The provisions of the Sheep Protection Act come into force at Indian Islands, under which all dogs except shepherd dogs or "coolies" must be destroyed.

2
1881. The brigantine, *H.B. Jones*, taking provisions to Bett's Cove, is wrecked at Cape Cove, near Fogo. Most of its cargo is saved.

1938. The two Sons of Ernest Hopkins, Kettle Cove, Twillingate South Island, are drowned near their home, aged eighteen and twenty-three.

3
The original St. Andrew's Presbyterian Kirk is opened on Harvey Road, St. John's.

4
1894. Thomas William Gordon Ashbourne, later a merchant, MHA, and member of the Canadian Parliament, is born at Twillingate to William and Lucy (Linfield) Ashbourne.

T.G.W. Ashbourne

5

1881. A local bucket brigade manages to save the Crow Head school house after its roof catches on fire.

1883. Charles Fox Bennett, former Premier and leader of Newfoundland's anti-Confederate forces, dies at age ninety.

1917. The three-masted schooner *Sydney Smith*, owned by the Ashbourne Company, sails out of Twillingate with a load of salt cod and is never heard from again.

Schooner Sydney Smith

1867. The 360 ton barque *Queen of Swansea* departs St. John's on its ill-fated voyage to Tilt Cove.

1917. The port of Halifax is rocked by the largest man-made explosion prior to the development of the atom bomb, after two vessels, one loaded with ammunitions and explosives, collide. Elmo Ashbourne of Twillingate and Chesley Miles of Herring Neck are both present and survive the blast.

7
1879. The original St. Andrew's Anglican Church, Durrell, Twillingate, opens for worshippers.

8
1832. Polling ends in Newfoundland's first election under "Representative Government." Thomas Bennett is elected to Twillingate and Fogo District by acclamation.

1889. Former mining entrepreneur, Chair of the Board of Works, and Twillingate and Fogo District MHA, Smith McKay, dies aged seventy-one.

1941. John Butcher of Twillingate, Captain of the Bay steamer *Clyde*, dies at the Notre Dame Bay Memorial Hospital after having taken ill on board ship while docked at Campbellton.

1941. Captain Alfred Elliott of Crow Head assumes command of the coastal steamer S.S. *Clyde*.

9
1876. Alfred Moores and four companions are awarded medals by Lady Glover for their role in rescuing survivors of the wrecked vessel, *Water Witch*.

10
1894. "Black Monday." Newfoundland's Union and Commercial Banks close their doors, leading to a serious financial crisis in the Colony.

11
1814. Hay Findlater is born at Perth, Scotland, to John and Isabell (Moncrieff) Findlater. Graduating as a doctor from the University of Edinburgh, Findlater would go on to practise at Fogo from the 1840s until his death in 1889.

Stories From These Shores

1842. The first service is held at Twillingate's second St. Peter's Anglican Church, which is still under construction. Rev. John Chapman officiates.

1891. The *Stanley*, owned by Hodge's of Fogo, arrives at St. John's. At sixty-nine tons, it is the smallest brigantine ever to enter the port.

1913. The top of the Fogo wireless station's mast is broken off and destroyed during a Winter gale.

1941. The Royal Navy steam yacht *Rosabelle* is torpedoed by the German submarine U-374 in the Straits of Gibralter. Most of its crew is lost, including Seaman Stanley Mahaney of Fogo.

1948. Newfoundland delegates, including future Premier Joseph R. Smallwood, sign the Terms of Union under which Newfoundland will join Canada.

12

1867. The *Queen of Swansea* runs upon Gull Island at 6:00am, leading to the slow and tragic deaths of her survivors.

1882. An intense gale hits Notre Dame Bay; twenty-two vessels are lost.

1894. Merchant James Byrne dies suddenly aboard his schooner at Seldom-Come-Bye.

1901. Italian inventor Guglielmo Marconi receives the first trans-Atlantic wireless messages atop Signal Hill, St. John's.

1908. A chapter of the Loyal Orange Association is formed at Barr'd Islands.

1911. Former Newfoundland Premier, Daniel J. Greene, dies at St. John's.

1912. Death of former Fogo MHA, Thomas C. Duder, now serving as Stipendiary Magistrate at Bonne Bay, aged sixty-two years.

1942. Fire erupts at St. John's Knights of Columbus Hostel during a servicemen's dance, resulting in ninety-nine confirmed deaths. Arson is suspected but the exact cause remains unknown.

13
1894. Daniel J. Greene is sworn in as Newfoundland's Premier and Attorney General.

14
1933. Doctor Charles Parsons, Chief Surgeon at the Notre Dame Bay Memorial Hospital, Twillingate, addresses the St. John's Rotary Club at the Newfoundland Hotel, on the condition known as beri beri.

15
1880. William Barnes of Herring Neck fails to return home after heading out to check rabbit slips. He is found dead the following day.

16
1947. The forty-two ton auxiliary schooner *Francis P. Duke* of Fogo is wrecked on the Shag Rock in the tickle between Pool's Island and Badger's Quay. All the crew are lost.

17
1864. Birth at Stockport, England of William Frederick Lloyd, a future Prime Minister of Newfoundland.

1887. Salvation Army Officer Thomas Henry Collier arrives at Twillingate, his coming marking the beginning of Salvationism in the community.

Stories From These Shores

18
1868. Captain William Jackman of Renews receives a silver medal and a parchment of thanks from the Royal Humane Society for single-handedly saving the lives of twenty-seven persons at Spotted Islands, Labrador.

19
1928. The late Frank Guy of Wild Cove is interred at Bear Berry Head United Cemetery, Twillingate, after his death at age thirty-two in a motorcar accident at New York.

20
1858. The Baccalieu light is lit for the first time.

21
1894. The Bank of Nova Scotia opens for business in St. John's.

22
1857. James Augustus Clift is born at St. John's. He will go on to serve as Twillingate District's MHA, and Minister of Agriculture and Mines.

23
1938. The schooner *Corsica*, of Catalina, is wrecked on South Side, Twillingate, near Hodder's Forge, after parting her chains at Path End.

24
1715. Early Twillingate settler, Mark Young, is (reportedly) waylaid by three Native men, who release him unharmed after learning that he had just rescued a Native youth from freezing in the snow.

1867. *Queen of Swansea* **survivor Dr. Felix Dowsley makes the last entry in his Gull Island diary before succumbing to exposure and hunger.**

1900. Joseph Roberts Smallwood, who will go on to lead Newfoundland into union with Canada, and become its first post-Confederation Premier, is born at Gambo.

1921. The new bell of Summerford's United Church is rung for the first time.

25
1863. A church bell cast in England to commemorate the "Great Seal Haul" of the previous year, is rung for the first time at St. Peter's Anglican Church in Twillingate.

1880. The *Kangaroo*, owned by William Waterman & Co., Twillingate, is wrecked on Harbour Rock, near Greenspond. While its cargo is ruined, both the vessel and its crew are saved.

1913. Long time ferryman, John Gillard, of Gillard's Cove (Bayview, Twillingate), who made regular runs from his hometown to Tizzard's Harbour, passes away.

26
1816. Merchant George Garland of Poole transfers his Fogo premises to Robert Slade, Jr. and John Slade, Jr. for the nominal sum of five shillings.

1883. The "Harbour Grace Affray," a clash between Roman Catholics and Orangemen, leaves five people dead and many others injured.

1885. Reverend (later Bishop) Michael Howley is appointed Prefect Apostolic of St. George's, on Newfoundland's west coast.

1934. Fogo merchant/politician Henry J. Earle dies at his Daughter's home in Glovertown, aged ninety-three.

27
1792. Pamela (Nancy) Simms, born near Fogo, marries Irish patriot Lord Edward Fitzgerald.

1895. St. John's new Masonic Temple opens on Harvey Road.

1931. A new bell for Twillingate's South Side United Church is unveiled, and officially rung for the first time, by Rev. W. Edgar Mercer. That night the bell rings again, conjointly with that of St. Peter's Anglican Church.

1937. The schooner *Bessie Marie*, owned by Ashbournes' Ltd., Twillingate, is damaged after breaking its moorings during a north east gale.

Schooner Bessie Marie *during a Winter storm*

28
1918. A public meeting is convened at Twillingate's Alexandra Hall, under Magistrate George Roberts, to initiate plans for a Memorial Hospital in the town.

29
1892. The schooner *Emeril*, returning to Twillingate from St. John's after dropping off a load of fish for merchant J.B. Tobin, is wrecked on or near Cann Island. All her crew are lost.

30
1864. Former Newfoundland Governor, Sir Alexander Bannerman, dies in London.

1922. Merchant William Ashbourne dies at Twillingate in his fifty-sixth year.

31
1890. Peter Samways of Twillingate is presented with a bound set of Matthew Henry's Commentary on the Bible, in recognition of his many years of service to the local Methodist Church.

1927. Death of former Newfoundland Prime Minister William Robertson Warren.

1934. In the midst of a gale of northeast wind, the end of Twillingate's coastal wharf breaks off, grounding on Pearce's Rock.

1940. Death of Dr. Charles Parsons, the first Superintendent and Chief Surgeon of the Notre Dame Bay Memorial Hospital.

Section 3 ~
A Few More Sunspots.
Wit, Wisdom & Whimsey from the
Twillingate Sun

6
Poetry Corner

Over its seventy year run the pages of the Twillingate Sun *saw an eclectic mix of items, ranging from world news received by telegraph, through to local events, and even some jokes and (later) comic strips. A frequent form of expression found in its columns were poems. A number of these were reprinted from other sources, sometimes the work of famous authors. Many of them were contributed by the Sun's own readers, and often reflected their thoughts, humorous or profound, about life on the Isles.*

....

Though published in the Twillingate Sun *in 1926, these poems on education at Twillingate, by the Reverend Thomas Harris, actually predate the paper by twenty years, having been originally composed in 1860. The Editor noted that the untitled compositions were*

[r]ead at a tea meeting...in March 1860, or sixty-six years ago. The meeting was convened in the interests of education in Twillingate, and was held in a store...on the Duder premises, now owned by Ashbournes Ltd. The verses were thrown together impromptu by the late Rev. Thomas Harris, stationed in Twillingate 1859-62.

> I quite appreciate the decision.
> Of everyone present without division,
> And seconded by Mr. Gillingham,
> That you, Sir, tonight should be our Chairman.
>
> I'm sure it gives you satisfaction, Sir,
> To see the friends of education stir,
> And that in this move I'm no intruder,
> I would appeal to John Congrow Duder.
>
> I think that in every great communion
> In education's cause there should be union;

DAVID J. CLARKE

I trust my boldness will be forgiven,
I'll ask the opinion of Mr. McMillan.

In this good work we've been long deferring,
With every mind and heart conferring,
However, I'll not stand demurring.
Not I, after the speech of Dr. Stirling.

To those around I cannot help referring,
I'd not have it said I am now preferring,
But many I'm sure would be deploring,
If they had not heard Mr. Alfred Stirling.

The ignorance of youth is much deplored,
But can we not a helping hand afford?
An act like this all Twillingate should applaud,
And none more so than Mr. Blandford.

We would let every Newfoundlander know
That in learning's path they have walked too slow,
But now sound knowledge we'd on all bestow,
And Mr. Bristow says it should be so.

The tree of knowledge we rejoice is growing,
How many the seeds of truth are sowing,
When next we meet I trust we'll hear a poem
From our respected Chairman, Mr. Owen.

....

Stories From These Shores

(Another read on the same occasion by the same author)

Many a tea party I've attended,
When love and harmony have sweetly blended,
And true friendships ties have been cemented,
And not a person there has been offended;
But never before in a store, Sir!

I have also listened to many addresses
Of complicated woes and distresses,
Of those lands where the slave trade oppresses,
But never before in a store, Sir!

I've spoken myself on various themes,
And often referred to most pleasing themes,
To mountains, plains and wandering streams,
And many of the ancient Kings and Queens,
But never before in a store, Sir!

I've stood on the ocean's pebbly shore,
And addressed three hundred souls and more;
I've mingled in audiences rich and poor,
And many have heard me here before,
But never before in a store, Sir!

I've listened to music soft and sweet,
In the home and on many a London street.
In the silent woods on the ocean sweet,
And many a time at a children's treat,
But never before in a store, Sir!

I wish it had been intimated sooner,
To pass votes of thanks to Muir & Duder,
But if proposed I would be a seconder,
Perhaps Charles Duder will be the mover,
And thank the owner of this store, Sir.

DAVID J. CLARKE

P.S. – The author of the above impromptu verses was the Father-in-law of the Rev. Charles Lench of Brigus, now attending the sessions of the Grand Lodge, L.O.A., July 30 – Aug. 3, 1926.

Rev. Thomas Harris died in Montreal about five years ago in his ninetieth year. He was twice President of the Newfoundland Conference and nine years Chairman of District, and spent twenty-five years in the Colony. C. L.[1]

....

Here are a pair of poems from "M. R."

(For the *Twillingate Sun*)
AUTUMN
Leaves are falling thick and fast,
Winter's coming, Summer's past.
Thoughts of sadness o'er me steal,
Yet some gladness still I feel.

Bees are humming soft and glad,
Birds are chirping, why thou sad?
Nature's lovely, oh they say!
Why so lonely, why not say?

Leaves are falling, this casts gloom;
Summer's passing, Autumn's come.
O'er me sadly steals the thought,
All that's earthly come to nought.

Summer, Autumn, Winter, Spring,
In succession vanishing.
Thus our treasures here below,
Fleeting pleasures come and go.

Stories From These Shores

Yet a gladness blends with all,
Robbing sadness of its gall.
For the cutting Winter's blast,
Frost so nipping cannot last.

Then comes Summer fair and bright,
Conquering Winter's dreary night.
After sadness here below,
Heaven's gladness may we know!

Trials earthly pass away;
Blessings Heavenly ne'er decay.
Ever prize then Heavenly lore,
This shall last when time's no more.

After earthly things are past,
Treasures Heavenly aye shall last.
When this passing scene is o'er,
Then bliss, lasting evermore.

     M. R. [1880][2]

....

(For the *Twillingate Sun*)
TO THE SEA.

Oh, who can describe the feelings of awe
Which steal O'er our hearts as we wander
alone;
Along thy rock boundaries or land girded
shore,
Old Ocean! and list to thy ceaseless
moan.

Should the day be fair and the breezes soft,
How placid thy bosom! thy wavelets
how bright!

DAVID J. CLARKE

Then thy voice is hush'd to a murmuring low,
And thy waters reflect a silvery light.

But, how changed thine aspect, and different thy sound,
When winds are high and a storm prevails;
Then thy thundering roar is heard on the shore,
And the bravest spirit before thee quails.

Sometimes, in the lull of the storm, is heard
The boom of a gun from a vessel distressed;
How the heart of the listener is thrill'd as he thinks
Of that lost ship's crew in their helplessness.

But standing there, on that storm-beaten coast,
Are men of true hearts and courage so brave.
That the life-boat's keel soon grates on the shore,
And those men set out to die or to save.

Oft is their purpose fulfilled, and the crew,
By those noble heroes brought safely to land.
Where everyone, be he stranger or friend,
Is ready to lend them a helping hand.

But there are times when a storm comes on,
And a noble vessel, all unprepared,
Is blown on the rocks or founders at sea.
And not one soul to tell the tale is spared.

Stories From These Shores

Right well, Old Ocean, art thou called a
grave,
For lives, hopes and fortunes beneath
three are laid;
But we know that thy reign at last will
be o'er,
When "the sea, death and Hell shall give
up their dead."

How sweet then to those who mourn for
dear friends,
Engulph'd in thy waters the promise
must be;
That in the "new heavens and earth" to
come
There is no more parting and no more
sea.

February, 1881.
M. R.[3]

....

DAVID J. CLARKE

During the second half of the 1880s one of the Sun's most prolific contributors of poetry was "Wilfred." Below are a selection of his submissions, which covered a wide variety of topics.

(For the Sun)
THE FISHER BOY
One light shone redly thro' the storm;
One cottage window on the cliff,
Gave out a radiance soft and warm,
And showed a waiting girlish form –
Where stayed the fisher's skiff.

Upon the fire the kettle sung.
The chairs were set, the plates were laid,
His Sunday clothes in order hung,
That when tomorrow's church bells rang
He might be soon arranged.

His cat, a speckled Maltese cat,
Lay half asleep before the fire,
But now it roused and listening sat,
Wild-eyed upon the doorway mat –
The winds were shrieking higher!

The boy had launched his boat at noon,
And drifted down, the waters still;
He said he would return as soon
As rose the white horns of the moon
Above the quarry hill.

No moon the Sister saw that night.
She heard the ocean seethe and roar;
And by the lightning's flashing bright,
She saw the waves that broke in white
Upon the yellow shore.

The fire burnt low, the room was cold,

Stories From These Shores

The cat kept mewing round her chair;
The rain beat down on cliff and wold;
She heard no whistle loud and bold,
    No step upon the stair.

Beside the sea at break of day,
A fisher's broken boat she found;
And on the sand not far away,
With calm dead lips, her brother lay –
    The bright waves dimpled round.

O Sabbath bells! ye ring so loud
Across the fields and glistening sands;
But yet with holy rest endowed,
He lieth smiling in his shroud
    At rest those weary hands!
                    WILFRED.
            Oct. 8 '85 [4]

....

(For the *Twillingate Sun*)
DAY
Day is time for life;
To speed its many cares,
Lead those we love thro' worldly strife,
And all the ills it wears;
To plant the smile and chase the tear,
And toil that they be happy here.

Day is the time for prayer.
Refreshed by balmy sleep,
The heart awakens devoid of care,
Its daily watch to keep,
To bend the knee to God, and raise
The grateful crisons of praise.

DAVID J. CLARKE

Day is the time for thought,
For cares that duty brings,
With what elastic freedom fraught
The mind to action springs;
Bounds lightly musing to her toil,
Unheeding the gay world's turmoil.

Day is the time for mirth;
To sinless joys resigned,
In union with the friends of earth
To wander, unconfined,
O'er sober pleasure's paths and glean
New rapture from each changing scene.

Day is the time for youth,
Life's new and busy Spring,
To lend a list'ning ear to truth,
And spread its zephyr wing;
Awhile mid sober scenes to dwell,
And bid the world a brief farewell.

Day is the time for Hope,
To troubled mortals given,
With dark despair to bid them cope,
And sweetly muse on Heaven;
To dying man a dawning light,
When life seems darkening into night.

WILFRED.
Twillingate [1886][5]

....

Stories From These Shores

(For the Sun)
LIKING AND DISLIKING

Ye who know the reason tell me
How it is that instinct still
Prompts the heart to like or like not,
At its own capricious will.
Tell me by what hidden magic,
Our impressions first are led
Into liking or disliking,
Oft before a word is said.

Why should smiles sometimes repel us,
Bright eyes turn our feelings cold?
What is that which comes to tell us
All that glitters is not gold?
Oh no feature plain or striking,
But a power we cannot shun
Prompts our liking or disliking
Ere acquaintance hath begun.

Is it instinct, or some spirit
Which protects us and controls
Every impulse we inherit
By sympathy of souls?
Is it instinct – is it nature
Or some freak or fault of chance.
Which our liking or disliking
Limits to a single glance?

Like presentment of danger,
Tho' the sky no shadow flings,
Or that inner sense still stronger
Of unseen unuttered things
Is it – oh can no one tell me
No one shew sufficient cause
Why our likings or dislikings
Have their own instinctive laws.

DAVID J. CLARKE

WILFRED.
Sept. 6 1886.[6]

....

MOONBEAMS
Over fields of thimy blossom,
Over beds of dewy flowers,
Now upon the streamlet's bosom,
Now within the whispering bowers,
Soft and slow
The moonbeams go
Wandering on through midnight hours.

Lightly o'er the crested billow
Where the heavy waters flow,
Where the sea-bird finds her pillow,
There the glistening moonbeams go
Soft and slow
Soft and slow
Ever wandering, soft and slow.

Queen of beauty robed in splendour,
Finds thy silent foot no rest!
Looks thy smile in accents tender
Ne'er upon a kindred breast!
Soft and slow
The moonbeams go
In their silver sandals dressed.

Silent moon! thy smile of beauty
Fainting hearts will oft renew
Teach me then thine holy duty
Waste and wild to wander through
Soft and slow
Still to go
Patient, meek, but lonely too.

Stories From These Shores

WILFRED.
Twillingate [1886][7]

....

THE CAPTAIN OF THE *CYPRIAN*
[*Editor's note*] On October 13, 1881, the steamer *Cyprian* sailed from Liverpool. She had just left the Mersey when she was met by a dreadful storm, and soon became a prey to the elements. A little stowaway, who had hidden himself among the cargo, terrified by the horrors of the gale, crept from below the mid-deck, where the sailors were all crowded together. The furnace fires were out, and the wreck was drifting near to the rocks of Plas Nevin, Carnarvonshire, Wales, where the waters were tossing and foaming in their angry mood. The Captain wore his life belt, but, looking at the helpless lad, he had pity on him. "Take me belt, I can swim," he said, as he threw it to the otherwise unprotected boy.

The Captain was lost, the boatswain dragging him down in despair, but the stowaway was saved.

> Broken and wrecked by the pitiless storm,
> The good ship *Cyprian* lay;
> Her timbers crashed as the hurricane
> Swept helm and mast away;
> And the sea sprang over her shivering side
> Like a tiger on its prey.
>
> The Captain stood on the vessel's deck
> That he might tread no more;
> He had fought the tempest manfully,
> Had fought but the fight was o'er;
> One hope, the life buoy, yet remained,
> And he might win the shore!
>
> Then from some hiding place there crept,
> All drenched with salt sea spray,
> A little ragged, half-starved child –
> A wretched stowaway,

DAVID J. CLARKE

Who wrung his hands and shrieked aloud,
In pitiful dismay.

Only a little stowaway,
With terror almost mad!
The Captain looked on the yawning waves,
He looked upon the lad;
He held the life belt in his hand –
The one last hope he had.

And far beyond the clamouring sea,
Beyond the blinding foam,
He saw the firelight gleaming bright
Within his English home –
He heard the voice of his love – his Wife;
It seemed to whisper – "Come."

The vision passed, as passing breath
That strives the steed to dun,
He turned towards the trembling child,
He gave the belt to him –
"Take it my lad," the Captain said,
"And I must try to swim."

They plunged together in the waves,
The stowaway and he,
But vain was swimmer's sturdiest stroke
As infant's strength might be;
His life-belt bore the lad to shore,
He —— perished in the sea.

Oh! never nobler deed was done;
Never on land or wave,
Shall the *Cyprian*'s Captain be forgot;
So tender and so brave,
Who gave his life so willingly
The stowaway to save.

Stories From These Shores

WILFRED.
Twillingate [1887][8]

....

(For the *Twillingate Sun*)
TO THE NEW YEAR
New Year, what hast thou that is new –
What themes and schemes to mark thy reign;
What great event, what social bent;
What pleasures new, and what new pain?

What new device for killing time;
And what for one another's killing,
What new surprise, in cant in crime,
What last new trick to turn a shilling?

And what new march on virtue's side –
Against the meanness, mockery, sinning
What rise in that slow, silent tide
Where hope and faith are surely winning?

What knowledge now to bless the race,
To solace suffering stem decay;
What new good cheer, which year by year,
May gladder make each New Year's Day?

What beauty new, what grace evolved,
From virtue's everlasting laws;
What purer thrills, what nobler wills;
What firmer bands with fairer cause?

What sign, New Year, of love's new sway,
What farther step, what clearer view
To prove old things shall pass away,
That all things are becoming new?

WILFRED [1887][9]

DAVID J. CLARKE

....

Here is a poem celebrating our native Isle, penned for the Sun by a resident of Pilley's Island.

OUR NATIVE LAND

Terra Nova, well we love thee
Land of peaceful summer calm,
Here we turn from foreign turmoil,
Here alone our hearts find balm.
How we longed while yet we wandered,
For our childhood's home again;
Thrilled our hearts with fond devotion,
As we crossed the bounding main.

Though of mighty deeds of valour,
We, her children cannot tell;
And the annals of our Country,
Show not where her heroes fell.
Yet upon our hearts main altar,
With a pure and steady glow,
Burns a fire that will not falter,
In the presence of the foe.

Newfoundland; we joy to own thee,
We will serve thee till the last;
Rise ye Sons of Terra Nova,
It is yours to make a past.
Brighter than the noontide glory,
Do it then in spite of frown,
Carry forward freedom's banner,
Break the chains that drag you down.
We have heroes grand and valiant,
Men who in the cause of right,
Would not fear to draw the falchion,
And for their beloved Country fight.
Some have passed into oblivion,

Stories From These Shores

> Graves unmarked by marble dome,
> We their children still will battle
> For the land we call our home.
>
> Clara A. Strong
> Pilley's Island, Nov. 17th, [1891][10]

....

In 1903 the Sun printed a poem titled the "Wadham's Song." In fact, this composition was more than a century older, dating from the late-1700s. According to the Shanties & Sea Songs *website, The Wadham's Song was sung to the tune of* I'll Tell Me Ma. *It was part of a genre known as "Pilot Verses," in which navigational directions were set to popular tunes as an easy way to memorize sailing directions. Apparently, the "Wadham's Song" was considered one of the best of these in the Newfoundland context.*

> From Cape Bonavista to Stinking Isles,
> It is due north about forty miles,
> Then you must steer away N.E.
> Until the Gull Island bears W.N.W.
> Then N.N.W. about thirty miles,
> Three leagues off shore lies the Wadham
> Isles,
> Whereof a rock you must take care,
> Which S.S.E. two miles from the land bear,
> Then N.W. by N. twelve miles or more,
> Lieth Round Head on Fogo shore;
> But N.N.W. seven or eight miles
> Lies breaking rocks round the Barrick Isles,
> Therefore my friend I would you advise,
> Since those rocks so dangerous lies,
> That you never amongst them fall,
> But always endeavour to weather them all.
> As you draw nigh to Fogo land,
> It's fifteen fathoms, nothing but sand.

DAVID J. CLARKE

From fifteen to eighteen, seldom more,
And that you will have close under shore.
And when off Round Head you be
Joe Batt's Point you'll plainly see,
And on your starboard side three or four miles,
A ragged parcel of rocks and isles.
When Joe Batt's Point you are abreast,
Then Fogo Harbour bears due West;
But unkind nature having laid
A sunken rock just in the trade,
That N.N.W. you ought to steer
Till Brimstone Head do plain appear,
Which over Pilley's Point you'll see,
Then, without danger you will be;
As you draw within a mile
You'll see the houses on Syms' Isle.
The Tickle is narrow and not wide,
The deepest water is on the larboard side.
When you are within the Tickle shot,
Three fathoms of water you have got;
Then port your helm and take good care,
That in the middle you do steer,
Till Pilley's Point you are abreast,
Then starboard your helm and steer S.S.W.
Till Pilley's Point covers Syms' stage,
You'll clear the harbour I'll engage.

Copied from an old document bearing date 28th day of October 1784.
(Signed)   J. COBB. Scrip.

and handed for publication by
Mr. ARCHIBALD ROBERTS,
Bluff Head Cove.[11]

....

Stories From These Shores

This composition, by "Jam Lover," celebrates the enjoyment many Newfoundlanders get from picking berries in the late Summer and early Fall. Whether it was blueberries, partridgeberries, or blackberries, harvesting the crop from their low lying bushes was such a part of the yearly round that in some places, including the Isles, pupils were given a "berry picking" day off from school to help their parents gather the succulent treats.

BERRY SONG.
Oh, the truck is coming!
Don't you hear her blow?
To take the people over
Where the partridgeberries grow.
Sweet alee, sweet alee,
You will hear the boys a singing
Sweet alee.

Some takes buckets, more takes pans,
But the ladies takes a bag,
Or a basket in their hand.
Sweet alee, sweet alee,
You will hear the boys a singing
Sweet alee.

The men that are in business
Will get the best of fun.
The time for selling sugar
Is only just begun.
Sweet alee, sweet alee,
You will hear the boys a singing
Sweet alee.

We people go a fishing,
The tom cod for to pull,
To get a little money
To take the ladies through,

DAVID J. CLARKE

Sweet alee, sweet alee,
You will hear the boys a singing Sweet alee.

When we are out a fishing
And the tommy cods go away,
"What is in the bread box?"
The other fellows say.
Pies baked in saucers that's just
The thing for me.
Sweet alee, sweet alee,
You will hear the boys a singing
Sweet alee.

The trucks are doing great work
They are on every call,
They will come to help you
To help you one and all.
Sweet alee, sweet alee,
You will hear the boys a singing
Sweet alee.

When you have fish to pull
Just listen unto me,
Here is luck, you can't be stuck
Get a truck, get a truck.
Sweet alee, sweet alee.
You will hear the boys a singing
Sweet alee.
              JAM LOVER.[12]

....

Stories From These Shores

Another tribute to our native Isle, Newfoundland, by Ethel N. Jacobs of Twillingate, 1935.

NEWFOUNDLAND

Beautiful island of freedom and
peace,
Engirdled by ocean blue — lashing
its shore.
With wild curling waves as soft as
a fleece,
Receding they echo a low,
solemn roar.

Its cliffs high and bare, like sentinels
stand;
For ages they've breasted the
storm and the gale,
Their bare rugged outlines revealing
to man.
The wonders of nature, which
never will fail.

Its forests are full of trees tall and
green;
Its seas teem with life – a blessing
to man.
Its wild rugged grandeur, by
thousands unseen,
Is typical of our loved
Newfoundland.

Oh dear island home, our thoughts
are of thee;
For thee there have toiled, for
thee there have died
The truest, the bravest and hardiest
men,

DAVID J. CLARKE

To their names, on the roll call
of war they replied.

They're lying asleep 'neath Flanders'
green sod.
They died for their Country,
their friends and their home;
And when shall we see them? On
that day when God
Shall arouse them from slumber –
they'll rise from the tomb.

Thy people are hardy, courageous
and bold.
They toil on the land; they toil
on the sea;
Enduring privations, hardships and
cold.
They're manly, they're true,
strong-hearted and free.
By E.N. JACOBS,
Twillingate.[13]

....

This next poem is another work by Ms. Jacobs in celebration of Newfoundland and its people, this time emphasizing their connection to the old union flag of the United Kingdom, the Union Jack.

BENEATH THE UNION JACK
Come every Newfoundlander who
toils on sea or main,
Help spread abroad the glories of
your honoured Country's name;
For we've a heritage to leave the
followers in our track,
That we were born in Newfoundland

Stories From These Shores

beneath the Union Jack.

Oh men of loyal hearts and true,
which beat in sympathy
For every poor unfortunate – how
fortunate are we.
Then we should all be thankful when
thinking of the fact
That we were born in Newfoundland
beneath the Union Jack.

For we've great wealth around us
in forest and in seas.
We face the foaming billows, the
wild, refreshing breeze.
And all the time we labour hard,
be glad that it's a fact
That we were born in Newfoundland
beneath the Union Jack.

A duty Newfoundlanders all
seamen brave and true;
To do the right, to live just lives,
is largely up to you.
Then the younger generation may
glory in the fact
That they were born in Newfoundland
beneath the Union Jack.
By ETHEL N. JACOBS [1936][14]

....

DAVID J. CLARKE

Another aspect of their lives with which Newfoundlanders were (and are) very proud was their connection with the sea, and their reputations as some of the world's best fishers and small boatmen. A downside of this life, at least as some saw it, was their dependence on the cash-less credit system, which often left Newfoundland's hardy Sons of the sea in debt to their local merchant houses.

In the early 1900s a new movement was founded to ensure that fishers received their fair share of the industry's bounty. Led by William Ford Coaker (1871-1938), the Fisherman's Protective Union was founded on the Isles in the community of Herring Neck. It soon spread to other outports, and over the years its main source of strength came from the northeast coast. The FPU eventually expanded into operating its own stores and formed a political wing. By the 1930s the movement may have been past its prime, but it was still able to inspire dedication. In the poem below "Union Man" urges the fishers of Twillingate to rally around the FPU and its President, Coaker's successor, Kenneth McKenzie Brown (1887-1955).

COME AND JOIN
Come all ye men of Twillingate,
Who to the fishery do go,
Come and join the Union
And make the Council grow.
For we have an able leader,
As good as ever stood,
Trying to help his Country
And do the people good.

Come all labouring people
And every fisherman,
Let's join our hands together,
And side by side to stand.
For it's just the labouring people
And the poor old fisherman,
Who barely gets a living,
In dear old Newfoundland.

Stories From These Shores

We have toiled both night and day
Trying hard to earn a living,
And to keep the wolf away,
We have done our best to do it,
And we have done most everything,
But we cannot get a living,
No matter how we try.

K.M. Brown is our President
And our leader strong and bold,
Come rally round his banner
And make our Council grow.
He is a man of honour
And a noble gentleman,
Trying hard to get a living
For every fisherman.

Now to conclude and finish
And to bring everything just right.
You can come and join the Union
On every Thursday night.
Fifty cents well spent,
It may be worthwhile,
So come and join our Union
And help the pot to boil.

Now my song is ended,
I have got no more to say,
But wishing that K.M. Brown
Would come down in Notre Dame Bay.
He knows that he is welcome,
As welcome as a lark,
For he is badly needed
Right down here in the north.

UNION MAN [1938].[15]

DAVID J. CLARKE

....

In 1945 Helen Kearney of Harbour Grace submitted this poem to the Sun about one of her favourite places, Twillingate, and its Hospital.

TWILLINGATE
While the moon shines down in
splendour
Over ocean, hill and lake,
My thoughts tonight are turning
To dear old Twillingate.
In fancy I can see again
That little northern isle;
Some memories bring me tear drops
While others bring a smile.

One very vivid picture
That oft returns to me,
Is the grand old Memorial,
As it nestles by the sea.
There in its wards are kindly forms
Clad in blue, pink and white,
Who patiently are ministering
To the sufferers day and night.

Again I see Miss Manuel,
So patient, wise and kind,
And Dr. Olds, a nobler man
On earth you cannot find.
May God protect and guide them.
He knows their wondrous worth;
And may they long continue
To perform their noble work.

While in the moonlight, dreaming,
I can see each well loved face,
And there amid the many

Are my kind friends on the Base.
The bout of dreams is over,
And now I kneel to pray,
God bless all those at Twillingate,
And all around its Bay.

By HELEN KEARNEY,
Harbour Grace.[16]

....

In this composition from 1948, Twillingate mariner Charles Froude recounts a trip to the icefields by one of his hometown's most famous schooners, the Bessie Marie.

Constructed by Eleazar Mills of Burlington, Green Bay, in 1929, the 208 ton vessel was the last three-masted schooner built in Newfoundland. It was later converted into a two-master with an auxiliary engine.

RHYMES ON THE BESSIE [MARIE]

Come listen and I'll tell you a story,
It won't delay you very long;
It's about our trip to the icefields
We enjoyed it with laughter and song.
On the 7th of March, left the City
All hands they were jolly and gay;
But we had to call at Bay Roberts
Where we ballasted our boat the next day.
We arrived at port that same evening,
The ice it was tight in the Bay;
But the *National* kept open the channel;
To keep us from being delayed.

DAVID J. CLARKE

We slipped our lines off from the wharf
Our engine turning fair;
We jammed the *Bessie* in the ice,
South east from Carbonear.
But never mind me jolly boys
Don't murmur, fret or fear;
The *Bessie* is a lucky boat,
And we will get our share.
We were not jammed there very long.
Before the wind did veer;
And with little extra power,
She wriggled herself clear.
We killed most everything we saw,
The young harp and the hood.
To kill three hundred seals each day
We thought was very good.
And now we're leaving the old harps.
We've get her underway.
We're heading for the whitecoats
That the plane spot yesterday.
Before I go much further
I'll make mention of the crew
And some of our officers
And what we've got to do.
We've got to obey orders
When the Captain says the word,
But every man is willing,
Yes, "as willing as a bird."
James Gillett is our master,
Cecil Stockley is our mate,
And his Brother Stan, the barrelman.
He scarce takes time to eat.

Stories From These Shores

Stewart Cooper's our chief cook,
And his Son Hayward second;
They cook the flippers of the seal
When they get short of bacon.
There are more men I can include
And that's the master watches;
Clarence Legge I'll mention first,
Fred Parsons he comes next.
Claude Churchill is in our watch,
He is a decent man;
He cuts our flippers in his watch
And fries them when he can.
And now the quartermasters
I'll try to bring in rhyme;
Harvey Earle in Churchill's watch
He always comes on time.
James Greenham and Andrew Troake
They stand there with their pole
They never do get weary
But shiver with the cold
Now there's another party
I think they are very nice;
The men that owns the *Bessie*
And fits her for the ice.
Now they are men of honour
And we know they do their best;
You can get a job to Ashbournes
When you are turned down by the rest.
And now getting near the Funks
Picking up seals each day;
We hope to get a bumper trip
Before the first of May.
And then there's our good doctor
I guess you know his name;

DAVID J. CLARKE

He now belongs to Twillingate.
From America he came.
There's three more men I don't forget
And that's the bridgemasters;
James Lambert and Stanley Troake
Also Raymond Bridger.
And now the engineers,
Their names are hard to rhyme;
They are the men that work below
Away from the sunshine.
Now we can trust George Burton
When things are going wrong;
Jack Greenham he's a comic
Pleasant as the day is long!
And now the other engineer
His name I'll not yet tell;
But I guess you all will know him
When we are back from the ice fields.
And then there's our ship's carpenter
I think I'll mention too;
He is the man that sheaths our boat
When the ice does cut her through.
His name is Walter Cooper,
He's one of the gunners as well;
A crack shot on a rifle,
He scarcely misses a seal.
And now it's April twentieth
In the early afternoon;
We are leaving the icefields
Our ship is homeward bound.
And here we are safely landed
Upon our native soil;
Back to our friends and loved ones
And they greet us with a smile.
And now you all may wonder
Who composed this song;
His name is Charles Albert Froude

Stories From These Shores

From Twillingate do belong.
I've crossed the broad Atlantic
And boldly took my stand;
I am a Diesel engineer
And bred in Newfoundland.[17]

....

DAVID J. CLARKE

The first Englishmen to visit Twillingate were not intent on settlement. Rather, the ships that arrived each Spring were wholly engaged in the migratory fishery. In that era their on-shore facilities were mainly concentrated in Hart's Cove (Durrell), near the mouth of the harbour.

Over time more and more people did *begin to overwinter in the community, and in the 1700s one Captain Primmer had the clever idea of bringing English soil to the settlement as ballast, so that it could be recycled for a garden, supplementing the thin, rocky product of Newfoundland's own shores. In the mid-twentieth century, when this poem appeared, the mariner's descendant was still tending his own piece of "Old England."*

OLD ENGLAND IN HART'S COVE
(By – Rev. Fred T. Fudge)
A ship loaded with English soil,
And guidance from above;
Sailed o'er the sea for many days,
And anchored in Hart's Cove.
The soil was landed with great care,
Soil that was brought from Dover,
To keep alive old England's pride
In new-found Terra Nova.

Generations have come, generations gone,
Two hundred years or more –
Since the soil was landed at Hart's Cove,
On Twillingate's south shore.
Now it is owned by my old friend,
In whose soul God's light doth glimmer,
A hero, sailor, sage and saint,
My Uncle Jimmy Primmer.

Guard well that English garden Jim,

Stories From These Shores

In Summer and in Winter;
Put the Union Jack on every side
And Churchill in the centre.
India is gone, Palestine is lost,
Egypt will soon be going,
But in God's name let England live,
In the garden you'll be sowing.

But I have something in Hart's Cove
Dearer than English soil –
The grave of Sister Harriet Jane,
My Mother's eldest child.
Please plant a flower for me Jim,
On the grave I shall never see,
And I will thank you when we meet,
My Sister, you and me.[18]

7
Royalty

(For the *Twillingate Sun*)

Every student of English history finds that a thorough acquaintance with the line of Sovereigns is one of the first and most important matters.

The Sovereign is the centre of the times in which he or she lived; hence, the circumstances or events of any particular time are more easily called up when we remember who reigned then, and for this, among other reasons, our historians have divided and sub-divided their work into periods, houses, and reigns.

The following simple rhyme, which gives in order all the British sovereigns from [the] Norman period down to the present [1884], will amply repay anyone who will take the trouble to memorize it;

Norman William stands first,
Then Will Rufus his Son.
Henry, Stephen, Henry;
Then Richard and John.
Henry the Third,
Edwards One, Two and Three;
After Richard the Second,
Three Henry's we see
Two Edwards, then Richard
With hump like an S;
Two Henry's, young Edward,
Then Mary and Bess.
Scottish James, then Charles
the Martyr's short reign;
Then Cromwell's Commonwealth;
Then a Charles again.
James the Second;
Then William and Mary appear.
After Anne reigned four Georges
Of Hanover here.
Then sailor King William
In peace wore the Crown,
Which Victoria has raised

Stories From These Shores

To unfading renown.[1]

....

In the year 1887 Victoria, Queen of Great Britain and Empress of India, celebrated her fiftieth year on the throne. The Sun's Editor and a number of correspondents reported on how the residents of Twillingate commemorated the occasion of the Queen's Golden Jubilee.

The present year is likely to be a memorable one in every known part of the vast British Empire, over which for fifty years our Most Gracious Sovereign, Lady Queen VICTORIA, has swayed the sceptre with such dignity and honour as was never excelled, or even equalled, by any Monarch that ever preceded her. In every corner of Her Majesty's domains the hearts of her subjects will be found throbbing with animation during this Jubilee year, at the remembrance of the long and peaceable reign of our beloved Queen, and in some form or other various demonstrations, as the outcome of love and loyalty to her, will nearly everywhere be made manifest. Her subjects in this insignificant part of her extensive possessions are no less ardent in attachment of loyalty for their Sovereign than those in any other part of the world; indeed, we believe as a rule Newfoundlanders are even more demonstrative in this particular than many other people, and we are proud to know that Britain has Sons here loyal to the British Throne, and who consider it a pleasure to engage in celebrating the Jubilee reign of our Queen. Hence, Tuesday next [24 May, 1887], being Her Majesty's birthday, is the day on which this community is invited to participate in the celebration of the auspicious event, and it is to be hoped that as loyal subjects, everyone who possibly can, will united in making it a real National Jubilee celebration. We need only call attention to the advertisement in today's paper to show that the Committee, managing arrangements, have spared no pains in endeavouring to prepare a programme, which, in order to be successfully carried out, requires the people's co-operation, which we would bespeak for it. The time named has been selected, as many of our men will be leaving for the Summer in a little while, and we think that the day fixed on is a very suitable one.

DAVID J. CLARKE

Queen Victoria

On the twenty-fourth of May next, Her Majesty the Queen will have attained her sixty-eighth year, having been born in 1819. Her age we are told, has been exceeded by only three Sovereigns of England, namely: George II [1683-1760], who lived to the age of seventy-seven years; George III [1738-1820], eighty-two years, and William IV [1765-1837], seventy-two years. Her Majesty ascended the Throne in 1837, and on the twenty-first [of] June next will have reigned over the United Kingdom fifty years – a length of reign that has been exceeded by two of the Kings of England only, namely, Henry the III [1207-72], whose reign extended to fifty-six years, and George III, who reigned for nearly sixty years, so that very many years have elapsed since the British nation has had occasion to celebrate a Jubilee year of one of its Monarchs. In whatever aspect we might view it, under no other potentate has the Empire made such strides as during the last fifty years, that Queen VICTORIA has ruled, and the feeling and desire of every true British subject is that her life may be long spared to sway the sceptre over the domains of her vast territories. Never have the skirmishes and direful consequences of war been less prevalent than within this period, from which in a comparative sense, it may be said

Stories From These Shores

there has been almost an entire absence, that is, to any proportionate dimensions. True there was the Crimean War and in later years the Franco-German War, and in other less important conflicts, in which minor sections of the United Kingdom may have been involved, but on the whole, absence of commotion involving or imperiling the interests of European powers is a distinguishing characteristic during the long reign of our Sovereign. The progress of truth, and the extension of civil and religious liberty has been greater under her sway than ever before known, while Christianity has extended and flourished to a degree unprecedented in the annals of English history. Wherever the British flag is unfurled thraldom and barbarism can have no abiding place, and perfect freedom and liberty of conscience is the common lot of Britain's Sons, wherever the Empire extends. Never was such a happy and prosperous reign known. Long may the health of our Queen permit her to adorn the British Throne, and when she shall be called to lay aside her earthly jewels, may she be adorned with a more endurable gem that will shine more illustriously through the illimitable ages of the future.

....

(To the Editor of the *Twillingate Sun*)

DEAR SIR, — No doubt all loyal citizens hail with pleasure the opportunity of doing honour to that paragon Queen, who for fifty years has swayed the sceptre with such acceptance over the British Empire.

Now, as Twillingate is the first place in Newfoundland to move in the Jubilee celebration, and as our leading men have consented to cooperate and suspend business for the day, it only remains for the general public to take an interest in the matter, and let every man, woman and child do their part to carry out the programme by joining the procession, &c., and then we feel the success of the day will be insured, and it will be a kind of red letter day in our history.

The Committee have made all arrangements possible, and the Societies are of one mind on the matter throughout. Therefore, let us have a good day, as it is only once in a lifetime that such an occasion occurs, and let us all pray, "God save the Queen."   Yours, etc.,
COMMITTEE MAN.

Twillingate, May 20 [1887]

DAVID J. CLARKE

....

May the twenty-fourth, 1887, will be a day long to be remembered in this community, it being the time set apart by mutual consent, for the celebration of Her Most Gracious Majesty Queen Victoria's Jubilee.

A joint Committee from all the societies had the arrangements for the day in charge, and under their management the day's proceedings were carried out in a manner which reflected great credit on the community; in fact, we venture to say that nowhere in the Island outside the Capital, could a finer demonstration be witnessed.

The day dawned favourably, and soon it was quite apparent that something unusual was on foot; for all business was suspended, and soon gay bunting in great profusion met the eye in every direction; and as busy hands gave the finishing touch to wreaths, garlands, mottoes, &c., the fact was clear that no trouble had been spared in making suitable preparations. The triumphal arches erected at different places were got up in good style, and the mottoes all betokened deep attachment to our Queen and Empress.

The first part of the day's programme was divine services at ten o'clock...Rev. R. Temple, R.D., conducted service in St. Peter's Church, and gave an excellent discourse [the subject being], "loyalty is the natural fruit of orderly subjection"...

...The Rev. A. Pittman occupied St. Andrew's pulpit [the topic of his sermon being] "parental authority developed as to the nation"

A large congregation was present in the South Side Methodist Church. The Rev. G. Bullen conducted the opening exercises and read the lessons. A Jubilee ode was sung as anthem by the choir. The sermon was preached by Rev. J.W. Vickers...

...Service was also conducted in the Congregational Church by Mr. Gillingham, in the absence of the Minister.

All services were well attended and a great interest was manifested.

At one o'clock the formation of the procession commenced, and soon a dazzling spectacle was presented to the hundreds of spectators who crowded every available elevation. Nearly all the Societies had provided elaborate "Jubilee Banners," some of them very large, and these, added to the regular stock of flags, banners &c., made an imposing sight. The design of mottoes and workmanship of the banners would do credit to a far more pretentious town. First in order was a carriage containing the Ensign and an old member from each of the three societies, drawn by a horse with streaming tassels in his ears, and a flag bearing the words "TERRA NOVA," over his head. Next came the Congregational School and Band of Hope, with several carriages to draw the little ones; their number was eighty-six. These were followed by the Methodist Schools and Bands of Hope, numbering 307. Next came the Church of England Schools and Bands of Hope, counting 235. Next we were glad to see the noble followers of Dorcas, who so lately have done so much good amongst the poor (work which Her Majesty also loves to foster) take their places, bearing a great banner of purple and white, with the inscription, "Dorcas Greeting." As many of their number were school teachers, only fourteen walked together, and we may here say the reason they are not mentioned in the cablegram to the Queen is, that when they had decided to walk, the message was framed and adopted by the Committee and no subsequent meeting was held. The Victoria Jubilee Band, under the management of Mr. Hitchcock, came next, and discoursed sweet music along the line of march. The Society of United Fishermen in their handsome regalia, musted well, 104 being their number, and they were followed by the Loyal Orange Association, counting 171. These looked remarkably well in the regalia of the different degrees, especially those of the Royal Scarlet Chapter. Representatives of the Church of England Temperance Society and Sons of Temperance showed respectively, twenty-one and twenty-six, and they were followed by Masonic members as private citizens wearing rosettes. The reason of this was, there being no Lodge here they could not appear in regalia. The rear of [the] procession was made up of one doctor, Government officials, and lastly the carriage of F. Berteau, Esq., Stipendiary Magistrate, containing himself and J.B. Tobin, Esq., J.P., attended by a Constable in full uniform on horseback.

    The total number in procession was 1,000. Starting from the Hall, they moved down through the arch near Mr. Williams' to Church Hill, and passing by Rev. R. Temple's decoration of bough, motto and flags erected near the Church, and on through the handsome arch on the top of Church Hill (designed and superintended by Chairman of Committee and built by voluntary labour, R.D. Hodge and J B. Tobin,

Esqrs. kindly lending material, and several young ladies making the attractive mottoes: "We honour Victoria," "1887," "Jubilee," "Terra Nova," &c.) They quickly passed by the new road, down around the premises of Messrs. Waterman & Co., and then on to the bridge, in the centre of which another arch was erected. Here a halt was made whilst the following cable-gram (in outline form) was dispatched from the telegraph office near by:

Buckingham Palace (Author's photo)

Twillingate, Newfoundland
TO HER MOST GRACIOUS MAJESTY
QUEEN VICTORIA,
Buckingham Palace, London.

The Brethren of Sons of Temperance, Loyal Orange Association, Society of United Fishermen, Church of England Temperance Society, also Bands of Hope, Sunday Schools, Magistrates, Doctors and others, celebrating Jubilee, extend their hearty loyalty and congratulations to their beloved Sovereign, who has been long blest by Heaven to the Nation's welfare, and invoke Divine favour richly to rest upon her whilst still swaying the sceptre over united and happy subjects, and that finally she may obtain that Crown which fadeth not away.

(Signed)
Wm. J. SCOTT, Chairman.

Stories From These Shores

Wm. HITCHCOCK, Sec. Com.

(At an early hour next morning the following reply was received, and the promptitude with which our dispatch has been replied to by Her Majesty is a matter of great congratulation: —

Balmoral, May 25th 1887.

TO WILLIAM JOHN SCOTT,

Twillingate, Nfld.

The Queen thanks you all, for your kind and loyal message.

Sir H.F. Ponsonby

Private Secretary

After the National Anthem was sung, and cheers given for the Queen, the procession moved on down the South Side, passing through the arches near Mr. A. Linfield's residence also near the premises of E. Duder, Esq., and lastly by the gate of the Methodist Church, all of which showed good taste and execution. Reversing order, they marched back to the Hall and dispersed, three cheers being given for the Magistrate, F. Berteau, Esq.

Long before the time named the spacious platform erected for the occasion on Church Hill was surrounded by an eager multitude, and at six o'clock the band, and Committee and speakers appeared. Mr. Scott introduced Josiah Colbourne, Esq., J.P. (As Chairman of the meeting), who opened with an appropriate speech...

The programme was enlivened by selections by the band and singing by a male choir under the leadership of J. Templeton, Esq...The meeting closed by singing the National Anthem, [and] cheers for the QUEEN, Josiah Colbourne, Esq., and Chairman Committee, and soon after the hills resounded with the reports from scores of guns fired in quick succession, and for two hours fireworks (of which a supply had been procured in St. John's) and illuminations of houses was the centre of attraction, and a more brilliant scene has never been witnessed here before. Many of the residences were in a blaze of light, but the palm must be given to J.B. Tobin, Esq., who had a large number of ships' side lights exhibited along the platform and over his porch, which added finely to his display.

We may say, in closing, that May twenty-fourth, 1887, was one of which we as a community may feel proud; for on that day we witnessed a union of all Societies and classes in a noble effort to commemorate in the best way the means at our disposal will allow, the Jubilee of that Noble Queen, whom we delight to honour, and whose name shall yet live in generations yet unborn, because of the noble traits of character which have endeared her to the Nation over which she has, in the wisdom of God, been permitted so gloriously to reign for fifty years. And there is a lesson we may learn from the day's success, and it is this, "what may be accomplished by union of hands and hearts in a good cause."

May England's Noble Queen long enjoy the loyalty of her loving subjects, both in the Colonies, yes even in cold Newfoundland, and at Home, is the prayer of
TERRA NOVA.[2]

....

Queen Victoria's Son, who reigned as Edward VII (1841-1910), wasn't on the throne long enough to celebrate any of the major Jubilees. However, her Grandson, George V, (1910-1936) did live to see his Silver Jubilee in 1935, the year prior to his death. As they had done for his Grandmother, Newfoundlanders celebrated the occasion in high style.

Victoria the Great was born in 1819, acceded to the Throne on June twentieth, 1837, was crowned the following year, 1838, on June twenty-eighth. She died Jany. Twenty-second, 1901. Edward the Peacemaker ascended the Throne on August ninth, 1902; owing to illness the coronation was postponed from January of the year before. He died May sixth, 1910, thereby bringing our present King to the Throne.

Prince George, upon the death of the Duke of Clarence and Avondale, became Prince of Wales. He was crowned May ninth, 1910.

Twenty-five years from the time of Accession brings the coming sixth of May [1935] as the Silver Jubilee Day. Let it be the beginning of a prosperous season to all in Newfoundland, and in view of the promise in Holy Writ of a Kingdom which will live while time lasts (note the falling off of Kings and democracies), England's reigning Sovereigns being in that line of promise, it behoves all His Majesty's subjects throughout the Empire to honour and obey. Fear God, honour the King, love the Brotherhood. Be loyal to all our rulers under our Gracious Sovereign, and it is possible the future will hold out something better than the past has ever given, and only if there is continual faith and loyalty.

....

King George V

On May sixth next [1935], the people of Newfoundland are asked to celebrate, with due enthusiasm, the Silver Jubilee (twenty-fifth anniversary) of King George's Coronation. It is just possible someone may ask, "why should we celebrate this occasion?" It is quite possible that when Joshua, amid much solemnity, ordered the erection of a huge cairn of stones in the middle of the Jordan, where the feet of the priests stood, that someone remarked "what's the use of piling those stones together?" That question was actually answered by Joshua, whether asked or not, because he pointed out that to keep the wonderful in remembrance it was necessary to have something to which the younger generation could be pointed in due time, and told just what the stones represented.

DAVID J. CLARKE

In the course of the journey through time of that very wonderful conglomeration of peoples who form the British Commonwealth of Nations (better known to young folk as the British Empire) there have been very many occasions upon which it was wise to set up certain milestones in history. Those of us who are now growing older will recollect one very important celebration in 1897, when the sixtieth year of good Queen Victoria's reign was celebrated through her wide domain.

But while Victoria's reign was marked by times of general world peace and comparative contentment, the reign of His Majesty, King George, has been set in times of world strife and depression, times that might well have tested the attachment of a people to their Sovereign. While many other thrones fell, the Throne of Britain's King became more firmly set in the affections of his people than ever, so that when death laid a threatening hand on the Throne a few years ago, the great heart of his people went out in affection and sympathy to their suffering King.

Throughout the twenty-five years of his reign the thoughts and sympathy of Britain's King have been ever for his subjects, and his heart was wrung as much by the suffering of his people during those times of depression, as by those of the men who served their Country in the war zone. He has visited among the humblest homes in his Country and done his utmost by advice, example, aid and precept to bring about a new social order.

As for the place in this great Empire, of which Newfoundland forms a parts, the King occupies the cornerstone position of the political fabric. In England, more powerful is the Prime Minister of the day, as regards the making of laws. But Father, advisor, central rallying point of the whole of the British people, the King is greater [by] far than the most popular Prime Minister could ever be, binding together in his hand the affections of peoples of different colour, language and climate.

Particularly is it the wish of the King that around the children of the Empire should centre the celebrations next month. They are to be the ones whose youthful hands can best build the memorial cairn in the stream of time, so that whatever stresses may arise during their lifetime they will ever have the memory of this great day in their young lives, when they did honour to a King who ruled not by force, but in love and affection.

....

His Most Gracious Majesty King George the Fifth will, on Monday [6 May, 1935], receive the homage of many millions of his subjects throughout the Empire and who, with Queen Mary, will enjoy the Jubilee Day as London turns out to meet him on his tour of the great City.

Their Majesties have won the respect and admiration because of their love and sympathy to the needy, the sick, and the children. Their peoples up and down the Empire, the Commonwealth of Nations, are making due preparation to the end that the Silver Jubilee will be fittingly celebrated.

The spirit of jubilation is already dominating the mind of the peoples under the British Crown, and they will, in their display of loyalty and devotion to the Throne, continue to be peaceful subjects hereafter. All English speaking people in the foreign countries and many others of different nations of earth, will send to the King and Queen, their congratulations. All the members of the Royal Family will receive the goodwill of everyone on this occasion of the twenty-fifth anniversary of the reign of George the Fifth.

Newfoundlanders who know of the King as a seaman will regard him as a friend to the mariner and fisherman. His career as a Navy man has brought him to the highest rank. First he spent several years cruising before he finally commanded HMS *Thrush*. On the death of the heir apparent, the Duke of Clarence, he left the Navy to prepare himself for his later duties.

DAVID J. CLARKE

Twillingate residents parade over Tickle Bridge to celebrate King George V's Silver Jubilee, 1935

"Though a student and fond of a quiet life, he has shown himself practical and progressive, and has promoted the interests of all members of the British Commonwealth."

"As a Nation we have much cause to give thanks for a ruler who has shown practical sympathy with every righteous cause, and who has sought to serve his God faithfully and well," says the [Salvation Army] *War Cry*. "His heart spoken 'God bless you all' on the occasion of his Empire-wide broadcast at Christmastide made a profound impression on his people, and testified to a man of deep religious experience."

We all, in return, join in saying
LONG LIVE THE KING.

....

Stories From These Shores

Jubilee day in Twillingate was ideal in weather conditions and idealistic as a time of celebration. In the morning, at the appointed time, the lines of flags and buntings were hoisted. Arches received their last touches and all preparations for the parade were finalized. At one p.m. the children met in the Parish Hall, S.A. School and the Marshall Hall, to participate in the parade; all under the age of seven and eight, respectively, met with the others at four p.m. to receive refreshments and candy.

The Boy Scouts, Girl Guides, Arm Lad's Brigade, Masonic Society, S.U.F., L.O.A., war vets, the Magistrate and Justices of the Peace, clergymen, children and citizens, formed in a huge line from the court house grounds. The A.L.B. Band gave prominence to the proceedings as the 1,284 members of the procession wended their way back from Yates' Hill, South Side to the North Side, and while nearing Mr. Linfield's residence a halt was made and the radio's transmitter was giving out the voice of the King. The calmness gave listeners across the harbour a chance to hear him. To the children His Majesty gave a special message, quoting from the message delivered by Queen Victoria on the occasion of her Diamond Jubilee.

"...As you grow up seek to become wise and devoted citizens." He thanked most heartily, the peoples of every part of the Empire for the many messages of loyalty, sympathy and kindness.

At Jubilee Corner (so called after 1887) and the Post Office grounds another halt was made to hear the address to be sent to His Majesty through His Excellency, Governor Anderson. Magistrate Roberts at this juncture spoke from the platform erected for the speakers. He was pleased with the loyalty shown in Twillingate and expressed his appreciation for the noble way in which the people were helping with the whole Country to celebrate the Jubilee, and made reference to the co-operation of the various organizations and committees in their tribute of devotion to the Crown. Also a few appropriate remarks in reference to the Silver Jubilee and the privilege we enjoy under such a Gracious Sovereign. After this Mr. T.G.W. Ashbourne, J.P., was called upon by the Magistrate to read the message to be sent to His Excellency the Governor. Mr. Ashbourne said: "We have met today to celebrate the twenty-fifth anniversary of His Majesty's Accession to the Throne – His silver Jubilee. We in common with the rest of the British Empire rejoice that Almighty God has spared the life of His Majesty and that it was our devout wish and prayer that for many more years he might be spared to guide his people. For many present this is the first occasion of its kind within their remembrance, but there are some in the parade who still remember the Diamond Jubilee of Queen Victoria, celebrating her sixty years' reign. The speaker then referred to His Majesty the King's speech which had been heard over the radio (the reception of which was excellent) as the parade was en route to Jubilee Corner.

Crowds gather at Jubilee Corner, 1936

His Majesty the King would in four weeks of the Jubilee reach the age of three score years and ten, and was known as the Sailor King and the People's King. He loved the sea, and at the age of twelve had joined a ship as a cadet with his Brother the Duke of Clarence. At the age of twenty-seven he was commander of a cruiser. His naval career had been temporarily interrupted by the death of his Brother the Duke of Clarence.

"By his life and example he has won the love of his people and has preserved through times encompassed with difficulties our historical inheritance of order and freedom."

It was with great pleasure that Mr. Ashbourne proposed that the following telegram be sent to His Excellency the Governor to be forwarded to his Majesty the King.

To His Excellency the Governor,
 St. John's,
May it please Your Excellency:
 We beg to ask you to convey to the King's Most Excellent Majesty the loyal greetings of the people of Twillingate. Our people respectfully offer their congratulations on the twenty-fifth anniversary of his accession to the Throne. We are deeply conscious of, and admire, his splendid example of personal and social excellence which has had a world wide influence in making for all that is elevating in human relationships. We are happy that Their Majesties are still spared to work for the consolidation of the Empire and in the interests of world peace. Recognizing the value of their exemplary lives in a position of such unique responsibility and effectiveness, we hope and pray that for many years to come Their Majesties may be vouchsafed health and strength to direct, by their wise counsel, their many subjects and to continue to exert their influence amongst the nations of the world:
 On behalf of the
  Citizens of Twillingate,
  F. ROBERTS, Chairman
   Committee.
  T.G.W. Ashbourne,
   Secretary.

Twillingate
 May 6th 1935.

 Mr. Robert Rice, J.P., who was pleased to second the motion, said in part:
 I have the honour on this historic occasion to second the motion that the address on behalf of the people of Twillingate be forwarded to His Excellency the Governor with the gracious request that it be sent to His Majesty the King...
 Three cheers were then called for His Majesty and was popularly responded to. The Royal Salute was then given by the A.L.B. and the Band played the National Anthem, the people joining in the singing of the same. The parade then dispersed and the children were taken to the Victoria and Alexandra Halls where the busy ladies and committeemen

did the serving to those who gathered, until six o'clock. A quantity of cake and candy was distributed to some parents of children at home, and also to the children in the Hospital.

The [Twillingate Athletic Association] T.A.A.'s arch of goalposts...erected above Jubilee Corner, gave a finishing to the street that did its bit of homage to the King. Many people around Twillingate turned out to take part in the day's proceedings, from all over the islands, and in all upwards of 3,000 showed their deep interest and patriotism.

At night public buildings and dwelling houses were illuminated, and also the arch near the Halls was lit up. The next night also saw several houses lit up and several bonfires; a pleasing spectacle to onlookers and passers by.

Both nights were well enjoyed by people who gathered in the court room, Masonic Temple, the Halls and club room, as some citizens, Scouts, Guides, and members of the T.A.A. took part in dancing and games until a late hour. At the Court House, which was handsomely decorated, refreshments were partaken of before the closing, baskets having been prepared. At the A.L.B. Armoury on Monday night a social time was held.

The Thanksgiving Services held in the various places of worship were all well attended. On Sunday at the United Churches and S.A. Citadel the clergymen, officers and laymen, conducted their services with prayers, hymns and subjects appropriate to Thanksgiving.

In addition to the various celebrations of the King's Jubilee held on May sixth, a Thanksgiving Service, according to that prescribed in the Book of Common Prayer, was conducted in St. Peter's Church at 10:30 a.m. on Monday. The service began with the singing of the first verse of the National Anthem, followed by Hymn 166...

At the United Churches Rev. Laite preached a sermon from the text, "Give the King thy Judgement, O God, and thy righteousness unto the King's Son" — Psalm 72 : 1...[3]

....

When King George died in early 1936 he was briefly succeeded by his eldest Son, who reigned as Edward VIII. The Sun carried a number of

Stories From These Shores

tributes to the late King, and well wishes for his successor.

Dear Mr. Editor: — Please grant me space in your paper to pay publicly, this last humble tribute of respect to my beloved Sovereign, the late King George V of England.

Today, every patriotic subject within the far-flung realms of the British Empire mourns the loss of our King. To some he was merely a historical figure, an English King occupying a throne like any other English King before him. To me he was more than that! It is one thing to hear of a man, to read about him or even listen to his voice over the radio; it is quite another to have a personal interview with him, to behold his face and expression, to feel his personal touch and share his thoughts in conversation. This was my pleasure in March, 1916. How, then, can I refrain from making known that he was, to me, a personal friend as well as my Beloved and Gracious Sovereign! During the Great War...we were officially invited to dine with their Majesties, King George and Queen Mary, at Buckingham Palace. We were there from 2:30 p.m. until nine p.m. Only those who have come in personal contact with him can estimate his appreciation, sincere love and veneration for the Newfoundland soldiers. Everyone knows that the days of grim Gallipoli and Beaumont Hamel were strenuous ones for our late King, and yet self was obscured in his care and unwearied devotion to the welfare of his soldier subjects.

It was his delight to ask us questions relating to ourselves and our service for him, and it was no matter of condescension for that Sovereign of perfect English to hear us give freely and easily our clumsy answers.

Today, he rests in his little oak coffin in the Chapel where he was wont to worship, awaiting burial in Windsor.

How much would we – Great War Veterans – give to be able to steal softly in and take one last look at that kind face that once beamed on us with cheerful courage! As Shakespeare makes Anthony say of Caesar, referring to the citizens – "Yes, beg a hair of him for memory. And, dying, mention it within their (our) wills, bequeathing it as a rich legacy."

In those war days we counted not our own lives dear unto us, but gave our limbs, our bodies, our hearts unreservedly in service for King and Country, and if we had again been called to defend our land, how willingly I would offer myself a second time, even as I am! Why? Not because of a love for warlike enterprise, human destruction and infinite bloodshed, but because of my love, devotion, respect and appreciation for my King. It grieves me that I do not see sufficient public manifestations of sympathy and sorrow in Twillingate. This is all the more so with me, I suppose, because experience leads me to believe that London mourns greatly and shows its due solemnity. How I desire to share it since it must be done.

"His life was gentle, and the elements so mixed in him that nature might stand up and say to all the world, 'This was a man!'"
Yea, my KING!
Undoubtedly, universal sorrow is felt for the Mother Queen!
1084 EDWARD WHITE
Royal Nfld Regiment

Twillingate,
Jan. 22nd 1935.

....

The new King Edward VIII, former Prince of Wales, comes to the British Throne at the age of forty-one years. A salute of forty-one guns was fired by the Royal Artillery at the grounds of St. James' Palace in London, on Wednesday, [22 January, 1936], as an ancient custom was performed, attended by much pomp and brilliancy, headed by the Lord Mayor of London, who read the Royal Proclamation announcing him as King. Many radio listeners here tuned in at 6:30 a.m. on Wednesday to the wonderful ceremony – reception being perfect – as the announcer in London kept pace in announcing every incident of this brilliant affair.

King Edward VIII as Prince of Wales

....

After an unbroken reign of twenty-five years the Empire is called to mourn the loss of a Sovereign. George the Fifth, whose health was somewhat impaired four years ago, has not been of a robust constitution, yet many were surprised to learn of his severe illness which seemed to have shown no improvement towards recovery as formerly.

The whole peoples of the Commonwealth of Nations deeply regret the passing of one of the most gracious of English Monarchs, and to Queen Mary and the Royal Families all the subjects join in sincere condolence. Not only do those of the British Empire mourn and offer sympathy but from all around the world come messages, in such high esteem and respect was the late King held by them also.

Before his death, after a few moments of unconsciousness, he rallied and asked: "How is the Empire?" Those gathered assured him and said, "it is well with the Empire." He then smiled and dropped off into his long sleep.

As a peacemaker the influence of George the Fifth was richly felt in the world, especially in times of difficulty, and no word can utter the value of such aid given to the difficult problems down through the years.

His broadcast speeches at his Silver Jubilee on May the sixth past, and his Christmas message of "good cheer" gave his subjects something of the inner nature of the head of "The Great Family." His wise counsel and advice to his subjects, given in a humble and very fitting manner has been the means to cement the cordiality and courage he wished for.

The funeral to be held on Thursday promises to be a memorable day for London, England, and the Empire, as well as an event to be remembered by the world at large.

Seventy years, the allotted span of life and a glorious reign of twenty-five years brings to a peaceful end a well beloved Empire ruler.

The accession of Edward, Prince of Wales to the Throne of England was proclaimed in England on Wednesday, and the display of guns, amid all the pompous ceremony, foretold the beginning of another reign – proclamation announced that the new King will be known as Edward the Eighth. The mantle of George the Fifth has thereby fallen on his oldest Son – Edward, Prince of Wales, Duke of Cornwall.

The loyalty and respect, common amongst all honourable subjects, will, and is already showing itself to King Edward. The thirty-eighth British Sovereign to ascend the Throne, he will, it was promised by him on Wednesday, follow in his Father's footsteps.

May his reign be long, and may the "Community of Free Nations" be prosperous.

Long live King Edward.[4]

....

Sadly, the prayers for a long and prosperous reign for Edward VIII went unanswered. Less than a year later, in what became known as the "abdication crisis," he renounced his Throne to marry a divorcee.

Stories From These Shores

What is termed as unprecedented in the history of English Kings and Queens has happened in connection with the Throne and Parliament, between a Sovereign and his subjects – a limited Monarch desires to marry a woman who has been twice divorced; should no evidence come up to annul the divorce within the six months set down by the Ipswich Divorce Court in October.

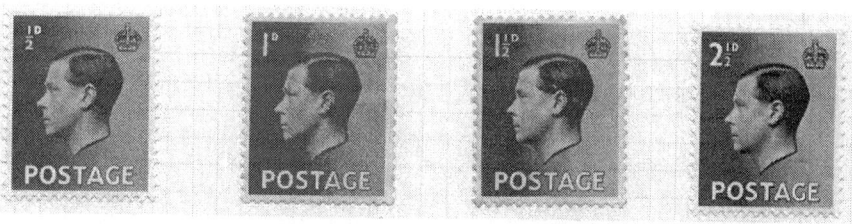

Postage stamps featuring King Edward VIII

It is unfortunate that abdication followed the crisis, and now, according to the despatches, the Duke of Windsor is evidently a sadder, if wiser, man in asking Parliament to pass the Bill. Had Parliament not passed the measure there could have been no voluntary abdication. Then, either legislation may have been passed allowing marriage in April, or the renouncing by Edward the Eighth of Mrs Simpson as a future Wife. One of the two, or a measure to force abdication. It is laid down, so say the press, that there can be no voluntary abdication without the sanction of both Houses of Parliament, after the refusal of the King to accept the advice of his Ministers, and asks the passing of an Abdication Bill. This was bourne out by Mr. Baldwin's fine speech after the death of George the Fifth, when he pointed out that "barring abdication, there is only one release for the King from duty and that is by death."

The advice of the London News Chronicle was to allow the marriage of Edward, and his Wife would need not be Queen, but the Duchess of Cornwall and Lancaster, and theirs heirs, if any, would not be in line for the Throne. This would want the passing of special legislation, as it would in the case of making her Consort. To affect such a change in the Constitution – not that it has not been amended – the Government of the United Kingdom, as per Statute of Westminster, must get the support of the Empire Dominions.

Prince Albert, Duke of York, Heir Apparent to the Throne, was proclaimed King on Saturday last [12 December, 1936]; his Duchess that of Queen Elizabeth.

May their reign be as illustrious as that of their Majesties, the late George the Fifth and Queen Mary, now the Queen Mother. We believe a loyal line of subjects will give Their Majesties and the Crown due homage.

The King was born on Dec. fourteenth, 1895, and celebrated in a quiet way his first birthday as King.

The announcement that a Christmas message is cancelled adds weight to the theory that the present condition of the Duke of Windsor is not very good.

Mrs. Simpson, according to a biography given in the press, is said to be a descendant of the House of Hanover, from which Edward is a descendant, on her Mother's side – from the Duke of Montague, the first to settle in Virginia in the United States in 1643. Of her twenty-five relatives, twenty-five are descendants of the Montague family. On her Father's side [she] is descended directly from Pagan de Warfield, an English knight of the eleventh century. The first Warfield settled in Maryland in 1662. Her maiden name is Bessie Wallis Warfield. [She] was born near Baltimore in 1896. Her first marriage was in 1916 to Earn Winfield Spencer, Jr., of the United States Navy, of Chicago, at Florida. He is now on an aircraft carrier, the U.S.S. *Ranger*. After going to England, following her first divorce in 1927, she met Mr. Ernest Simpson, an Anglo-American, born in New York, but with his ship broker's business in London; she is considered one of England's leading hostesses. In 1932 [she] was presented to Court. She is now a British citizen – having lost her United States citizenship when she married Mr. Simpson.[5]

....

When Edward VIII abdicated, his place was taken by his younger Brother, who reigned as George VI (1895-1952), and Elizabeth (1900-2002), his Queen Consort. Here's a short biographical look at their

Stories From These Shores

Majesties from "J. C. L." (John C. Loveridge), Secretary of the Twillingate Publicity Committee, prior to their upcoming coronation.

Ascending the Throne of England in a time that is destined to be one of the most momentous in history, George the Sixth, King and Emperor, and Queen Elizabeth, have already won the esteem and devotion of their millions of subjects throughout the empire. This manifestation of loyalty and devotion has not been lacking in Newfoundland, and we, of Britain's Oldest Colony, will join with the rest of the British Empire in celebrating in a fitting manner the coronation of their Majesties on May the twelfth [1937].

GEORGE VI

The second Son of the late beloved King George V, and Queen Mary, our King was born on December fourteenth, 1895, and was christened Albert Frederick Arthur George. He received his early education in England and entered a naval training school at the early age of fourteen. Two years later he had his first experience afloat as a cadet on HMS *Cumberland*, and served in the Battle of Jutland during the First World War. In 1920 he was created Duke of York and appointed to the Privy Council five years later. In 1923 he married Lady Elizabeth Bowes-Lyon, and today is the Father of two children, Princess Elizabeth, the heir presumptive to the Throne, and Princess Margaret.

Like his Father, our new King is essentially a family man; a man possessed with the ability for serious and painstaking application to the many and varied problems which will confront him. Throughout his life as Duke of York he has never ceased to work for the well-being of his people, not only among older people but his interest in the younger generation led him to form a Boys Camp in 1921. Since that time he has met annually with some hundreds of boys in a week or more of happy comradeship and is rarely happier than during the carefree hours he spends among them. Much can be written about the characteristics of our new Monarch, but in conclusion should it be said that in no way has he exemplified his gracious Father more than in his desire for divine service, to which he attends regularly with other members of his family.

DAVID J. CLARKE

ELIZABETH

Lady Elizabeth Angela Marguerite Bowes-Lyon, as she was before her marriage in 1923, was born in Hertfordshire on August fourth, 1900, and is the youngest Daughter of the Earl and Countess of Strathmore. With her pleasing manner and disposition she has endeared herself to all. Since early in life she has devoted herself to the welfare of others and every charitable cause has not only her sympathy, but wherever possible, her presence and help as well. She has travelled extensively and has made many tours throughout the Empire with her Husband, and was with him when he opened the first Parliament held in the new capital of Australia. Her position as the Wife of the King of England means an appreciable increase in her public work, but which she has undertaken with the smiling good nature that is so typical of her.

J. C. L., Sec.

TW'GATE PUBLICITY COMMITTEE.[6]

King George VI and Queen Elizabeth visit Canada, 1939

....

And here's how Twillingate celebrated their Majesties' coronation in May of 1937:

Stories From These Shores

The part Twillingate took in the Dedication, Homage and expression of Loyalty to Their Majesties, on Coronation Day, was a decided success.

The services in various places of worship were fairly well attended. The display of bunting, decoration, long parade – with the police on horseback – blowing of horns, and cheering, fireworks, boom of many guns and illuminations, proved that loyalty to King and Country is, as through the years, still abounding. The Committee's program...was carried out in good order.

The King's address was heard over the radio at 4:30 by most of the children, after their tea in the Alexandra Hall – the full text of which we give below:

"It is with a very full heart I speak to you tonight. Never before has a newly crowned King been able to talk to all his peoples in their homes on the day of his coronation. Never has the ceremony itself had so wide a significance, and I felt this morning that the whole Empire was in very truth gathered within the walls of Westminster Abbey. I rejoice that I can now speak to you all, wherever you may be; greetings to all peoples in distant lands, and I hope new friends in those parts where it has not yet been my good fortune to go. In this personal way the Queen and I wish health and happiness to you all. And we do not forget at this time of celebration those who are living under the shadow of sickness or distress. The example of courage and good citizenship is always before us, and to them I would send a message of sympathy and good cheer. I cannot find words with which to thank you for your love and loyalty to the Queen and myself. Your goodwill in the streets today; your countless messages from overseas and from every quarter of the islands have filled our hearts to overflowing. I will only say this, that if in the coming years I can show my gratitude in service to you, that is the way above all others I should choose. To many millions the Crown is a symbol of unity. By the Grace of God and by the will of the free peoples of the British Commonwealth, I have assumed that Crown. In me, as your King, is vested for a time the duty of maintaining its honour and integrity. This is indeed a grave and constant responsibility, and it gave me confidence to see your representatives around me in the Abbey, and to know that you all were enabled to join in the infinitely beautiful ceremony. Its outward forms come down from distant times, but in their meaning and message are always new. For the service of others and to the ministry of kingship I have dedicated myself, with the Queen at my side, in words of the deepest solemnity. We will, God helping us, faithfully discharge our trust. Those of you who are children now, will I hope, retain memories of this day of carefree happiness such as I still have of the day of my Grandfather's coronation. In the years that are to come, some of you will travel from one part of the Commonwealth to another, and moving thus within the family circle will meet many of those whose thoughts are coloured by the same memories, and whose hearts unite in devotion to our common heritage. You will learn, I hope, how much our free associations mean to us, and our friendship with each other and with all the Nations of the earth to help the cause of peace and progress. The Queen and I will always keep in our hearts the inspiration of this day. May we ever be worthy of the goodwill which I am proud to think surrounds us at the outset of my reign. I thank you from my heart, and may God bless you all."

> Taken in shorthand and transcribed by Mr. J.C. Loveridge.
> The message from people here, to their Majesties is as follows:
> To His Excellency the Governor, St. John's.
> May it please Your Excellency: —
> We beg to ask you to convey to Their Most Gracious Majesties, King George the Sixth and Queen Elizabeth, on this the day of their coronation, the loyal greetings of the people of Twillingate, Newfoundland.
> We, your loyal and faithful subjects of Twillingate, Newfoundland, assembled for the celebration of your coronation, approach Your Majesties with the dutiful assurance of our devotion to your Majesties' Throne.

Twillingate citizens celebrate King George VI's coronation. L-R: Major Pike (Salvation Army), Stephen Loveridge, Chesley Roberts, Magistrate B.J. Abbott, ?, Rev. J. Goodland, Rev. J. Burden, and local school children

    We join with all British subjects throughout the Empire in the widespread and wholehearted expression of loyalty universally extended to Your Majesties on this historic occasion.
    We participate in the solemnity of Your Majesties' coronation with heartfelt prayers that by God's blessings Your Majesties' subjects may be united with one heart and will in loyalty to Your Majesties and in Brotherly charity one towards another, dedicating themselves with renewed devotion to Almighty God. And we shall ever pray that His Blessing may rest abundantly upon Your Majesties, upon the Queen Mother, and upon Your Majesties' whole family and Realm.
    GOD SAVE THE KING.
Signed on behalf of the citizens of Twillingate:—
    B.J. ABBOTT, S.M.
    J. GOODLAND, Priest.
    J.A. BURDEN, B.A., U.C. Clergyman.
    MAJOR J. PIKE, S.A.
    FREDERICK J. WHITE, Act. W.M.A.F.A.M.
    CECIL SIMMS, W.M., L.O.A.

DAVID J. CLARKE

Wm. HARNETT, Sec'y
Citizen's Committee.[7]

....

Only two years after their coronation, and on the eve of World War II, King George and Queen Elizabeth toured a number of their Dominions, including Newfoundland. It marked the first visit by reigning Monarchs to Britain's Oldest Colony. This was how the Sun saw the historic visit.

Being a maritime Country, we figure well into the Empire structure and so fit into the system of democratic institutions that we can command a front rank line in the Royal Visit. Why is this so? In the first place the greatest military force Britain has is her Royal Navy, that from which our Kings have so ably sprung when training to fill their places as Admiral of the Fleets. Secondly, because of our being the oldest outpost of the Commonwealth and that from which the Nation spread to its great extent of being the mightiest.

Apart from our place as a principle part of the Empire, Nfld. offers to be a defence unit for western peoples...because of her place in the Atlantic. It would become in short time a bulwark against foreign aggression.

The visit of Their Majesties ought to cement us more fully to the ties of the Crown in that we may in a real and special manner reap a prosperity that will be more than lasting; it ought to give a far more enjoyable and easy existence than prevails today in many quarters of the Country. There ought to be a reconstruction of our economic and social services to uplift the masses. It will be done if the strangling competition is beaten down by goodwill amongst those who can make it possible.

Before another issue their Majesties will have entered St. John's for the welcome prepared for them. May their visit and their associations with the people have an effect to put into effect a more spontaneous loyalty amongst people in the position to do it, and then it can be expected that the masses will show their sincere appreciation. May the visit, though a short one, be the means of more contact between those who govern and those who are governed, and the outcome of it all mean more wealth, health and tranquillity to all our people in this cornerstone of Empire.

In the realm and throughout its great extent we have no semblance of intimidation as in dictatorship countries, and socialism as they have it would not become suited to a free people under a Sovereign who is not a despot, or who holds his or her reign by putting fear into the hearts of the subjects over whom they rule – by the cruelty of a concentration camp or the block and axe.

As a people, who in the main are loyal and devoted, we join to extend to the King and Queen a right Royal welcome, and also wish them in the close of the Royal Tour a pleasant passage from our shores to their home in "Olde England," and many years of Health, Joy and Peace in which to reign over us.[8]

....

Little more than a decade after he and his Queen visited Newfoundland, and after steering his Nation through the dark days of World War II, King George passed away at the age of only fifty-six. Here's how the Sun memorialized a beloved Monarch:

A universally beloved Sovereign has passed to his eternal reward. George the Sixth of England, who captured the hearts of his subjects as had no other ruler in the Empire's long history, died peacefully in his sleep on Wednesday night [6 February, 1952]. To a world which for the past six months had entertained deep anxiety over his health, had prayed for his recovery from a serious lung operation, and given thanks for its success, the news came as a distinct shock.

A simple, family loving, unpretentious man, our late King found the Throne thrust upon him sixteen years ago when his Brother Edward abdicated. Unlike his Brother, who from the time of his birth had been trained and guided in the sovereign role he would someday occupy, he had been content to live simply outside the glare and limelight of court and palace. But his keen sense of duty, his unswerving devotion and affection for his people, sustained him thorough the troubled years which followed, through a long a bitter war and a long, uneasy peace. The strain of sixteen years of Kingship under circumstances more troubled than those of any predecessor in England's long story, undoubtedly shortened the life of this conscientious, selfless man.

During his reign he saw his beloved England stripped of her wealth, brought down from her former high position as a world power. But to him, as to many others, this was a price to be cheerfully paid for a victory over oppression and evil. England had come through with clean hands and untroubled conscience, bearing honourable scars, and imbued with the will to live. And her King, by his innate goodness, his natural simplicity and impeccable character, had woven between the Throne and the Empire a cord of loyalty stronger and more lasting than any former tie.

George the Good has laid down the heavy load of Kingship. He has entered into well-earned rest. With their expressions of sorrow at the passing of a beloved ruler, the people of the great Commonwealth of Nations pledge unswerving loyalty to his Daughter, Queen Elizabeth the Second. The King is dead. Long live the Queen![9]

8
"Local & General"

In its early years the Twillingate Sun *featured a column titled "Local & General." This section presented a selection of short articles detailing events of interest to readers living in, or with connections to, the Districts of Twillingate and Fogo. Almost any topic might find its way into the column, though items relating to shipping and the fishery were especially prominent.*[1]

Nautical Notes

1880

[8 July] During the past week our harbour has worn a very naval aspect. On Saturday last [3 July, 1880] HMS *Contest* came in, to hear tidings, if possible, as to the whereabouts of HMS *Druid*, but being unsuccessful they left us on Sunday at 10 a.m.

On Tuesday about 5 p.m., the *Druid* arrived from Gander Bay in expectation of the mail, which came in on Wednesday morning. Their next destination will be Hall's Bay, and thence slowly up the coast to Battle Harbour on Labrador.

We understand that orders have been received to destroy all saw mills as they are injurious to the salmon fishery.

Captain Kennedy has shown great kindness to the numerous visitors who have visited the *Druid* during her stay. She left this morning at 9 a.m.

....

[19 August] W. Waterman & Co.'s schooner, *Branksea*, returned yesterday from her trip around Green Bay in which she has been engaged for the past seventeen days collecting fish, oil, salmon, & c. The weather and winds having been favourable for the work, the crew were successful in completing it in a short time and bringing back 1,050 qtls. fish, and also a deck load of cod oil, & c. The salmon fishery has been nearly a blank, but the cod fishery has been fair, and still there is a little doing. W. Waterman, Esq., was aboard the whole trip and expressed himself highly pleased with the different places, and the kind reception given by the people. Services were conducted by him in several localities...

....

S.S. Plover *in dry dock*

[25 November] The coastal steamer *Plover* arrived here [Twillingate] this afternoon, having been detained a little after her usual time in consequence of the adverse winds and heavy seas with which she had to encounter since leaving St. John's. Taking into account the tempestuous weather so often met with along the shore we think that the *Plover* performs her work well, under the command of Capt. Blandford. It is true that when the sea is running high she may be pronounced by some as being a great "roller," though on such occasions we have known the Captain to quaintly remark that she is a "pretty little duck," and perhaps he's about right. It would be difficult to find many steamboats that would steam along more steadily than the *Plover* does in the heavy seas with which she is brought into contact so repeatedly while engaged in the northern coastal mail service, and if the Captain had the same control over the elements of nature as he has over his good ship, so that he could always command a smooth time, it is not at all probable that anyone would be disposed [to] find fault for her rolling.

....

[23 December] We understand Mr. J.H. Tavernor intends opening a night school at the Arm [Durrell], for the purpose of imparting instructions to the young men of schooner owners, and others, who may be desirous of obtaining knowledge of the chart, and of receiving such information in relation thereto as may qualify them to navigate their craft in safety in any direction. This we think is a great privilege placed within the reach of our young men, and let us hope that numbers will see the wisdom of availing of the means thus extended to them, so that they may possess such desirable instruction as shall fit them for their avocation. Terms will be given on application to Mr. Tavernor, and all who wish to attend must give in their names by the first week in January next [1881].

1881

[3 February] We understand that on Wednesday there was a meeting at the government wharf of the Commissioners – F. Berteau, Esq., J.P., J.W. Owen, Esq., J.P., and R.D. Hodge, Esq. – to take into consideration the advisability of filling up the intermediate spaces in the wharves already built, so as to make the wharf more suitable for the steamer to lay by in rough weather, and also to be more secure from the pressure by drift ice in the Spring of the year. It was unanimously decided to commence this work, and also to build a slip at the government wharf for the accommodation of parties landing in small boats.

....

[12 May] The coastal steamer *Plover* made her first appearance here for the season on Wednesday morning, in charge of Mr. Manuel, the senior officer of the ship, Capt. Blandford not having arrived from the ice on [his] second trip in time to take command. Mr. Manuel is well acquainted with the dangerous creeks along the coast, and is in every way competent to take charge of a ten or fifteen knotter, which we hope in time to see him commanding.

....

[2 June] The *Alpha*, Captain Leonard, of Swansea, arrived here on Saturday last *via* St. John's, with a cargo of salt to the firm of the late E. Duder, Esq. She left the Capital on the twenty-fourth ult., and the following morning experienced a snowfall, some five or six inches having fallen upon the deck. The winds were very light and variable nearly all the distance, so no ice was encountered. The *Alpha* is about 500 tons, barque rigged, well founded, and is in every respect adapted to encounter the dangers of the sea. Being built specially for the copper trade, she is constructed of the most substantial material that could possibly be secured. The Captain expects to be in port five or six weeks, and after leaving here will proceed to Bett's Cove, whence he will sail for an English market with a load of copper ore. We are glad to welcome the Captain to our shores for the first time and hope that he may enjoy pleasant weather during his short sojourn in our port.

....

[23 June] Having visited the light-house at Long Point the past week in company with a friend, we were at once struck with the excellent, cleanly appearance which every part of the beautiful apparatus presented. Whatever else the District may lack, it can boast of having one of the finest (if not the finest) light-houses in the Colony, and credit is due to the Keeper, Mr. S. Roberts, for the superior style in which it is attended to.

....

Stories From These Shores

[25 August] The schooner *Paragon*, owned by M. Osmond, Esq., J.P., of Moreton's Harbour came here on Thursday last with a cargo of dry fish, having been previously engaged on a trading venture. The *Paragon* was built on the premises of the owner the past Winter, and is in every respect a most suitable craft for the general trade of the Country.

The *Presto*, owned by the same, also arrived at Moreton's Harbour on Friday from the French Shore, where she had been similarly engaged the last few weeks. The *Presto* was as far as Quirpoon and reports that the fishery thereabouts has been good, but there ha[s] been such a continuance of wet, disagreeable weather that fish curing operations were entirely retarded.

....

[13 October] The schooner *Wild Rover* arrived from the Bay today with a cargo of timber for the new coastal wharf, which is now nearing completion [at Twillingate], and which will prove quite an acquisition to that part of the harbour.

....

[21 October] The Revenue cruiser *Rose*, from Labrador, on her way to St. John's called here on Friday last, having on board the Collector of H.M. Customs for that coast, Mr. Berteau, Son of our worthy Magistrate, F. Berteau, Esq.

....

[21 October] HM ship *Fantome* came into port on Saturday evening last, and left again on Wednesday morning. She has been engaged in protecting the fisheries on our coast the past season, and had lately left the Labrador coast.

On Saturday night, while a number of the *Fantome*'s men were on shore, they appeared to be conducting themselves somewhat disorderly, and having been spoken to by Sergeant Wells, some insult, we understand was given, whereupon the Sergeant attempted to arrest a couple, and resistance having been made by them, a struggle ensued, when the prisoners received a good deal of injury. The matter was heard before the Magistrate on Monday last, but no decision was arrived at regarding the justice or injustice of the course adopted by the officer.

....

[28 October. This item comes from the Sun's "Correspondence" section, but is included here to round off the *Fantome*'s story]. DEAR SIR — I notice on your paper of the twenty-first inst., an article in reference to the disorderly conduct of some of the seamen of HMS *Fantome*; that the matter was heard before the Magistrate on Monday last, but that no decision was arrived at regarding the justice or injustice of the course adopted by the officer.

HMS Fantome *(R), with HMS* Opal

Allow me to correct that error, as the facts are these: that on the Monday you allude to, [Seaman] Jones was fined two dols. and costs, and [Seaman] Sheean one dol. and costs by me, the other seaman concerned in the rabble not having been arrested by Segt. Wells. Three of them, on their return to the ship to save themselves from a scrape, made a charge against Sergt. Wells of the police.

Commander Karslake, having to investigate the charges, and

report the conduct of the seamen to the Admiral, I consented to Sergt. Wells' going on board the *Fantome* to enable the Commander to do so, which after the inquiry proved to be an unfounded charge against Sergt. Wells. Commander Karslake reprimanded the seamen, and said before them on the quarter-deck, that I had very justly fined the two men, and that he was sorry that I had not fined Jones, being the ringleader, ten times more. Yours truly, F. Berteau, J.P.

....

[11 November] On Tuesday evening three individuals belonging to the Arm [Durrell], left Capt. Wrey's wharf in boat for the South Side. Having previously indulged a little too freely in beverages of an intoxicating tendency, the trio could not refrain from displaying [?], and when a few yards from the land, the boat tipped over, plunging its occupants into the water. Had it not been for timely assistance afforded, the result of their "dip" would have been most serious.

....

[11 November] The schooner *Vivid*, owned by Messrs. Hodder & Linfield, returned from the French Shore on Tuesday last, where she has been employed in a trading venture the past season. This is the second time the *Vivid* has come back with a full cargo of this year's produce. She arrived late in September with 1,600 qtls. of fish, sixty tierce of salmon, and seven tuns [of] oil. This time her cargo consists of 1,600 qtls. fish and a quantity of oil, both trips being remarkably good. Three or four other craft have also arrived from the French Shore within the past few weeks with cargoes of fish, etc., to the same firm.

The *Vivid* formerly belonged to the firm of E. Duder, Esq.; is well and substantially built, and is a fast sailor, as is well known from the quick trips made while running for her former owner. She was purchased last Spring by Messrs. Hodder & Linfield, and it is pleasing to know that the speculation has thus far proved so successful. We trust that the enterprising firm may have continued success in the future.

She left for St. John's on Wednesday morning last, Mr. T. Linfield, one of the partners of the firm, taking passage by her.

DAVID J. CLARKE

....

[25 November] Monday night of the twelfth inst., was one of intense darkness, and in fact seldom is it that we realize such a dark mantle as overspread our Harbour at that time, and remembering that unlike most places, we are without a single artificial ray to guide the pedestrian in his wanderings around our shores and wharves, coupled with the fact that about this season our harbour is generally full of strangers from all parts of the Bay transacting their business before the Winter closes, it is a matter of the greatest wonder that so few accidents of a serious nature occur.

Hodges (former Waterman's) premises, Twillingate, c.1920

About nine o'clock on the night mentioned, Messrs. Michael Byrne and his Son James proceeded to the wharf of Messrs. Waterman & Co., in order to board their schooner, of which the latter is Master, and who at once laid hold of the mainstay and swung himself out so as to drop on deck, where he landed safely. But not so with his Father, who, in the act of boarding in the same manner, was precipitated into the water by the schooner giving a sudden roar. Fortunately, however, he went clear of any obstruction that might have inflicted injuries of a serious nature, and not having forgot the art of swimming, acquired in his younger days, he at once struck out for the shore where he landed safely, after a complete ducking.

At about eleven o'clock the same night Mr. Thomas Boyde and Daughter, of Little Bay, left the shop of Messrs. Waterman & Co. (Where they had been transacting business during the day) in order to go to lodgings for the night, but wishing to give some instructions to men on board a craft at the wharf, they both walked down, the Father being on the outside. In the act of turning a corner, he told his Daughter to take his hand, so that she should not go astray, and scarcely had the words been spoken when he walked right over the wharf, leaving her terror stricken. She, however, was equal to the occasion, and being called back to consciousness by the splash in the water, she at once gave a good pair of lungs fair play, and her cries with those of her Parent, quickly summoned men from the schooners lying close by and from the establishment which they had just left, and assistance being quickly at hand, the struggling man was rescued from a watery grave. It was the most miraculous thing that he escaped, for in the fall he just brushed a projecting half-way platform used for passing fish from small boats upon the wharf, which if he had struck might have inflicted injuries of a fatal character. However, all's well that ends well...a quick change of clothing...a good rub down, and a little fainting, brought the tragic event to a termination.

1882

[10 February] A large crew of volunteers were engaged at times the past week in endeavouring to get the *Ja. G. Jones* upon the ice in order to make repairs, and after two or three attempts on various days, they succeeded in accomplishing their object on Thursday. This schooner belongs to Mr. Thos. Avery, and was purchased by him last Summer on what use[d] to be termed the French Shore. Fortunately, however, it is to be no longer known by that name. The craft is about twenty-five tons, built of good oak, and not being very old, will, when put in good order, be suitable for trading purposes, for which we think the owner intends her.

DAVID J. CLARKE

....

[24 February] — Sch. *Edward E. Webster*, Cap. Solomon Jacobs, is high line of the mackerel fleet, having landed 4,500 bbls. mackerel this season, 2,900 bbls. fresh and 1,600 bbls. salt, making a net stock of 24,270 dols. Her gross stock was 26,570 dols. This is the largest stock ever made in the mackerel fishery. Last year the *Webster* led the New England fleet with a stock of 19,745 dols. and seventy-six cents gross, her catch being 3,900 bbls. – 2,600 salt and 1,300 fresh – *Cape Ann Advertiser*, Dec. 2.

Solomon Jacobs

The Captain Jacobs above referred to, who has been so successful among the mackerel fleet, is a native of Twillingate, and connected by family ties to Mrs. Titus Linfield. He left here some years ago, and like most Newfoundlanders who make a residence in foreign lands, he had made his mark in the avocation pursued, being pronounced by the above journal (printed in the place where the fishery is prosecuted) as "having had the largest stock ever made in the mackerel fishery." We wish him still further prosperity in future.

....

[23 June] ...A new schooner named the *Garfield*, and owned by Duder's house, was brought here [Fogo] from Exploits a few days ago. She adds *one* more to the large number of vessels owned by that firm, registers something over forty tons, and is intended to replace the *Daisy*, lost at sea last Fall. She is finely modelled, well finished, and is a credit to her builder, Mr. Frederick Jewer, of Exploits. She is equipped for the Labrador fishery, and is to be commanded by Mr. George Brown of Exploits.

....

[23 June] On Monday evening last, a number of the crews of vessels in port were rather noisy on the public street, and on being spoken to by Constable [Benjamin] French, one or two of the gang gave insolence. He allowed them to pass, notwithstanding, without taking any notice of the unbecoming expressions used, and in order to see that the public peace was observed, he followed them to Messrs. Waterman & Co's wharf, where fifteen or sixteen of them attacked him, and would probably have inflicted severe bodily harm, had it not been that some of the Constable's former acquaintances, belonging to Spaniard's Bay and Carbonear, interfered and seemed determined that he would not come off the worst. One of the ringleaders in the crowd, Stephen Maddock, was taken into custody, the officers being guarded to the gaol by about 200 men from different craft, the greater part of them being friends of the Constable.

Maddock was brought before the Magistrate the next morning and fined eight dollars and costs. The others got clear as they left port the next day before a warrant for arrest reached them.

....

[14 July] On Sunday night last John Campbell, boatswain of [the] barquentine *Voyager*, of Brixham, deserted said ship as she lay in

Twillingate Harbour. At the time of his desertion a valuable ship's jolly boat, painted white topsides, copperpaint bottom, black gunwales, pea green inside, with varnished bottom, and with the name *Lizzie*, cut in rudder and yoke, and also rigged with mainsail and jib, was taken from the premises of Messrs. Waterman & Co.

The Captain describes him as follows: He is a Scotchman about five feet four inches high, of dark complexion, black hair tinged with grey, slight moustache and whisker same colour, not very stout, is round shouldered and has a peculiar gait. When he left [the] ship was clothed in monkey jacket, black wide-awake hat, badly shod and altogether a conspicuous figure.

Any person who shall give such information as shall lead to the discovery of either the boat or man will be suitably rewarded by sending such to the Sun Office, Twillingate.

....

[18 July] The pleasure yacht *Shamrock*, belonging to Messrs. Waterman & Co., was despatched on Thursday last in search of the jolly boat that was taken from their premises a day or two before by seaman Campbell, who deserted the *Voyager* a few days previous. On the arrival of the *Shamrock* at Fogo the crew gleaned that a white whale boat with a sailor in charge was at Hare Bay, they wisely surmising she was the jolly boat instead, at once despatched a crew for said place, when the following account was given by a man who had the boat in charge. The sailor put in here, jumped ashore, leaving the boat adrift, on being remonstrated with by the fishermen nearby, he told them they might have the boat, as she was no good to him, and his vessel was to sail that day. He was afterwards seen at Fogo, but as it was impossible to communicate with Twillingate, no one had authority to detain him, although suspicion was aroused.

....

Schooners in port, Battle Harbour, Labrador

[16 September] It is pleasing to be able to chronicle the arrivals of many of our craft from Labrador within the past week. In most instances they have come back with good fares, and it is a cause for much thankfulness to a kind Providence that so many of our people have thus been prospered, and permitted to return somewhat enriched with the treasures of the deep.

The following are some of the arrivals :—

Fawn, Albert Spencer..........................	540
Kangaroo, J. Moors.............................	590
Somerset, J. Stuckless.........................	500
Rover's Bride, J. Rideout.....................	500
Jewel, A. Knight, do.	
Village Belle, S. Rideout, fair.	
Betsy Purchase, J. Purchase................	500
Guerilla, John Anstey.........................	550
Queen of the North, W. Waterman.....	600

Wild Rover, J. Roberts...	550
Sullian, Josiah Clarke...	450
Turtle, Thos. Hicks..	400
L.P. Pond, Josiah Pond...	300

....

[22 September] The following craft have returned from the fishery at Change Islands:

Guiding Star, Joseph Elliott...............................	400
Lash, Samuel Saunders..	60
Wild Rover, John Chaffy.....................................	120

This was the second trip for the last two named...the *Guiding Star*'s crew had 500 qtls. on shore before going north, which make[s] 900 for nine men.

Although in the early part of the season, the prospect in that vicinity appeared gloomy, we are glad to find that it did not turn [out] so bad as was anticipated. We understand that the average catch there will be fifty qtls. per man.

Here are some of the lucky ones besides the *Guiding Star*, mentioned above:

Wild Rover's crew — 100 qtls. per man.
Steadfast, Thomas Ginn — 100 qtls. per man.
Thos. Wm. Taylor — seventy qtls. per man.
The catch for Thos. Elliott and Son was 330 qtls. shorefish; total, with boy and one shareman, 450.
The following were shoremen — John Parsons, 600 qtls. for six men.
Henry Seamile & Son — 400 for six men.
James Havens & Bros. (Three) 230.

Abraham Bowen — 240 for five men.

Change Islands, early 1900s

1883

[20 April] Vessels Cleared for the Seal Fishery 1883:

SUPPLIED BY J P. TOBIN

Vessel	Master	Tons	Men
Sunbeam........................	Wm. Murcell	36	15

SUPPLIED BY HODDER & LINFIELD

Vessel	Master	Tons	Men
Abyssinia......................	John Hellier	49	18

DAVID J. CLARKE

SUPPLIED BY EDWIN COLBOURNE

Vessel	Master	Tons	Men
Annie Laura	Chas. Young	39	17

SUPPLIED BY W. WATERMAN CO.

Vessel	Master	Tons	Men
Success	Mark Brett	72	12
Welcome Home	Chas. Brett	55	18
British Queen	James Dalley	46	19
Wild Wave	Elias Dalley	34	17
Lily Dale	Geo. Snow	48	19
Bellorophen	Sam. Fox	42	17
Volunteer	Sam. Wells	42	17
Rover's Bride	Jas. Rideout	45	18
Endurance	John Hackett	41	16
Pretorious	Wm. Wheeler	34	14
Rosetta	Jas. Hodder	34	14
Betsy Purchase	Jas. Purchase	45	20

SUPPLIED BY EDWIN DUDER

Vessel	Master	Tons	Men
Brothers	Elias Warren	49	19
Lady Blandford	Esau Blandford	43	15

Stories From These Shores

Vessel	Master	Tons	Men
Porcupine............	James Young	60	22
Turtle............	Thos. Hicks	44	18
Delta............	Thos. Ashbourne	32	15
Mary Jane............	John Keefe	31	15
Queen of the North......	W. Waterman	45	21
H.W.B.............	Reu. Blackmore	20	10
Erebus............	Chs. Vatcher	30	13

SUPPLIED BY OWEN & EARLE

Vessel	Master	Tons	Men
Blooming Queen............	John Warren	52	21
L.P. Pond............	Geo. Pond	50	20
Isabel............	Thos. Lacey	72	16
Regent............	Wm. Pond	36	16
Lucy............	Philip Freeman	51	18
1883 — 29 Vessels		1,277	499
1882 — 26 ditto		1,203	451
Increase		74	48

....

[6 July] The schr. *Flying Mist*, Butler, Master, with a cargo of material for the construction of the light house on Gull Island, Cape John, came into port on Saturday last. On Wednesday a favourable time offered and the *Flying Mist* took her departure for her destination.

DAVID J. CLARKE

1884

[13 September] The following schooners have returned from the fishing voyages since last paper. The catches in most instances are exceedingly small, as may be seen from the figures furnished, considering, too, that the crews of these craft consist of from six to ten men, respectively :—

Vessels and Masters	*Qtls.*
Jewel, Mark Brett	100
Bellorophon, Robert Aden	300
Greyhound, Mark Cook	140
Rose, Thomas Manuel	90
Summerset, Joseph Stuckless	120
Five Brothers, Robert Young	170
Rose of Sheron, George Clarke	350
Kangaroo, Jacob Moors	170
Fawn, Albert Spencer	200
[Illegible], Matthew Elliott	350
Erebus, Charles Vatcher	300
Loyalty, George Guy	100
Success, Samuel Fox	250
Rover's Bride, James Rideout	300
Fortuna, Daniel Blackler	200
Brisk, Job Luther	400
Rise and Go, Thomas Warr	100

J.S.O., Philip Freeman... 140

Schooner in full sail

....

[20 September] The Moreton's Harbour fishing fleet has returned...The average catch for these craft is equal, if not ahead, of any belonging to other ports. It will be seen that over 4,000 qtls. of fish have been carried into Moreton's [Harbour] by this number of craft, which must be considered good for so bad a season.

Vessel and Masters	*Qtls.*
Combat, Ephraim Small...	190
Precuraer, William Small...	190
Outstrip, Abraham Knight...	625
Rambler, James French...	575
Welcome Home, Charles Brett...	480
————, Joseph Taylor...	380

Sunbeam, Abel Jones...	180
Brilliant Star, Hercules Rideout..........................	320
Village Belle, Samuel Rideout.............................	160
X X X, Uriah Osmond..	250
A.J.O., Joseph W. Osmond..................................	250
Princess, Richard Boon B.B................................	300
Speed, Solomon Hand..	200
Harvest Home, Joseph Woolfrey........................	400
Branch, John Woolfrey...	300

....

[1 November] The Cunard steamer *Delta* arrived here yesterday morning from Montreal *via* St. John's, with part cargo of provisions for Messrs. W. Waterman &Co. She left St. John's on Wednesday morning and experienced a very rough time. J.B. Tobin Esq., came passenger in her.

1885

[2 May] Sailors call the sea "Davy Jones' Locker" because the dead are thrown there. Davy is a corruption of "Duffy," by which name ghosts or spirits are known among the West Indian Negroes, and Jones is a corruption of the name of the Prophet Jonah, who was thrown into the sea.

    Locker, in seaman's parlance, means any receptacle for private stores. So when a sailor says, "He's gone to Davy Jones' Locker," he means, he is gone to the place of safe-keeping, where Duffy Jonah was sent to.

1886

[23 October] The largest codfish ever taken in these parts, or perhaps in any other part of the Newfoundland coast, was caught on Tuesday last by an old fisherman, Mr. James Rogers, of Durrell's Arm. This fish, we learn, weighed one quintal [1 quintal = 112 lbs], and what makes it the more remarkable is that it was caught by well nigh the oldest inhabitant of the place, Mr. Rogers being over eighty years of age. The perseverance of this industrious "toiler of the sea" at his advanced age is worthy of example by young fishermen nowadays. He must have come from the good old English stock to be so smart and active at his time of life.

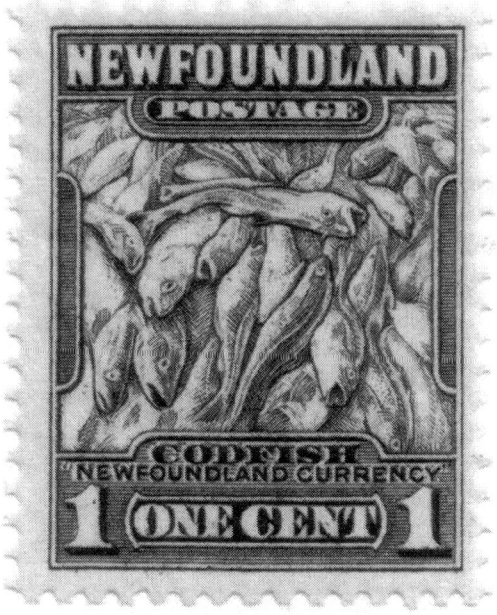

1887

[30 April] The following schooners have been cleared for the Bank fishery by the firm of E. Duder, Esq. This is the first that have ever prosecuted the industry from Twillingate, and it is to be hoped that the results of these pioneer reapers of that deep sea fishery from this port will be abundantly remunerative for all concerned:

Iris..........................	51 tons	......E. White, Master
Gaspereau...............	66 tons	......I. Churchill, Master
Annie Roberts..........	44 tons	......J. Roberts, Master
Sulieau.....................	66 tons	.....J. Clarke, Master

"On the Banks"

....

[20 August] On Monday last an exciting sailing contest was witnessed on our harbour between the boat of the schr. *Clementine*, Capt. Ball, and that of the *Pearl*, Capt. Lower. The race came about in this way: sometime ago the boat of the *Ensign*, Capt. Pieré, bore a pennant, but in a recent match this was taken from her by the *Pearl*'s boat, the *Clementine* also competing, but being amongst the losers, she was determined to try her luck again and wrest if possible the flag of honour from the *Pearl*, which she barely succeeded in doing in the race on Monday. Never mind. "Lower" at her again, old friend and keep up the valour of North Side, remember, "faint heart never won fair lady."

....

[1 October] All the schooners of Farmer's Arm [Durrell] have returned from Labrador, and we are glad to say the most of them have done pretty well. These are among the number:

Porcupine, Thos. Ashbourne....................	750
Jessamine, Abraham Earle........................	600
Bianca, Thomas Earle...............................	500
Delta, Isaac Pond.......................................	400
Regent, William Pond...............................	270
Queen of the North, William Waterman....	250
Silver Stream, J. Jenkins...........................	280
Abib, John Minty.......................................	240

....

[26 November] ...Capt. Solomon Jacobs, Son of Mrs. Wm. Hudder, has recently embarked in a new enterprise, having equipped two fine vessels owned by himself, and dispatched them to the Pacific coast, where he thinks there is a good opening for prosecuting the fisheries and doing a general trading business. Capt. Jacobs was previously engaged in...mackerel fishing, and was one of the most successful men connected with it. He appears to be a man of great enterprise and energy, by which he has gained a position for himself, [of] which us [as] Newfoundlanders...ought to feel proud. We hope that this new venture will prove even more remunerative to him than any that he yet embarked his capital in.

DAVID J. CLARKE

1888

[4 February] We are glad to learn that on February second, Mr. William Hudder received a cablegram informing him that his Son, Captain Samuel Hudder, and men, who left here [Twillingate] some time ago, have arrived out to Seattle all right, and Captain Solomon Jacobs leaves for there on Monday next. It will be remembered that mention was made in previous papers regarding the new project which these two enterprising Captains intended engaging in, namely the prosecution of the seal fishery &c., in the Alaskan waters, on the Pacific coast. The departure of their vessels from Gloucester for these waters was referred to some time ago, and now the owners themselves, with a number of men whom Captain Hudder selected when here not long since, are proceeding overland. The voyage which they have undertaken will extend a year or more, and we trust that a large measure of success will reward the industry of our enterprising natives, who were heretofore so exceptionally fortunate while engaging in the mackerel business.

....

[28 July] The new steamer *Matilda*, belonging to R. Scott, Esq., made her first visit here lately, coming from Fogo on Saturday evening last and returning on Monday, having the enterprising owner on board. She is about as large again as the *Tibbie* was, being some twenty-seven tons gross. Her length is fifty-two feet, beam twelve feet, depth eight feet. When properly fitted out, there will be considerable accommodation for a number of persons fore and aft, while the freight capacity of the *Matilda* doubles that of his first steamer, which will make her far more convenient, and profitable, we should say, as the *Matilda* only consumes the same quantity of coal. We wish the energetic owner every success in his speculation.

Stories From These Shores

Sealers on the ice near their vessel

1889

[23 March] Vessels Cleared for the Seal Fishery to Date

Supplied by E. Duder:

Vessels & Masters	Tons	Men
Sisters, Wm. Richards	43	19
Niobe, Elias Warren	32	17
Mary, James Young	52	19
Porcupine, Thos. Ashbourne	60	21
Advance, Joseph Taylor	41	16

Supplied by W. Waterman & Co.

Emeline, Chas. Brett	41	17
Welcome Home, John Hellier	53	18

DAVID J. CLARKE

Outstrip, A. Knight	46	17
Muselift, Matthew Elliott	55	20
Pretorious, Thos. Whellor	34	18
Flamingo, James Seviour	71	18
British Queen, Samuel Fox	46	17
Lilly Dale, William Snow	48	18
Volunteer, Elias Dally	42	17
Supplied by Owen & Earle		
Lady Blandford, E. Blandford	43	17
Blooming Queen, John Pride	52	20
Lucy, Phillip Freeman	51	17
Regeat, William Pond	36	16
Supplied by J.B. Tobin		
Sunbeam, William Murcell	36	14
Patience, Stephen Newman	43	16
Olivette, Samuel Young	33	14
Total......................	963	366

1892

[2 January] While the [coastal steamer] *Curlew* was in St. John's this last trip she had undergone a real transformation in the passenger accommodation and is now fitted up on the same principal as the *Conscript*. The saloon is made in the fore part of the ship and provides accommodation for twenty-eight or thirty passengers. It is not quite completed yet as time would not admit of doing so, although while the work was going on there were some one hundred labourers employed about the ship. The steerage will accommodate thirty-five or forty, and looks as though it will be preferable even to that of the *Conscript*'s. The alterations will be a capital improvement to the steamer and will make her a better passenger boat than she originally was. Two steamers a little larger, but equipped for passengers in the same style, running weekly, would answer the northern coastal service much better than a larger one fortnightly, and this is what we have always advocated.

S.S. Curlew *steaming out of port*

....

[24 September] Several craft returned from Labrador on Tuesday, the *Brisk*, Mr. Job Luther, of Back Harbour, Master, being one of the number. He was fortunate in securing 450 quintals, which is very good indeed considering the large number of fishing craft that have done so poorly this season. This year was Mr. Luther's Jubilee trip, he having been to the Labrador fifty Summers successively, which is more than

DAVID J. CLARKE

can be said by many of the veteran planters or fishermen now prosecuting the fisheries. Some may have been fifty years going to the Labrador, but it would be difficult to find many who have gone annually and never missed a Summer for that period, either by illness or other causes. For a greater part of the time he has been Master of a schooner, and has generally been fortunate in bringing home at least saving trips. Although nearing three score and ten years, he is as smart and active as the great majority of young men who are in their teens. We have much pleasure in congratulating him on attaining this Jubilee, and of the success that has crowned his long fishery career.

Stories From These Shores

In Peril at Sea

1880

[8 July] The schooner *Challenge*, Captain Dingle, from Bristol to Messrs. Owen & Earle, arrived here on Friday last [2 July, 1880], in a disabled condition. The Captain states that on Wednesday the thirtieth June it was densely foggy, and at 11 p.m., while near Little Fogo Island, bearing W by N about thirty miles, the *Challenge* struck an iceberg, whereby considerable damage was sustained. Her jib-boom was carried away, unshipped bow sprit, and lost night heads, pall and windless bits and box, spritsail yard, figurehead and fore companion. It was fortunate that the ship was going at a slow rate at the time, otherwise much greater damage, would in all probability, have resulted.

....

[22 July] The schooner *Bismark*, belonging to E. Duder, Esq., was lost at the Wadhams on the night of Sunday last [18 July, 1880]. She left Fogo on the previous Wednesday for St. John's, discharged a full cargo and was returning when the accident occurred. She was only left Fogo three days and ten hours, so that had she arrived safely the trip would have been the quickest on record. The craft and goods were covered by insurance. The *Bismark* was a very fast sailer, having on one occasion travelled thirty-three miles in three hours. Her loss to the trade at this season of the year...will be considerable.

....

[7 October] It is our painful duty...to record [a]...very sad accident which occurred near Fogo about a fortnight since. It appears that two men named Robert Waterman and Richard Mason had been up Gander Bay, shooting, and whilst returning in a small boat, over a heavy sea which was running at the time, she was upset and the occupants were buried in a watery grave. The boat and oars were afterwards picked up. We learn that Waterman was a young married man...

DAVID J. CLARKE

North Side, Fogo, c.1900

1881

[13 January] A correspondent writing from Fogo, under date of the seventh inst. says: "A sad gloom has been cast over this place in the now almost certain loss of schr. *Maggie*, E. Duder Esq., owner, over six weeks from St. John's, having on board provisions, £150 cash, and a quantity of ship-building material, said to be uninsured. The loss of the provisions, it is feared, will entail considerable distress upon poor families the ensuing Winter.

The crew, consisting of six men, together with Dr. Oke, a passenger, were all, with one exception, married persons, thus leaving Widows with eighteen Fatherless young children, to suffer and mourn their irreparable bereavement. The above will be eleven untimely deaths by drowning from our midst since June last [1880], and a loss of ten members from St. Andrew's Lodge, SUF, Fogo.

....

[24 February] We are sorry to have to chronicle the loss of two men named James Jones and Eli Atkinson, belonging to Herring Neck, which sad event happened on Thursday, the seventeenth inst. The morning being fine, several boats left that place in search of seals and about noon a sudden storm of wind and snow set in. As soon as it commenced, they all ran for land and reached home safely after experiencing great difficulty and danger, with the exception of the above mentioned...The following day their boat was found bottom up, with one gun tied fast to it, having drifted into Merritt's Harbour during the night. Search has been made for the bodies, but up to the nineteenth they could not be found. It is thought that the boat upset while running for the land, as it was impossible for a small boat to stand very long in the wind and sea then prevalent. James Jones was about sixty years of age, and leaves a Wife and large family to deplore their loss. The young man was about twenty-four years and Son of Mr. Thomas Atkinson of Herring Neck. We tender our sympathy to the sorrowing relatives in the painful dispensation of Providence they have just sustained.

....

[26 May] The S.S. *Hercules*, when leaving [St. John's] for Bett's Cove yesterday afternoon, collided with the schr. *Guerilla* from Twillingate, and tacking in the harbour at the time. She was struck on the port quarter, which, driving her stern to leeward brought her in collision with the jib-boom of the barque *Era*, lying at anchor in the harbour, tearing away her mainsail and carrying away her main-boom. The *Hercules* on clearing from the *Guerilla* ran into the *Era*, striking her in the port quarter, and breaking in her bulwarks. The was no injury done to the *Hercules*, and she proceeded on her journey. — *Ledger*.

....

[30 June] We are sorry to hear that a craft belonging to Mr. William Richards of Herring Neck, when beating out of the harbour last evening, bound for Labrador, mis-stayed and went ashore near Rages Rock, becoming a total wreck.

....

[7 July] It will be remembered that some time in February the loss of two men belonging to Herring Neck was reported in our columns, having been overtaken by a snow storm when out gunning. The boat was afterwards picked up, but no sign of the bodies was seen until Wednesday last, when that of James Jones was discovered floating on the surface of the water near Merritt's Harbour, being, we learn, a good deal mutilated, caused no doubt by the ice.

Blandford's Point, Herring Neck, early 1900s

[14 July] The following is the Captain's statement of the accident which resulted in the loss of the [schooner *A.D.O.*] about the fourteenth inst: — "Left Twillingate at 11 o'clock a.m., and at 3 o'clock next morning neared St. Anthony under foresail, jib and reefed mainsail. The high southeast wind which prevailed all night, veered to the northeast, with fog. Tried to make harbour, but the schooner mis-stayed three times, when we bore up and ran for Goose Cove, she mis-stayed again and drifted on Irish Point; let go anchors but could not save her, and she capsized and sunk. The crew were rescued by a skiff sent off by Henry Pynn, ot whom great credit is due for the timely assistance rendered."

We understand the *A.D.O.* has been replaced by the *Mallard*, a fine schooner recently built by Mr. F. Warr. She left for the Labrador yesterday evening.

....

[15 September] The *Annie Harris*, Capt. Jordan, arrived [at Twillingate] from Cadiz this morning to the firm of Messrs. Owen & Earle. She anchored a short distance outside the premises of the consignees, and having afterwards left the position to go nearer the wharf, she grounded on the Harbour Rock where she remains as we go to press.

....

[22 September] The English schooner *Annie Harris*, which arrived from Cadiz to Messrs. Owen & Earle on Thursday last, and which grounded on the shoal near Harbour Rock, floated off soon afterwards without sustaining the least damage. The water was lower at the time the vessel was going in, and being deeply laden, she just caught on the shoalest [*sic*] part.

Henry J. Earle, partner in the firm of Owen & Earle

....

[9 December] It is sad to learn that so far no account has been received of the schooner *Daisy*, belonging to Fogo, which left St. John's for that port about three weeks since. She reached as far as Cat Harbour Island on the evening of Friday, the second inst., where she was anchored, in company with the *Five Brothers*, Capt. Samuel Young, of the place, who got there on the following Tuesday evening. When the gale increased the *Daisy* was seen dragging her anchors, and it is to be hoped that intelligence of her safety may soon reach us.

....

[23 December] We regret to learn that no account of the schr. *Daisy*, has yet been received. The *Mary*, belonging to Mr. Butler of Exploits, is also missing. It is now more than four weeks since both these craft left St. John's, the former for Fogo and [the] latter for Exploits.

1882

[7 January] Mr. James Winsor received a telegram from Queenstown this forenoon acquainting him with the fate of the schr. *Mary*, about which so much anxiety had been felt. The *Mary*, it will be remembered, left this port nearly five weeks ago with a cargo of "supplies" for Exploits, Notre Dame Bay, but having failed to reach her destination after a reasonable time elapsed, it was feared she had "gone-down" with all on board. It now appears the schooner [was] driven off by the strong westerly gales experienced all along the coast shortly after her departure; that she was reduced to a helpless wreck somewhere between this Island and the Irish coast, and that Captain Butler and his crew were rescued by a passing vessel and landed at Queenstown. — St. John's, Telegram.

....

[24 February] ...The *Rosanna*, Nicholas Penny, Master, of Seldom-Come-By, left St. John's on a Thursday in November [1881] previous to the heavy gales that were experienced about that time. When about half way across Conception Bay she was overtaken in a snowstorm, and ran for Bay-de-Verde Bight. Being unacquainted with the locality, and wishing to secure safe anchorage, the Master made a signal of distress, and sent a boat ashore for assistance to direct him to [a] good holding ground, and to render aid in putting the schooner in a good position for riding out the storm, which was raging fiercely at the time. Two [men] belonging to the place went on board, but being in [a] state of intoxication, they could not afford the necessary help. The Master then called on others, but the next who responded to the request were just as bad, if not worse, than the first. However, with his own crew, the Master managed to secure the craft, but while he was busily engaged in doing so, the parties who had been on board took from the craft a reefer jacket belonging to the Master, a spare compass which was in the cabin, a can of paint and a flask of powder, and it was not until after they had left the place that [the crew] discovered that these things had been stolen. To take such a thing as a compass out of a craft, at a time like that was an act of downright villainy, and if the parties could be ferreted out they should be severely punished, and it is to be hoped that they may yet be brought to justice. It was just a short time afterwards, while going from Catalina to Greenspond, that they were near being in [a] bad predicament, by only having one compass on board. When near Gooseberry Rock, and about to shape course for harbour, the jibing of the mainsail caused the compass they were steering by to fall about the deck, breaking the binnacle in pieces, but fortunately, however, the instrument sustained no serious injury. If it had, the removal of the spare one might have resulted disastrously.

DAVID J. CLARKE

Seldom-Come-By, pre-1930

....

[16 June] The following facts of an accident which occurred at Black Island, a few weeks back, were only given to us a day or two since by one of the survivors: — While Ambrose and Thomas Hill, two Brothers, were out sealing a pan struck the boat, causing her to capsize, near Red Point Cove. Both were plunged into the roaring sea. Ambrose was driven back and forth with the waves two or three times, and says that once he was on bottom, but at length succeeded in reaching the shore, being well nigh exhausted. His Brother, Thomas, was also in the water all the time, but could not combat with the elements as he did. Fortunately, however, a boat came to his rescue just in time to save him from a watery grave, as he was then sinking beneath the waves. He was immediately taken to his home, and thus the two of them narrowly escaped drowning.

....

[23 June] The schooner, *Trial*, from St. John's bound to Labrador, which struck a pan of ice off Twillingate about two weeks ago, and sank immediately, was picked up about two miles off Barr'd Islands and towed into port. When found she was floating, her stern about five or six feet above water and bows downward, spars, mainsail and foresail gone. Tuesday the schooner, anchors, chains, seines, nets, traps &c., were sold at public auction by Mr. William Fitzgerald, Wreck Commissioner for Fogo [Island], for the benefit of owners, underwriters, and those claiming salvage. As the fish have struck in well on our shores, and the prospects of a good fishery [are] more hopeful, as might be expected, the cod traps and seine, realized their full value; sundry other articles sold at fair prices. The *hull*, which is not many scores short of a hundred years old, and certainly modelled after "Noah's Ark," as it lay on the beach with a hole about *eight* feet by *three* in her starboard bow, sold for the sum of two pounds. The sum total of sales, amounted to £231. The sale was well represented by the mercantile body of Fogo or their guests.

....

[16 September] We are sorry to have to announce the death of a promising young man, Mark Linfield [aged twenty-five], youngest Son of Mr. George Linfield of this place; which sad event happened on board the schooner *Loyalty* at Hopedale, Labrador, on the thirtieth July. He left home apparently in robust health on the fourth of the same month and about two weeks after he was taken ill, which led to inflamation. The craft being down the coast at the time, the Master deemed it expedient to run back to Hopedale, or near by, where a missionary, who has been in the habit of treating for sickness was then residing, but as he had no medicines that would answer the complaint of the sufferer, death speedily ensued. Here we might allude to the great necessity there is for a medical practitioner to be sent on the Labrador coast during the fishing season, a subject that was before spoken of, and one that we shall again give attention to in future publications.

  The remains of the above deceased were preserved in salt and conveyed home to the sorrowing relatives in the *Loyalty*, which arrived here last night.

  The funeral will take place from his Father's residence, South Side, tomorrow (Sunday) afternoon. We tender our sympathy to the bereaved.

[14 October] The fore-and-aft schooner *Lily*, John Murcell, Master, arrived in port on Wednesday morning from Herring Neck, having on board between three and four hundred qtls. fish, the property of J.B. Tobin, Esq., J.P.

When she first dropped anchor near the premises of the owner there appeared to be no danger of disaster, but in the afternoon, the wind blew very strong from the NE, [with] a heavy sea running, and notwithstanding the precautions that were made for the craft's safety, she afterwards drifted upon Pearce's Rock further up the harbour and became a total wreck. Some of our fishermen, on first seeing the danger, immediately went to the rescue of the craft, and with great difficulty succeeded in saving the canvas and other gear. A good deal of the cargo was spoiled.

The *Lily* was owned by Mr. Tobin, and classed No. 2 in the Twillingate Mutual Insurance Club.

1883

[5 January] A Fogo correspondent, writing under date, Dec. 29, 1882 says :—

A few lines of Fogo correspondence may not be amiss, especially after the late, disastrous gale of twelfth December [1882]. In Fogo Harbour, the only real loss of importance was E. Duder's schr. *Emily*, excepting a small and old craft belonging to Mr. H.T. Simms. The wreck of [the[former was sold at public auction, Mr. Scott being the purchaser of [its] hull at £40. Mr. Scott's schr. *Lassie*, full laden with fish and oil from St. John's, had a narrow escape, driving from her moorings and striking heavily on Wiseman's Point, when fortunately the anchors brought up; the said craft left for St. John's, eighteenth Dec., Mr. Scott taking passage by her. Mr. Rolls' schr. *Willie* also went ashore with a quantity of goods, valued [at] £500...*Lassie*...sustaining £100 loss in damage of goods, but not much injury to [the] craft. A number of stages and flakes were carried away, and debris scattered about the harbour and drifted through the canal. At J.B. Arm and Barr'd Island[s], similar losses [were] reported, the principal one being a new schr. belonging to Mr. James Mew, which became a total wreck, and many other large boats and small craft [were] partially wrecked. No report from Change Islands.

....

[27 April] the schr. *Abyssinia*, belonging to Messrs. Hodder and Linfield, was lost on the seventeenth inst., whilst engaged in the seal fishery. The *Abyssinia* was running through loose ice when she came in contact with a heavy pan, thereby damaging her stem and starboard bow, and filling with water within three hours after the accident. The vessel was at the time about fifty miles east of the Gray Islands. The Master and crew, seeing no possibility of saving the vessel, took their clothes, some wrecked gear, &c., and proceeded on board the schr. *Flamingo*, of this port, which was lying some distance from them in the ice. The latter vessel arrived into port on Sunday last, have on board the shipwrecked crew.

  The schr. *Porcupine*, Young, Master, brought into port on Sunday last the crew and wrecked gear of the schooner *Avalon*, which was lost a short time since. The *Avalon* sailed from Random, Trinity Bay, early in March, and succeeded in getting as far north as Belle Isle. She was afterwards driven south, and was lost about sixty miles NE of Cape St. John. She had no deals.

  We have also been informed of the loss of the schr. *Havelock*, of St. John's. This vessel "came to grief" about seventy miles off Fogo, into which port the crew were taken.

....

[11 May] Just before going to press we have received information of two melancholy accidents, which occurred during the heavy snowstorm of Wednesday last. A boat belonging to Mr. Ashbourne of the Arm [Durrell], left here on the morning of that day for the purpose of going in the Bay for a cargo of wood. She was overtaken by the storm, and sad to relate, one of the crew, Mr. Richard Burton of the Arm, was knocked overboard by the main boom and was drowned...

DAVID J. CLARKE

Tizzard's Harbour, early 1900s

We have also received information of the loss of the schr. *Annie Jane* during the same storm. The *Annie Jane*, Jospeh Carley, Master, was bound to this port from the Bay with a cargo of lumber. About seven o'clock in the evening, it being very thick at that time, she ran into Webber's Bight, Tizzard's Harbour, and became a total wreck. The crew with little difficulty succeeded in reaching the shore. The cargo and vessel's gear were all saved, the men of Moreton's and Tizzard's Harbours giving the crew every assistance.

....

[18 May] The schr. *Four Brothers*, Robert Boyd,, Master, was upset by a squall of wind, on Monday night last, while tacking near Matthews Island. The *Four Brothers* left here in the afternoon of the above day for Tizzard's Harbour, but it being calm until after nightfall, she did not make much headway. About ten o'clock, however, a good breeze of wind upset her; two of the crew were precipitated into the water; the remainder held onto the vessel. One of the men, the Master's Son, narrowly escaped drowning, being covered with the foresail of the vessel, and when extricated from his perilous position was quite insensible. The other managed to grasp the mainboom, which he held until rescued by his shipmates. The cause of the disaster is attributed to the vessel having no ballast on board. She was subsequently towed into Manuel's Cove for the purposes of freeing her, &c.

Stories From These Shores

....

[30 June] The schr. *Minnie Tobin*, Jonathan Burt, Master, struck on the "Black Rocks," situated between Fogo and Change Islands, on Monday last, causing considerable damage to her keel and stern post. The *Minnie Tobin* was returning home from Hare Bay, whither she had been on a fishing voyage, when the accident occurred. At the time of the disaster the vessel was making good headway, but fortunately, with the aid of the swell which was on at the time, she passed over the rock, else a total wreck would have been inevitable. The vessel made water freely and the crew were kept at the pumps until she reached port. The *Minnie Tobin* had on board about twenty qtls. of fish per man, at the time of the disaster.

....

[16 November] A melancholy accident occurred at Crow Head on Wednesday last, by which William Hamilton [Hamlyn?] found a watery grave, and his Brother, Uriah Hamilton, narrowly escaped the same untimely end. It appears that the two men had launched a punt for the purpose of boarding their large boat, which was moored off in the Cove. They had just stepped on board the punt, when a sea upset her, and both of them were precipitated into the angry surf. For some time they were struggling with the boiling sea and strong undertow that prevailed, when a friendly billow landed the survivor on the shore. About an hour afterwards the lifeless body of the other poor fellow was washed in by the sea. At the time of the accident several persons, attracted by the cries of the drowning men, rushed to the spot, but it being quite impracticable to launch a boat in such a sea, very little assistance could be rendered by then. The deceased was married and leaves a Wife and child to mourn their loss.

His remains were interred in the Church of England Cemetery today (Friday), and attended by an escort of the Society of United Fishermen, of which deceased was a member.

The afflicted relatives and friends have our deepest sympathy.

DAVID J. CLARKE

Lower Head, near Crow Head, 1930s

....

[7 December] The schr. *Patience*, belonging to Thos. Hodinott of Seldom-Come-By, left that place on Monday morning last for Friday's Bay, for the object of herring catching. When off Vincent Point, Purcell's Harbour, she was upset by a squall of wind, and the crew with some difficulty escaped in their boat. A boat manned by Mr. John Anstey and crew put off to render assistance, but the strong wind and heavy sea that prevailed compelled them to retreat. The vessel afterwards drove on Lower Main Tickle Point, where she soon went to pieces. The *Patience* had on board at the time a quantity of salt, five herring nets and some other fishing gear. She was not insured.

1884

[30 August] The schooner *Self*, belonging to Messrs. W. Waterman & Co., having a valuable cargo on board, left Fogo harbour on Monday morning last on a trading and collecting expedition to the Strait Shore and other localities. After getting outside the harbour, it was found that the high north west wind which had been blowing strongly, caused a heavy sea to heave in, and as the wind was adverse, it was deemed advisable to return to port, and await a more favourable time. While "boating" in through the Middle Tickle, she grounded on the Harbour Rock, damaging her keel and becoming leaky. In consequence of the sea which was running high at the time, she was in a very dangerous predicament, but no sooner was she thus seen from the shore than assistance was rendered. The other business firms promptly sent men from their employs who, with many other volunteers, quickly succeeded in taking the cargo out of the craft, which was safely conveyed to land in boats, and in a short time she floated off. Had it not been for the timely assistance so willingly rendered, it is probable that the fate of the craft and property would have been very different from what it fortunately was, as the continuous bouncing of a loaded craft on the rock would soon have beat the bottom out of her, and both become a total wreck. The injury the *Self* sustained rendered her unfit for the work intended for her, and another craft had to be provided for the business.

....

[4 October] A serious accident occurred near Little Fogo Islands on the twenty-fifth ult. Two young men of Seal Harbour, Change Islands, named Henry Evely [Eveleigh] and Nathaniel LeDrew were out on the fishing ground in a small boat. They were just about starting for home, and one of them was in the act of pulling up the grapnel, when a heavy sea went over the boat, which swamped her and cast her unfortunate occupants into a watery grave. Other boats were fishing some distance from them, but there was a strong wind and lop at the time and before they could reach them, the angry waves had carried them out of sight. The bodies have not yet been discovered.

Both of these young men were unmarried. Evely was twenty-one years of age, and was the only support of a widowed Mother who had four small children to be provided for, in consequence of which she is left in rather distressing circumstances, which we trust will be taken into consideration by the proper authorities.

DAVID J. CLARKE

Catalina, c.1900

1885

[13 June] The schr. *First Fruit*, bound from St. John's to this port [Twillingate] with a cargo of provisions for W. Waterman & Co., was lost at Catalina during the gale of Sunday last. Her cargo, some of which was considerably damaged, and the wrecked gear which was recovered, were brought hither by the steamer *Plover*.

The schr. *Planche*, Philip Young, Master, became a total wreck at Farewell, near Dildo, during the late gale. Their supply of salt was lost, but the crew managed to save all available gear, which was brought hither by the schooner *Restless*, Loyte [Leyte?], Master, on Monday last. This latter vessel had a large part of her keel knocked off.

The schooner *Rose of Sharon*, George Clarke, Master, and the *Fawn*, Albert Spencer, Master, left port last week for the prosecution of the fishery. They returned to port on Monday last. During the gale of Sunday both these vessels lost their trap skiffs, and had their traps considerably wrecked, which necessitated their returning to port. They were anchored at Cape Cove, near Fogo, and had to run for another port, the *Rose of Sharon* having to slip her anchor, and the *Fawn* beat into Stag Harbour with five reefs in her sails.

The schr. *Wild Rover*, John Roberts, Master, was lost at White Point, Strait Shore, on Sunday last. She was bound from St. John's to this port [Twillingate], and on Saturday night was in the vicinity of the Wadhams. It was very thick and the vessel hove off for the night. On

Sunday morning the wind increased to a gale. The vessel's forestay was carried away, and being off a lee shore, had to run for White point in order to save their lives. She had on board a large quantity of freight for Messrs. Hodder & Linfield; 100 brls. flour for E. Duder, and a Summer's supply of salt, all of which [were] saved, with the exception of the salt, which was lost. The recovered property was brought here by a craft on Thursday last.

....

[22 August] The steam-ship *Sunnyside*, bound from Montreal to Fogo with a cargo of provisions, ran on the rocks in Western Tickle (just at the entrance to Fogo) on Thursday last. Yesterday she was half full of water, but a large part of the cargo had been landed with little or no damage, and there were good prospects of getting the remainder ashore safely. It is thought that if the weather keeps moderate she may be got off, and not become a total wreck. The *Sunnyside* was chartered by the firm of Messrs. J. & R. McLea, of Montreal and consigned to Messrs. Owen & Earle, Fogo and Twillingate. She is of 2,300 tons burthen, and it is not known whether she was insured. Mr. McLea, representing the firm of the Messrs. McLea, arrived here from Fogo last evening in Messrs. W. Waterman & Co.'s yacht *Snowbird*, en route to Little Bay for the purpose of communicating by telegraph with the firm at Montreal, and the steamer owners.

DAVID J. CLARKE

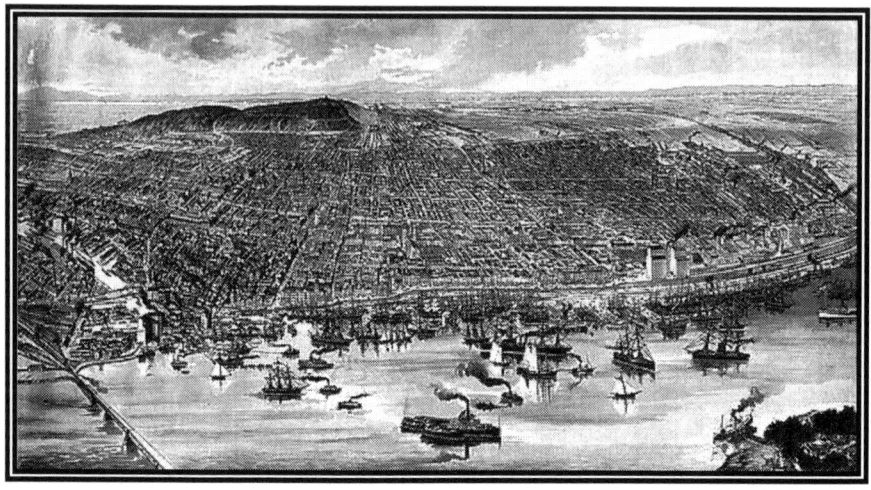

Montreal, 1880s

1886

[27 November] The steamer *Hercules* met with a serious misfortune on leaving Fogo harbour early on Wednesday morning, the seventeenth inst. When going out the Western Tickle she struck on what was supposed to be the wreckage of the steamer *Sunnyside*, lost there about two years ago. At first it was thought that part of the steering gear had given out, and the Captain continued his course, not thinking that anything serious had occurred, but after a little while it was discovered that water was quickly making in the hold. The steamer proceeded as far as Dean's Rock, some three miles from Fogo, and had to return in a very dangerous condition. The steam pumps would not work, and before arriving back to the harbour one of the fires was out, and the water had reached the cabin floor. The *Hercules* was put in the beach near Messrs. Waterman's premises, where she now lies. It is not known yet whether she will be a total wreck. If so, it is very much to be regretted, as her loss to the northern trade will create a void that will be sorely felt by the public.

·······

Stories From These Shores

[18 December] The steamer *Hercules*...is afloat again, and will likely be brought...here this or next week after being temporarily repaired. The job of emptying the hold of water was a most difficult one, and were it not for the ingenious method adopted by Condon, supplemented by the diver's all-important services and the powerful pumping apparatus, the boat might have lain there forever, so far as the ordinary plans of getting her to the surface would have availed. Once...the workmen could work on the fractured hull from the inside, the task of keeping her afloat was assured. We congratulate those concerned in her purchase on the success of their enterprise.

1887

[1 January] The steamer *Hercules* came here on Friday evening last. She brought the American mail and a few local papers and letters. This was the steamer's first trip north since being repaired, and her appearance seemed familiar. She was in charge of Capt. Christopher, who was formerly Second Officer on board. The *Hercules* had a large quantity of freight for this and other ports north. She called here, returning on Monday evening, and, being rather stormy, remained until next morning, when she left for Fogo and St. John's.

....

[17 September] It is with regret that we have to record a painful drowning accident which occurred at Cut Throat, Labrador, on August twenty-ninth. The schooner *Erebus*, whose crew consisted of seven, four of whom were Brothers (Sons of Mr. George Vatcher, an old and respected resident of this place) was fishing at the above-mentioned place, and early on the morning of the date mentioned, three of the crew, namely, Charles Vatcher (Master of [the] craft), James Vatcher and James Young, went to take up their trap which was in danger of being carried away by the sea. While endeavouring to clear the leader, which they had partly in the boat, two seas had come towards them, and before they had time to escape a third one broke upon them with terrific violence, and in the twinkling of an eye the poor unfortunate men were buried beneath the surf. Two of them were never seen or heard after, but a hand of the other was once seen rising above the foaming billows when it instantly disappeared, and nothing more was known of them. Search was made a couple of days for the recovery of the bodies, but all in vain. The boat and leader of trap were also lost.

Schooners at Labrador, pre-1921

Both the Brothers drowned were married, and leave Wives and children to mourn their irreparable loss. James Young was about eighteen or nineteen, and of late was living with the Vatchers. The sad event has cast a gloom over the community, and much sympathy is felt for the families so suddenly and unexpectedly bereft of their loved ones.

．．．．．．．

[1 October] Very serious reports reach us of destruction caused by the gale of the eighteenth Sept. A boat that was anchored at Change Islands is said to have been lost with all hands. A worthy correspondent from Fogo, writing on the twenty-eighth, furnishes the following rumour which is current there: —

On Sunday morning, eighteenth inst. (During the gale) a boat drove from her anchors at [the] southern end of Change Islands, and became a total wreck; supposed all hands to be lost. Since then a considerable quantity of wreckage has been picked up on the Strait

Shore, also a board or a piece of the stern with the name "Brothers" upon it. A report in circulation this afternoon says that some men belonging to Island Harbour discovered the bodies of four men and a boy near some rocks, and also a considerable quantity of fish lying on the bottom...

Change Islands View (Author's photo)

[1 October] The boat *Fear Not* of Change Islands was driven from her anchors at Fogo Island, and it was thought she was lost, but a telegram from Capt. Wm. Windsor, Greenspond, informs us that she was picked up on the twenty-ninth September, twelve miles off Cabot Islands, so that the poor man, Thomas Peckford, is not likely to be deprived of his little craft, which was about fifteen tons.

Two smaller boats from Change Islands were also driven away. The men losing their Fall's catch of fish are reduced to complete distress for themselves and their families.

....

[10 December] The schooner *Bianca* left here on Wednesday week for the Bay. In rounding Herring Head, the mainsail jibed, and one of Mr. Thos. Earle's feet (the Master) got caught in the rope belonging to [the] main sheet, bringing the leg in contact with the steering gear and bruising it severely. The craft had to return to Back Harbour to land him, whence he had to be taken home with a horse and slide.

1888

[14 January] We are sorry to learn that during the gale and sea that prevailed on the fifth inst., the schooner *Springbird*, belonging to M. Osmond, Esq., Moreton's Harbour, which was moored in Pearce's Harbour for the Winter, with the intention of prosecuting the seal fishery, was driven ashore and broken to pieces. There was such a tremendous sea running that the anchor was lifted from the bottom and landed ashore on the beach. The vessel was nearly new, and there being no insurance on her, the loss is a very serious one to the owner.

....

[14 January] The steamer *Tibbie*, [owned by Robert Scott, Esq.,] came from Fogo on Tuesday, and on returning was lost in Western Tickle, at nine o'clock last night. She struck on Western Rock, immediately filled with water, and quickly sank, the lives barely escaping. We are sorry that the enterprising owner should meet with such a misfortune, as we understand there was no insurance on the steamer, which cost between seven and eight hundred pounds.

....

[21 January] The following are the particulars of the loss of the steam launch, *Tibbie*, reported in last paper:—

*Home built by merchant Robert Scott of Fogo.
(Now known as the "Miller House"), early 1900s*

At nine o'clock on Tuesday morning the twelfth inst., the steam launch *Tibbie*...left Twillingate for Fogo, *via* Beaver Cove. She had [on board] the owner, [Mr. Scott], and four passengers, besides the crew consisting of two men. She landed three of the passengers at Beaver Cove at one p.m. and as it got very thick she went no farther than Change Islands that night. Next day, Friday, she left Change Islands at one p.m., and was seen from Fogo at two p.m. A crowd of men with John Scott, Son of the owner, went up on a hill to signal them to go back, but their signals were misunderstood, and the *Tibbie* came on and tried to enter the harbour by the Eastern Tickle. The men were all down at the Tickle but the *Tibbie* could not get far enough to communicate with them. She then went round to the Boatswain's Tickle and the men had to walk round shore. While John Scott was crossing the ice to the North Side he fell through, and sprained his thigh. When the men got round to the Western Tickle, the *Tibbie* was being tossed by the waves, and those on shore thought every moment that they had seen the last of her. It was nine p.m. when she got round to the Boatswain's Tickle, and just as she got into the worst part, some part of her machinery refused to do its work, and she was at the mercy of the waves. Once those on shore heard screams and thought that all was up, but one of the men called Robert Irish got his boat, and with the willing help of the North Side men under the superintendence of John Scott, they got out lines and rescued those on board, but none too soon, for just after they left her she turned bottom up. It is not known if she blew up, as amid the confusion and noise of the waves a report could not have been heard. A quarter of an hour after she struck, there was not a sign of her to be seen. The boat with the rescued was hauled ashore, and those in her helped to a house near by, where restoratives were given to those that required them. None of those on board were seriously hurt.

....

[7 April] The schooner *Isabella*, Thomas Lacey, Master, from the firm of Messrs. Owen & Earle, which cleared for the seal fishery some time ago, was lost on Friday last about two or three miles from land. The ice went off from the land and the schooner, taking advantage of the same, left Herring Neck to proceed on her voyage, but before getting very far the ice ran together and crushed the schooner to pieces. They succeeded in saving the tackles, &c., which [were] taken to Herring Neck, on Saturday, the day after the unfortunate occurrence took place.

....

[12 May] The new steamer *Conscript*, which was intended for the northern coastal service, left the Clyde on the thirteenth ult., for St. John's, and being two days out was caught in a heavy breeze of wind, sustaining serious injury, and had to put back to Dumbarton, Scotland, where she is now on dock. We understand it is the hull of the ship that is damaged, which appears to be of such a serious nature as to make it probable, according to latest advices, that the steamer will be condemned. If this is so, it is a very unfortunate affair for all concerned, and looks strange that a steamer which was intended for such a service as the *Conscript* should have been so frailly constructed.

....

[19 May] A boy named Albert Greenham was drowned in Durrell's Arm on Tuesday morning. There was some wrecked gear near Burnt Island Tickle, and the lad attempted to reach it by walking on the ice, but when about 200 yards from the land, he fell through, and before help could be afforded, he disappeared beneath the ice. The ice moved off, and [a] search was made, which resulted in the finding of his body, which was interred on Thursday. The boy was about fifteen or sixteen years of age, and Son of Henry Greenham, Manuel's Cove, but had been living in the Arm with James Hillyard.

View of Durrell, Twillingate, 1930s

....

[17 October] We learn that on the night of Sunday the eleventh inst., a small craft belonging to Mr. John Anstey of Purcell's Harbour, drove from her anchors in Long Tickle, near Dildo. Leaving Purcell's Harbour on the previous Friday, she was struck by a heavy squall while beating up the run, which split her jib and foresail. The craft put back to Long Tickle, and on Sunday night the wind veered to northwest and blowing a gale. She dragged her anchors and the crew left her at daylight. No sign was seen of her on Monday morning, and it was supposed that she was lost, but a few days after she was picked up at Island Harbour nearly full of water, but very little damaged. The schooner was bound in the Bay for the Winter and had supplies on board for two families, in addition to household property, and if the craft had been a total wreck, the families would have been entirely destitute.

1889

[2 February] Although the ice has not been very strong connecting the surrounding settlements, many ventures have been made over it, and several persons have fallen through, and very narrowly escaped drowning. One instance, particularly, was that of Mr. Jacob Keefe and his Son, Abraham, of Burnt Cove [Newville], Friday's Bay, on Tuesday morning last. They were on their way to Moreton's Harbour, with dogs and slide, and fell through near Samson's Island. They were in the water some considerable time, and were at length rescued with great difficulty, both being nearly exhausted. Some of the dogs perished in the water. The men reached Mr. Samson's where they received a warming and refreshments.

....

[23 February] A very narrow escape from drowning occurred at Purcell's Harbour last Saturday morning, the particulars of the case being something like this: David Ginn, who had been gunning, happened to see a seal just outside the point, which he was fortunate in killing, but while in the act of getting it on board, the boat capsized, and the occupant was precipitated in the water. He managed to get on the bottom, but the boat being very light would not bear up and it capsized over and over again, and the unfortunate man was struggling in the water for some time, and though within sight of persons on shore, felt that he must perish in the water. When he thought that there was no hope of being rescued he managed to tie the painter of the boat around him, so his body might easily be recovered. But, providentially, Mr. Evely [Eveleigh] took a gun and left his house to look for birds, and...he saw the drowning man, and immediately got a boat and crew, and went to his rescue. Mr. Ginn, who had then been in the water nearly thirty minutes, was in an almost exhausted condition, and in a minute or two longer he would doubtless have been drowned. His hands and fingers were all drawn up with the frost and cold where he had been holding fast to the boat, and this week he was confined to his bed for the most of the time suffering from the effect of the accident. However, it is a providential thing for his Wife and family that he was seen in time and rescued from a watery grave.

....

Eastern Tickle, c.1900

[17 August] A sad accident occurred at Fogo on the first inst. William Elliott, of Eastern Tickle and his Son William, went out early in the morning to haul a herring net. A strong NNE breeze with a heavy lop was prevailing at the time, and while taking the net in the punt a heavy lop broke on board which turned the boat over. The young man sank, and was not seen afterwards, but his Father held on to the boat for a considerable time, and when taken off was much exhausted. William was a fine young man of twenty-two years, and great sympathy is felt for the Father and family.

1891

[21 March] On Tuesday last, the seventeenth inst., several of our boats went off to the ice, as is usual this time of the year. On this day the morning was fine and promising, the wind about SE, blowing a light breeze, and nothing, seemingly, to cause the slightest uneasiness about the weather. There were several punts out from Herring Neck on the same occasion, and for the same purpose. The wind increased in the afternoon, accompanied with snow drifts, when experienced hands on shore began to fear for the safety of those in the boats. We presume the boats must have been a long way off, as they all had a desperate struggle and task to reach the shore. In this, they all, with one exception, succeeded eventually, but sad to state, the cold and exposure was so intense that it caused the death of one young man named Philpot, of Herring Neck, who died before assistance could reach him, and many of the others suffered dreadfully, and could not possibly have overcome the strain if it continued a little longer. The punt of which we alluded is still missing, and the men on board were, one of them a Son of Mr. Francis Roberts, the other a Son of Mr. Phillip Rideout, the former a married man with a family. Every enquiry has been made by telegraph and other means to discover whether there is any hope of them having been fortunately driven into any of our outharbours, but we cannot hear of such being the case. And at the present moment a boat and five men have been dispatched to Fogo and intermediate places to ascertain if there is any hope of them being seen or heard of. We sincerely trust that they may turn up alright, but regret to say, the prospect at present is very gloomy.

1892

[14 May] We learn that the schooner *Forward*, Capt. White (owned by Messrs. Hodge, Twillingate), was lost at Cadiz on the twenty-second of March. On that day a heavy gale of SE wind prevailed and caused considerable damage among the shipping. The *Forward* was driven ashore in the breeze and became a total wreck. She had no cargo in at the time – *H.G. Standard*.

....

[18 June] News was received here [Twillingate] yesterday of the loss of the schooner *General Booth*, belonging to Mr. Jacob Moores, near Cape John, which occurred on Thursday morning. The schooner only left here on Wednesday and encountered the ice the following morning, which knocked a hole in her causing her to sink almost immediately. The crew barely had time to escape with their lives and could save nothing, everything going to bottom with her. We regret to hear of the unfortunate occurrence just at the commencement of the fishing season, which is a severe loss to Mr. Moores, and will likely put him and his crew out of a Summer's voyage.

....

[22 June] What was supposed to be a wreck was seen off in the Bay on Sunday morning by a number of men from Crow Head. Several of them proceed to the object seen from the shore, which was a long distance from the land, and which on reaching it, proved to be the hull of the *General Booth*, reported in our last [issue] as having been lost near Cape John on Thursday morning last. The crew towed it into Back Harbour, reaching there in the evening. The schooner was not in the ice at the time of the accident, neither did any of her crew perceive that she had knocked against an ice flow. She was steadily sailing along when it was discovered that the water was up to the cabin floor, and in a few minutes...she went down. The supposition is that a sharp lumper underneath the water must have unperceivingly struck her bottom and quietly put a hole through it, which caused the damage. As soon as she filled with water she went down, but having only a little ballast, it is apparent that when the salt dissolved she partly floated again. It was evident, however, that before the Crow Head men got to her, the wrecked schooner had been met by some other craft, as she had been stripped of her rigging and gear. There is only a little more than the hull of the *General Booth* remaining, and the cost of repairs would nearly be as great as the first cost of the craft. She was insured in the Twillingate Mutual Insurance Club.

....

[25 June] Our reference to the loss of the *General Booth* in our last issue, as to her not having been in ice just about the time the accident occurred, was incorrect, and we are glad to be able to give the facts of the case today. She had been sailing through a skirt of ice, but during all the time there was no heavy concussion with the ice to cause any alarm or to lead to the suspicion that any accident had occurred. Shortly after the schooner got clear of the ice, however, it was discovered that the water was up to the cabin floor, and then it was not long before she filled and went down.

The *General Booth* was nearly a new craft of twenty-one tons. She was strongly built and well founded, and was very convenient for her owner for carrying on the fisheries. By the unfortunate event Mr. Jacob Moores sustained a considerable loss, all his Summer's supplies and the greater part of the outfit being lost at the same time, besides the chances of doing well with the fish the early part of the Summer.

1894

[1 December] The schooner *Rabbi*, Wm. George Woolfrey, of Moreton's Harbour, left St. John's for home previous to the gale of the twentieth ult., and was driven off over 100 miles, but the wind veering more in their favour, they afterwards succeeded in making in near Greenspond. A terrible time was experienced. The bulwarks had to be cut away, decks were swept, all the sails except part of the mainsail were blown away, and they were at the mercy of the raging billows and gave themselves up for lost, but providentially they were brought once more to land. They succeeded in obtaining sails to enable the schooner to come along whenever the time is favourable. Mr. Samuel Small, of Moreton's Harbour, who was coming passenger by her, went to Gambo and took the train, and got home by way of Burnt Bay.

1895

[5 October] The coastal steamer *Virginia Lake*, Capt. Taylor, called here early Thursday afternoon going south. She was detained longer than usual as she had to go to the assistance of a wrecked steamer called the *Mariposa*, which came to grief at Forteau in the Straits of Belle Isle. The *Virginia Lake* had a full load of sheep &c., saved from the wreck, and was crowded with passengers, this being her last trip to Labrador [this year]. Mrs. Tobin, Mrs. Samuel Hudder, Mrs. William Hudder,

Miss Smith, and others, embarked here for St. John's.

Steamer Virginia Lake *(R), and other vessels, in harbour*

DAVID J. CLARKE

Merchant Matters

1880

[1 July] Messrs. Waterman & Co. have formed a Mutual Insurance Club, including all their masters, and by which insurance is effected to an amount of over £15,000. Should there be no losses a large amount of money will be saved by premiums, etc.

....

[5 August] On Tuesday last [27 July, 1880] at the firm of Messrs. W. Waterman & Co., a very serious accident occurred to one of the assistants, by a fall through the trap-hatch in the shop, a height of nine feet. It appears that the young man was engaged in getting a box up through the hatch when the ladder slipped, and he fell, his chin taking the edge of the hatch, and afterwards falling on the side of his head and face to the bottom of the store, where he lay insensible for some time. But when discovered, we are glad to say that the wound inflicted was not of a serious nature, and he is now doing well.

1881

[3 February] On Saturday last Path End was the scene of great excitement occasioned by the launching of a large salt store and rigging loft, on the extensive premises of Messrs. Waterman & Co. The building was hauled from the old site, bordering the Government land, where it has stood for the last thirty or forty years, over wharves which took some nine or ten days to build for the purpose, and it now stands in close proximity to the other stores of a more recent structure. It must be always pleasing to patriotic minds to notice improvements, either of a public nature, or the result of private enterprise, and here we have an instance which embraces both, for while Messrs. Waterman's premises are made more compact and commodious, the Government property near the coastal wharf, in course of erection, is infinitely improved, both in appearance and convenience.

Over 300 men from all parts of the island testified their good will by lending a helping hand on the occasion, and their united assistance proved how much may be accomplished by a "long pull, a strong pull, and a pull altogether." we congratulate R.D. Hodge, Esq., on the success of his undertaking, and trust that it will be remunerative to him in his business. After the work was over refreshment in the shape of coffee, tea, biscuit, &c. was provided on the premises of Mr. James Hodder, foreman of the undertaking.

Merchant premises near Path End, 1930s

....

[26 May] R. Scott, Esq., one of the principal mercantile gentlemen of Fogo was here a short time the early part of the week. Mr. Scott has a shrewd business fact, and after years of assiduous toil and close attention to business has gained an elevation in mercantile status worthy of commendation. The branch of his trade here conducted by the Agent, Mr. J.G. Lucas, Jr., is somewhat extensive. Mr. S. was on a visit to the Old Country during the past Winter. We were glad to see him looking so well after his return, and wish him every success in his future business speculations.

....

[28 July] Yesterday afternoon the schooner *Daisy* arrived to the firm of E. Duder, Esq., having on board A. Duder, Esq., and Bride, who are on a short visit here. The schooner was gaily decked with bunting and looked very pretty as she glided in under full sail. The premises of E. Duder were also decked with flags, and several guns were fired on the arrival of the schooner. We congratulate the happy couple and wish them a pleasant honeymoon.

1882

[7 January] The following statement of the Committee of the Terra Nova Mutual Insurance Club shows that fortune has attended the vessels connected therewith, notwithstanding the storms that may have been encountered during the past season. The Club comprises some fifty or sixty craft, principally engaged in the trade of Messrs. W. Waterman & Co. :—

TWILLINGATE, Dec., 30th 1881.

We the undersigned Committee of the Terra Nova Mutual Insurance Club hereby state to those concerned that at the termination of the time limited, twenty-first inst., no loss had occurred to vessels entered in the Club the past season: Simon Warr; Matthew Elliott; John Purchase; George Snow; William Starke; Charles Brett; Albert Spencer; Joseph Stuckless; John Dwyer, Jr., George Porter.

R.D. HODGE,
Secretary

....

[10 February] On Friday last, a building owned by Mr. James Hodder, and formerly situated on his premises on the side of the hill, just past the [Tickle] Bridge, was hauled near the water-side, close to the bridge, and when put in proper repair, will make a capital business stand. A large number of volunteers assisted in the launch, which was superintended by Mr. James Fifield, who has undertaken and successfully carried through other similar projects in the past.

....

[4 July] The English schooner, *Vistula*, Capt. Andrew, arrived from

Liverpool last evening with a cargo of goods &c. for James Byrne, Esq., at the Arm. This, we presume, is the first direct importation to that part of Twillingate. We must congratulate our enterprising friend on his business "pluck," and wish him every success in his undertakings.

View of Liverpool, UK (Author's photo)

....

[4 August] We are pleased to note the arrival in town of W. Waterman, Esq. (of the firm of W. Waterman & Co.) and Son. They took passage from England on a steamer bound to Bett's Cove, where they arrived on Monday, twenty-fourth ult., after a fine passage of ten days. They then proceeded to Nipper's Harbour and came here per schr. *Emeline* on Saturday evening last. We understand that Mr. Waterman intends remaining here during the Summer months. Mr. Waterman, Jr. left for Fogo on Monday last, where he intends remaining for a few days.

1884

[23 August. Edwin John] Duder, Esq., principal of the well-known and long established mercantile firm of E. Duder, Esq., arrived here per last

DAVID J. CLARKE

Plover, from St. John's, and having spent a few days in this part of his extensive business domain, left in Messrs. Waterman's yacht, *Snowbird*, on Monday last to pay Fogo a short visit previous to the *Plover*'s return from the north. We hope that Mr. Duder, who is a Son of the late, lamented E. Duder, Esq., whose memory will not soon be forgotten, will be as successful a mercantile gentleman as his respected Father proved to be.

Edwin John Duder

J.W. Owen, Esq., came here on Saturday last from Fogo, having arrived there per last *Plover* from St. John's. Mr. Owen has been on a visit to the Old Country the past few months, and is looking well after his trip.

Stories From These Shores

1885

[31 December] The steam launch *Tibbie*, belonging to R. Scott, Esq., came here from that port on Tuesday afternoon, having its enterprising owner on board. She brought a quantity of merchandise for his branch trade here and left again the next morning for Fogo.

1886

[9 October] We are sorry to have to record the death at Moreton's Harbour on Saturday last, of George K. Osmond, at the early age of twenty-six, Son of M. Osmond, Esq. He was a young man that was much beliked [sic] by the whole community. He left home about three weeks before on a trading venture to White Bay, and was taken ill shortly after leaving, and the schooner returned with him. His funeral took place on Tuesday, and was one of the largest ever known there. Being a member of [the] Loyal Orange Association, the brethren of the "Arctic" Lodge, of which [deceased] was one of its founders, paid their last respects by attending in processional order, being borne by Companions of the Royal Scarlet Chapter, to which he also belonged. An appropriate sermon was preached on the occasion by Rev. H. Hatcher...

1887

[23 July] We learn that a brisk business has been done in the Lobster factory, Fogo, the past few weeks by the enterprising proprietor, R. Scott, Esq. Up to the eighteenth inst., 800 cases had been finished, and it is contemplated to put up 400 more, which will represent about sixty or seventy thousand tins. The preparation of this article has been superintended by Mr. Scott himself, and every precaution has been taken in its manufacture so as to send a superior product into foreign markets, which it is to be hoped will prove to have been the result. The cod fishery having been such an utter failure there, as well as in other places around here, where lobster factories are in operation, many have been kept alive by the employment they afford in preparing lobsters, etc.

We understand that good work is also being done in the Lobster

DAVID J. CLARKE

Factory, Exploits, by Messrs. Foote Bros.

....

[26 November] W. Waterman, Esq., Sr., who has been spending the past few months in Newfoundland, left per *Robert Morris* for Lisbon, whence he will take steamer for Great Britain. During his stay, Mr. W. has visited various localities familiar to him in these parts, and no doubt his numerous friends and acquaintances have been highly pleased with his visits to their respective communities, and would have liked that his stay could have been much longer than time would admit. We unite with his many friends in wishing the respected gentleman a pleasant passage in crossing the Atlantic, and a safe and prosperous return to him home in England.

1889

[25 May] The steamer *Swallow*, now owned by Messrs. Owen & Earle, came from Change Islands yesterday. This is the first trip that this little steamer has made since being the property of its present owners. No doubt this mode of rapid intercourse between the different branch establishments must prove a great convenience to the trade, and we must congratulate this old and well-known firm on their new departure in thus keeping pace with the times.

1892

[3 December] ...We regret to record the demise of one of the leading men of South Island. On Thursday Mr. And Mrs. Thos. Ashbourne drove to North Side on business, and at their usual time retired to rest. About eleven o'clock, Mr. Ashbourne (who last year had been very ill but recovered sufficiently to prosecute the Labrador voyage as usual, and since his return has been in fairly good health), complained of being ill, at once medical and other aid was at hand but in less than two hours the end had come, and today we mourn with the friends in the loss of a useful citizen, kind Husband and indulgent Father. Deceased was a prominent member of the LOA and SUF. We extend our sympathy to the family in this severe visitation of Providence.

Thomas Ashbourne

....

[10 December] The funeral of the late Mr. Thomas Ashbourne took place on Sunday afternoon last, and was one of the largest ever witnessed in the community. The Orange and United Fishermen Societies, of which he was a worthy member, attended in procession, and crowds of persons from all parts, which shows the great respect in which [the] deceased was held. His remains were interred in the Church of England cemetery, connected with St. Andrew's Church, the ceremonies being performed by the Rev. R. Temple, R.D., who preached a very suitable and impressive discourse on the occasion.

....

DAVID J. CLARKE

Churches & Religion

1880

[1 July] Within the past two or three weeks a new rostrum has been put in the Methodist church of this town [Twillingate]. The one formerly there was so low as to preclude some of the congregation worshipping in the furthest parts of [the] gallery from seeing the speaker. The one recently placed there is on a more improved style and at such an elevation as to admit of the speaker being observed from any part of the building. The work, which was undertaken by Mr. Andrew Linfield, is creditably performed. We understand that he was the accepted contractor for the finishing of the building some two years since, but in consequence of the depressed circumstances of the people, resulting from a succession of bad voyages, the work was rather protracted, and it was not until the past twelve months that the woodwork has been completed. The interior is now ready for painting and staining, which, when accomplished, will greatly enhance its appearance and will be a credit to the Methodists of this community. It is to be hoped that no time will be lost in undertaking so desirable a work.

BUSINESS NOTICE.

Andrew Linfield,

SOUTH-SIDE, TWILLINGATE.

Carpenter, Builder & Contractor.

DOORS & SASHES

of all sorts and sizes made to order.

ALSO ;

Mantlepieces, Handrails, Newel Posts, &c., &c.

CABINET-MAKING--a specialty.

☞ Orders from all parts of the Bay executed at low prices and at short notice. Anything in the Furniture line can be supplied.

1881

[26 May] We understand that the annual Missionary Meeting in connection with the Methodist Church of Canada, was held [at Fogo] on the evening of Friday, the thirteenth inst., commencing at half-past seven. The meeting having ben opened with praise and prayer, the Chairman, T. C. Duder, Esq., J.P., gave a suitable address. A report was read by the Minister of the circuit, Rev. A. Hill, after which the Rev. T.W. Atkinson, of Twillingate, and J.G. Lucas, Esq., Sub-Collector [of Customs], addressed the audience in a pleasing style, and the occasion throughout was one of interest.

On the following Monday evening the Missionary Meeting was held at Indian Islands. The Chair was taken by J.G. Lucas, Esq., who having addressed the meeting, was followed by the Revds. Messrs. Atkinson and Hill.

....

[16 June] On Tuesday night, May twenty-fourth, a very interesting missionary meeting took place at Merritt's Harbour, the first of the kind ever held in that place. In almost every seat there appeared faces beaming with delight and expectation. It really seemed as if the scriptural declaration was realized in their case: "Arise, shine, for thy light is come, and the Glory of the Lord is risen upon three." Mr. Samuel Card took the Chair, who after describing the habits of the Esquimaux on Labrador, in a very interesting manner, was followed by the Rev. W.H. Edyvean, who spoke of the spread of Christianity in various parts of the World, and the demands of the Methodist Church for increased liberality to extend the Redeemer's Kingdom in the Earth. A collection was made, after which this most interesting meeting was brought to a close by singing the doxology.

On the thirtieth [of] May, the annual Missionary Meeting was also held at Change Islands, which was a time of great spiritual blessing. The meeting was presided over by the Minister of the Circuit. After the opening exercises and the reading of the report, the meeting was addressed by the Rev. Anthony Hill of Fogo, who gave a very earnest speech on Christian Missions showing the contrast between the Gospel system and heathenism, followed by the Rev. W.H. Edyvean, urging the financial claims of the Missionary Society, and reminding them that a work cheerfully done cannot fail to secure its reward. The increased liberality of the people of Change Islands shows their interest in the spread of the Gospel, the collection being in excess of last year.

*Interior, Change Islands United
(Methodist) Church (Author's photo)*

....

[14 July] We understand the Revd. James Nurse of Moreton's and Tizzard Harbours preached his farewell sermon at the latter place on Sunday last. The discourse was earnest and practical, and many of the hearers were moved to tears during the delivery. The Rev. Gentleman leaves with his Wife in a few days for his new sphere of labour at Grand Bank, where they will be followed by the best wishes of the people, and we hope be continually blessed in their labour of love, by the All-wise Ruler of the Universe.

....

[29 September] The Rev. William Temple, arrived here in the mission yacht *Snowdrop*, on Tuesday last, from White Bay, where for the past

Twelve months he has been zealously working in the holy office to which he has been called. We are glad to see him looking so well after encountering the hardships peculiar to the performance of the important duties connected with his mission.

1882

Congregational Church buildings, Twillingate, late-1800s

[27 January] On Wednesday evening last, a children's quarterly entertainment, in connection with the Congregational body, was held at their church. The exercises commenced at 7:30, by singing a hymn from Sankey's Collection, and then of an earnest and importune prayer by the Pastor, Rev. G. Whyte, who, since his assumption to the duties of his sacred office here, has worked zealously for the promotion of Christian principles among his congregation. A programme replete with interesting and instructive recitations, &c., was unfolded to the audience, and each of the performers acquitted themselves in so creditable a style that it might be invidious for us to mention anyone in particular. The gathering on the occasion was good, the church being comfortably filled, and the audience appeared to be much interested while the various pieces were rendered. Three months hence a similar entertainment may be expected to take place in the same place...

[Recitations and readings were given by, John Stowe, Katie Hughes, Mary Jane Mitchard, Edward Hayward, George Mitchard, Maggie Hughes, James Stow, Walter Hodder, Laura Hodder, Lavenia Stowe, Phoebe Jacobs, James Hodder, Ross Mitchard, Eliza Hughes, George Gard. A solo was performed by "Mr. William Hughes."]

....

[23 June] METHODIST CHURCH AT CHANGE ISLANDS. — A correspondent informs us that the reopening services of this Church took place on the third ult. The Rev. W.H. Edyvean, Circuit Minister, was kindly assisted by the Rev. A. Hill, and J.G. Lucas, of Fogo.

During the Spring, in company with a friend, we had an opportunity of spending a short time with Mr. Solomon Roberts of Change Islands, who invited us to look at the building. It is one that was erected some years ago, but of late it has been thoroughly renovated inside at a cost of about 350 dols., free of debt. The new gallery rostrum, &c., greatly improve its appearance. The Church is nicely situated, the work neatly done, and will cost about 450 pounds 1s. It reflects credit upon the Methodists of Change Islands, and the Pastor, who has attended to their spiritual necessities for the past three years.

....

[29 September] The Rev. R. Temple, R.D., left here [Twillingate] in the mission yacht *Snowdrop* on Wednesday morning for White Bay on a visitation tour to the Church people in the many scattered harbours and coves of that extensive part of the coast. The Rev. Gentleman's indefatigable labours in these parts during the years he ministered to the spiritual needs of his flock in that direction, will doubtless ensure for him a most warm and kindly greeting from the old friends of the Bay.

The Clergyman for White Bay, Rev. Wm. Temple, Brother of the Rural Dean, arrived in the *Snowdrop* on Saturday evening last, and will remain during his absence. He will preach in St. Peter's Church on Sunday next.

Stories From These Shores

1883

[30 June] His Lordship the Right Rev. Dr. McDonald, Bishop of Harbour Grace, accompanied by the Rev. Fathers Brown, Flynn and Walker arrived here from Fogo *via* Herring Neck on Thursday afternoon last. His Lordship is at present paying his first pastoral visit to this portion of his Diocese. Proceeding as far as Fogo by last *Plover* from the south, His Lordship began his work at that place, and visited the adjacent localities, for the purpose of administering to his flock the Rights of the Church as invested in one holding the office of Bishop. On Thursday, the Bishop, accompanied by three of his clergy, proceeded to Herring Neck, where a service was held; after which the party came from thence to this town, arriving here early in the afternoon of that day. Next morning a service was conducted by the Bishop, assisted by the clergy, at the residence of J.B. Tobin, Esq., after which His Lordship and priests left here in the schr. *Oliphant*, belonging to J.B. Tobin, Esq., for Leading Tickles and other localities to the northward.

His Lordship and Rev. Fathers Brown, Flynn and Walker were the guests of J.B. Tobin, Esq., during their stay here.

....

[4 August] On the occasion of the Bishop's recent visit, the first mass was celebrated in the Church of "The Holy Family" at Joe Batt's Arm. Silently and unknown, save to the people of the Parish, the Rev. Father [James] Brown laboured the last two years in collecting funds and material for this new church. The result is a neat and carefully finished wooden structure sixty x thirty foot, with vestry. On Saturday, June twenty-third, the Catholics of the Arm gave a day's fishing – a catch of 100 odd quintals – to liquidate the small balance of debt remaining on the Church – *H.G. Standard*.

....

[31 August] We are pleased to note the return per *Plover* of the Rev. Mr. McKay (Pastor of the Congregational Church) who has been to St. John's the past few weeks, supplying for the Rev. Mr. Beaton, who was on a missionary tour to Labrador. It is pleasing to know that Mr. McKay met with so many generously disposed friends in the Metropolis who were willing to assist our Congregational friends here in their praiseworthy undertakings, as the following item from a late number of the *Evening Telegram* will show :—

"The Rev. Mr. McKay of Twillingate desires to express his very sincere and heartfelt thanks to the friends in this city for their liberal contributions towards the erection of a school house and the purchase of an organ to be used in connection with his missionary labours at that place. He says the liberality of the gentlemen upon whom he called far exceeded his most sanguine expectations."

1884

Anglican Church yacht Lavrock

[26 July] On Monday at 5:30, the Church of England mission yacht, *Lavrock*, entered our harbour. On board were His Lordship the Bishop of Newfoundland, and Rev. T. Nurse, His Lordship's Chaplin pro term. They were on their way to Labrador, and had a very fair run so far, the Church yacht sailing at her usual excellent speed. She anchored near the public wharf, and Mr. W.S. Rafter proceeded on board, and, in the absence of the Rural Dean, welcomed His Lordship once more to our town. The rain and high wind did not prevent His Lordship from coming on shore and visiting St. Peter's Church. He expressed pleasure at the needful alterations which have lately been made. His Lordship then visited the Rectory. The next morning the *Lavrock* proceeded on her noble mission north.

Llewellyn Jones, Anglican Bishop of Newfoundland

....

[23 August] We are pleased to note the rapid improvements being made in the picturesque Church of Moreton's Harbour. On Sunday, Aug. third, a large congregation were pleased to find that an organ (Mason & Hamlin Cabinet) had been placed in the Church. It was only the old people who could remember the last one that was there, and then that was the property of the Minister, while this belongs to the Church. The people in and around Moreton's Harbour can well appreciate good music, and already there is a regularly formed choir, who on the Sunday referred to, performed their part very well, considering they only had one hasty practise previously. The Hymns chosen were the brightest, and ye tones that the "old folks" knew, and many a one who has not been able to take part in the Church service for years, blended their voices in the praise of God.

Mr. W.S. Rafter undertook both the duties of Minister and organist, having composed a voluntary in honour of the day. The sermons preached were very appropriate to the occasion, the text of one being Psalm, lxxxix, 1 (Prayer book version) "My song shall be always of the Lord."

We learn that the Church is to be repainted, the paint having arrived here by the *Mary Parker*.

1886

[16 January] We are indebted to an esteemed Fogo correspondent for the following interesting Church items: —

"Two handsome carved oak Glastonbury chairs, the joint gift of a...parishioner and a lady in England, were placed in St. Andrew's Church on Christmas Day."

"At a meeting held last Spring, it was decided to erect a building to the memory of the late Rev. C. Meek, to be called the "Meek Memorial School." Work was commenced last Fall, and has been progressing steadily, and what was promised to be a very handsome building is now sheeted in and shingled. Length, fifty feet, breadth, twenty-four feet."

"The members of the Church of England at Seldom-Come-By commenced a fortnight ago, to build a Church. It is already sheeted in. The principal dimensions are: Nave — length, twelve feet; breadth, twelve feet. The workers deserve all praise for the very rapid progress which is being made. The design for this building is by Mr. Southcott."

....

[16 January] Forty years ago on Thursday last, the remains of the late Rev. Mr. Marshall (the first resident Methodist Minister at Twillingate) were laid to rest in the South Side cemetery. Mrs. Marshall, we learn, still survives, and resides at Newcastle on Tyne, England.

....

[13 February] We are sorry to learn that the Rev. J. Hewitt, of Herring Neck, was found in a precarious condition on the ice one day last week. When about half a mile from land he fell through the ice and had some difficulty in getting out, as it broke away in under him. It was snowing at the time which rendered the position more perilous. After some difficulty, he managed to scramble on a bearable part of the ice, remaining there until the weather cleared and he was seen from the shore and soon afterwards rescued, being in a somewhat exhausted condition. The Rev. Gentleman is an indefatigable worker, and in his zeal for the performance of his parochial duties, it may be that he ventured to travel over ice at a time that he would not have risked under other circumstances.

Herring Neck, c.1910

....

[6 March] ...[A] fine building is now in course of erection at Fogo, to serve as a Church of England Sunday School, as a memorial to the late Rev. C. Meek. The building is covered in, roof shingled, gable ends of roof finished and ornamented, and clapboard prepared for second covering, under the superintendence of a carpenter and architect, Mr. Blackler, assisted, hitherto by voluntary labour only, cost of material and carpenter hire being defrayed by subscriptions from Church of England members.

....

[26 June] As a result of the tea meeting and cantata held some time since, in order to furnish the rostrum in the North Side Methodist Church, that object is now nearly accomplished, in a very neat and substantial manner.

The carpets, rods, cushions, &c., were imported from a London firm, and are very tastefully executed, and a handsome pulpit Bible was presented by Wm. Waterman, Esq., Poole. The chairs for [the] inside communion rail – the work of the Messrs. Jacobs, Brothers, South Side – are gems of workmanship in their way, and certainly a great credit to the makers, and a testimony to the genius of our Twillingate young men. The rostrum itself, and the table, are the production of the Nfld. Furniture Factory, St. John's, and are of chaste design

The Committee take this opportunity of conveying to Mr. James McIntyre, Standard Marble Works, St. John's (member of George Street Church), who (whilst being a stranger to Twillingate), made them through John B. Ayre, Esq., the recipients of a very handsome marble Christening Font, executed at his well equipped establishment, and his generous act commands him to the well wishes of any who may require anything in the line of business. The communion service, light branches, &c. and chairs for [the] rostrum, are yet to be supplied, when the whole will be complete, and present a very pleasing appearance. — *Com.*

1887

[19 February] The settlement of Fogo was taken somewhat by surprise on Thursday the tenth inst., when flags suddenly went up here and there, and it was discovered not only that there had been a wedding, but that the esteemed Incumbent of St. Andrew's Church had taken to himself a Wife. The Rev. R. Temple, an old friend of the Bridegroom, had been asked to perform the ceremony, but the uncertainty of his arrival, in the present early part of the season, prevented such preparations as might otherwise have been arranged. However, ice and weather being not too forbidding, the affair was accomplished in due order. Fogo did not like to be prevented from holding a festival, and, determined to do *something* to honour the occasion. So, salutes were fired, and a bonfire kept blazing till late into the night, and we suspect that when the happy pair returned from Barr'd Islands, whither they retired for a few days to enjoy the hospitality of friends equally kind to those at Fogo, there was a hearty reception in true style.

Old St. Andrew's Church, Fogo, Pre-1916

Rev. Mr. Wood had made many friends in the two years he has resided at Fogo, and his Bride has always been beloved and respected by Fogo people, being herself, we believe, a Fogo woman by birth.

This makes the *fourth* clerical wedding solemnized by the present Rural dean of Twillingate. The late Rev. C. Meek was the first; next the Rev. C. Winsor, now of Burin; then the Rev. T.W. Temple, now of St. Pierre, and the Rev. C. Wood of Fogo. We wish all happiness to the newly married pair.

DAVID J. CLARKE

....

[11 June] The Rev. J.F. Geddes arrived here per steamer *Kite* on Thursday last to take charge of the Congregational Church, which has been without a pastor for the last few months. Mr. Geddes has lately been ordained for the work of ministry...We welcome him here, and wish him every success in his mission.

....

[20 August] By a recent arrival from Change Islands we are glad to hear that very successful services were being held by the Methodists there, and that many conversions had been recorded, especially amongst the Sunday school children. The Rev. J. Embree, President of Conference, and T.C. Duder, Esq., had visited the settlement, also Wm. Waterman, Sr. Esq., who was spending a time with Mr. J.C. Waterman, the manager of his branch establishment. The latter visitor occupied the pulpit, and conducted some of the Sunday services recently. We hope the good work will continue and that grand results will be tabulated.

....

[27 August] The first of the annual treats was held on Wednesday last, when the children of the Church of England Sunday Schools united in celebrating theirs with characteristic enthusiasm. The morning opened dull, but as the day advanced it showed promise of brightness and sunshine, which tended to make the weather agreeable and added happiness to the day's recreation. As customary, the children assembled in St. Peter's Church shortly after one o'clock, where a service was held. A short address was given by the Rev. W. Pilot, B.D., Superintendent of Church Day Schools, with whose presence our Church friends were favoured on this occasion, and who contributed much to the enjoyment of the young folk during the evening. On leaving the Church, the children formed in procession and proceeded up Church Hill, down the new road by Messrs. Waterman's and Tobin's, turning the corner near Mrs. Taylor's new shop and back to the Parsonage grounds, where games and amusements of various kinds were participated in until the alarm for tea was given. The children were then admitted to the schoolroom in divisions, and partook bountifully of the good things liberally provided for them. After they had been supplied, the teachers had their tea, and were joined by a number of friends who were present by invitation, among them being Hon. A.F. Goodridge, MHA for this District, who favoured the event with his presence during the day. The children amused themselves on the field until dark, and then returned to their homes evidently delighted with their day's fun. The Rev. R. Temple, R.D., spared no pains to make enjoyment for the children, and a lively interest was also manifested in them by the Rev. A. Pittman and Rev. Theo. R. Nurse. The grounds were beautifully decorated, and here we are required to say that the Committee desire to thank the Captains of English vessels in port for kindly lending their bunting, in assisting to decorate the grounds, in contributing towards the fund, and in their usual jovial style, uniting to make the day's entertainment a success, which it certainly proved. The Committee also beg to thank the friends who helped with their contributions of any kind.

1888

[28 January] A Barracks for the Salvation Army followers is in course of erection on South Island, on ground given for the purpose by Mr. James Whitehorne.

....

[29 September] The Salvation Army Barracks which has been in course of erection for some time on Whitehorne's Hill, South Side, is so far completed as to permit of service being held in it, and the building was opened for that purpose on Sunday last for the first time.

DAVID J. CLARKE

Twillingate Salvation Army Barracks (Centre), c.1950

....

[13 October] Besides the improvements which have been carried out during the Summer, and which are finished so far as to the carpentry work, St. Peter's Church has been presented with two additional stained glass windows for the chancel. These are the gifts of Mr. Owen, merchant of this place, and are placed there in memory of two of his late intimate friends, Rev. Thos. Boone, Incumbent of the Church for many years, and Mr. A.A. Pearce, Clerk of the Peace in former days. The two windows add considerably to the appearance of the chancel, since the opening out of the end on each side.

1889

[14 September] The Methodist Church was filled last evening to listen to the baccalaureate sermon delivered by the Pastor, Rev. W. Jennings, to the senior class of the High School. The sermon was not lengthy, but it was an able and comprehensive one, delivered in a manner to at once convince and charm his hearers. The wholesome advice given to the class of '89, who are just about to begin life in earnest, will, if followed, make their lives a success. Mr. Jennings advised them to put their faith in the Bible, to let their aim in life be high, and to remember that in the bright lexicon of youth there should be no such word as fail.

The Rev. W. Jennings came to this Colony in 1874, and laboured on the Moreton's Harbour, Herring Neck, Little Bay Islands, Lower Island Cove and Greenspond circuits. He married the eldest Daughter of M. Osmond, Esq. In 1887 he resigned his connection with the Newfoundland Conference, receiving a complimentary vote from his brethren. He is now labouring at Grand Haven, Michigan, and is a member of the Michigan Conference of the Methodist Episcopal Church.

Twillingate United (Methodist) Church, 1950s

....

DAVID J. CLARKE

Educational Edits

1880

[5 August] In another column will be found an account of the yearly entertainment of Halifax Mount St. Vincent Academy, taken from the Halifax *Acadian Recorder* of the twelfth ult., the receipt of which, with other papers we beg to acknowledge per *Bessie*. Among other Newfoundlanders we are very pleased to notice the name of Miss Lizzie Tobin figuring conspicuously as one of the successful competitors of that Institution. It will be seen that prizes were awarded her for proficiency in three or four branches. Miss Tobin, who is a native of this town, is a Daughter of one of our leading merchants, J.B. Tobin, Esq., and we are happy to congratulate him on the satisfactory manner in which she is completing her studies. As a native of Twillingate we should feel proud that this young lady has been able to compete with so many others from different cities and towns whose advantages of receiving an early educational training may have been far superior owing to the very defective school system which formerly existed here. We wish the young lady every success in her future studies.

1881

[18 August] The Rev. [William] Pilot, B.D., Superintendent of the Church of England day schools, paid Twillingate a visit last week. He preached in St. Peter's Church on Sunday morning, delivering an eloquent and impressive discourse; in the afternoon he addressed a gathering of Sunday School children and friends, and at 6:30 he conducted service in St. Andrew's Church [Durrell].

    None of the teachers on Twillingate North Island, acting under the Church of England Board, have hitherto had *Grades*, and at the present moment no graded teachers have commenced work since the vacation. But there is a temporary school, kept in the mornings by the clergyman, numbering some fifty-eight children, which was examined by Rev. W. Pilot, the Inspector, during his late visit. The Herring Neck schools were also examined by him on Monday as he passed southward.

Rev. William Pilot (Second from left), and family

....

[18 August] The Rev. G.S. Milligan, M.A., Superintendent of the Methodist day schools, has been in town the past few days. He has inspected three schools namely, North Side, Durrells Arm and Little Harbour. We understand that a pleasing demonstration of advancement was apparent in the respective schools. The status already attained by many of the schools under his jurisdiction is to be attributed largely to the indefatigable interest evinced by Mr. Milligan for the spread of education among the people, and we trust that he may long be spared to discharge the onerous duties which such an important office necessarily involves.

1882

[14 January] The Church of England Board of Examiners, St. John's, have awarded certificates of the THIRD GRADE to Mr. S. Colbourne and Miss Martha Blackler, pupil teachers of this place. Mr. Colbourne was trained at the St. John's Academy, Miss Blackler has been entirely educated at Twillingate, where she is now in charge of North Side Infant School. Mr. Colbourne takes...the school usually maintained by the

Colonial and Continental Church Society, but for the present discontinued by them for want of funds.

1883

[4 August] We are pleased to notice that Miss M. Tobin (Daughter of J.B. Tobin, Esq., of this town), who is attending Mount St. Vincent Academy, Halifax, was awarded a gold medal at the recent examination and distribution of prizes held in connection with that institution...

1884

Twillingate schoolboys, early 1900s

[23 August] The North Side Methodist Day School, which was in charge of the late Mr. W.T. Roberts for several years, and which has been closed since his decease, was reopened on Monday last, by the newly appointed teacher, Mr. J. Hillyard, who arrived here per last

Plover. He is a trained teacher from the St. John's Wesleyan Academy, and holds a first grade certificate. He attained considerable proficiency while attending that institution, as is evident from the fact that at the annual examination a few weeks since he was awarded the scholarship prize, being $25.00.

In consequence of the illness and decease of the late teacher, the day school has been closed for a long time, and as many of the children have not attended other schools, they have been deprived of receiving such secular instruction as was hitherto imparted in this school. Now, however, that it has again been opened, and supplied with so well qualified a teacher, it is to be hoped that parents will make an effort to send their children, so that they may be enabled to avail of the excellent opportunity, which is thus put within their reach, of obtaining valuable knowledge...

1886

[6 February] We understand that the Arm Methodist Day School is being largely attended this Winter, upwards of 100 pupils being present at times. Many of this number, we learn, are adults – young men who are desirous of improving their intellectual endowments, and it is greatly to be commended that there is such a disposition on their parts to raise themselves to a more elevated degree, educationally. The Teacher, Mr. J. Davis, manifests a deep interest in training the scholars, as the proficiency to which they have attained in the past fully indicates.

Durrell Academy School, 1940

....

[26 August] The Rev. G.S. Milligan, M.A., Superintendent of Methodist day schools, arrived from Moreton's Harbour on Monday. The Doctor left St. John's in the *Hercules* when she went to Labrador, and has been as far north as Groswater Bay, visiting and inspecting the schools under his supervision in the intermediate localities between there and this place.

1887

[8 January] In the visitation and inspection part of the Rev. [William] Pilot's report, we are much pleased to note that the Back Harbour Church of England Day School is so highly spoken of by the Superintendent. Miss Blackler is a young lady belonging to the place and, indeed, it is very creditable to her to bear such a reputation as a teacher, as it must be gratifying to the people to know that the school has attained such a degree of proficiency. This is what the last report says:

"*Back Harbour.* Present, thirty-six, out of forty-eight on the register. This is by far the best school in the District – the Teacher is competent and industrious, and the improvement in the scholars was decided and good. In Fourth Reader, reading was clear and expressive – the dictation was generally good, and arithmetic in simple and compound rules satisfactory. Order and discipline excellent.

Back Harbour, 1921

[15 January] We made a mistake last week in according to Miss Blackler the credit given Back Harbour School in the report of 1885, which had only just come to hand, Mr. G.B. Lloyd having, at the time of the Inspector's visit, been in charge of the School, which Miss Blackler, the present teacher, wishes us to inform the public. Nevertheless, we believe we are safe in saying that the Back Harbour School now is in as creditable a condition as when the Inspector last visited it, while the number in attendance is much larger.

....

[12 March] one good example excites others to follow it. The ladies having so actively set to work to clothe the poor of Twillingate, the children are beginning to take an interest in the same good cause. We understand that the girls of Miss Blackler's school, Back Harbour, have...formed themselves into a small "Dorcas Society" of their own, with the object of spending a part of their sewing hours in making clothes for destitute children on North Island, irrespective of denomination...School children have not much means to buy material with which to work, and the ladies have already gathered as much as could be expected in the way of subscriptions. Therefore, Rev. Mr. Temple kindly and properly provided a part of the means for them out of the collection lately made in St. Peter's Church at the Orange Anniversary, which was announced "for charitable purposes and for clothing the poor," adding to it from his own small funds. By this means the work is more widely spread, and the poor little ones will have an additional chance, besides the greater interest given to the school children in their work, when it is done for so beneficial a purpose...and it is gratifying to know that the children of Back Harbour School have this object in view, as well as all who take an interest in them.

....

[27 August] The schooner *Evangeline*, Captain Roberts, returned from St. John's last Sunday afternoon, having nine passengers and a full cargo of freight, principally for J.B. Tobin, Esq., J.P. Among the number were Mr. Tobin and his three Daughters, Misses Lizzie, Minnie and Gertie, the two latter having recently arrived at St. John's from Halifax, where they had been attending college. Miss Minnie Tobin has been away from here about ten years, the last six of which she has spent at Mount St. Vincent, Halifax, where she graduated with honours, finishing her course the last term which ended this Summer.

....

[24 September] On the afternoon of Saturday, the twelfth inst., the pupils of Crow Head Day School, of which Miss Mary Roberts is teacher, passed quite an enjoyable time on the green near the school. A tea was generously given to the children by the worthy Lighthouse Keeper, Mr. S. Roberts, and different kinds of games entered into by the children, who amused themselves heartily until the time came for them to go home. Such an act of kindness on the part of Mr. Roberts will no doubt greatly tend to encourage the scholars to their studies.

Long Point Lighthouse, early 1900s. The people in front are most likely members of the Roberts family

....

DAVID J. CLARKE

Matters of Law

1882

[4 August] At two o'clock on Saturday morning last, Widow Ann Jones of [Herring Neck] was awakened from her slumbers by a noise on her stage near the house, but at first thinking it was her Son she paid little attention to it. Afterwards, her suspicions being aroused, she arose and went outside to ascertain the cause, when she saw two persons who were in the act of stealing fish, &c. On being remonstrated with they made an attack on her person, striking her on the head with a stick and otherwise inflicted injuries of a cowardly nature.

The matter is being investigated by the Police, and we hope that ere long the offenders will be brought before the authorities, where they will receive the severe punishment which their dastardly conduct merits.

1883

[30 March] On Good Friday last, while the occupants were at Church, the dwelling house of Messrs. Waterman & Co., Fogo, was entered by some person or persons, who took the office key from its usual place when the business premises are closed, and proceeded to enter the office and from thence to the shop where considerable pillage was made. The cash drawer was found on the floor minus some few shillings, which had been taken the previous evening after the transfer of the day's receipts to the safe, and several pairs of kid boots and gloves were picked up which had evidently been dropped by the depridators [*sic*] in their hurry to escape. A hole was cut up through the retail store floor, which gave access to the pork, molasses, &c., of which no doubt a considerable quantity was stolen. It is not often we have to chronicle such daring acts of lawlessness, and it is to be hoped that through the efforts of the Police, or otherwise, speedy justice will o'er take the perpetrators. We are glad to see that Messrs. Waterman & Co. offer a reward of *twenty pounds* for such information as shall lead to the conviction of the parties, and as it is a matter which concerns the public generally, we feel that the people of Fogo will do all in their power to bring to punishment those who thus destroy that feeling of safety and confidence which settlers in all localities ought to have in one another.

....

[12 October] Two or three cases of assault have lately been tried before the Stipendiary Magistrate at Fogo, James Fitzgerald, Esq.. One was that of James Morgan, who was charged with an assault upon Cornelius Whiteway of Musgrave Harbour, whose schooner, *Newfoundland*, was then loading with fish for St. John's. In his deposition before the Magistrate, on the eighth inst., the complainant said :—

"I was keeping tally of the fish going on board of my vessel for St. John's, on Mr. Duder's wharf about half past twelve o'clock, when James Morgan, aged thirty-two years, a shareman, came and asked me for money. I refused to give him any as he was drunk. He then left the wharf and went down into the hold of the vessel. I heard him making a noise with the people who were stowing the cargo. I told him to be quiet or I should go for the Policeman. He then began to rear and curse me and got up out of the hold of the vessel and followed me upon the wharf. I told him to go on board, but he came close up to me in a threatening manner, swearing and cursing. I pushed him away and then went up to look for the Police, and to make a complaint. He then followed me and overtook me near Mr. Peter Pickot's [Pickett?] and raised his hands over my head in a violent and threatening manner. I pushed him away again. He then took up a stone about the size of a man's hand and threw it at me with all his might; the stone struck me on the back of my head, just under my hat, and cut and bruised my head. He then came up to me again to assault me. I caught him again, and pushed him away.

The evidence of a witness, Mr. John Hoddinott, fully corroborated the statement made by the complainant, and Morgan was fined $20.00 for his improper conduct.

DAVID J. CLARKE

Lion's Den

Another case before the Magistrate was that of Joseph Waterman against a fisherman named George Hillings of Lion's Den. From the evidence it appeared that [as] Joseph Waterman was going from his work between five and six o'clock, Hillings came out of a shop nearby, making use of very unbecoming language; Waterman told him quietly not to be swearing. Hillings, however, did not regard his kindly advices, but thereupon assaulted him without any provocation, pushing him off the street and striking him a heavy blow on the mouth. Hillings was fined $6.00 and costs.

1886

[11 December] We learn that Mr. [James] Rolls' office, Barr'd Islands, was broken into on the second December, and money to the value of over £80 [was] taken from the desk. The robbers took [the] cash box, and all contents.

1887

[3 September] On the night of twenty-third August, a store that was used by Mr. Joseph Osmond at Tizzard's Harbour as a shop was feloniously entered by some party or parties, and goods to the value of about £12, stolen therefrom. It appeared that the miscreants entered through a window which was found partly up the next day. Mr. Osmond is, unfortunately minus of his right hand, with a large family, and the commitment of an act of this kind on him is the more dastardly. No clue can yet be ascertained of the perpetrator, but it is hoped the guilty one will be brought to justice. To put persons on their guard, we have been asked to mention that among the goods stolen were such articles as follows: twelve yards white eslade serge; some gold and silver colour lockets; pearl necklets; one roll floor canvas, and one roll tapestry carpet.

1891

[9 May] A melancholy occurrence occurred at Tizzard's Harbour on the seventh inst., resulting in the death by hanging of Edward Cantwell. This...event terminates a sad list of casualties occurring in one family, which seldom falls to the lot of the journalist to record. The deceased was the only surviving Son of the late John Cantwell, merchant, well and favourably known. The deceased's Brother, Nicholas, was killed last Fall, at Little Bay Mines, by falling down a shaft 200 feet. Another Brother was accidentally shot on his Father's room, another was drowned, and a forth and fifth died of consumption; of their Sisters, two of whom died of consumption, only one survives. The deceased, no doubt, being unable to bear up under such sad family afflictions, as also the death of his Father and Mother all within a few years, became so despondent that the burden of life was too heavy to bear, and while labouring under temporary insanity, terminated his existence in the cool manner in which the insane so often evince. Since the death of his Brother Nicholas he ceased to take an interest in his affairs; during the Winter he was the prey of melancholy. For some time nothing unusual occurred. The arrival of his Brother's effects by the steamer, from the Mines, evidently added to his former grief. On the day of his death, the deceased took his dinner with his family as usual. Some time after he went into his net loft and selected a suitable cord, prepared the noose, and stepping on his Brother's trunk, affixed it by three turns around a beam, and holding one end of the cord in his hand, stepped into eternity. He was found with his feet resting on the floor, his body reclining, and his neck within the fatal noose...[His] eldest Daughter, about fifteen years old who, missing her Father, [found] him in the loft. The sight produced such cries as soon alarmed the neighbours, who instantly came to her relief, and on going to the loft cut down the lifeless remains.

> **LEGAL CARD.**
> **FRS. BERTEAU,**
> NOTARY PUBLIC,
> And Commissioner of Writs of Attachments and Affidavits,
> will execute Protests, and other ship's papers, Wills, Mortgages, Leases, Bills of Sale, Indentures, Adjustment of Accounts, and other documents on most reasonable terms.
> OFFICE:
> Back Harbor, Twillingate.
> June 16.

A magisterial enquiry was held by the Stipendiary Magistrate, F. Berteau, Esq., at the house of the deceased, on the eighth inst., when, after examining several witnesses, and Dr. Scott who was present, arrived at the conclusion that the deceased completed the act while labouring under temporary insanity.

The grief stricken Widow, and his three young Daughters have the heartfelt sympathy of the neighbours and community.

1892

[10 December] Information having been given to Constable Burt of Fogo that John Hynes of that place sold intoxicating liquors, contrary to the spirit of the Local Option Act, which is in operation, he proceeded to prosecute Hynes, who was summoned before the Stipendiary Magistrate (S. Baird, Esq.), on the charge made against him. The case was to be tried on Tuesday last, but in the meantime the accused acknowledged his guilt, and when he appeared before the court all that the Magistrate had to do, was to pronounce sentence, and for the unlawful selling of spiritous liquors he was fined twenty dollars and costs. The Magistrate warned him, as well as all others, against the illicit sale of liquors, and gave them to understand that he would not deal so leniently with the guilty parties in the event of another breach of the Local Option Act coming before him.

Stories From These Shores

....

DAVID J. CLARKE

Healthcare Happenings

1881

[2 December] There have been several cases of measles in this community [Twillingate] of late; not, however, of a very bad type. Through skilful medical treatment and proper care and attention on the part of those interested, all have convalesced, or are in a fair way for doing so, and we are not aware that in any one instance a case has proved fatal.

Diphtheria still prevails at Herring Neck, and some cases of measles are also reported there. We are sorry to know that Mr. T. Connor, teacher of the Church of England day school, has lost his only Son from the effects of both...

1883

[27 July] By reference to the professional card of Dr. Scott...it will be seen that he has recently removed from his former residence to his new surgery, a little to the west of the town hall. Dr. Scott has been practising his profession in this community for upwards of a year, with much acceptance. He has now succeeded in completing a surgery, which he has neatly fitted up for the dispensing of medicine, &c., which will no doubt prove of great benefit to him and his patients.

CARD!

THADDEUS SCOTT, M.D.
(Harvard University, 1860, U.S.)
Member of the College of Physicians and Surgeons New Brunswick.

TWILLINGATE, Notre Dame Bay.

Office and residence at Mr. Titus Manuel's, nearly opposite the Temperance Hall.
Office hours from 8.30 to 9.30 A.M. And from 1 to 2.30 P.M.
A ledger will be open for yearly patients.

[26 October] On the arrival of the *Plover* on Thursday last, Mrs. Embree left home in carriage to meet the Rev. Mr. Embree, who was returning from St. John's (whither he had been for the purpose of attending a committee meeting in connection with the Methodist Church). During the absence of Mrs. Embree, the servant went to the back yard for a few moments, leaving the children alone. In the meantime, a little girl about four years old, approached the stove and held her pinafore to the fire. The fringe quickly caught and almost instantly the little creature was enveloped in flames. The servant was soon on the spot, but was powerless to render any assistance towards suppressing the blaze. Fortunately, however, the Rev. Mr. Duffill was in the study at the time, and hearing the screeches from the little one, was speedily to the rescue, and with some difficulty succeeded in extinguishing the fire. If it had not been for his timely assistance, fatal consequences would, no doubt, have attended the painful circumstances. As it is, the little one was much disfigured, the hands and head being a good deal burnt. Dr. Stafford, who resides nearby, was promptly in and applied the necessary remedies for the relief of the unfortunate little sufferer. She is still in a painful condition, but it is hoped that skilful care and attention will restore her to soundness in a few weeks.

We tender to Mr. And Mrs. Embree our deepest sympathy in this their hour of domestic affliction.

....

[2 November] M.K. Langill, Dentist, is now on a professional visit to Twillingate, and may be consulted for two weeks at Mr. Titus Manuel's (near the Town Hall).

....

[9 November] Dr. M.K. Langill, Dentist, as announced in last paper, is here on a professional visit and can be consulted at Mr. Titus Manuel's. His stay is limited to a few days only and we would advise all who may require his professional services to give him a call at once. This is a first rate opportunity for all who may be suffering from bad teeth to have them removed and replaced by new ones at a very moderate cost. Mr. L. is highly recommended and we believe that satisfaction will be given to all who will favour him with their patronage. We understand that after leaving here he intends visiting Bonavista and Trinity.

Titus Manuel

1885

[6 June] A very painful accident occurred at Jenkins' Cove [Durrell] on Sunday last. A young girl (Daughter of Mr. Geo. Slade of the above place) was carrying her little Sister of two years over a flake near their dwelling house, when the former accidentally tripped and both fell violently on the sticks on which they were walking. The eldest girl was not much hurt, but the poor little one was seriously injured. The front part of her lower jaw was broken, one part overlapping the other, and her face somewhat contused. Dr. Stafford was promptly in attendance and set this jaw, and the little one, we are glad to know, is doing as well as can be expected.

....

[31 December] We are sorry to hear that Mr. Henry Shave, an employee in the firm of Messrs. W. Waterman & Co., met with a severe accident on Tuesday morning. He was employed on board the English schooner *Golden Fleece*, loading with fish, when he slipped off the planks and fell down the hold of the vessel, a distance of about twenty feet, fracturing a couple of the ribs of his right side. Dr. Stafford was quickly in attendance through whose skilful treatment we are glad to learn the patient is doing well.

1886

[9 January] We understand that a very critical surgical operation was performed by Dr. Stafford on Saturday, the second inst. Wm. Clarke, Son of Mr. Richard Clarke, Farmer's Arm [Durrell], had been suffering from an abscess or a gathering of matter within [the] outer layer of skull. The symptoms were of a very severe character, and their being no other chance of saving his life, the Doctor decided on perforating or boring the skull, which critical operation was done on the date above mentioned. The patient has been doing well ever since, and we are glad to learn that there are now good hopes of his ultimate recovery.

NOTICE.

To the Inhabitants of Twillingate, Herring Neck, and Adjacent Settlements.

HAVING now come amongst you I am prepared to receive all parties who are desirous of becoming annual patients and shall be pleased to place their names on my books.

My residence is the House recently occupied by JOHN DUDER Esq., on the South Side of Twillingate.

SURGERY HOURS.—9.30 to 12 A.M., and 7 to 8.30 P.M.

F. STAFFORD, M.D.C.M.

Tilwlingate, Dec. 15th, 1882.

....

[16 January] ...On Thursday, Dec. twenty-fourth, Mr. Nathaniel LeDrew of Change Islands, while out in a punt gunning, and drawing a loaded gun towards him, by the muzzle, accidentally struck the hammer against the side of the punt, discharging it through the middle of his hand, carrying away half the metacarpal bone of the middle finger, and nearly all of the muscles and skin on the back of the hand. It is thought the hand will probably be saved.

On Wednesday, Dec. thirtieth, while out at Gabby's Island, duck killing, John Head of Lock's Cove, near Fogo, accidentally burst his gun, blowing away part of the thumb of the left hand. He was brought to Fogo where his thumb was removed. The wounds are healing rapidly, and he is expected to be seen soon at his post of duck and fish killing – minus the thumb.

....

[3 April] Some time ago a little boy named Arthur Ashbourne, aged twelve years, Son of Mr. Thomas Ashbourne, Farmer's Arm, was suffering from a crippled leg. The cause at first appeared to be unknown, but on examination by Dr. Stafford, he discovered that the hip was out of the cup, and that the little fellow would have to undergo the painful operation of having it set, which was afterwards successfully performed by the Doctor. The boy bore the operation bravely, and we are pleased to learn that he has since recovered and is as nimble as ever he was.

Arthur Ashbourne in later life

Stories From These Shores

1887

[26 February] Elijah Whitt was coming over Indian Hill, Friday's Bay, on Tuesday, with a load of wood when the slide capsized, and he sustained serious injuries. A stick ran into his thigh causing a dangerous wound which we understand has been attended to by Dr. Scott, whose medical aid was sought soon after the accident happened.

     Joseph Chinn, of Friday's Bay, also met with a bad accident on the day following, we are told. He had been engaged for some time cutting sticks for the Shoal Tickle work, and while in the act of paring one, the axe slipped, and cut his toes, separating one, we learn, entirely.

....

[4 June] We are sorry to learn that a serious accident occurred at Tizzard's Harbour on the twenty-fourth of May, which happened something like this: Two young men, Sons of James and Andrew Locke, while amusing themselves with a loaded gun, suddenly discharged the same, the entire charge passing through the right hand of Kenneth, aged thirteen years, Son of Mr. Andrew Locke, carrying away most of his right hand, and injuring the remainder to such an extent that amputation had to be immediately performed by Dr. Stafford. We learn that the poor little fellow is now progressing favourably.

....

[30 July] The *Tibbie* came here from Fogo on Tuesday night, bringing a quantity of merchandise for the owner's branch trade at this place. While lowering a puncheon of molasses over her side into a boat the next morning, a sudden jerk caused an iron block to break off which fell from a height of fourteen or fifteen feet, striking Mr. Mayne on the back of the head, and leaving him almost insensible for a time. The cap fortunately warded off the blow somewhat, but not withstanding the head was not much bruised, and cut to the extent of a couple of inches. Dr. Scott was promptly in attendance and administered the necessary applications, and we are glad to learn that at present no serious consequences need be despaired of.

DAVID J. CLARKE

1888

[24 March] We are sorry to learn that while on the ice last Saturday, a sad accident befell George Young, a married man, and Son of Mr. George Young of South Island, Twillingate. While firing at a seal the gun [he was using] burst...injuring his left hand to a considerable extent, fracturing nearly the whole of the fingers and otherwise bruising the parts. Dr. Stafford was soon in attendance, and not wishing to sacrifice the entire hand, decided on saving part of the thumb, to together with the whole of the little finger. But on Monday afternoon symptoms of mortification were setting in, and in order to save his life the Dr. decided on amputation of the arm above the wrist, since which time he has been progressing very favourably, and hopes are entertained of his ultimate recovery...

1890

Herring Neck, 1950s

[22 February] On January twenty-fourth, Jacob Warford of Herring Neck, poorly clothed and considerably worse fed, while in one of the

Arms procuring wood, had one of his feet severely frozen. Nevertheless, he managed to walk home where he remained for a week when, symptoms of mortification setting in, he was brought to Twillingate and placed under the care of Dr. Stafford. The Doctor, after administering chloroform, amputated about half of the foot. The patient, owing to the enfeebled condition, nearly succumbed to the operation, however, under careful management the poor fellow rallied, and since then had been progressing very favourably. In about two weeks more he will no doubt be able to return to his family at Herring Neck. There were present at the operation the Rev. R. Temple, Mr. Josiah Colbourne, and Mr. Thomas Ashbourne. This adds another to the list of skilful operations performed by the Doctor since his residence amongst us.

....

[10 May] We are sorry to report that two accidents have lately occurred to members of our community. The first one happened about three weeks ago. Philip Fifield (Son of Mr. James Fifield of North Side), living with Mr. Hicks of Durrell's Arm, and lately employed at Loon Bay, on passing a bulk of lumber, caused by the loosening of some of the board, which, on falling, caught the young man's right leg, fracturing one of the lower bones, and he was brought to Twillingate.

The second one occurred only a few days since, Mr. John Roberts of Wild Cove, on removing an oar from the upper part of his stage, carelessly walked backwards, and in doing so walked over the edge of the stage, falling a distance of about ten feet. He was removed to his house, and on the Doctor visiting him found he had received a severe dislocation of his right shoulder, together with other internal injuries. We are glad to learn that up to the present, under the skilful treatment of Dr. Stafford, both of the above named injured persons are doing as well as can be expected.

1891

[7 February] We are glad to note the return to [Twillingate] of Dr. Scott, who has been on a protracted visit to Fortune Harbour (We understand at the insistence of the Government), where diphtheria has been prevalent. We are glad to hear that the Doctor's efforts have been very successful, and that the dread disease [has] been stamped out, there being no case when he left. The people speak highly of the services rendered, and we learn that every attention and kindness was shown to the professional gentleman whilst in that important settlement.

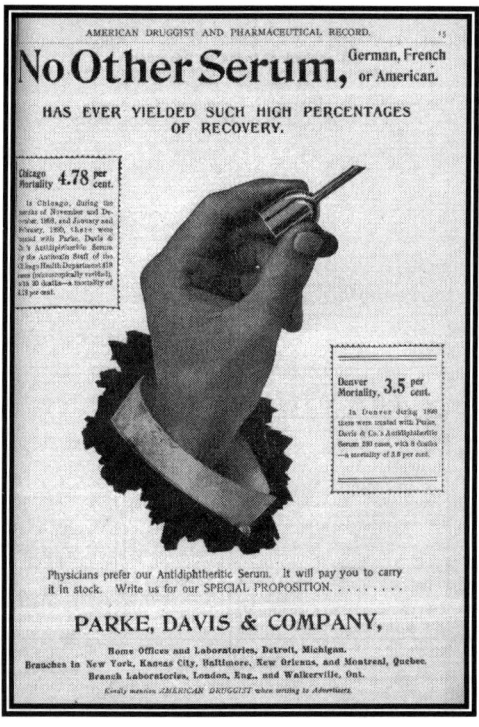

Anti-Diphtheria ad, 1900

From every hand in our town we hear golden opinions of Dr. Scott's success in this disease (which alas seems in some cases to be so fatal), the thorough manner in which he enters into the details of treatment being especially commented upon by the families, who have been fortunate to have his services. We hope we shall secure his services and valuable experience for many years to come.

[11 April] Last Monday afternoon a young man named Albert Harris, aged nineteen years, Son of Mr. Thomas Harris, of Black Island, on firing at a target, burst his gun immediately under the palm of his left hand, carrying away nearly the entire hand. The following morning he was conveyed by boat to Sansom's Island, and thence to catamaran to Twillingate, coming by way of Cottle's Island, Carter's Cove and Trump Island Necks to Gillard's Cove, arriving at Twillingate by nine o'clock in the evening. The poor fellow was immediately conveyed to Mr. James Boyd's of North Side, and was a few minutes afterwards seen by Dr. Stafford, who on careful examination decided not to operate until the next morning. Wednesday morning Dr. Stafford, assisted by Revs. Temple and Kelly, and the Relieving Officer, Josiah Colbourne, Esq., amputated the remainder of the hand to about three inches above the wrist joint. Last reports state that the young man is progressing very favourably.

1892

[14 May] During the past week several cases of diphtheria have appeared in our midst, three resulting fatally...Among the number is one whose name only a short time since appeared in this paper as taking part in a concert for the purpose of a Sunday School library; Ellen May Temple, youngest Daughter of the Rev. R. Temple, who died on Thursday morning, just completing her eighth birthday. She was a very intelligent little girl whose winsome manner made her beloved by all who knew her. The funeral took place yesterday, and was attended by a large concourse of sympathetic friends. Today her little grave is beautified with the presence of many tokens of sympathy with the bereaved family in the shape of tastefully arranged floral designs. To those bereft of their loved ones we tender our deepest sympathy.

DAVID J. CLARKE

Fire!

1881

[10 December] Crow Head school house, the property of the Church of England Board of Education of this District, had a narrow escape from destruction on Monday last. The gale of Friday had probably shaken the stove pipes, which were somewhat worn, and at the dinner hour the roof was found to be on fire. An alarm having been raised, the men soon reached the building with ladders, buckets, hatchets, &c., and their promptitude saved the building. Much credit is due to the Crow Head people, not only for their alertness and ready aid, but for the manner in which on the next day they repaired all damages to the roof, and cleaned the building, so as to enable the usual Tuesday evening service to be held. A crowded congregation proved the estimation in which these fishermen hold their school house, living as they do at so considerable a distance from the Church.

Crow Head, 1920s

1885

Stories From These Shores

[13 June] We regret to learn that the premises of Mr. Thomas Dally, Herring Neck, were destroyed by fire on Thursday night. It appears that the servant girl went into the stage with a lighted candle, and while there she snuffed it with her fingers, throwing the contents on the floor. She soon afterwards left the place, and as the floor must have been oily, a spark from the candle quickly ignited, and the building was in flames. The fire extended to the store close by, and from that to the dwelling, some two or three hundred yards distant, by reason we learn, of a quantity of gunpowder that was in the store. Every exertion to arrest the flames proved unavailing, and in a little time everything was destroyed. The loss is a very severe one for Mr. Dally, having been deprived of his fishery gear, as well as household valuables, which for a lifetime he has been accumulating. We deeply sympathize with him in his great loss.

....

[20 June] Just as we were going to press last week we received information that Mr. John Dally of Herring Neck had all his property – dwelling house, store, and stage – destroyed by fire. We are glad to know that it was not so disastrous as then reported – the stage and dwelling house were not consumed.

1887

[5 March] The dwelling house of Mr. Wm. Fox, Back Harbour, narrowly escaped being burnt down on Thursday night. About twelve o'clock his Wife woke, and thinking she smelled smoke, aroused her Husband, who on making search, found the kitchen in flames of smoke. It was so bad that he could not pass through where the water was, but soon procured some from a neighbour, and with assistance managed to arrest the fire. A large hole was burnt in the floor which fortunately was about the only damage done, but if a few minutes more had interfered before being discovered, the whole building would have been destroyed.

....

[5 March] On Friday morning last, a very unfortunate occurrence took place at Wild Cove, a dwelling house belonging to Mr. Benjamin Roberts, with nearly all its contents, including a little money, having been destroyed by fire. It broke out upstairs about eight o'clock, and before being discovered, had spread so rapidly that it was impossible to extinguish the blaze, and in a quick time the dwelling was in ruins. The origin of the fire is unknown, but it is supposed that a little boy, five or six years old, was playing with matches and set fire to some clothes. The loss sustained by Mr. Roberts is very heavy, and assistance in any shape we doubt not would be most gratefully received. We know that there are many calls on the public, but it is seldom that an event like this happens, and when it does it deserves sympathy and support, which we trust will be extended in this case.

Wild Cove, Twillingate, 1960s

....

[30 July] Two or three little children were playing in a store belonging to Mr. Joseph Moores on Tuesday morning last, where there [were] a lot of shavings, which they set fire to, and had it not been for the timely assistance rendered, the building would have been totally destroyed. As it was, the store was a good deal damaged and a net partly destroyed.

[26 November] A small dwelling house belonging to John Froude, Hart's Cove, was destroyed by fire on the night of Tuesday last. It occurred about eleven o'clock and was caused by defective funnelling. The family were very poor, but whatever few things were in the house were all lost. The poor man has been quite a long time sick, and was incapacitated when the fire took place.

Hart's Cove, Durrell, c.1940

1889

[6 July] The roof of Mrs. Hannah Colbourne's house, near the chimney, was discovered to be on fire about two o'clock, Thursday afternoon, and had it not been for the timely assistance rendered and energetic efforts of neighbours who were prompt in attendance, the house would have burnt down in a very short time. As it was, considerable damage was done, as part of the roof had to be cut away to arrest the fire which had made good headway, and was smouldering underneath the shingles. The rooms being flooded with water as a consequence many articles were spoiled, which, altogether, is a serious misfortune for a Widow to meet with. Mrs. Colbourne is a most industrious person, and having met with this misfortune, we think that she is entitled to a little practical sympathy from the public, which we would take the liberty of pleading for on her behalf.

Stories From These Shores

Miscellany

1880

[1 July] We are requested to announce that a meeting of the Twillingate Cricket Club will be held in Mr. Oakley's Boot Store on Saturday evening at eight o'clock. A full attendance is requested, and any persons wishing to join will have an opportunity of so doing.

....

[29 July] We are very pleased to notice the various steps taken by our local authorities towards the improvement of our town, and the convenience of pedestrians, especially of the gentler sex, who can now promenade thro' the streets without fear of any four-footed obstructions, and with the happy thought that, however long their trains, there is now no fear of spoliation by dust or dirt.

We should like to suggest that, not only should the pigs be kept *in*, but also kept *back*, for the effluvia arising from these styes which border on the public road, are very unpleasant to the olfactory nerves.

Is this within the power of any of the town authorities? If so, we should certainly like to see some measures adopted for the removal of such abominable nuisances.

....

SUF Hall, Twillingate, 1950

[7 October] We understand that the Worthy Grand Master of the Society of United Fishermen, Rev. W. Pilot, B.D., addressed a very fair attendance of the brethren of the Twillingate Lodge No. 12, on Monday evening last, upon the rise and progress of the order since its establishment in 1873. Looking at this Order which "has for its object the welfare of fishermen, the inculcation of temperance and morality, the preservation of peace and harmony, obedience to the laws and legally constituted authorities, and the development of the fisheries," and which is also a Mutual Benefit Society, we cannot but regard it as one worthy [of] the attention of the fishermen of the Country. That it has already done, and is still doing a vast amount of good, we know upon the testimony of many associated within its ranks, and we wish not only the order generally, but the Twillingate and neighbouring Lodges prosperity and progress.

1881

[13 October] Within the past eight or ten days a number of men have been employed in mining on Cann Island. Several blasts have been made, and indications of copper ore are apparent. We understand that a good "find" has also been discovered there recently.

....

[2 December] Henry Brown, a servant to Reuben Blackmore, while in the Bay a few days since, with other of the boat's crew, after fire-wood, met with an accident by inflicting a large wound in his right arm. He rested his axe down a short distance from where his "turn" was, and when starting the hauling rope gave way, and [he] fell backwards, his elbow striking the sharp implement, thereby sustaining the injury. He returned in Mr. Blackmore's craft yesterday, which brought a full load of wood-fuel.

A young man named William Poole, of Little Harbour, while cutting timbers for a boat near Rocky Pond, Friday's Bay, on Wednesday last, accidentally cut his foot across the instep, which had a like to prove serious. He was taken to his home yesterday morning.

1883

[27 April] Messrs. G. Hodder and J. Templeton recently made some examinations of a vein of ore at Moreton's Harbour, for which they have a license, and as the resultoftheir labour were rewarded with some rich specimens of lead and silver, and well as indications of a large quantity of it in that vicinity. We have no doubt but this will prove a valuable *"find"* for the prospectors.

Moreton's Harbour, 1960s

....

[30 June] During the past week the property, &c., of the post office have been removed from the former building to that of Mr. Josiah Colbourne's. Mr. A. J. Pearce, the former Post Master having resigned last Spring, Mr. Colbourne was appointed to the office, which he now occupies for the first time. It is needless to say that Mr. Pearce proved himself an efficient officer in all matters connected with that important post, and it is a matter of regret that one so long in the service and consequently familiar with matters generally, which is an essential point in...successfully filling...any office, was not indeed to retain the position. We have no doubt, however, that every effort will be made by our recently appointed Post Master for the purpose of giving general satisfaction.

1884

[13 September] ...On Monday last, in company with George Hodder, Esq., Manager of the [antimony] mine, I paid a visit to Moreton's Harbour. On the side of the road leading to Moreton's Harbour a shaft has been sunk to the distance of thirty feet, but which is now stopped, for what reason I do not say, but it is best known to the proprietors themselves. The last ore taken from the bottom of the shaft is of a good quality, and will pay well if worked. About 400 yards to the west of this, on the same lode, a shaft is being sunk, its greatest depth being about twelve feet. The lode in the bottom of this shaft will average six inches in width. The ore is of a good quality and contains a small percentage of lead and silver. Between these two shafts, the surface having been removed, show the lode to be eighteen inches in width. This hole from highwater mark, can be traced to the distance of half a mile, running a due course east and west, which proves it to be the regular lode. All regular lodes containing rich minerals, viz, gold, silver, copper, lead, &c., run east and west. Any branches diverging from this line are called shoots, cross leads and fissure veins, which in some cases are very rich, but do not run to any depth. This mine can be worked with a very small expense, as the ground is chalky and of the nature of limestone, and under the management of a skilful Foreman would proved a success to the proprietors. This lode, as well as others that have been named, diverge a few feet from the main lode, but will eventually resume its own course again, and in all probability the ore will be of a richer and better quality. A mine shaft sunk on the centre of the property, and a tramway built of one quarter of a mile, hundreds of tons of ore could be shipped daily if required. This property, if managed properly and worked with prudence and economy, will prove a mine of wealth. I have every confidence in the gentleman who is Manager at present of this fine property, and with skilful men at his command, would work it to the best advantage possible...RENFREW.

Stories From These Shores

....

[8 November] We understand from good authority that T.J. Every of Twillingate has opened up a gold mine in Bay Verde, White Bay. He has at present five men employed, and will employ from ten to twelve during the Winter months. We believe the property is a very valuable one, far superior to anything seen in this Country. He has procured the service of a Nova Scotia gold miner, to take charge of the mine, who understands mining in all its different branches. This same gentleman, T.J. Every, has shares in a number of mines in White Bay and other places, some of which have shown up very valuable deposits of copper and gold bearing quartz, which have been proved by Prof. Holloway. We heartily wish that further success may follow — *Evening Mercury*.

1886

[24 July] The steamer *Plover* called here on Sunday afternoon for mail and passengers on her way south. Mrs. [Kate] Putzki, Daughter of Wm. Stirling, Esq., M.D., of this town, who was married at Chicago, Il., within the last few months (whose Husband is [an] artist of Altwasser, in Schlesien, Germany), and who has been here on a visit to her friends, took passage by the *Plover* for St. John's *en route* for the city of Chicago. The Sun unites with her many friends and acquaintances in wishing this fair Daughter of dear old Terra Nova a safe and pleasant journey to the land of her adoption, and trust that length of years and prosperity may be the portion of the newly married couple.

....

[26 August] We have lately seen specimens of paints manufactured by Mr. T. Every which appear to be a very good kind. The earthy ingredient which it contains was discovered by him some time ago, and seems to combine excellently with the other mixtures used in its manufacture. The paint made by Mr. Every has been tested and proves itself so far to be all that it is recommended for the exterior of vessels or dwelling houses. The residence occupied by himself was painted with his own manufactured article in the first part of the Summer, and it seems to endure the weather first rate. It cannot be recommended for indoor work, as the raw material requires a refining process that the inventor has not the means of procuring at present, but we hope that the invention may prove successful, and that he will be warranted in making the outlay necessary to procure all the outfit required. However, we are told that the article now made is excellent for the bottoms of schooners and all outdoor works, and can be put in the market cheaper than any other. Testimonials of its worth could be given by different persons who have used it. That subjoined from Dr. Scott is given here by request.

Twillingate, August 26th, 1886
This is to certify that I have used paint procured from Thomas J. Avery [Every] of this place. One kind on the bottom of my boat in place of copper paint, and find it to wear better than any in use by me formerly; the other kind I used for [the] top sides, and find it to mix and wear well.

Thaddeus Scott, M.D.

1887

[16 July] A deed worthy of note was accomplished the past week by an old sire of the soil. Mr. Abraham Dean, aged eighty-four years, left Seldom-Come-By on Wednesday, in a small, cross-handed paddle boat, and rowed to Twillingate, a distance of some thirty miles or more. He landed at Little Harbour, and walk[ed] nearly four miles across the island, reaching here Friday morning. The task performed by this old resident, shows that the strength and energy of former years have not entirely forsaken him, but that the measure still retained would be to shame many of the younger race in the accomplishment of such a task as that done by this old man.

1888

[14 January] We are requested to say that on Tuesday evening next, seventeenth inst., in the [Twillingate] Town Hall, the scenery of "Ten Night in the Bar-room," "Rip Van Winkle," and other views (comic) will be shown by an Electro Radiant Magic Lantern. Doors open at seven o'clock. Exhibition to commence at 7:30. Admission ten cents, Nfld currency.

The stage is set, for a theatrical at Twillingate, 1934

....

[25 February] Within the past fortnight three stores belonging to F. Berteau, Esq., Stipendiary Magistrate, were successfully launched from his late residence, Back Harbour, to the premises he now occupies in Front Harbour. The undertaking was superintended by Mr. James Fifield. The hauling of the stores engaged part of two days, and on each occasion large numbers of men, from various parts of the place, freely gave their services to assist the work, thereby evidencing a kindly spirit towards our esteemed Magistrate.

As Mr. Berteau was prevented, through indisposition, from personally thanking all the men who kindly assisted in the launches, he desires through the columns of the Sun to publicly thank everyone who so willingly gave their valuable assistance to remove his stores.

....

[27 October] Among the passengers per *Conscript* who embarked here this morning was Miss G. Stirling, youngest Daughter of Wm. Stirling, Esq., M.D., who goes to St. John's *en route* for Italy. This young lady is endowed by nature with no ordinary musical talent, and being desirous of excelling in the art of music, she has decided to take a thorough course of studies from first class Italian professionals, who are renowned all the world over for their proficiency in the musical art. Miss S. has many amiable qualities, and by her genial disposition is a general favourite, and will be greatly missed in the community, especially by many of the poor, to whom it was her delight to administer deeds of kindness. We wish our young friend a safe and speedy journey across the Atlantic, and every success in the future. Miss Rose Stirling accompanied her Sister as far as St. John's.

Georgina Stirling illustration, from the Twillingate Sun

1889

[10 August] A meeting of commissioners for Shoal Tickle [Twillingate] was held in the Court House on Wednesday morning last, when it was decided that the work connected therewith should commence at once. It was agreed to employ twenty or twenty-three men, who were to be selected by the mercantile firms. This is conducting public affairs on "sound commercial principles." We cannot see why a larger number of men should not be employed, and an opportunity given to others to earn a little for their families, considering the fishery has been so poor, and by this means the work would be got through much sooner. Machinery for deepening the Tickle is expected here in a few days. This part of the work will be superintended by Mr. S. Peach, who is a first rate man for the business.

....

[17 August] The machinery for dredging Shoal Tickle arrived here per *Flamingo* on Monday evening. It has been put together and is now in working order. Rocks at the entrance of the Tickle are being removed by dynamite and other means.

Shoal Tickle, Twillingate, early 1900s

1890

[26 April] A club has lately been organized here [Change Islands], known as "The Change Islands Labourers' Secretary." Several important matters have been brought up for discussion, the following are some of the resolutions passed:

DAVID J. CLARKE

1st: That no lobsters shall be sold for less than $2.00 cash per hundred.

2nd: That all labour shall be paid in cash, strictly in advance.

3rd: That no man shall work on the roads, or elsewhere, for less than $1.00 per day.

4th: That the merchants, instead of issuing goods on credit, shall be compelled to give cash to their dealers, payable at the end of the voyage, with three percent interest.

1892

[9 January] During the year 1891 over 12,000 letters were posted in the Twillingate post office, more than 500 of them being registered. This number does not include those that go there from the [Durrell's] Arm way office, and besides those hundreds of others [that] pass through the office.

9
"High Spirits" ~ Alcohol and Temperance

Up until the early nineteenth century alcohol was a (generally) accepted part of life for Newfoundland fishers – it was common practise for merchant firms to serve grog or rum to their employees, even young boys. At the same time, many Newfoundlanders, who had little ready access to alcohol, made their own home brewed beer and produced wine from the native berries. According to the Encyclopedia of Newfoundland & Labrador, as early as 1726 the Colony's capital, St. John's, had some forty-six licensed taverns, that number growing to eighty in 1775 (In that year St. John's was home to only 1,500 residents). The presence of a drinking culture led to numerous reports of violence, and in the 1840s the use of alcohol ran up against a powerful anti-drinking, or temperance, movement, which had accompanied a religious revival in Western nations such as Britain and the United States.

As of 1843 Newfoundland's temperance movement had grown to some 10,000 members, with groups like the Sons of Temperance active by the 1850s. In the 1880s temperance was a major factor in Newfoundland party politics, and on 18 April, 1887 a resolution to introduce total a prohibition on alcohol sales was defeated in the House of Assembly by a single vote (that of the Speaker).

We observe that an amended Intoxicating Liquor Bill, introduced into the House of Assembly by the Hon. J.S. Winter, was lost in committee on the fifth ult. This is to be regretted as the adoption of the Bill would have given any town, harbour or settlement in either of the Districts in the Colony, the privilege of prohibiting the sale of intoxicating liquors, providing one-fifth of the resident electors in any one place were to object to it. It is the more to be regretted because it is the poorer classes of our people that mostly have to suffer from the baneful consequences arising from the evils of intemperance in many communities. When measures are introduced calculated to improve the tone of society one would think that they would receive the warm support of every Hon. Representative, and there may be few others likely to prove more conducive to this end than these having for their object the promulgation of total abstinence principles.

James Spearman Winter

We are therefore sorry that so many Hon. Members were unfavourable to the Bill brought in by the learned member, Mr. Winter, the passage of which, we believe, would have been looked upon most favourably by the great majority of our people. If we remember rightly, petitions were sent from this and other Districts last year praying that a measure something similar to the one embodied in Mr. Winter's Bill might be put into operation, but owing to the late stage of proceedings when the matter came up for consideration, it had to remain over until this session, when it was brought before the House at an early date, with unsatisfactory results.

The following are the names of those who voted for and against the measure: — For the Bill — Hon'bles, Receiver General, Mr. Rorke,

J.S. Winter, the Speaker, the C.B. Of Works, Messrs. Watson, MacKay, the Financial Secretary, and Messrs. Saint, Rice and Penney. Against the Bill — Hon. Surveyor General, Hon. Mr. Shea, Messrs. Collins, Dwyer, Norman, Little, McLoughlan, Kent, Scott, Nowlan, Parsons, O'Mara and Goodridge.[1]

....

During the last session of the Legislature a Bill was brought in by the Hon. J.S. Winter to amend the law relating to the sale of intoxicating spirits, which was rejected by a small majority. Had the Bill been adopted it would have given "any town, harbour, or settlement in either of the Districts of the Colony," the privilege of prohibiting the sale of intoxicating liquors by a vote of one-fifth of the electors in any one locality in a District. By this means we imagine that it would not be a very difficult task to have this great evil banished from many (if not from all) of the settlements of our Colony, as we are of opinion that there is scarcely any locality, especially in the northern Districts, but where a required majority would be found to bring about such a satisfactory condition of things. The aim of the introduction of the Bill in this particular having been defeated, as already stated, numerous petitions, we understand, will be sent to the Legislature from the various Districts during its next sitting praying for the adoption of some such measure for prohibiting the sale of spirits as was embodied in the Bill rejected last term. It is not too much to expect that every Hon. Member who may be animated with ambitions of patriotism will give their hearty support to these petitions; for one would suppose that all would be unanimous in making laws that might save the Country, or any portion of it, from the degradation and blight into which the bane of intemperance is calculated to emerge it. Even many who may be inclined to favour the use of alcoholic stimulants in moderation would (and have done so by appending their signatures to petitions for the same) raise their voice to suppress a vice that has resulted in so much wretchedness in many families in the past.

It is to be desired that the time may come, ere many years elapse, when not only will a law be enacted to prohibit its sale (by vote) in any one particular section of a District, but when we shall hear of total prohibition being demanded all over the land, and when the laws of the Colony will not tolerate the importation of ardent spirits, except for medicinal uses, for which they might be more in place than if used by men to destroy health, and entail all the misfortunes that [are] possible to befall human beings. But let us hope, however, that for the present the prayers of petitioners, on behalf of a measure such as that referred to will receive the most favourable consideration of the House the present term.[2]

....

Eventually, the "local option," mentioned in the piece above, was introduced, and in 1883 Twillingate residents went to the polls to decide whether or not to ban alcohol sales in the community. While Twillingate had become a bastion of the anti-alcohol movement – a local Sons of Temperance branch, the North Star Division, had been founded in 1864 – opinion was not unanimous.

Sir, — Prohibition, a question that will be tried in a few days at the polls in this "Twillingate of ours," is not sufficiently understood by the majority of the people of the District, and knowing one or two facts relating to the question, I take the liberty of bringing them forward, and I feel certain there are many who, knowing something of this matter, and the "island we live in," will agree with me.

1st Financially: — The revenue of this Colony is derived from duties levied on nearly everything imported, and strange to say, principally on all *staple* articles that we cannot do without, and *cannot possibly produce* in any quantity to ameliorate our wants. Take, for instance, flour. We import over 300,000 barrels per annum, and on this great article of consumption there is levied a tax of twenty-four cents per barrel; pork, of which we consume a great quantity, is dutiable to the extent of 5/9 per barrel; sugar, 11/6 to 17/6 per cwt, according to quality; molasses, tea, tobacco, &c., &c., to a certain extent, and on some articles the duty is more than the first cost.

Now, the revenue of the Colony is only 1,000,000 dols. per annum, and of this nice sum, spirits alone pay 250,000 dols., or one quarter of the revenue! Now, my dear Prohibitionists, don't lift your *pious* eyes to Heaven, and cry Oh! Horror! Don't, I say, for there is no necessity. It is not by the quantity drank, but, by the exorbitant duty of four times its value levied on this article of import that brings in such a sum (and a necessary help) to the revenue.

The former Temperance Hall, Twillingate, 1971

Now, if the sale, and then the importation, of spirits, is prohibited, how is this great deficit in the revenue to be paid? Are our merchants and then, of course, our hard-taxed and hard worked fishermen to pay up this quarter of the revenue when every penny of it is wanted for the support of the Country, and the existing railway and dock subsidies? No, certainly not, and it would be unfair to say so.

The Prohibitionists will say yes! And how? Why, it is easily answered. The fisherman, having more money to spend, not spending any on liquor, will have more to lay out to te merchants. Will he – the fisherman – that is the question.

Now, I know from some experience in the general business of the Country – which is a credit business – that the fisherman won't spend these few pence, saved by not indulging in his customary glass, by purchasing with *cash* from his merchant, when he can get, as he always could, a year or two years credit! No, a fisherman won't buy a barrel or a bag from a cash dealer, even at 7/6 cheaper, when he can get either from his merchant on unlimited credit.

The credit system is the principal factor in the glaring poverty well-known in any of our most populous fishing Districts, not the quantity of rum bought and sold!

Now then, can the fisherman, who is taxed and charged for his goods at such exorbitant rates, afford to pay any more for his flour, pork, tea, sugar, molasses, &c., &c.? Is he able and is he willing to pay? These questions I leave to the fisherman, and to the Prohibitionist to answer.

I can answer for the merchant that he won't be willing to pay an addition to the already high tariff.

I daresay you recollect some two or three years ago, the stern, and almost frantic attitude of the merchants, when the additional "fifteen per cent" was added to the amount of all duties? Do you think for a moment, that they will stand idle and allow another fifteen per cent to be added? I am afraid not...

...[I] will now take a commercial view of [prohibition]. What benefits will accrue to us if the Prohibition Act be passed? None, in relation to the Act.

In the first place, liquor will be consumed, and in far greater quantities than before. It is easily procurable, and will be purchased in larger packages than heretofore. Our R.M. Steamer will be a conveyance used in this illegal traffic; besides the many opportunities by sailing craft. Now, all this money will go to "outsiders," who have no stake in the place, and so there is a certain amount of evil attached to liquor, we will be debited with the *loss*, while they – the sellers or smugglers – will have the profit, so that in a monetary way of business we will be the losers.

Again, this port is largely visited by strangers, at all seasons of the year, and they naturally put up at the hotels. Won't they look astonished when told they can't have their glass of spirits? And won't it be astonishing, that the landlord or lady hasn't a good stock on hand for their boarders? Pray, why should strangers who come here for business or pleasure be made to suffer for our misdeeds? It is a question that the "Prohibition Act" leaves no margin for an answer.

Yours with respect, H.³

....

Despite the opinions of persons like "H," the temperance advocates generally had the upper hand in this era, and prohibition soon became the norm at Twillingate.

A meeting was held in the Town Hall on Thursday evening, under the auspices of the Sons of Temperance. The Hall was crowded in every part, and many were unable to obtain admission at all. Mr. Andrew Roberts, W.P., occupied the Chair, and discharged its duties with dignity and wisdom. In his opening address he removed any prejudices that might exist and assured the audience that the Society (S. Of T.) had not been actuated by selfish motives, but had gone to work solely for the good for their fellows.

The Chairman introduced the Rev. J. Embree (Methodist) as the first speaker, who delivered a powerful and pointed address. He said there were times when the world's pulse beat fast, as for instance when it rose to demand the emancipation of the slave...They were now seeking to abolish a slavery more galling than Africa's swarthy Sons ever felt. The song, *Yield Not to Temptation*, was sung, after which the Rev. Charles McKay (Congregational) spoke. He contended that there was a fitness in the people demanding the closing of public houses; alcohol was a poison as really as arsenic or strychnine – to obtain the later you must carry a physician's order to the drug store. Alcohol should be sold only by medicinal permission.

Another hymn was sung, after which the Rev. R. Temple, R.D., addressed the meeting. He said he was not thoroughly familiar with the terms of the bill. He thought it did not go far enough. It robbed the poor man of his "beer," but put no restraint upon the rich. He regarded the closing of public houses as a questionable good; it would generate smuggling; it would not effectually check the consumption of strong drink; men who had an appetite for it would get into their punts and row to Tizzards Harbour for it, &c.

Dr. Stafford here sang a solo with good effect, accompanying himself on the organ. Rev. F.R. Duffill (Methodist) appeared to dissent from the opinions expressed by the last speaker.

The greatest decorum prevailed throughout, and evident interest was felt in the topic under discussion.

The battle that is won without opposition can hardly be called a triumph. The temperance workers may not expect unanimity at the pools on Monday, but they may rely upon the support of all who have the well-being of the people at heart.

The people of Twillingate will have an opportunity of checking a traffic, which happily has never attained to very serious proportions here, but if they do not now deal the enemy a death blow there may be circumstances that will tend to develop it, and when it is too late the coming generations will sigh for an opportunity which once past may not soon return.

"Of all and words of tongue or of pen
The saddest are these – It might have been."
PARAKLETOS[4]

....

According to a proclamation issued from the Colonial Secretary's Office, Dec. 15th, 1882, a poll was taken at the Court House, on Monday last, for the prohibition of the sale of intoxicating liquors. The total vote was 247 – 212 for prohibition, thirty-five against. This community is now free from the sale of liquors.[5]

....

For some years past there has been a great reformer in our midst in the shape of a Temperance Society, known as the Sons of Temperance, the members of this worthy Brotherhood have been shaping to a large extent the sentiment of the public on the drink question, and that sentiment has at last given itself satisfactory expression.

After a stern battle the Newfoundland Parliament passed the Local Option Bill, which has already been of benefit to the Country. Twillingate has been notorious as a stronghold of religion and temperance, and yet in our midst strong drink has been freely sold, and as a consequence not a few have sold their manhood to the publican.

Nineteenth century Twillingate, "...notorious as a stronghold of religion and temperance"

What the future might bring forth if this traffic were not checked, it hardly needs a seer's vision to foretell. Many of the youth in our midst who are now reputable and worthy citizens, would be lured by the seductive whisper of this most pleasing of the family of sirens, and the enchanted isle would be a prison of despair, in which all that was best in them would be immolated, and all that was worst would be maddened. Few towns in the Country grow more rapidly; an important fishing village only a few years ago, today it is probably the third seaport on the coast of Newfoundland. This progress may be expected to continue; there may be an influx of population from other countries; that population may be worse than the native population, bringing with it the habits and vices of other more thickly peopled and more iniquitous neighbourhoods. If the public houses had been suffered to remain, before many years there would have been an increase in the number of rum shops, and the drunkenness that now creeps out at night would walk the streets at noontide as unabashed as the sun.

Monday decided the question. Drink and temperance went to the pols, and the issue was one for which all who feel for the woes and weaknesses of men must be thankful.

Many conjectures were ventured prior to the contest; the general impression was that the temperance element was the strongest; some veteran tipplers anticipated a rebuff for temperance; some doubting souls on the right side hoped they would be successful, but feared the majority would be a small one. About eight o'clock in the morning a grey headed Englishman, who for many years has resided in the neighbourhood, walked with quick decided steps to the Court House and voted vehemently against rum; later on crowds began to walk towards the poll; we could notice the faces of those strong men as they walked to the bloodless contest. It needed not the Magistrate's question to assure us on what side they were to vote. Some of them had been scourged by the plague; some had felt the chafing of the fetters; some were poor men living from hand to mouth, permitted to vote because they lived in some humble shed they called their own. "A man's a man for 'a that."

Manly men they were, most of them not likely to give the family physician much trouble for some yeas to come, proving that health and tea-totalism are not avowed enemies after all.

The first 156 voters, with only four exceptions, gave their vote against public houses. In the afternoon we noticed another class of men, and we said to ourselves and others, these are the men that are going to vote against themselves, and their Wives, and their town, and their God – they were emitting clouds of smoke, there was less manhood in their gait, and a forced tranquillity in their faces. They voted apologetically, and the better nature struggled through the skin and blushed a little.

Their force was feeble and their resistance useless. The victory is won! Out of 247 votes polled, 212 were polled against rum. The most sanguine did not anticipate a success so thorough. All honour to the men who have who have brought about this magnificent result...

F.R.D.[6]

Stories From These Shores

....

All of the local fervour for temperance didn't mean that Twillingate lacked its free thinkers, unwilling to go along with what was usually touted as the majority opinion. This writer saw the events of the meeting described above by "Parakletos" from a very different perspective.

Sir, — An account in your last issue of the proceedings of a meeting held in the Town Hall, for the purpose of bringing before the public of Twillingate the Local Option question, was, I think, in the first place *partial*. The author, "Parakletos," was there, and must have known when he was penning his letter [that] he was trying to misconstrue some things that were said.

I was there, as a matter of course, and took a little notice of the performance, having expected some fine arguments on the question, but was uniformly disappointed. Without commenting on the "dignified and wise old man" who filled the Chair, I will pass on to the general features for the meeting.

There was quite a crowd there of all sizes. The meeting was opened with a Hymn, and the speakers were introduced, in the order given by "Parakletos." Now, what did we get drummed into our ears? Not the question [of] prohibition, but a lot of time-worn talk about intemperance, with the exception of one Rev. Gentleman, who came to the point and honestly gave his opinions to the audience, and questioned very much the benefits that would accrue from prohibition.

Another speaker then rose dissenting from this sentiment, but without convincing me and many others that prohibition would benefit this community.

Now that the question in the meantime is settled and the Bill is sustained, the victors are jubilant over their victory! But I ask is it a victory? Was it a fair contest, and does the result show the feelings of the people of Twillingate? No, and I venture to say that if the ballot system was in operation it would not have been carried.

Is there no other evil more glaring than the "drinking habit," crying out for ostracism in the community? Ask the "powers that be," my dear friends, for a five minutes glance at the "judicious records" kept in the *proper place*, and you will be astonished, aye! Shocked, not

at the use of alcohol, oh no. Prohibition is necessary.
Yours &c.,
VERITAS[7]

....

Despite being generally favourable to the temperance cause, the Sun and its Editor came under criticism for allowing the opinions of both sides of the debate to appear in it's pages, through the correspondence section. Mr. Thompson felt compelled to respond to public censure of what he felt was simply fairness in journalism.

On Thursday evening [22 February, 1883] while attending a public meeting, under the auspices of the Sons of Temperance, we were a little hurt at some of the remarks made use of. One Rev. Lecturer, for whom we have the greatest respect, in the course of his remarks drew the attention of the audience to some articles that have recently appeared in this paper, some of which he severely criticized. So far so good. But there were some remarks we take exception [to], and they are these: "Since the Local Option Bill has passed, there have appeared in the Sun some dark spots that have marred it, and would have been better off out of it." We are sorry that the Rev. Gentleman did not point out the dark spots more clearly, but we infer them to be those articles that have appeared in the Sun adverse to prohibition. We will give the view taken by the present Manager, and the motives by which he was prompted in pursuing the course he did.

Stories From These Shores

Twillingate Sun *Editor, Jabez P. Thompson*

Prohibition was about to be tried in Twillingate, and it was a well known fact that many were not conversant with the nature of the Bill, and that the feeling in favour was *not* unanimous. The Sun had advocated prohibition through correspondents and otherwise, and a portion of the community were strong for it. At the same time there were some who were opposed to the system of prohibition, and who took different views of the question. Some did not believe in making men sober by the law; some thought it would not advance the temperance cause; some believed in persuasion not force; some thought where it would remove one temptation it would create twenty, &c., *and we give both parties credit with honest convictions*. And while the latter view might have been held by a minority of the community (which we do not say it was, as we do not think 212 votes a large majority of the voters in this community), would it be right to ignore them? Would it be consistent? Would it be honourable? Would it be fair on the part of the Sun to shut its door against them, and not allow them to express their opinions, or if they thought they were harshly judged, seek for redress through it? And again, where is a more suitable place for any subject touching the public weal to be discussed, turned and twisted, its weak points shown up as well as its strong, as through the press, leaving an intelligent public to judge for themselves. Right is certain to succeed eventually, and the cause that cannot stand on its own merits, ought not [to] stand at all. These were the views taken by us, and consequently the "dark spots." But it seems to be since the Bill has passed that these "spots" have particularly appeared on the Sun's disc. Now have not those in favour of prohibition been able to give full vent to their views and exaltations through this paper? They certainly have! And while there was an Opposition Party, we ask again would it be honourable or just to that Party, if they thought they were harshly judged, or wrong motives attributed to their actions, would it be right for them to be denied the privilege of defending themselves? Certainly not!

But if we have acted injudiciously in giving publicity to any letters (as we do not think we have), we are willing to abide by the decision of an enlightened and unprejudiced public. But at the same time we wish it to be distinctly understood that we do not hold ourselves responsible for the opinions of our correspondents, nor do we, by publishing, endorse them, *nor charge those who do not agree with the method of prohibition as being in sympathy with intemperance*, for we hold that a man may advocate temperance and not advocate prohibition, and that they are not necessarily ONE. And we are not aware that the Sun is the organ of any Party, but is an independent public journal, and as such, "is open to all, and influenced by none," and in pursuing the course we did, we cannot see where we have "marred" its rays, and merited the censure cast on its present youthful and inexperienced Manager at a public meeting.

With all due respect to the Rev. Gentleman's opinion's, we think his remarks on this occasion were quite uncalled for.[8]

....

...The Sons of Temperance acted the part of statesman and warrior in the late struggle [for local prohibition]...The Temperance Society not only led the battle, but also supplied the "sinews of war." An abstract of their expenditure which is laying before me, shows that the expenses were considerable. The Society spent upwards of £13 in connection with the passing of the Local Option Bill. All this money was directly drawn from their own exchequer, and we understand their funds were pretty well drained. They paid $22 to the Returning Officer and Roll Clerk, spent $32 for refreshments to voters and other incidental expenses. It need scarcely be said that if such a Society did not exist, the people would have to pay these expenses, if they wished to test the Bill in this community. The public, therefore, ought to know that they owe a debt of gratitude to the Sons of Temperance, not only for conducting the campaign, but also for supplying the "sinews of war." Therefore, all who approve of adopting the Bill should not forget their indebtedness to the Society, and of course we only undertake to express the sentiments of those who supported the measure. Long may this noble Society exist in our midst, to guard our hearths and homes from the dreadful invasion of intemperance.

X.Y.Z.[9]

....

Although Twillingate was the first area of the Isles to enact local prohibition, it was not the last, and temperance advocates felt the fight must be continued as long as any communities in the area still allowed the sale of the "demon rum." Between 1883 and 1889 practically all of the towns of the Isles (excepting a few such as Tilting and Change Islands) went dry.

A short time since we adverted to the fact that the good people of Fogo purposed at an early day to test the Local Option Bill at the polls, and that the advocates of the measure were quite sanguine that it would be adopted. Polling day was on the ninth inst. [February, 1884], when, we learn, the results of the poll were: —— ninety-seven for; nine against. Notwithstanding the favourable view that was indulged in appertaining to the success of the measure, we think this signal and complete victory must have surpassed the expectation of the least sanguine, and must be very gratifying and encouraging to the promoters of the movement.

Some parties, however, having considerable faith in the credulity of their neighbours, endeavoured to gull those who were in unison with the object of the measure, by telling them that they were influenced by the mercantile body. But it proved a "little too thin." People now-a-days are too enlightened and independent to be made dupes of by such twaddlers, and while the mass of the people will act in unison with the merchants, or any other class, whose object is the furtherance of the public good, they will, we believe, at the same time, think and act for themselves, notwithstanding the cry of prejudiced parties to the contrary. The only ones apparently, if any, that were influenced by this absurd argument, were the nine that voted against the measure. The expenses of the campaign, which are something considerable, were paid by the "Rising Sun" Division, Sons of Temperance. The voters from Seldom-Come-Bye were provided with a dinner by their Fogo friends. Fogo proper and Seldom-Come-Bye have now decided against the legal sale of liquor, and we hope that the efforts put forth to secure this boon will be crowned with thorough and lasting success. We learn that Joe Batt's Arm and Barr'd Islands intend at no distant day to follow in the steps of Fogo and Change Islands, by testing [the] Local Option at the polls. The universality of feeling in favour of [the] Local Option, shows clearly that people are becoming more and more alive to the evils that are the fruits of intemperance, and are determined on using every legitimate means in their power for its suppression, and banishment. It is not perhaps that at the present period the effects of intemperance in all the communities that are adopting [the] Local Option seem to demand immediate and powerful action to counteract its ruinous course, for, in point of fact, some have every reason to be thankful that a better state of things exists, but probably the deplorable spectacle that the past and present history, if not of their own humble settlements, those of more importance and affluence, remind them of what may be their's or their children's in the future...[10]

....

Barr'd Islands, pre-1930

We are pleased to notice that in response to a petition from over one-fifth of the registered electors of the Settlements of Barr'd Islands and Joe Batt's Arm, including Shoal Bay, His Excellency the Governor has appointed Thursday next, the thirtieth inst. (October, 1884) for the taking of the poll at Barr'd Islands, to decide whether the sale of intoxicating liquors shall be legal in the settlements mentioned. This is a step in the right direction, and it is gratifying to know that our friends in these places have thus manifested a desire to banish from their midst the great giant of intemperance, which must be looked upon as the greatest evil that can exist in any civilized community, and which is doing more at the present time throughout the world to undermine society and bring to degradation and ruin thousands of our fellow creatures, than all other evils combined.

There may be some who are not altogether in unison with the spirit of the temperance movement, and who contend that such measures as the Local Option Law are not calculated to further the design of the advocates of temperance principles. This in some measure may be true in communities where there is a laxity on the part of public officials in enforcing the law, but in places where the authorities strictly and impartially carry out the spirit of the Act, it cannot be denied but that very beneficial effects follow the introduction of the Local Option Act wherever it has been accepted by the people. The temperance sentiment seems to be gaining ground in this Colony, as [is] evident from the fact that petitions from several other localities have also been presented asking for a poll to decide against the sale of liquor in their midst. We are proud that our friends at Barr'd Islands and the surrounding places have resolved on coming to the front in this noble movement, for the suppression of the liquor traffic, and fervently pray that the poll which is shortly to be taken will result in a grand victory for the temperance cause in that section of our District.[11]

....

All interested in the temperance movement will be pleased to learn that the poll taken at Barr'd Islands on Thursday, the thirtieth ult., resulted in a grand victory in favour of [the] Local Option, which prohibits the legitimate sale of intoxicating liquors in that and the surrounding localities. It affords us pleasure to congratulate our temperance friends there on their success in thus endeavouring to banish the evil of intemperance from their midst, and hope that the authorities will not be dilatory in enforcing the law in reference to this measure. At Fogo the Local Option Act is in operation, still we have been informed that spiritous liquors have been frequently bought there, as well as in our own and other communities where the sale of such has been prohibited, excepting for medicinal purposes. It behoves the advocates of the movement to be vigilant in assisting the enforcement of the temperance laws, and thus aid the authorities in the discharge of their duties in respect to this matter.

It is a cause for thankfulness that with one or two exceptions, there is not a licensed public house in this extensive District, and we are sorry to know that Change Islands should be one of these; not, however, that it is the wish of the people that it should be so. We understand that an attempt was made on the part of some of the inhabitants to introduce [the] Local Option there, but being led to believe that a license would not be given to any person to sell intoxicating spirits, the matter was abandoned. When, however, application was afterwards made to the Stipendiary Magistrate for a renewal of a license, the exaction of a large license fee appeared to be the primary consideration, and the sale of spiritous liquors is still tolerated at Change Islands. On the whole the residents of this place may be considered as temperate and law abiding a class of people as can be found in any community, and it is not for fear of their becoming otherwise that we would like to see the nefarious liquor traffic discontinued there. But as this is the only place now within a radius of many miles where a licensed house is to be found, we have been informed that it is not an unusual thing, especially in the Winter season, for persons to congregate there from distant settlements for the purpose of having a "spree," and causing a disturbance, to the great annoyance of the peaceable and well-behaved residents of Change Islands. It is to be hoped, therefore, that our good friends there will imitate the example that has already been set by many other communities, and rally to the front in suppression of the liquor traffic, and in the advancement of the temperance cause in our land.[12]

Rally at Fogo, early 1900s

....

A Festival in connection with the [Prevention Division, Sons of Temperance]...was celebrated at Morton's Harbour, on Wednesday last, March fourteenth. The weather was all that could be desired, which added much to the enjoyment of the celebration. Tea was provided in the school-house, which was neatly adorned with bunting, and about four o'clock the tables, which were profusely decorated with numerous kinds of good things, very acceptable to the appetite, were surrounded by a goodly company, who appeared to heartily enjoy the feast, the preparation of which reflected credit on the ladies connected with it. When tea was over, the gathering dispersed for a little while to allow the room to be got ready for the entertainment. At seven o'clock the building was pretty well filled and the meeting was commenced by singing an appropriate hymn, after which the Rev. J. Heyfield was asked to lead in prayer. Mr. Osmond then intimated that as Mr. T. French was the W.P. of the Division for this quarter, he would take the Chair and preside over the meeting. The Chairman gave a short and appropriate address, and closed with an appeal to the parents to strive and instil into the minds of their children total abstinence principles, and asked for the support or sympathy of all present, in the noble cause in which they were engaged. The programme, as will be seen, consisted of addresses, dialogues, choruses, &c., all of which were performed in a very efficient manner, and reflected a good deal of praise on the part of those who had the management. The addresses were practical, and the temperance cause was advocated in an earnest and forcible style by the various speakers, especially by the Rev. J. Heyfield, who, in a masterly speech, adduced many facts and figures bearing on the enormous evils resulting from the use of intoxicating liquors, and spoke of the enthusiasm and sympathy that are being manifested in the movement throughout the world at the present day. The organ was well played by Miss Jessie Osmond and Miss Jane French, and the singing was creditable. Owing to the lateness of the hour, two or three items on the programme had to be omitted, and do not appear in the copy appended. The singing of the National Anthem brought the interesting proceedings to a close.

Chairman's Address. Chorus — *Dash it Down*, Choir. Recitation — Mr. Robert French. Reading — Mr. George Bennet. Solo — Miss A. Mills. Address — Mr. Elijah Jennings. Dialogue — A Changed Housewife. Trio — *The Social Glass*. Recitation — Mr. Robert Bartlett. Chorus — *Love at Home*, Choir. Reading — Miss R. Osmond. Chorus — *Appeal from Intemperance*. Address — Mr. Mark Osmond. Recitation — Miss Lily Bartlett. Solo — *One Day Nearer Home*, Miss Milly. Dialogue — "Trapped." Singing — Three Total Abstainers. Address — Rev. J. Heyfield. Chorus — *Gather Them in*. Vote of thanks — proposed by Mr. J. B. Osmond, seconded by Mr. R. French. National Anthem.

Joseph B. Osmond business premises, Moreton's Harbour

The above is the first celebration that has been given in connection with "Prevention" Division, which has only been working little more than a year. At present its membership does not number largely, but is on the increase. There is no doubt the presence of such an institution is a power for good in any community, and although the immediate necessity for temperance organizations in communities where strong drinks are not sold, may not be apparent to many, it is well that such a safeguard should encircle the young, so that when they go out in the world and are brought into contact with the deadly foe, they may be the better prepared to desist all persuasions to indulge in a practise which in thousands of instances proves ruinous to both body and soul. We wish "Prevention" Division a long existence, and hope it will be the means of preventing many from pursuing so dishonourable a course.[13]

....

DAVID J. CLARKE

To temperance advocates there was probably no more sinful profession on earth than that of a "publican," those who made their living selling alcohol, either at licensed taverns or hotels. In the context of nineteenth century Twillingate, one of the most well-known of these would have been Captain Richard Wrey, who operated a hotel on the town's North Side in the 1870s and 1880s. Even before the local option came into effect, Wrey and his Wife Catherine found themselves in trouble with the authorities for breaches of the Liquor Act, and their problems didn't end in 1883.

Twillingate North Side, c.1905. The Stirling family residence is at right. Richard Wrey's business was located to the left of this shot

BEFORE MAGISTRATE BERTEAU. October fourth [1880] — Richard Wrey, for breach of [the] License Act, 1875, was fined four dollars and costs.

....

BEFORE MAGISTRATE BERTEAU. Tuesday, Sept. twentieth — R. Wrey having been summoned by Sergeant Wells for breach of [the] License Act, sections twenty-one and twenty-five, was fined ten dollars and costs.

....

January 20th, 1882.

An appeal case was tried today before the Court of Sessions, in which Mr. Wrey was appellant and Sergeant Wells respondent. The latter objected to the appeal on the grounds of its being illegal. He opened the case with the following address to the Chairman and gentlemen of the Quarter Sessions: —

The first case on the docket for your consideration this morning is an appeal case in which Richard Wrey (Licensed publican) is appellant and I am respondent. This is a case, gentlemen, as you are aware, in which the Police Magistrate gave judgement against the defendant on the twenty-second day of November last [1881], for a breach of the twenty-first sec. of the License [Act] of 1875, committed by him on the eighth day of the same month, in which case I was complainant, and the appellant R. Wrey) was defendant. He was then convicted and fined the sum of ten dollars and costs, which he refused to pay, and appealed to a Bench of Magistrates at the Quarter Sessions, and I am sure that the appellant must be more than pleased today to see such a "full Bench."

Now, gentlemen, on what grounds he appeals from the Stipendiary Magistrate's conviction to the Justices sitting in Quarter Sessions, I am entirely at a loss to know. And, gentlemen, Mr. Wrey...has managed to keep me totally in the dark...But now, Mr. Chairman and gentlemen, it is my duty as respondent in the case, to state for the information of all whom it may concern, that Mr. Wrey's "notice of appeal" is informal, and not at all in accordance with the law made and provided in such cases, and consequently, not worth the scrap of paper it is written upon. You will see, gentlemen, by referring to the thirty-third sec. of the License Act of 1875 (the sec. under which my friend, Mr. Wrey, claims an appeal). That section reads as follows: "All persons convicted under this Act, who shall think themselves aggrieved by such conviction may appeal against the same to the next Court of Quarter Sessions holden in or nearest to the place where such conviction shall have been made, Provided (Here is a provision gentlemen) that such person shall give to the convicting Justice, notice in WRITING of his intention to appeal; and of the cause and the matter thereof, and to abide the judgement of the Court thereof; and to pay such costs as by the Court shall be awarded; and the judgement of the said Court shall be final and binding to all intents and purposes." And again, gentlemen, if you will turn to page 130, sec. sixteen, of the *Magistrates' Manual*, you will see there what an able an learned gentleman of the legal profession (Judge Prowse), who compiled that little book, says in reference to appeals under the License Act. That learned Judge says: "The cause and the matter of the appeal must be given in writing." Mark you, he says, "it MUST be given in writing." He don't [*sic*] say it may be given, but he says, gentlemen, "it MUST be." It is very easy for any person who may think himself aggrieved by such conviction to ask for, or demand, an appeal, but when he is called upon to state the cause and the matter of his appeal, he is at a loss to find any real "cause or matter" for such appeal, and so you see, gentlemen, that were not the law thus wisely framed, the Sessions Court would be subject to endless trouble with "frivolous" cases, a specimen of which we have here today. And again, gentlemen, if the appellant were not bound to state the "cause and matter of the appeal," how could the respondent be prepared to meet the case; he could not be prepared at all, gentlemen, but he would find himself the same as I do today – in ignorance of the cause and the matter of this appeal, and I most emphatically object to this illegal notice of appeal. No doubt, gentlemen, but my friend Mr. Wrey will tell you by and by that he was ignorant of the law in this respect. But, gentlemen, as an Irish lawyer said one time, "the law presumes every man innocent till proven guilty, but a policemen presumes everyone guilty until proven innocent." So it is presumed that every man (including publicans and sinners) should know the law, and especially the License Act of 1875, and I am sure, gentlemen, that my friend, Mr. Wrey, who prides himself (and justly so) [on] his well known ability to conduct his own affairs as regards matters of law, knew well that his notice of appeal was not what the law required it to be. But, gentlemen, whether he knew or not we have nothing whatever to do. And now, for this very offence which has brought Mr. Wrey here today; he was liable to a fine up to forty dols., and what does Judge Prowse say in reference to this twenty-first sec.? He remarks: "Selling liquor to drunken persons or permitting them to consume liquor on the premises are offences which, when proved, should be punished severely." But, gentlemen, I have no doubt but that my friend Mr. Wrey will have the audacity to tell you that he gave them no liquors at all in his shop, except a bit of bread and cheese and a drop of porter; and he may tell you that he gave them a drop of brandy for peace and quietness sake, but will he tell you that he gave one of the three men a whole glass of his best "Old Tom," or as the boys call it, "fire water," which is able to kill an "old dog hood [at] 600 yards?" Will he tell you that this man (Samuel Rogers) whom he gave this glass of "fire water" to, was so drunk at the time that he did not really know whether it was the pleasing countenance of the old landlady, Mrs. Wrey, or whether it was the "austere man," my friend Mr. Wrey himself, who gave him this full bumper of "fire water"? But gentlemen, the other two men who were not so drunk state on oath that it was Mr. Wrey who gave them all the liquor, including the glass of "Old Tom" drank by friend Samuel, in his shop the time in question, which I am sure will satisfy you on that point. And what do we find that this glass of "fire water" did to its recipient? Why, like the "evil spirits" of old, threw its victims sometimes in the water and sometimes in the fire, so the "fire water" threw our friend Rogers out of his punt in[to] the water. I was an eyewitness, gentlemen, to Samuel Rogers being thrown overboard by the evil spirits or fire water, and it was I who helped them to go home on their way rejoicing, not to the disgust of all present...but perhaps to the disgust of...all friends of the "Northern Hotel." Was it, indeed, very disgusting to see these unfortunate creatures rescued from what might have been a watery grave? Now, gentlemen, I shall conclude by referring you to the thirty-fifth section of the License Act, which states as follows: "In all cases where a person is convicted for a breach of the provisions of this Act, the Justice before whom such conviction is had, may, in addition to or in substitution for, any penalty, declare the license of every such person so convicted to be forfeited." Allow me, gentlemen, to quote a few words from that learned Judge again, in reference to this section. He says: "This valuable provision should seldom be put in force for a first offence. The defendant should be warned that he will lose his license for a second conviction." But, gentlemen, I must tell you that my friend, Mr. Wrey, has been convicted twice [under] this very same section within the last fifteen months. He was convicted and fined four dols. on the fourth of October, 1880. On the twentieth [of] Sept. last he was convicted and fined ten dols. and costs; on the twenty-third of the same month his Wife [Catherine] was fined two dols. and costs for a breach of the twenty-fifth sec., namely, for obstructing the police in discharge of their duty, and again on the twenty-second of Nov. last, he was fined ten dols. and costs for a breach of this twenty-first sec., and I may add that this offence is a most glaring, and I had almost said, an aggravated one. I shall trespass no longer, gentlemen, on your valuable time by going farther into details, as I should otherwise do were it not as I have already stated, that this notice of appeal is altogether illegal; therefore I shall content myself by leaving the matter, gentlemen, in your hands, feeling assured, from the evidence procured on behalf of the Crown, that you will confirm the decision of the Magistrate on twenty-second of Nov. last.

The appellant, Mr. R. Wrey, then replied by stating [that] the men were not drunk, and that he gave them no liquor, but only some bread and cheese, and thought it very queer to be fined for doing that. He having no witnesses to be examined, the Court in Sessions confirmed the judgement of the Court given on the twenty-second of Nov. last, whereby Mr. Wrey was fined ten dols. and costs, and also the costs of appeal. Mr. Wrey then stated in open Court that he would not abide by the judgment of the Court of Quarter Sessions, and would appeal to the Supreme Court, and that he would not pay a farthing, as the men were not drunk.

....

February 9th, 1887.
Constable Burt: — On the third February, 1887, I was informed that Thomas Fifield bought spirits at the dwelling house of Richard Wrey. On the fourth Feb., 1887, I had an interview with Thomas Fifield. I said to him, "I am informed you bought spirits at Richard Wrey's." He said, "I did." I asked him whether he had bought any spirits within this last six months from Richard Wrey's, he said, "Yes, the last I bought was last Wednesday fortnight, which was the nineteenth [of] January, 1887." I asked him to give me full particulars. He then told me that on last

Wednesday fortnight he went into the dwelling house (in the kitchen) of Richard Wrey's, between seven and eight o'clock in the evening, and asked Richard Wrey whether he would sell him a half pint [of] rum. Richard Wrey went out of the kitchen, and after a short time returned with the bottle containing a half pint of rum, and gave it to him (Thos. Fifield). Then Thomas Fifield gave him (Richard Wrey) one shilling in cash to pay for the pint of rum. I then asked Thomas Fifield whether he had bought any spirits from Richard Wrey previous to this time, and within the last six months. He (Thomas Fifield) said, "I have on several occasions, and on one occasion Ethelbert Vatcher bought spirits from Richard Wrey's for me (Thos. Fifield), and I gave Ethelbert Vatcher two shillings and sixpence in cash to pay for the half pint [of] rum. Ethelbert Vatcher went into Richard Wrey's, and after a short time, he came out with a bottle containing a half pint [of] rum, and one shilling and six pence in cash, which he gave to [me]." This was sometime in December of 1886, to the best of his (Fifield's) knowledge and belief. On the fifth [of] Feb., I made complaint to you.

TOHMAS FIFIELD, sworn: This day three weeks [ago] (I think it was the nineteenth of January, 1887), between seven and eight o'clock in the evening, I went and knocked at the front door of Mr. Wrey's house. Mr. Wrey came to the door. I went into the kitchen and then asked Mr. Wrey for a half pint [of] rum. Mr. Wrey went out somewhere, and after a short time returned and brought back the half pint [of] rum in the bottle which I gave him. I then paid Mr. Wrey one shilling cash for the rum. Mr. Wrey told me to mind what I was about, and not let anyone know anything about it, then he opened the door and let me out.

Questioned by MR. BERTEAU: I was there about a quarter of an hour. I did not drink any liquor in the house. I have bought liquor there several times within the last six months from Richard Wrey. I paid cash for the rum each time to Mr. Wrey. Once I shovelled away some snow for Mr. Wrey, and he gave me a glass of rum for doing it. He gave me a glass of rum of his own free will, and there was no arrangement made before hand between us. A little while before Christmas last [1886], I sent Ethelbert Vatcher to Mr. Wrey's for a half pint [of] rum. He got it at Mr. Wrey's. I gave him two shillings and sixpence cash, and he brought me the half pint [of] rum, and one shilling and sixpence cash change. He did not get a certificate from Doctor Stafford at that time. I never got a certificate from the Doctor to get any spirits at Mr. Wrey's at any time. I gave Ethelbert Vatcher a bottle to put the rum in. I did not tell Ethelbert Vatcher to tell Mr. Wrey that the rum was for me. I positively swear that I only had spirits given to me once at Mr. Wrey's for a present. I always paid for the liquor I had at the time, with the exception of the time Mr. Wrey gave me the glass of rum for shovelling the snow away. He gave me the liquor within the last six months. I can't remember the date.

Questioned by CONSTABLE BURT: Mr. Wrey said to me where have you been so long, as I have not seen you for some time? I told him I was in the Bay. The last time I was in Mr. Wrey's was this day, three weeks, I think it was the nineteenth [of] January. I remember Mr. Wrey asking me the question within the last six months, whether I was living with James Hodder (Coastal Wharf) as usual. He asked me whether a young man by the name of Bishop was living with James Hodder. I told him he was. Ethelbert Vatcher did not tell me that he had an order from the Doctor when I asked him to get me the rum or that he would get an order. Mrs. Wrey did not give me any spirits within the last six months. I got it from Mr. Wrey every time.

ETHELBERT VATCHER, sworn: I went to Mr. Wrey's and bought some liquor for Thomas Fifield. [I] bought a half pint [of] rum. I had a bottle to put it in, and I paid one shilling cash for it to Capt. Wrey when he gave me the half pint [of] rum. I do not remember the date, but it was somewhere about a week before Christmas last. Thos. Fifield sent me for the liquor. When Thos. Fifield sent me for the rum he gave me a bottle and two shillings and sixpence cash. I brought back the half pint [of] rum and one shilling and sixpence cash, which I had got at Mr. Wrey's and gave it to Thomas Fifield. When I asked Mr. Wrey for the rum he asked me if I wanted it for sickness, I told him no; I positively swear that I said no. Mr. Wrey asked me if I had a bottle. He told me to keep the bottle under my jacket so as no one should see it. He went inside and got the rum. I paid the shilling in the shop. I had no certificate from Dr. Stafford when I got the rum for Thomas Fifield. When I was going to the herring fishery with my Brothers last October, I got a certificate from Dr. Stafford for a half gallon [of] rum. Instead of having the half gallon then, I got a pint, and James Young got a pint, making a quart at that time. I never mentioned to Mr. Wrey anything about the order that I gave him when I got the rum for Thomas Fifield. The reason we took only the quart was because we had not enough money to buy any more. That is the only time I bought liquor for Thomas Fifield. I bought a half pint [of] rum for myself about a week after New year's Day. I paid Mr. Wrey a shilling cash for it. He asked me whether I wanted it for sickness; I told him no. Mr. Wrey told me to put it under my jacket and keep it snug so as not to let any person know it on the road. I positively swear that I did not tell Capt. Wrey anything about the certificate (that I gave him previously) the last time I had rum for myself and Thomas Fifield, neither did I mention it to him or he to me.

Question by CONSTABLE BURT: I only took one order from Doctor Stafford within the last six months. I bought no liquor from Richard Wrey for anyone else within the last six months, except what I have stated before. Mr. Wrey never said directly or indirectly anything about the Doctor's order when he gave me the half pint [of] rum.

Question by Mr. Wrey: did you say to me that you would come again, and get the remainder of the half gallon [of] rum after taking the quart on the day you did?

VATCHER: Yes, I did tell you that I would come for the remainder of the half gallon [of] rum some other time.

No plea was offered by [the] Defendant, and His Worship fined him the next morning, in the sum of twenty-five dollars. Costs $6.50. $31.50.[14]

....

Even as the Local Option came into force in many Newfoundland communities, the idea of total prohibition for the Island had not gone away, and continued to be debated by politicians and Twillingate Sun *readers alike.*

Information has been received here during the week that a measure is now before the House of Assembly having for its object the prevention of the importation of spiritous liquors into the Colony, excepting for medicinal or Holy Communion purposes. We are not aware what form the Bill assumes, but imagine that it provides for the sanctioning of a law whereby a vote of the whole Colony shall be taken to decide the important question. This move is being made, no doubt, in response, to the prayers of numerous petitioners from almost every part of the Colony, who have petitioned the Legislature asking that a prohibitory law might be enforced, preventing the importation or sale of alcoholic beverages in any part of Newfoundland. No question, a great deal has been accomplished in checking the torrent of evil caused by intemperance, but the step that is now being taken is the only effectual means of banishing from our land the monstrous foe, because if the roots are disturbed and annihilated the whole fabric must soon fall into decay, and this is what temperance workers and all sympathizers of the noble cause are striving for.

We are in favour of total prohibition for this Colony, believing that the measure is a *right* one, and one that is calculated to be fraught with many blessings to our people, particularly the working classes. How many homes there are in poverty and misery that would be comfortable and happy were it not for the drinking habits of the parents, who, instead of spending their earnings for family needs, visit the dens provided to decoy them into, where they spend their money, leaving their families penniless and without the real necessities of life. Some persons in places like this may be inclined to ask, what do we want total prohibition for? Is not the Local Option already in force? Certainly it is, but this is only a partial remedy for the evil, for so long as the ruinous beverages are imported and allowed to be sold elsewhere, we are in danger of being entrapped in the snare and of becoming a prey to the demon, and it should be the duty of all sober-minded persons to endeavour to banish King Alcohol from our shores altogether. It may be that some St. John's people wonder why the outports that have [the] Local Option are so anxious for total prohibition. But the reason is clear enough. Many of our people frequently go there, and while the temptation is removed from them in their own localities, there are powerful inducements presented to them nearly every step they take while transacting business in the Capital, to partake of the "maddening bowl," which some unfortunately fall victims to. Besides, so long as it can be procured in the Metropolis, places that have [the] Local Option cannot be free from the baneful consequences. But supposing communities such as ours do not suffer to a very large extent from the liquor traffic, there are others in various parts of the Country that do, and wherever our fellow creatures are known to suffer therefrom, it should be the common aim of persons elsewhere to endeavour to relieve them from such thraldom as intemperance assuredly is.

In attempting such a sweeping measure there is a good deal to be considered, but there will be other opportunities later on of discussing the question. Meanwhile, we might venture the opinion that the large majority of this District would be in favour of total prohibition, and as requests have gone to our Representatives from the Sons of Temperance and the leading residents of the place...(and we doubt not other communities would do likewise were they within reach of wire), it is to be hoped that the Hon. Members will give the measure their fullest support, and thereby carry out the wishes of their constituents.[15]

....

The question of total prohibition has for some time past been engaging the attention of temperance advocates in various parts of our Colony, and for two or three sessions petitions numerously signed have been presented to the Legislature imploring legislation prohibiting the importation and sale of intoxicating liquors into this Colony. The measure of success that has thus far attended the labours of advocates of the movement is well known to our readers. Last session the prayer of petitioners was only defeated by a casting vote, and so now they are resolved to make another appeal, which we hope will be more successful than either of those previously made. With this view, petitions have lately been...signed by many of the inhabitants of this community, ladies included, and will be forwarded to our Representatives for presentation to the Legislature in a few weeks, and it is hoped that the subject will have their warmest advocacy. Petitioners only ask that a law may be made for the taking of a vote on the question throughout the entire Colony, so as to allow the people to decide for themselves whether they shall have the privilege or not of purchasing ardent spirits. Surely this is not an unreasonable demand on the part of our temperance advocates, and we can see no just grounds why the Legislature should refuse to comply with such a moderate request. If this were done then the campaign would be fairly opened, and those who may be opposed to the measure could come out boldly and advocate their cause, but we imagine that their best arguments in favour of the abominable traffic would prove very fallacious when compared with the benefits to the people directly and indirectly, which the supporters of the prohibition movement could produce as a result of total prohibition. The evils of intemperance are too well known by our readers to need dilation on here. It is hoped that the petitions soon to be presented to the Legislature will meet with a more favourable reception than any that have yet been received there on the subject of prohibition, and that a law in compliance with the wishes of petitioners will be enacted.[16]

....

Dear Sir, —
I noticed in your last issue that no less than seventy-six puncheons of rum had been recently imported into St. John's. This doesn't look much like prohibition...I believe the time is not far distant when the Legislature will see the wisdom of prohibiting the manufacture and sale of intoxicating liquors in Newfoundland. A prohibitory law is the only logical and adequate remedy for the grievances under which the whole Country is at present suffering, with respect to strong drink. We are convinced that this question is one essential to prosperity, and the well-being of this Colony.

Suppose the Government gets $18,000.00 duty on these seventy-six puncheons of rum, what about the expense of keeping our jails, court houses, etc. in repair? What about the salaries of Magistrates and policemen, who are being paid principally for the purpose of bringing to justice, and the prosecution of culprits, for the atrocious crimes committed whilst under the influence of the demon drink; generally the most heinous crimes are committed by men whilst under the influence of the "liquid fire." We may mention a few – arson, embezzlement, forgery, homicide, etc. The Government expends thousands of dollars more than the amount of duty collected on liquor, for the prosecution of parties who are guilty of crimes when influenced by liquor; besides the wasted health and strength, heart-aches, heart-breaks, misery and poverty, caused by its use. According to my calculation those seventy-six puncheons of rum would realize $27,360.00 (allowing ninety gallons to each puncheon), that is taking into consideration the advantage gained by retailing it over the counter, it would realize at least $4.00 a gallon; the publicans and shebeeners secure (after deducting $18,000.00 duty), $9,360.00 We have given a meagre description of the "Evil Beast."

St. John's warehouses, pre-1892

The question is, who will hunt him down, and how can he be killed? We answer, first by getting our children right on this subject; let them grow up with an utter aversion to strong drink; we will battle with this evil by voting only for the men who will give us the power by law to protect ourselves, our families and our Country, from the attacks of the "Evil Beast." We will war upon this evil by organized societies; we wish we could lay upon the rum casks a train, which when once ignited would shake the whole Country with the explosion of this monstrous iniquity. Do I address one whose regular work is to administer to this appetite? If a woe is pronounced upon the man who does this during every hour of the day, Sundays included. Do not think that because human Governments license you, that therefore God licensed you. Higher than the judicial bench at St. John's is the Throne of the Almighty; no enactment, national, state, or municipal, can give you the

right to carry on a business whose one effect is destruction, whether you sell it in a dungeon, cellar, or behind the polished counter of a first–class hotel, the Divine curse is upon you. We tell you plainly that you will meet your customers one day when there will be no counter between you, when your work on earth is done, and you enter upon the reward of your business, all the souls of them whom you have destroyed will crowd around you, and pour their bitterness into your cup; they will show their wounds and say you made them, and point to their unquenchable thirst and say you kindled it, and with their united groans will smite your ear, and with the hands from which you took the silver dimes, they will push you off the verge of the great precipice, while rolling up from beneath and breaking among the crags of the pit, will thunder, "Woe unto him that giveth his neighbour drink."
        Thanking you for space,
           I am, yours truly,
              PROHIBITIONIST[17]

....

Dear Sir, —
I venture to send a few comments on the letter signed "Prohibitionist," appearing in your issue of twenty-eighth March [1896]. I suppose there is no more sober community than Twillingate, though the letters appearing from time to time in your paper would lead outsiders to think quite the contrary. There are many absurd and misleading remarks made by "Prohibitionist" which ought to be contradicted. The use of drink in excess is no doubt a great evil, but at the same time there are many greater sins than taking a glass of spirits, though our teetotal friends may not think so. Does your correspondent mean to suggest that the Magistrate, two constables and Court House in this, and I may say, every other outport in the Country are maintained "for the purpose of bringing to justice and the prosecution of culprits for the atrocious crimes committed whilst under the influence of the demon drink?" And can he give any instances of any atrocious crimes that have lately been committed in this Country by any persons under the influence of drink? The list of crimes given as committed by men under the influence of "liquid fire" is rather peculiar. If at any time a man should take

particular care to keep sober it would be, I should say, while he was meditating and committing such crimes as arson, embezzlement or forgery. If he were not sober his chances of escape from detection would be very small. Experience shows that most great crimes are committed by cool, long-headed, temperate men, frequently I may add, under the guise of religion, as witness the numerous building society frauds lately exposed in England. Free drinkers are, as a rule, happy-go-lucky sorts of individuals, who seldom commit great crimes. Let it not for a moment be thought that I am defending intemperance. I am simply trying to put the matter in a fairer and less bigoted light than "Prohibitionist." It is a mistake to attribute all crimes and immorality to one cause and overlook the others. The statement that the Government spends thousands of dollars yearly more than is received in liquor duties in the prosecution of drunkards, and in keeping policemen, etc., on their account is absurd on the face of it. I have statements for '92 and '93 by me, in which it states that the expenditure on the whole judicial force is about eight per cent of the custom's revenue, while the receipts from liquor duty are nearly twelve per cent. In addition, I suppose no one would say that the prohibition of the sale of liquor in this Country would do away with the necessity for *any* judges, magistrates, police or gaols. At the very best it would only do away with a few of them, and it is quite possible that a much larger staff of police, and more judges, would be wanted to detect and prosecute the keepers of shebeens, which would inevitably crop up. How then would the deficiency in the revenue be made up? Are the teetotallers willing to subscribe the $170,000.00 or so among themselves? They certainly do not pay their share of the revenue now. Another thing is that prohibition would undoubtably injure us in our fish markets on the "if you don't buy from us, we won't buy from you" principle. "Prohibitionist" seems rather rough on publicans. I have known many of them – honest, respectable men, ever ready to help a friend in distress, and paying heavy licenses to the Government. I cannot see that their calling is any worse than many others. People will have drink, and it is better for it to be sold in licensed houses under the inspection of the police, and for the Government to benefit by the business done, than it is for it to be sold *sub rosa* in shebeens. It is a certain fact that there is nothing a publican objects to more than seeing a drunken man in his house. The talk about souls is of course not worth the notice of practical men; no soul will ever be lost on account of its owner taking an occasional drink. It may be interesting to note that the revenue on tobacco, which article was also lately attacked in your paper is about $110,000.00 per year.

I am, Sir, yours very truly,
A LOVER OF FREEDOM.[18]

....

By the start of World War I the temperance movement began a new phase, with advocates successfully persuading the Government to call a plebiscite on total prohibition. If this passed, not just individual towns, but the whole Dominion, would be dry. In November, 1915 citizens went to the polls. A large majority opted for prohibition, though well under half of eligible electors even bothered to vote. On 1 January, 1917 prohibition became the law of the land, and the only alcohol permitted to be sold in Newfoundland was for medicinal purposes.

During this time the Sun ran a "Prohibition Column," edited by Rev. R.S. Stirling, J.D.S. Barrett, and George Roberts. Its purpose was not only to boost the cause of "total prohibition," but also to inform electors on questions surrounding the vote and what would happen if and when prohibition came into force.

If Manitoba and British Columbia go dry, and indications are that they will, it will mean, with Alberta and Saskatchewan recently declaring in favour of temperance, that no license[d] bar will exist west of the Great Lakes. Adding Prince Edward Island, where prohibition has been in force for several years, more than half of the Provinces in the whole Dominion of Canada will be rid of the loathsome saloon and all its attendant evils...

Many persons are asking the following question: "If we have total prohibition in Nfld, will it be possible to obtain intoxicating liquors in case of sickness?

The question is fully answered by the Prohibition Plebiscite Act, sections of which will be published in this column from time to time...it shall be lawful...to grant a license to any qualified druggist [to sell]...intoxicating liquors for medicinal purposes, to any person presenting a prescription...signed by a duly qualified medical practitioner...

Another question being asked is "What affirmative vote is necessary to bring the prohibition law into effect?"

The reply is found in section. seventeen: "If the number of votes polled in the affirmative be a majority of the total number of votes polled at the election, and amount to at least forty per cent of the total number of registered voters upon the revised list of electors, taken for the purpose of the general election of Members of the House of Assembly held in the year 1913, the Government in Council shall issue a proclamation prohibiting the importation, manufacture and sale of intoxicating liquors into or in this Colony at any time after the first day of January, 1917, except as hereinafter provided.

Note: the above section may be briefly stated thus – it will be necessary for 25,000 men to vote "Yes" if Nfld is to have total prohibition (eds.)

Will *you* be one of the 25,000 on polling day, Nov. fourth?...

Names of the Members of General [Prohibition] Committee

Crow Head – George Hamlyn; John Mills; Henry Hamlyn; Samuel Dove

Wild Cove – Benj. Roberts; Jno. Elliott; Edwin Roberts; Jno. Roberts; Walter Roberts.

Back Hr. – W. Rideout; George Murry; Jno. Anstey; Jno. Rideout; James Anstey; James Janes; Lewis Purchase.

North Side – Rev. A.B. Stirling; George Roberts; W.J. Scott; Jacob Moores; F. Linfield; Arthur Manuel; W. B. Temple; Edgar Sweetland; A. H. Hodge; Stewart Moores; J. D. S. Barrett; Jas. Preston; Fredk. White; Alex. Moores; Fredk. House, Jr.; S. Loveridge; J.A. Templeton; Cons. Tulk.

South Side – S. Bennett; Adj. Sainsbury; W. Ashbourne; Ed. Hayward; Geo. Blandford; Walter Young; Gordon Rendel; W. Hughes; Saml. Watkins; C. White.

Farmer's Arm and Jenkins' Cove – W. Pond; Edgar Hawkins; A.G. Ashbourne; Peter Parsons; Jas. Gillett of Geo.; Joseph White; Hannibal Churchill.

Durrell's Arm – J.W. Minty; W. Snow; H.J. Howlett [Two other names are illegible]

DAVID J. CLARKE

*George Roberts, North Side representative,
General Prohibition Committee*

....

Though the catch may not have ben so good as could be desired, "cheer up," for there's life in the old land yet, and our turn will come again some day.

It's good to be home, safe and sound, and in time to bless our Country by a *solid* vote for prohibition on the fourth [of] November. Don't forget, the booths open at eight o'clock in the morning, and close at four o'clock in the afternoon.

Every make citizen to twenty-one years and upwards is entitled to vote. A resident of any District can vote in any booth within his District. Booths will be open in St. John's for all the Districts, for the convenience of those who may be there on polling day.

If it were by a majority prohibition would be carried easily, because the sweeping majority of the electors of this Country would not think of voting for the drink traffic.

But in this election a *vote not cast*, is a vote for liquor. And if prohibition is lost for the *want of the votes of professing Christians*, or any others, they will find themselves, after polling day in the awkward position of being responsible for the continuation of the *rum business* in this Country, with all its attending evils. A very uncomfortable position, certainly. Save yourselves from such a *guilty position* by voting *YES* for prohibition...[19]

....

(For the Sun) if two large halls packed to twenty-five per cent beyond normal seating capacity by audiences of childhood youth and mature manhood gathered in the centre of a circumference of many miles, not including visitors who had come by motor[boat] from outside harbours, may be taken as a criterion, then our people are rising splendidly to the occasion of the most important decision at the polls that has ever called for the exercise of that glorious talent entrusted to every man of twenty-one years – his vote. And would to God our women had come into their right to use the same power, then what a terrible cyclone would strike the Devil and his faithfully ally, "King Alcohol," whose throne is tottering and will fall ere closes this year of Grace by the help of God and the guardians of morality.

In Alexandra Hall, Mr. Ashbourne, Chairman, was very ably supported by the Campaign Committee on the platform while the massed choirs with organ, and Mrs. Temple, Jr. and Miss Scott. Organists were grouped below the dias.

The speakers were Adjt. S.A. Sainsbury, Revs. Bennett and Stirling, and Captains Isaac Young and Andrew Roberts, Jr., who in the meridian of life spoke at a public meeting for the first time and with no uncertain sound, and what temperance platform would be complete without Mr. Stephen Loveridge, a life[long] worker for the cause.

Needless to say, many sledgehammer arguments in favour of the abolition of alcohol were driven home by the speakers, and the immense audience joined heartily in specially printed Hymns, the effect being truly inspiring. Miss Margy Scott sang the touching solo, *Pass it On*, with original verse as follows:

DAVID J. CLARKE

In the prohibition fight.
Help it on.
Hear your weaker Brother's call.
Play the game.
Give your vote to help him rise,
And restore life's shattered joys.
Banish Wife and children sighs.
Play the game.

Stephen Loveridge, a "life[long] worker for the cause" of prohibition, and Wife Lilian, at Battle Harbour, Labrador, 1923

    The children were happy and well served in Victoria Hall. Rev. Stirling led opening devotions, Mrs. Stirling was in the Chair with Mr. Scott as right hand supporter. Catchy talks were given by Mesdames R. Temple and Facey, and Misses Batstone and Roberts, and Preston and Superintendents Sweetland and White. Hearty singing of selections from Sankey's Ed. by Miss Young, organist, kept all in good tune, and how they sang.
    A message was sent to Alexandra Hall by Rev. Stirling, and fully determined to win, Daddy and big Brothers, Uncles, and Cousins, to vote YES on polling day, the crowd dispersed after [the] National Anthem and Benediction.
    CORRESPONDENT[20]

....

(Special to the Sun)
Moreton's Hr. Saturday.
The Moreton's Harbour Prohibition Committee held [the] first meeting of [a] series at Bridgeport last night. [The] school house [was] crowded and much enthusiasm manifested. [A] unanimous response [was] made in favour of prohibition.

Several other meetings in this neighbourhood will follow in quick succession. This Sub-District will poll [a] practically solid vote for prohibition.

J.D.S. Barrett[21]

....

From the start, prohibition proved to be something of a farce. The law was widely flouted, with Newfoundlanders substituting patent medicines containing alcohol, like "Beef Iron and Wine," for their usual fare. At the same time, a lucrative bootlegging trade developed with the French island of St. Pierre, while closer to home moonshine stills and home brewing of beer proliferated. If all else failed, it was common for doctors to issue prescriptions for medicinal alcohol. In 1919 the authorities even had to call in a Royal Navy warship after the Constabulary was prevented from investigating alleged moonshine stills in Bonavista Bay. By the 1920s it was reported that members of the Newfoundland Government were in on the action, making money from the provision of illicit booze to a thirsty populace.

In 1924 the new Administration of Walter S. Monroe (1871-1952) repealed prohibition in favour of an Alcoholic Liquors Act which tightly controlled, but did not prohibit, the trade in beer and spirits. Few realized it at the time, but their seeming victory in 1915 marked the beginning of the end for the temperance/prohibition movement in Newfoundland.

A few years after the dust had settled, Twillingate Sun *editor Stewart Roberts offered a pragmatic perspective on this chapter in Newfoundland history.*

DAVID J. CLARKE

Newfoundland Prime Minister Walter Monroe (Rear-left) attends the Imperial Conference of 1926

"Temperance" was until a few years ago, the only word applied in reference to people who kept sober. Nowadays the word is more or less ignored, and for a substitute is "Prohibition." This recalls to mind a wise saying gleaned from a paper recently: "A greater thing than prohibition is sobriety."

There was for years no such a topic as prohibition; it was either temperance, or free or moderate drinking. Today the problem of carrying out prohibitive laws in connection with spiritous liquors becomes more acute, and only recently over 1,300 American clergymen (against about 600 – two to one), voted that prohibition does not settle the liquor problem in the United States. While [the] sale of hard liquor and rum running is an offence against the law, and to a great degree there is a change as regards the use of such liquor, yet beer and moonshine making, and drinking, is being carried on as never before; a new frame up, which is even worse than smuggling the real stuff, which is far better to use than poisonous substitutes. The new abuses cropping up [are] making it a greater problem to enforce, what a few years ago could be carried out with some measure of success.

To get to the root of the matter we must agree that there are many things that make for intemperance, when that which is good is abused, whatever it may be, and when it brings about excesses. The abuse of anything does not destroy its proper use unless it be something that is manufactured that cannot be used for...other than immoral purposes.

Where then is the end to be of the ever increasing problems regarding intemperance? Would it be wise to say "let every man be free to use his own conviction," and at the same time use all the exhortation possible in the cause of temperance, and as St. Paul said, "in all things"?

It has been said that were it not for a few, who make themselves drunkards, there would be no need of appealing to the arm of the law. Cannot moral suasion have the old time effect to cause this one or that one to be self-respective?

A point in connection with the Liquor Law now in vogue in this Country is that what brought about the formation of the Control Board was not in the main to control drunkenness, but to properly govern the sale of liquor. It is of course understood that prohibition carried out, would only allow sales for medicinal purposes, but there were loopholes enough in that law to bring all the abuses that came when the Controller desired to take advantage. Therefore, seeing that some are bound to have intoxicants – by fair means or foul – it means that a form of control of sale is better, even if there may be an odd loophole, which only the most clever may detect, except where breaches are allowed for the sake of getting revenue, and not to regard, the full proper control![22]

DAVID J. CLARKE

Not inserted by the Board of iquor Control

A sign of changing times – Twillingate Sun *whiskey advertisement, 1927*

10
"Memorials of the Past" ~ Early Religion on the Isles

*T**he nineteenth century was a time of great religious fervour in Newfoundland, and in fact, throughout much of the Western world. Pieces on religion and the various Churches appeared in every issue of the* Twillingate Sun. *In 1881 the paper published a series of articles, contributed by an author identified only as "T," that detailed the early years of Church activity on the Isles, allowing readers to reconnect with the faith of their ancestors.*

...There cannot but be much in the old past of the Church in Newfoundland that would be interesting to revive in the memories of Church people. The growth of the well-known settlements; the spiritual doings or the spiritual wants of our forefathers, and graded accomplishments of plans for their benefit; the gratitude due to the venerable [Anglican] Society for the Propagation of the Gospel in Foreign Parts; the increase of Churches and Church ministrations, as population has increased; all this, and much more, cannot fail, one would imagine, to interest our people, if only placed clearly and truthfully before them. The writer of these memorials was clearing out some old Reports of Newfoundland Church Mission work the other day, and a glance at some of the papers interested him so greatly, that, he ventures to publish some of the contents in the Church column.

Care shall be taken in the Memorials to give facts as actually repeated by writers of the reports themselves, and not mere hearsay or tradition. The earliest date found among the papers is the year 1822, at which time this Colony was still a part of the immense Diocese of Nova Scotia, one of the first American Colonial Dioceses for which Bishops were consecrated by the Church of England (Quebec being the other).

This great Diocese then included Nova Scotia itself, New Brunswick, Cape Breton Island, Prince Edward's Island, Newfoundland, and Bermuda, while the other Diocese of Quebec included all Canada. This year there are in the former territory *three* Bishops, and in the latter, *fourteen* Bishops of the Church of England; SEVENTEEN in place of two in sixty years.

In Newfoundland itself, in 1822, there does not appear to have been even an ARCHDEACON, but only an *Ecclesiastical Commissary*, whose name was the Rev. John Leigh.

The only settlements which were the residence of Church of England clergy seem to have been then, *St. John's, Harbour Grace, Trinity* and *Twillingate*, most, if not all of whom, were in the pay of [the] SPG. Rev. Mr. Blackwell was also tutor to the Governor's family.

Bishop A.G. Spencer

In the report for that year, we find names of clergymen, since celebrated in other Dioceses. *Mr. Spencer*, afterwards Bishop Spencer of Newfoundland, and then of Jamaica, now gone to his rest; *Mr. Ballock*, afterwards well known in Nova Scotia, but with respect to Notre Dame Bay itself, and Twillingate in particular, the report shall speak in its own words:

> The Rev. J.G. Laugharne, Missionary at Twillingate, continues to discharge the duties of his situation with

exemplary zeal; and notwithstanding the severity of the climate in that northern district, he was only precluded twice from officiating in the Church when the state of his health would not permit him to venture abroad. The congregations both at Twillingate and Fogo increase, and he flatters himself [that] the efforts of his ministry are visible in an improved state of morals and devotion throughout his Mission. The Society had placed at his [illegible] the Mission of Trinity; after some hesitation, Mr. Laugharne has declined to avail himself of the offer, and continues to reside at Twillingate.

Besides this description of the local Missionary's own work (one man for all the Bay), we have also the account of a visit to the District from the Commissary himself, in August, in a man-or-war —

On Mr. Leigh's arrival at St. John's, Lieut. Hose politely offered him a passage to Twillingate in His Majesty's brig *Snap*, which, in the anxious hope of making some arrangement for the liquidation of the debt incurred in building the Church and Parsonage there, Mr. Leigh accepted, and determined on commencing his travelling Mission by visiting the northern part of the Island, where he had begun his first Missionary labours. The prospect of settling anything definitely as to the payment of the debt on the Church and house being very little, he was obliged to leave Twillingate, after staying there nearly six weeks, with no other arrangement having been made than a meeting of the inhabitants should take place in the fall of the year, for the purpose of disposing of the pews. Mr. Leigh is extremely sorry that his stay at Twillingate was protracted longer than he should have wished by his not being able to get a passage to the southward, there being no communication or intercourse between Twillingate and any southern part of the island but St. John's, and none with that at that season. Mr. Leigh's route was to Greenspond, between which and

Twillingate there is no intercourse at any season; and the fishery being then in its height, a boat could not be obtained on purpose, without materially injuring the proprietor. Mr. Leigh is in hopes that this delay was not altogether unproductive as he had an opportunity of visiting some of the adjoining harbours. At Exploits Burnt Island, the Protestant inhabitants, who are partly of the established religion, and partly Protestant dissenters [sic], have commenced building a place of worship, in which the service of the Church is to be alternately read with that of the dissenters. The person who performs both services is a Mr. William Manuel, a planter of sober, pious habits, who receives no remuneration for his services.

How matters prospered afterwards, we shall probably learn from further reports. The Twillingate Church people seem to have been at that time in some difficulties respecting the debt upon their Church and Parsonage. Let us hope we shall find that means were forthcoming to defray the whole expense. It is to be presumed that the buildings were not those at present existing, for they cannot have been built so long. It is also evident from Mr. Leigh's report that he had himself been once the missionary at Twillingate.[1]

....

In referring to the report of 1825, it is found that Mr. Langharne had been removed from Twillingate and was assisting in visiting the outharbours around St. John's; Rev. Mr. Carrington being the permanent clergyman. How different matters were in the neighbourhood of the capital from their present state may be judged from Mr. Langharne's description of his ride to Portugal Cove. He says "It was an arduous journey, even on horseback." Now, so excellent are the roads around St. John's that *the walk* to the Cove is quite enjoyable for average pedestrians. And to reach Petty Harbour Mr. Langharne then had to proceed by sea. His successor at Twillingate was the Rev. John Chapman, of venerated memory in Notre Dame Bay, who is said in the report [to] have been received with great attention and respect.

In 1827 the then Bishop of Nova Scotia, Rev. Dr. Inglis, paid a visit to the Island in a man-of-war, the *Orestes*. This was the first voyage of visitation round the coast by a Bishop of our Church, but to how many was this the prelude! Bishop Spencer followed in his track; Bishop Feild made the work *biennial*; our present Bishop, in the rapid increase of population, will almost find an *annual* visitation necessary, in order to grasp all parts of the Diocese.

Bishop John Inglis

When the Bishop arrived, he found only eight clergy in all Newfoundland, none of whom were westward of Cape Race. Of these eight were, 1. Archdeacon Coster, in *Bonavista*; 2. Mr. Carrington and 3. Mr. Langharne in *St. John's* 5. Mr. Blackman and 6. Mr. Burt in *Conception Bay*; 7. Mr. Bullock in *Trinity* 8. Mr. Chapman in *Twillingate*. It would be interesting to follow his Lordship in his voyage. He appears to have been very successful, in all places, consecrating churches and cemeteries, and confirming large numbers of persons; in one place (Harbour Grace), as many as 339, and in another (Trinity), 367. He found the [illegible] from settlement to settlement difficult for want of roads, and mentions the fact that the clergy (among them Mr. Chapman) had persevered very laudably in improving the paths.

Trinity, pre-1892

But...our extracts must be confined to Twillingate and the neighbourhood, Bishop Inglis writes:

> Saturday, June 30th. The night was fine and the ship was under topsails only, as there was a very rocky and dangerous passage ahead, which could not be attempted till the morning. Through this we passed safely, and anchored at Toulinquet before noon. The missionary, Mr. Chapman, came on board, with his principal churchwarden, Mr. Pearce; and after completing arrangements for a preparatory service in the evening, and for the duties of the following day, we landed, and visiting the church and parsonage, which are large, and unhappily encumbered with a debt of £1500, which never will be paid. This amount is due chiefly to three

mercantile houses, and I could not have consecrated the church, if these houses had not kindly and properly consented to [illegible] the property to the Church...

Sunday, July 1st. We had a better congregation in the morning than we expected. St. Peter's Church and burial ground were consecrated, and the Archdeacon presented a very interesting sermon, but many of the people seem uncouth and wild, with little devotion and much apathy. The congregation, as is usual in Newfoundland, was large, in the afternoon, and I endeavoured to rouse them. Ninety-three were confirmed...but the church was so busy...that after the close of the services, the principal persons and I spoke...so sincerely on these points, that with much apparent sincerity they promised their best endeavours for improvements...Here, as at Greenspond, there is much jarring; and some very wild religious opinions have been introduced. Mr. Chapman seems earnestly desirous to promote their best interests, and discharge his duties faithfully.

The same evening the ship sailed further up the Bay. The Bishop continues,

Mr. Chapman accompanied us, and I greatly regretted that we were unable to visit Moreton's Harbour...
Monday, July 2nd. A current during the night had taken us out of our course, and but about ten o'clock we entered Exploits Bay, which forms the mouth of a...river of the same name. We landed on Burnt Island, where there is a...settlement and a church, but has no clergy...We left Mr. Chapman on shore to prepare the people for confirmation, and returned to sup with Mr. Peyton, the principal magistrate of the place...who was leisurely in the Navy Pay Office, but came to this place because his father required his assistance. We hardly reached the ship when a violent gale of wind arose, in

which several boats and some lives were lost, and we ran very rapidly for twenty-five miles up this magnificent river, with the topsails on the cape, when we anchored in a very safe harbour.

Tuesday, 3rd. This was the first day since I left Halifax that was devoted to personal gratification. The weather was fine, but as hot as I ever felt it. While the ship was being provided with wood, we went in the boats about thirteen miles up the river, to a rapid, where we landed, and walked to a splendid waterfall. The land is good, nicely wooded with large timber, and the scenery is rich and picturesque. Mr. Peyton, who was with us, has twelve fishing stations for salmon along thirty miles of the river, and the abundance of seal, deer [caribou], wild fowl, and game of every description is surprising. But our interest in all we saw was greatly increased by knowing that this was the retreat of the Bœthick [sic], or red or wild Indians, until the last four or five years. We were on several of their station and saw many of their traces. These stations were admirably chosen on points of land, where they were concealed by the forest, but had long views up and down the river, to guard against surprise. When Cabot first landed, he took away three of this unhappy tribe, and from that day to the present they have had reason to lament the discovery of their island by Europeans. Not the least advancement has been made towards their civilization. They are still clothed in skins, if any remnant of their race be left, and bows and arrows are their only weapons. English and French, and Mic Macs and mountaneers, and Labradors and Esquimaux shoot at the Bœthick as they shoot at the deer. The several attempts that have been made under the sanction of Government to promote an intercourse with this race have been most unfortunate; though some of them had every prospect of success. An institution has been formed in the present year to renew these praiseworthy attempts, the expense of which must be bourne by benevolent individuals; and while I am writing, Mr. Cormack is engaged in a search for the remnant of the race; but as it is known that they were reduced to the greatest distress by being driven from the shores and rivers, where alone they could procure sufficient food, and none have been seen for several years, it is feared by some that a young woman who was brought in about four years ago, and is now living with Mr. Peyton's family, is the only survivor of her tribe.

Bishop Inglis afterwards called at Fogo and then returned to St. John's and thence home to Halifax.[2]

John Peyton, J.P.

....

In the days which followed the visitation of Bishop Inglis, we still find that the clergy of Newfoundland were very few. Here and there one, in the chief settlements of the great Bays, but even up to 1832, not more than nine in all.

Of these, Rev. J. Chapman was in *Twillingate*; alone in charge of...Notre Dame Bay, there being no person in Holy Orders of the Church of England nearer than Bonavista (southward), and northward from Twillingate none. Even in our day, we sometimes complain of the labour and burden of missionary work, but how little real cause have we to murmur, when we find this man (Mr. Chapman) willingly paying a visit to Greenspond at the request of the Archdeacon, because they had no resident clergyman there.

With respect to his own mission, and Twillingate more especially, Mr. Chapman wrote as follows, describing first, the *State of Education*:

> No regular day school, as I am informed by all my neighbours whom I have consulted, and by my own observation since I came here, has ever, at any time, existed in my mission; nevertheless, many can read a little, some can write, and a few have acquired a trifling knowledge of arithmetic, especially at Twillingate, where the best means have been afforded; and since the year 1825 a Sunday school has been established at Twillingate; since 1826 at Fogo and Change Islands; and since 1827 at the Exploits Burnt Islands.
>
> Schools taught by old women and fishermen's servants, and those taught by planters in the winter months, when the severity of the weather necessarily prevents many small children from attending them, must be of very contracted influence; not to say that most masters who seem to have made the attempt here have been very incompetent, and in short, have wanted a master themselves. Our Sunday schools seem to thrive very well in summer, but in winter our numbers are, comparatively, very small.
>
> STATE OF RELIGION. — Since the time that the dissenting preachers began their ministerial labours in this neighbourhood, especially in Twillingate, there has always been a spirit of opposition manifested by a few to the Baptism, prayers, and as they call them, forms of the Church of England.

I think that a moderate, gentle, and mild carriage towards them, on our parts, will gradually unite most of them to us; though I am satisfied there are some incapable of being reasoned with, and unable to give an explanation of what their tenets are, and yet are too self-opinionated ever to alter. Upon the whole, our churches, generally speaking, are well attended, and the number of our communicants increasing. Our congregations are always the largest in the afternoon; this is common in all the outharbours. The Sabbath day is as much reverenced in Twillingate as in most places in this country, but in every harbour we have great reason to lament that it is not more strictly observed.

Mr. C. would have been less sanguine as to the result of his "gentle carriage" towards the dissenters, could he have seen Twillingate as it appears to a Churchman's view at this present moment. *Verbum sapienti satis est.*

In the Newfoundland School Society's report for 1828, is found as interesting extract:

Among several important applications for teachers received by your Committee that from Toulinguet or Twillingate claimed their first attention. The population of this harbour is large, and the inhabitants have undertaken to build schools and dwellings for the teachers at their sole expense. At Twillingate, which is 210 miles north of St. John's, a most encouraging prospect of usefulness presents itself: there are nearly 600 children, whose parents earnestly desire the blessings of Christian instruction for them. Mr. Willoughby arrived at twillingate on the 9th September, and quitted it on the 17th. In that short time a suitable building and sufficient land for a garden were freely given and duly conveyed by deed to the Society, and the sum of £160 was subscribed to build a dwelling-house for the Teachers, and put the building into a fit state for

conducting the school.
And in that for the following year, 1828, another:

> Mr. Walker, the Teacher appointed to take charge of the Society's School there, reached it in October last, and met with a very kind reception from the inhabitants.
> Owing to the great distress caused by the failure of the fishery, the new school room still remain[s] in an unfinished state. Mr. Walker, however, called upon the principal inhabitants, who expressed themselves very anxious for its completion. A public meeting was held, and subscriptions have been subsequently raised, amounting to above £70. Mr. Walker expected to occupy the new rooms in about a week after the date of his letter, in the beginning of December last. Meanwhile the attendance at the temporary school-room amounted to 40 day scholars; in the adult school, 28; in the Sunday school, 41. Mr. Walker has also a Catechetical Class. He speaks in very grateful terms of the cheerfulness with which the merchants and inhabitants generally render him every assistance in their power. He had received a good supply of wood. A haul was also promised, on which occasion the merchants had engaged to send men to assist.

It would be a subject worth enquiry, as to how far the Newfoundland School Society now called [the] "Colonial and Continental Church Society," is fulfilling its engagement in return for such conveyances as the above extracts mention. The school-house and ground have been alienated, and a simple £40 per annum is the extent of the present assistance afforded, far less than (one would imagine) ought to be the case where so good a foundation was laid. And it is a question whether the loss of this Central School on North Island, and the correspondent multiplication of schools in every cove, has not acted to the detriment rather than the increase of education.[3]

*Samuel Codner, founder of the
Newfoundland School Society*

....

Very little difference appears to have arisen in the position of the various Newfoundland missions during the latter part of the decade which ended with the appointment of the first Bishop in 1839. Rev. Mr. Chapman thus describes his mission in 1833: —

> The extent of my mission, or rather of the district I am employed in, is from this one end to the other, about sixty-four miles, including Twillingate, nearly in the centre; Tizzard's Harbour, Morton's Harbour, Exploits Burnt Island, and Fortune Harbour, on the west, and Herring Neck, Change Islands, Fogo, Barred Islands, Joe Bat's Arm, and Tilting Harbour on the east; altogether embracing a population of about 4000. In this

amount, however, the settlers in several little creeks are estimated. You will please observe also, that Tilting Harbour and Fortune Harbour I never visit, the settlers there being all Roman Catholics, and their number about 800. The churches are four; one at Twillingate, one at Fogo, one at Morton's Harbour, and one at the Exploits Burnt Island.

In this same District are now (1881) *five* clergy and *fourteen* churches, besides schoolhouses and other buildings used for services in various places. Mr. Chapman would have had a still more arduous and anxious work had he not found such lay-helpers as the following: —

> Mr. Pearce is kind enough to read for me at Twillingate when [I am] absent in other parts of my mission, and that without any kind of remuneration.

Material help in subscriptions appears then to have been very small.

> The contributions to the support of the Missionary are small. Six hogshead of coal have annually been given by Mr. Pearce; besides which, I know not of any thing except in itself of every trifling value. For marriages I demand ten shillings each; all other services are free. The people here always complain of their circumstances, and doubtless many of them are poor; therefore I have never solicited their contributions, while I am happy to say that the provision made by the Society is fully equal to all my wants.

Mr. Chapman did not exercise his usual far-sightedness in this particular of making no *annual* collection. He seems to have thought that the SPG grant which sufficed for himself, would never be reduced, and forgot that (like other kinds of education) by *giving we learn to give*. Habits of self-support in religious matters are as requisite in the Colonies as other habits of self-dependence. He who exercises his skill in every trade as far as he is able, or finds it a saving of expense becomes more self-reliant (and more handy) than the man who has to send for a tradesman to perform every smallest price of mending or making. And so he who forms a habit of giving regularly and liberally of his means for the support of his religion, takes an interest in his Church, and has a fuller right to speak in Church matters, than he who fancies that all should be done for him without cost to himself. Had Mr. Chapman established an Endowment Fund *then*, Twillingate might by this time have ceased to be dependent on missionary aid, for at least *one* clergyman, and have had the (much needed) services of a second.

Very different was the forethought and prudence which he showed in agricultural matters, as follows: —

> The extent of the glebe land is about thirty acres, all adjoining the parsonages. About six acres of it I have enclosed, and two acres of this is in an excellent state of cultivation now. The expense has been great, but it will in a few years make suitable returns. My plans have been as economical as possible, and I trust my example in agriculture has had considerable influence in bettering the condition of many families in this neighbourhood. The people here are generally very deficient in this permanent branch of independence, and they need both precept and example to make them comfortable against their will; for they had rather undergo any hardships at sea, generally, than seek support from the tardy efforts of the soil. They out their winter fodder for their cattle near the ponds and rivers in the uninhabited bays, and bring it home in large boats to dry. The trouble thus thrown away for three or four years, would cultivate as much ground at home as would serve their turn much better. In front of my house I have grown as much excellent fodder as will serve two cows this winter; besides, our crop of potatoes has been about sixty bushels. This autumn I have had three, four, and sometimes five men at work, cutting up trees and breaking up new ground than the quantity already fenced

in, about six or perhaps seven acres. Thus we enjoy many comforts which perhaps you may not have expected attainable in this inhospitable climate. I have seen this season samples of very good wheat raised by some of my neighbours, but it requires to lay in the ground twelve or thirteen months. It is my intention to enclose a little in this letter.

The merchants are giving less and less credit; and this, while it impels agriculture, will, I hope, finally show the planter how to become independent. The potatoes grown in Twillingate cannot be much less than 12,000 bushels yearly.

The agricultural reputation of Mr. Chapman has long survived him, as also his road making, and tradition points still to a certain enormous rock on Church Hill, which Mr. Chapman (who was a very large and strongly built man) is said to have rolled from off the road with his own hands, the workmen being unable to move it even with their combined strength. But the Mission Registers show that the Missionary not only acted in these capacities of promoter of tempered good, and encourager of improvement, but was diligent in visitations (so far as he could be) to all parts of Notre Dame Bay, holding services and performing offices for any who needed them.[4]

·······

In the report of a speech made by the (then) Bishop of Nova Scotia at the annual meeting of the SPG in 1838, we find His Lordship alluding to this Colony in very affecting terms:—

I must allude to another very engaging topic – the religious destination of the island of Newfoundland – a destitution most deplorable, and most difficult of full relief.

But there is no part of the British dominions where the services of devoted Clergymen are more affectionately welcomed, and no place where such services appear to be more eminently blessed. I have seen boat after boat follow the visiting Missionary from settlement to settlement, and it is impossible to behold a more becoming and cordial regard for the ministers and ordinances of the Church than is manifested by these warm-hearted people. It is most deplorable, therefore, that large numbers of them should be left entirely destitute of the spiritual instruction which they desire above all things. Thousands of them remain for years, for ten, twenty years, without seeing a Clergyman, and without the consolations of the Church of Christ.

It can scarcely be wondered at, that steps were immediately taken, to disconnect this Country from the overgrown Diocese of Nova Scotia, and to procure the consecration of a separate Bishop of Newfoundland. A fit and proper person was found in the Rev. Aubrey G. Spencer, Archdeacon of Bermuda, who (with the new Bishop of Toronto) was consecrated in England in August, 1839. Thus Bermuda gave Newfoundland her first Bishop, and in return Newfoundland gives episcopal care to Bermuda, and although the climate of the one is sub-Arctic, and that of the other sub-tropical, yet the Church and the Episcopate being one all over the world, climate makes no distinction.

The immediate effects of the appointment of Bishop Spencer will be seen from the following extract: —

> So much was done by the Society, in adding to the number of missionaries, and aiding in the erection of churches and parsonage houses, during the first three years after the erection of Newfoundland into a separate bishopric, that little, comparatively, remains to be reported this year. At the time of the consecration of the Bishop, in 1839, the whole number of clergy in the island was ten, it is now twenty-six. The missionaries in this diocese have, probably, more difficulties and privations to endure than in any other; while so great is the poverty of the people, that they can expect but little pecuniary support from them in any of their

undertakings. The general report, however, of the aspect of religious affairs is very encouraging, compared with what it was but a few years ago.

Seal of the Society for the Propagation of the Gospel

His Lordship, however, evidently found great difficulty in visiting his Diocese, for want of a Church-ship.

> But if, with all the aid that was afforded to my predecessor by the abundance of one of her Majesty's frigates and her well-manned boats, his lordship found the visitation of Newfoundland to be by far the most perilous and difficult of his laborious [sic] duties, you may suppose how fearfully these difficulties are aggravated to me who am deprived of the facilities which the Bishop of Nova Scotia, the Admiral Sir George Cockburn, and the Governor of the Province have all declared to be essential to Episcopal visitations in Newfoundland.

The only special mention which I find during these years of Twillingate, is the following:—

> Mr. Wood will relieve Mr. Chapman at Twillingate, as early as the opening spring will permit.

Now, as the Rev. Mr. Wood never came here, it may be presumed that Bishop Spencer's failing health, and consequent translation to the warmer climate of Jamaica, and the consecration of Bishop Feild in 1844 to succeed him, altered the contemplated arrangements. There appear to have been at the end of Bishop Spencer's episcopate in Notre Dame Bay, three clergymen:

Rev. J. Chapman, *Twillingate*.
Rev. J.C. Harvey, *Fogo*.
Rev. Wm. Hoyles, *Moreton's Harbour*.

By Mr. Chapman's own computations there were in 1842 in Twillingate (possibly including Herring Neck), 2,364 Church-people, and only 114 dissenters. At the present moment, it is a question (which the next census will probably in a measure show), whether dissent may not be almost or altogether in the majority. Possibly this will satisfy the writer of the letter in the Sun, who complains of "innuendo." But, seeing that Mr. Chapman puts down only forty communicants out of his high figures, and there are at least 216 in Twillingate alone, there is not the same appalling decadence from the Church that there seems to be.

To proceed with these "Memorials" into the Episcopate of the late, lamented Bishop Feild would be encroaching upon a subject which has already been taken up in a far more able manner by [Rev. H.W. Tucker,] the writer of the *Life and Episcopate of Edward Feild, Bishop of Newfoundland* [1877], which ought to be read by every Churchman. Suffice it to assert, that we the present generation of Church Missionaries are favoured above those who went before us, in having less physical difficulties to overcome, and may take courage in our prospect of the work set before us, having a worthy head and leader in our present Bishop, and a bond of support in the Diocesan Synod...[5]

DAVID J. CLARKE

"Morning Glory," St. Peter's Anglican Church, Twillingate, Newfoundland (Author's photo)

Section 4 ~
An Isles Miscellany.
Stories From These Shores

11
Stories From These Shores

The Wheelbarrow Man

Joseph "Joey" Strickland

In old Newfoundland it seemed that every settlement, ranging from the Capital down to the smallest outport, had its "characters," those individuals who always seemed to do their own thing, and made a name for themselves. Sometimes this was a good thing, and a local character might be noted for his or her talents, like the entertainer Mickey Finn was in early twentieth century St. John's. By the same token, one might become a local character for some less desirable traits, like extreme stinginess. For the most part, one simply had to march to the beat of their own drummer to become immortalized in community lore. Probably the most famous example of a "character" in Newfoundland fiction is Pigeon Inlet resident Jethro Noddy, created by Ted Russell. (1904-77) By some accounts, Change Islands was especially noted for its characters, and Canon George Earle (1914-2000), who later played one of the residents of Pigeon Inlet on TV, was renowned for his after dinner speeches that focussed on the amusing doings of Change Islands' most unique inhabitants.

Sometimes it was the special nature of one's work that earned a person the status of local character, and that seems to have been the case with Joseph "Joey" Strickland (Always pronounced "Stickland"). Joey was born at Twillingate around the year 1859, the Son of John and Hannah Strickland. He married twice, first to Rose Quenton (Quinton), and later to Anne (Jacobs) Legge, of Pound Cove, White Bay. A member of Twillingate's Congregational Church, Joey made his home in Robin's Cove, near the site of Twillingate's modern hockey arena.

During his lifetime the only way one could travel to or from Twillingate (apart from over ice in the Winter) was by boat, and coastal steamers made regularly scheduled stops in the "Capital of the North." To their passengers Joey Strickland was a familiar sight. Although he made part of his income as a labourer, Joey also filled a need in the community for portering services, bringing travellers' luggage back and forth from the steamers to their hotels or boarding houses. Depending on the distance to be travelled, he charged from ten to twenty-five cents. Strickland was familiarly known as the "Wheelbarrow Man," using his blue-painted conveyance, known (oddly enough) as the "Red Cross Express," to transport his customers' belongings. Joey's express barrow also served him in carrying water from local wells for other clients.

Like any good character, Joey Strickland was the subject of at least one, if not more, poems composed by local wits. While these have mostly been forgotten, at least one verse can still be recited by a few people today. It goes as follows:

> Onward Christian soldiers,
> Washing out their clothes.
> When they wants some water
> Joey Stickland goes.

Stories From These Shores

> Down past Moores'
> In through Wells' Lane,
> Dips it with a spudgel,
> and then goes on again.

Joey died on 18 January, 1922, apparently from the effects of an accident he'd had some time earlier. It seems that alcohol was a factor in his mishap, and the defenders of temperance –prohibition was still in force – couldn't resist getting in a dig at poor Joey as he went to his eternal reward. As the Sun reported:

> On Saturday last the remains of the late Joseph Stickland [sic] were laid beneath the sod by Adjt. Marsh of the Salvation Army. A goodly number of people attended the services, both at the Barracks and at the graveside.
>
> The Adjt. delivered a very able and eloquent address from the words found in Ecclesiastes, "He that breaketh the edge, shall be bitten by the serpent." He referred us back to the days of 1915, when Newfoundland voted in Prohibition and made its laws, which he claimed was the edge which we were to keep inside of, as if we broke the edge, and fell over the precipice, we surely would be bitten by the serpent. He visited Mr. Stickland while lying in his lamented condition on more then one occasion, and the deceased admitted that he was under the influence of liquor when the accident occurred, and therefore had been bitten after breaking the edge.
>
> Honourable in his confession, penitent in his humility, he at last claimed to have made it right with his Creator, through the influence and prayers of his spiritual advisor.
>
> The note was struck in order when the Adj. brought us face to face with our duties as a people, including the duties of the legality, the duties of the press, as well as the pulpit and platform, in seeing to it

that no repetition should occur in this particular, and to probe the sore and let the matter out. It is rightly demanded, and although hard obstacles will have to be mounted, yet right must prevail.

The remains were laid in the cemetery at Platter's Head, and all were sorry and lamented with the whole population of Twillingate the losing of a citizen in such an unwarranted manner.[1]

....

The Mysterious Mountaineer

Schooner Mountaineer

Newfoundland's modern Isles of Notre Dame District had longstanding ties with England's West Country, including the Counties of Devon, Dorset and Hampshire. Perhaps no city of the region maintained closer connections to the Isles than did Poole in Dorset. With a current population of around 150,000, Poole was first inhabited in pre-Roman times, and became an important port starting in the Middle Ages. By the

1500s Poole was noted for its involvement in the Newfoundland fisheries, with its trade in salt fish peaking early in the nineteenth century.

Starting in the seventeenth century, a number of Poole merchant houses established premises in Newfoundland. In the context of the Isles, one of the most important firms was the Slade Company, founded by John Slade "The Elder" (c.1718-1792). As early as 1773 John Slade & Company had a branch at Battle Harbour, Labrador, and its main headquarters on Newfoundland's northeast coast was at Twillingate (Branches were maintained at Fogo, Tilting, Moreton's Harbour and other locales). When Slade the Elder retired back to Poole in 1777, his Nephews assumed control of the business, continuing to trade in the Colony until the 1860s, when their assets were sold to a number of successor companies.

An important part of the Slade enterprise was its fleet of ships, used to transport cargoes of salt cod back to Europe, and returning to Newfoundland with fishing supplies and many of the goods the Island's fishers needed to carry them through the Newfoundland Winters. As early as the 1770s the Slade fleet consisted of about fifteen to twenty vessels, averaging about 100 tons each. By today's standards, such craft were incredibly small to be making the trans-Atlantic crossing, and it seems that the Slade Company was not averse to running its vessels for many years, sometimes well past their prime. These factors, combined with the notorious treachery of the North Atlantic, meant that the loss of a vessel was by no means uncommon. Still, the story of one Slade craft, the *Mountaineer*, provides us with a genuine maritime mystery, presaging the more famous case of the *Mary Celeste*.[2]

The *Mountaineer* was owned by the "Northern" branch of the Slade family, that most closely associated with the Isles. At eighty-seven tons, the schooner-rigged craft was small, but of about average size for the Slade fleet. She was constructed in 1836 at Hamworthy, Poole, by William Cox and Thomas Slade, Sr. At nearly seventy-seven feet in length, the *Mountaineer* was ornamented with the figurehead of a man, and Jenny Oliver of the Poole Museum Society speculates that it may have been named for the "Mountaineer," or Montagnais, people of Labrador (Innu). By the time the vessel was launched England's salt cod trade with Newfoundland was already on the wane, and according to Oliver, the Slades were one of the last West Country merchant firms active in the business.

The *Mountaineer* spent fourteen years plying the Atlantic between Newfoundland ports and European destinations such as Cadiz and Gibralter. In December, 1849 the schooner arrived at Poole from Newfoundland with a cargo of fish and oil, setting out for Gibralter with fish the following March. In April the vessel, under Captain John Tilsed, aged thirty-three, returned from Figuera with a cargo of salt and wine. Tilsed's crew consisted of six men, mostly English, but including a Nova Scotian and a Newfoundlander, Robert Warburton.

On 26 June, 1850, most likely manned by the same crew, the small craft set sail for Newfoundland with her cargo of salt. A voyage that should have taken weeks dragged into months, and by the Fall of that year the *Mountaineer* was given up for lost, most likely having foundered with all hands. Then, in October, the little schooner reappeared, floating largely undamaged about twenty-six kilometres from the Newfoundland coast.

She was discovered by a Jersey fishing craft named the *Canopus*. Strangely enough, there was no sign of the *Mountaineer*'s crew. The vessel's cargo of salt and provisions were intact, but the boats and anchors were gone, along with all personal possessions, save three miniature portraits of Queen Victoria's Daughter, Princess Alice, found in Captain Tilsed's locker. *Canopus*' Captain Duheaume put a crew of six on board the *Mountaineer*, bringing the abandoned vessel back to St. Helier, Jersey in tandem with his own craft. After their arrival in November, the ill-fated schooner was returned to Poole and, following the payment of salvage fees to *Canopus*' owners, once again pressed into service by the Slades.

In June, 1851 the *Mountaineer* was re-registered by Robert Slade, for John Slade & Company. For a another dozen years the old vessel faithfully made the Atlantic run with its cargoes of fish and provisions. In 1858 she had another close call, making it back to Poole after a stormy eighty-two day crossing. Starting in 1863 the *Mountaineer* was reassigned to the less arduous coastal trade, mainly carrying foodstuffs, clay and iron to ports such as Bristol and Southampton. The long-serving schooner's luck finally ran out on 26 January, 1873, when she was wrecked off the Isle of Man.

For the families of those seven men who set out on *Mountaineer* in 1850, however, there was never any word of their fate; even today descendants wonder what happened to their ancestors. A contemporary newspaper account from the *Poole and Dorset Herald*, uncovered by Ms. Oliver, speculated on what may have been the cause of their disappearance. The paper felt that the schooner might have run aground in fog, with her crew taking to the boats to determine their whereabouts, bringing along their personal effects as a precaution. Perhaps with a sea running, the little craft broke her anchors, leaving the men to fend for themselves on the pitiless Atlantic. They may have been quickly swamped by the waves, ending their suffering quickly, or just as likely, the luckless crew might have perished slowly of exposure, unnoticed by any potential rescue vessel, or unable to find their way to a port of refuge. Whatever their exact fate, the details remain unknown more than 160 years later, and may never be determined, yet another strange mystery of the sea.

....

Adventures on the Grace Boehner

The Grace Boehner *(L) at Twillingate's Coastal Wharf, c.1934*

With a maritime history of some 300 years, Twillingate has been home to many storeyed fishing craft, including the *Bessie Marie*, celebrated in verse in Chapter Five. One of the most interesting of the sailing vessels owned in the port of Twillingate, and probably the last to survive, was the *Grace Boehner*. The old schooner's career has been recounted in at least two unpublished articles written by former Captains, and through the reminiscences of her last skipper, W. Donald Linfield.

We can begin the proud vessel's story through the recollections of Angus L. Tanner, who was her Master from 1925 to 1927. He notes that the *Grace D. Boehner*, as she was then known, was built in 1919 by Boehner Ship Builders, based at LaHave, Nova Scotia, once the capital of Acadia. The schooner was 125 feet in length and of 157 gross tons. By this date, Captain Tanner notes, the use of large sail craft in the foreign trade was declining, and the vessel was laid down as a two-masted schooner, using stock materials on hand, that had originally been intended for a three-master.

The *Boehner* was constructed for Thomas Mossman, who served as her first Captain, using the vessel for cod fishing. However, the salt fish business was not a paying affair, at least not in those years, and in 1923 she was operated under charter by an American group which used her for rum running, under the command of Captain Amiel "Paddy" Mack.

In 1924 the schooner was sold to Captain Tanner, who at the time had been in command of the *Maud Thornhill*, another rum runner. After buying the *Boehner* from W.C. Smith & Co. Ltd., Tanner chartered her to an American, who used the vessel for running liquor from the French island of St. Pierre, off Newfoundland, to the United States. Her commander on that voyage was Fred Tanner who, upon arriving off Atlantic City, New Jersey, ran into severe weather, forcing him to anchor offshore. Captain Fred was finally forced to head to Lunenburg, Nova Scotia, arriving there with a full cargo of liquor on 10 February, 1925. Having lost his anchor, and being unable to discharge any of his illicit cargo, he refused to take the *Beohner* back to the American coast. At this point Captain Angus Tanner took command of his schooner personally. Effecting repairs, he sailed to Atlantic City where the cargo was discharged, or so he thought, and the vessel made it back to Lunenburg after a round trip of ten days. At this point, Tanner encountered another potential source of trouble, and we'll let him take up the story in his own words:

> At that time it was (as now) unlawful to have unsealed liquor coming in from a foreign port. I was not aware that, during the transfer of liquor to another ship, the crew had stored many cases of liquor in the fore-peak. This was made known to me when we were about to enter Lunenburg harbour. After being in the business for such a long time I was reluctant, after spending many stormy days and nights protecting the precious stimulants, to order them disposed of over the side.
>
> Instead we removed some of the plank flooring over the rock ballast, then dumped enough ballast to hide the liquor and then placed the planking back in its proper place. The job was completed just before tying up at the wharf in Lunenburg.[3]

With this adventure behind her, the *Grace D. Boehner* returned to the fishery under Captain Tanner, from 1925-7. He records that during this time the schooner was a "lucky ship," taking as much as 4,700 quintals of fish in a season. In 1927 she was sold to Zwicker & Co., and Captained by St. Clair Tanner, who was her Master until the vessel was sold once more in 1933. During this time the letter "D" was dropped from the schooner's name, as it was considered unlucky to have a vessel with thirteen letters in its name.

The vessel's new owners were John Gillett and Silas Facey of Twillingate, who paid $3,500.00 for her. The *Grace Boehner*, as she was now known, came under the command of C. William "Billy" Gillett, whose own account takes up the story at this point. Captain Gillett sailed to Twillingate with a crew of six men, four of whom slept up front in the forecastle. While the crew were accommodated below deck, the steering in those days was done in the open, exposed to all the elements. During heavy weather the man at the wheel would have a rope attached to him to prevent his being swept overboard by the surf.

Captain Gillett remembers that navigation was of the most basic type. The *Boehner* had no electronics in that era, with only a compass, ship's log and charts to rely on. He would often navigate with a sextant, using the sun to calculate latitude, with a chronometer for longitude, methods that had been in use for well over a century (Much longer in the former case). Still, Captain Gillett recalls that the "*Grace Boehner* was a wonderful sea boat, especially in bad weather – handle her right and she would bring you back safely to land."[4]

During her first Summer under Twillingate ownership the schooner made a trans-Atlantic voyage, taking a cargo of salt cod, loaded at English Harbour West and Harbour Breton, to Oporto, Portugal. With very light winds, and the vessel reliant on sail, she made a slow crossing, taking a month to reach her destination. After spending nearly three weeks in Oporto, Gillett and his crew headed to Cadiz, Spain loading salt for Battle Harbour, Labrador. By the time they made it back to the western shores of the Atlantic, however, it was considered too late in the year to head north, and the salt was discharged at Moreton's Harbour, with a cargo of fish from the community then taken on to St. John's.

In his eight years on the *Grace Boehner* Captain Gillett had many adventures, including one storm-tossed December run south from Twillingate that saw the vessel brought into St. John's under tow on 10 January. On a 1934 voyage between Halifax and Sydney, Nova Scotia, storms turned what should have been a twenty-four hour trip into an ordeal lasting some ten days.

During these years the schooner made a number of voyages to Gloucester (Massachusetts), Halifax and North Sydney, transporting coal for Newfoundland. The *Boehner* was also used in taking salt fish from Labrador to St. John's.

Life was made somewhat easier for the vessel's crew in the Spring of 1935, when the owners installed a thirty hp engine which made it easier to manoeuver around the coast, and get in and out of harbour during moderate seas. Still, this did not mean that all dangers were past, and in December, while making about 9.5 knots, the schooner nearly ran into Ragg's Island near Walsh's Point, clearing the rocks by only some thirty metres.

Captain Gillett recalls that of all the difficult trips he made in the *Grace Boehner*, perhaps the worst came in late November, 1940, on one of the coal runs from North Sydney to Twillingate. Off Cape Race the vessel encountered a SE gale, with heavy seas washing all her deck cargo over the side, and breaking out the cabin house's skylight. Sadly, the ferocious storm also resulted in the death of Mate Harry Oxford, Captain Gillett's Cousin. Oxford was swept overboard by the waves, just as the seas turned the vessel around. Gillett notes that it took considerable time and skill to get the *Boehner* back on course, and by that time it was far to late to do anything for Oxford, who was never seen again. Donald Linfield points out that it was the only time in her long career that the trusty schooner ever lost a member of her crew. Unable to save their colleague, Captain Gillett and the remaining crewmen pushed on through winds of over fifty knots. They were finally able to make port at Petty Harbour around three pm the next day. After several days of repairs, and reporting the loss of Mate Oxford, they proceeded to St. John's before heading back to Twillingate with a load of deck cargo, and then going north. After further adventures, including another fierce storm, the vessel finally docked back at Twillingate on 10 January, 1941.

About two months later Captain Gillett received his Master's Ticket and decided to move on to other challenges. Tendering his resignation, he headed to Halifax, taking up command of the steamer *Fernfield*. At this point the mariner's Brother, George Gillett, assumed the Captaincy of the *Grace Boehner*. In this period Linfield remembers that the schooner was used to bring bombs from Halifax to the American base at Argentia, Newfoundland.

One of the vessel's strangest adventures occurred while George Gillett was in command. The tale is recounted in contemporary newspaper accounts, and recalled by the *Boehner*'s then-Mate, Mr. Linfield. Strangely, the schooner was not even at sea when this event took place, but was instead docked at North Sydney. Accompanying Linfield (who had just been married), were Captain Gillett, Chief Engineer Chesley Ings, Second Engineer Gerald Farthing and cook George Holwell, along with sailors Harold Bulgin and Vernon Woodford. Farthing, Holwell and Woodford hailed from Herring Neck, with the remaining crew calling Twillingate home. Linfield remembers that the vessel docked about midnight, and that they heard a great bang around three am. Unbeknownst to the *Grace Boehner*'s crew, a heavily loaded flat car, weighing some twenty tons, had gotten loose, running out of control from the CNR Yards a distance away. Crashing into the vessel, the flat car snapped off the *Boehner*'s foremast at deck level (A second flat car had also broken loose but was brought to a halt before reaching the vessel due to track damage caused by the first car). That all the crew survived unscathed was something of a miracle, the tide being just right for the runaway car to land atop the deck without crashing down from a height or smashing into the superstructure. Had the *Grace Boehner* been any lower or higher in the water, it is likely that Farthing, Holwell, Bulgin and Woodford would never have made it home. It took about eight weeks to get the damaged schooner repaired since, as Linfield states, she "was beat to Kingdom Come in the forward part." He also laughingly notes that the vessel "must be the first schooner to get run down by a train!"

This wasn't Linfield's last harrowing experience on the *Grace Boehner*. In December, 1958 the schooner was caught in a massive hurricane, with recorded wind speeds of 100 knots. The storm saw a rogue wave smash all of her dories, the only thing the crew had in the way of lifeboats. After battling the seas for about twenty-four hours, they finally made Sydney, where a week's worth of repairs were needed to get the craft in order.

By 1959 Don Linfield was working on other vessels, like the Ashbourne-owned *Bessie Marie*, on which he also served as Mate, but he eventually returned to the MV *Grace Boehner*. In 1963 the venerable craft had made its last run to Sydney for coal, but the following year, under Linfield's command, it returned to the port, also stopping in Lunenburg, to unload a cargo of salt fish from Nipper's Harbour.

After that the schooner made one or two trips to the Labrador fishery, but was by then considered too old for the run across the Gulf of St. Lawrence. She was then moored at Purcell's Harbour on South Twillingate Island, but in the 1970s it was decided to put the vessel to a new use as a tourist attraction. Brought into Twillingate's main harbour, it was surrounded by fill with the idea of it being permanently docked for visitors. Unfortunately, the old vessel soon began to deteriorate, and within a few years it was decided to dismantle the once proud craft. As Mr. Linfield laments, it was "a sin what finally happened" to her, as parts of the schooner were simply brought to the dump. Instead, he feels, the *Grace Boehner* should have been taken back to sea and let sink with flags flying, a more fitting end for a vessel with so many adventures under her belt. Given her many trials and tribulations, and the number of men she brought safely to port (perhaps as many as 100 over the years), I couldn't agree more.

....

Change Islands' New Church

The old Change Island United (Methodist) Church, built, 1897 (Author's photo)

For most people living on the Isles in the nineteenth or early twentieth centuries, religion was part and parcel of daily life. The temperance movement, detailed in Chapter Nine, largely grew out of the strong religious temperament of the period, and which manifested itself in many aspects of daily life. It was common for members of a congregation to band together and perform volunteer work when their church needed to be repaired or cleaned. The same was true when it was decided that they needed a new church building. From the mid-1800s through to the turn of the century, the area saw the construction of a number of churches, many of which are still standing. Today, none of those who helped see the work completed are still living, and the written records of church construction are sparse indeed. In some cases, accounts have survived which give at least a some insight into the "who, when, where and why" of a congregation's efforts to provide themselves with a new place of worship. Such is the case for Change Islands' old United (Methodist) Church, constructed in 1897. To mark the fiftieth anniversary of its completion, a short history of local church life was prepared, with specifics of the first few years provided by Mr. Horatio Taylor, and the remaining details filled in using Church records. This document is one of the few surviving, detailed accounts of the building of a church on the Isles, although their experience was probably typical of many of the outport faithful at that time.

According to the history, in October, "some fifty years ago," a public meeting was called to discuss the possibility of erecting a new Methodist Church for the citizens of Change Islands. The well-attended gathering was chaired by Rev. Ackroyd Stoney, the incumbent of Herring Neck.[5] Taylor reported that every man at the meeting was in favour of proceeding with the new church building. A Building Committee was quickly established, consisting of the following: T.W. McGinn (or MacGinn), James White, Frank Taylor, James Waterman, William Diamond, Archibald Elliott, John LeDrew, William John LeDrew, John Porter, John Pelly, Solomon Roberts and Edgar Taylor (The only Committee member still living in 1947).

By late November the Committee had organized an expedition to secure the wood needed for their new church, and a fleet of seven schooners set off for Gander Bay. They were: *Beulah* (T.W. McGinn, Master), *Thrasher* (A. Elliott), *Ocean Home* (Benjamin Taylor), *Fidel* (Frank McGinn), *British Lion* (William Diamond), *Flying Mist* (John Diamond), *Jessie* (Frank Taylor), *Columbia* (James White). Arriving at Big Bight, the little flotilla's men set to work in earnest selecting and cutting all the material they needed.

Despite their good intentions, the elements seemed to conspire against them. Just as all the materials had been cut and ready to be loaded onboard the schooners, a fierce storm blew up, with northerly winds which soon veered to the NW. A number of the little vessels were blown ashore or had their booms broken, while their crews barely escaped the gale with their lives. This ordeal was barely over when intense cold set in. Soon the Bight was beginning to coat with slob ice, preventing the men from loading any of the material they had worked so hard to secure. For the moment they were forced to abandon the expedition, returning to Change Islands with little to show for their work.

Still, they were undaunted, and in May, 1895 they set off once more to see their church completed, not just for themselves, "...but for the rising generation..." [6] This time the little fleet succeeded in getting the materials back from Gander Bay, landing it near the road opposite the chosen building site. They then proceeded to chop and saw the wood into suitable boards for construction. That same month, master builder Josiah Roberts of Twillingate arrived to oversee the project as foreman. Roberts then spent the Summer making boxes and sashes, and otherwise preparing the materials for the Fall when work could begin in earnest.

Soon after the Change Islands men returned from the Labrador fishery they set to work again, and by 1896 the foundation had been laid (Hence, the date of 1896 was mounted over the door). Rev. Stoney's successor, a Welshman named William Harris, was chosen to lay the cornerstone. Work on the Church continued throughout the Winter and Spring of that year. By June the building had been "...framed, rough boarded, clapboarded, shingled and all windows and doors put in their places." [7] That Summer Roberts continued on alone, completing the fine detail work on both the inside and outside of the new house of worship. In the Fall of 1896 local men, once more returned from the Labrador, helped dismantle the community's old Methodist Church, with services being conducted in the South Side schoolhouse pending the opening of the new Church.

Work continued into the Winter of 1897, with both the older and younger members of the Parish taking a great interest in the project. For a time their spirits may have been dampened somewhat following a serious accident on-site. "Uncle" John Porter, a longtime Church stalwart, Class Reader, and member of the Building Committee, had been working on the top scaffold when he lost his balance, falling to the floor beneath. All work came to a standstill, and the history notes that

Porter was "entirely disabled." He was carried home, and it was a considerable length of time before Uncle John fully recovered. Despite this setback, building went on into the Spring, and over the Summer Foreman Roberts and a crew of three men finished the remainder of the job.

On 18 October, 1897 the day parishioners had "...so long anticipated and longed for..."[8] arrived, as the Change Islands Methodist Church opened its doors for worship the very first time. Presiding over the service was the Rev. Albert J. Holmes, successor to Rev. Harris. Other principal speakers were Rev. William Henry Browning from Fogo, along with Levi Perry, and Solomon Roberts, who served as Chair. Along with addresses by each of these men, a number of hymns were sung, including number 403, *How Firm a Foundation*.

Sadly, three men who dedicated many hours to seeing the Church completed did not have long to enjoy their new place of worship. Eli Diamond died in June, 1897 before the Church was even opened, while Jonathan Bursey followed in February, 1898, his funeral being the first conducted in the new building. Two months later Parishioner Frank Ginn was the victim of a tragic accident, shot while seal hunting off the White Islands. He survived only a few hours after the mishap. Ginn's funeral was attended by some 600 persons, the Church being filled to capacity. The history notes that the deaths of three of its members in so short a time cast a gloom over the congregation, but they would solider on.

With the opening of their Church, the Building Committee evolved into a Board of Trustees. Some of those active with the Board in this era included Levi Perry, Solomon Roberts, John Porter, Frank Taylor, Matthew LeDrew, George Bursey and James White. Within a few years some of their number were gone, Levi Perry moving to Joe Batt's Arm, and John Porter taking up residence in Grand Falls. Around 1920 Frank Taylor had immigrated to the United states, while Solomon Roberts passed away in July, 1919. Even so, there were always others ready and willing to take up the torch from their predecessors.

It should also be kept in mind that it was not just the men who performed invaluable service to the Church. Mrs. Susan Roberts was responsible for organizing a Ladies Aid Society, which was still going strong as the Church marked its fiftieth anniversary. For many years

Mrs. James Waterman of North End was the Church's organist and choir leader, shaping her charges into what many described as "...the best choir outside St. John's."[9]

An important development occurred in the Summer of 1900, as Change Islands' first resident Methodist Minister arrived. Rev. William Patterson lived on the South Side, in the house of T.W. McGinn, owned in the 1940s by T.W. Peckford. In 1904 the congregation started work on a parsonage, which was completed two years later, Rev. W.J. Morris being the first Pastor to occupy the structure. Change Islands' Methodist Congregation saw many Pastors come and go between the opening of their new church in 1897 and the commemoration of its golden anniversary. Fifty years on, their faith had not flagged.

A United Church congregation is still active on the islands, though there are now far less inhabitants to attend services, a common problem for all religious denominations in the community. Even so, the spirit of the early builders is not forgotten, and we will end our retrospective on Change Islands' new church in the same way as the 1947 history did, by taking "...a glance back once more to the Fall of 1897..."[10]

> October 18th, the first Sunday this church was opened; as you can imagine it was a big day for old and young. Rev. Browning from Fogo conducted the evening service and all who could possibly attend did so. The evening service was even more largely attended, being conducted by our own Pastor, Rev. Albert Holmes. His text was, "Upon this rock I will build my church and the gates of Hell shall not prevail against it"...Hymn forty-six in the Hymnary was very heartily sung with such feeling and thankfulness to God.[11]

....

DAVID J. CLARKE

Fire and Ice

Thermite charge exploding an iceberg off Twillingate, 1926

With the decline of the northern cod fishery and the cod moratorium of 1992, Isles towns were concerned with finding a new economic pillar to replace that which had supported their inhabitants for well over two centuries. Governments at all levels could take some lessons from history, reflecting on the way then-Premier Smallwood had tried to graft heavy industry onto the Newfoundland economy in the post-Confederation era, with less than stellar results. Located far away from larger markets, and with a limited population at home, the Province was clearly not marked out for this kind of development. The discovery of offshore oil reserves provided a good deal of relief for a beleaguered populace, even erasing the "have not" status the Province had carried since it became part of Canada. Still, the industry created little employment outside of St. John's and its hinterland on the Avalon Peninsula. For outport Newfoundland & Labrador, another solution was clearly needed.

    Both citizens and politicians focussed on the region's natural advantages to create a new source of revenue for rural areas, drawing on the spectacular beauty and unspoiled vistas of the extensive coastline. While tourism hasn't entirely filled the void left by the fishery, or even replaced it altogether, it has provided another much-needed economic pillar for rural Newfoundland. Some locales on the Isles, such as Twillingate and Fogo Island, have become especially busy Summer tourist centres, with the former community receiving some 70,000 visitors per annum, according to some sources. The focus of tourism marketing is often on the ever present sea, which has shaped and defined the Isles since time immemorial. Whale watching from tour boats or kayaks has become a popular draw for visitors to Twillingate. An even bigger attraction (perhaps) are the icebergs that drift southward from northern waters, their huge, crystalline shapes a source of endless fascination, and countless photographs, in the Spring. So much have icebergs become a part of the Twillingate experience that the town now bills itself as "The Iceberg Capital of the World" (A title also claimed by St. Anthony on the Great Northern Peninsula).

That being said, icebergs weren't always viewed in the positive light they now are, as natural wonders. In the days of the cod fishery they were considered at best a nuisance, at worst a real danger. With ninety percent of their vast bulk lurking beneath the surface, the bergs could easily "founder," rolling over to swamp any vessel unwary enough to stray too close. Even if they didn't present an immediate danger to life and limb, the giants might still drift into a fisherman's nets, carrying them away or destroying them. For those eking a precarious existence from the sea, with its razor thin margin between success and failure, the loss of a good portion of one's gear could be ruinous. This would create untold hardship for the family, and Newfoundland fishers were always concerned with getting their gear out of the path of the icy behemoths, or even with towing the smaller ones away from fixed gear like cod traps.[12]

On the international scene, icebergs weren't taken much into consideration, or so it seemed, at least not until the Spring of 1912. In April of that year the brand new White Star liner *Titanic* went down off the coast of Newfoundland hours after striking a large iceberg, the disaster resulting in the loss of some 1,500 souls. In the wake of this most famous of maritime tragedies the Coast Guard International Ice Patrol conducted experiments to see if it would be feasible to simply destroy any large bergs that were threatening shipping. As early as 1913 a US Revenue Cutter fired its six-pounder gun at a berg on the Grand

Banks, to little effect. The experiment was repeated with more guns, but no more success, than the earlier attempt. In 1923 the United States Coast Guard tried to destroy a fast moving iceberg in the shipping lanes using underwater mines, but it was found that conditions had to be ideal in order for this to be a viable solution.

It was at this point that Professor Howard Turner "H.T" Barnes entered the picture. Born at Massachusetts in 1873, Turner's family moved to Canada in 1879. After completing his Doctorate in Science at McGill University in 1900, he joined the institution's Physics Department, becoming the Department's Chair in 1919. Throughout his career Barnes took a special interest in iceberg research, and in attempting to reduce ice on the St. Lawrence River. Taking very much the "old school" opinion of icebergs, he considered them an enemy of humanity.

While it was decades away from claiming the title of "Iceberg Capital," Twillingate was already known as a place where the masses of ice gathered during the Spring/Summer, and so it became a focus of Dr. Barnes' research. He had been present for some of the attempts to destroy icebergs with mines, and felt that there was a better solution at hand. Barnes advocated the use of thermite, a mixture of aluminum and iron oxide, to destroy the bergs from the inside out. When ignited, thermite reacts violently, burning at temperatures of up 3,500° C. Hot enough to melt steel, this would, in Barnes' opinion, be just the thing for quickly reducing a dangerous iceberg.

The Summer of 1926 found Barnes taking up quarters at Twillingate's Notre Dame Bay Memorial Hospital, with laboratory space provided by the facility's Director, Dr. Charles Parsons. Barnes and his colleagues conducted tests on three bergs, starting with the largest one they could find. The researchers placed about forty-five kilograms of thermite about a metre into the iceberg and fired the compound. Barnes reported that the result was:

> ...the emission of flame and fire to a height of 125 feet or more with a great explosion of the ice and the throwing off of great masses of the ice from the sides and ends of the main plateau tested. This iceberg was, we estimated from our survey, 500 feet long by as many

wide, and its mountainous cliffs rose on one side to a height of between 75 to 100 feet with a second plateau 60 feet up. These measurements were made all from the water line and no estimate was made of the mass under the water. The whole berg was stable and oscillating very slowly from the swell with a period of from 4 to 5 minutes. As anticipated, the effect of the intense heat in direct contact with the hard ice was to send a temperature wave into the mass which produced a great deal of cracking and visible disruption, apart from the explosive shock...of the dissociated ice itself. This cracking went on all the evening after we returned to the village and could be distinctly heard out at sea 5 miles away. Toward the early morning a very loud report resulted which woke many of the people of Twillingate, and when we visited the berg the next day we found the great bulk of the interior had come away...[13]

The next berg targeted by Dr. Barnes was a smaller example aground in the harbour at Jenkin's Cove, Durrell. This time the researchers used some 225 kilograms of thermite, which they inserted slightly farther into the berg. The charge was fired near sundown so locals could see the effects of the disrupting ice, "...like Vesuvius in eruption."[14] A third, mushroom-shaped berg aground off North Island was the next to be tested. In this case, less thermite was used, but this was distributed between two charges. Though explosions resulted, the berg didn't break up in earnest until the next day.

While Professor Barnes was generally pleased with the results of the thermite tests, he concluded that the compound would have to be inserted much deeper into a berg – perhaps fifteen to thirty metres – for the result to be truly effective. Even so, some journals were soon predicting that Barnes might have hit onto the solution for ending the menace of icebergs.

However, the experiment had an obvious drawback; closely approaching one of the unstable masses of ice in the notoriously stormy North Atlantic to insert the thermite just didn't seem feasible. With that in mind, the Ice Patrol turned its attention towards what they saw as a more practical way to destroy the bergs – bombing from aircraft. By 1960 more tests, including new experiments with thermite, were judged to be failures, and the Ice Patrol turned their efforts from destroying bergs toward tracking them and issuing warnings to mariners. In the end the efforts of men like Dr. Barnes produced few results, though he did give the residents of Twillingate one of their only opportunities to see an "erupting" iceberg. These days, thousands of visitors are probably just as glad his experiments did not bear fruit.

....

Be it Ever So Humble...
By Ernest G. Clarke

Newfoundland Ranger E.G. Clarke of Twillingate

(This story, which took place in the 1930s, is recounted from Mr. Clarke's years serving with the Newfoundland Ranger Force). [15]

Stories From These Shores

Be it ever so humble, there is no place like home. And to Uncle Sam Blake and his Wife Lottie their dilapidated cabin of rough hewn logs, burrowed into the side of a hill in a sheltered bay of central Labrador, was as precious a possession as the finest mansion to its millionaire owner.

As a young man Uncle Sam had toiled long and hard to prepare this "Winter house" for his bride. In Summer they lived near other families on bleak Bolter's Island in a dwelling even less pretentious, but in Sam's opinion quite good enough for the few months they spent there fishing for salmon and cod. A true Labradorman, he lived only for the freeze-up when with his family and his few possessions he snugged himself down in his Winter home and lived "off the country" until break-up in May.

Uncle Sam had chosen his isolated Winter location with care and wisdom. Firewood, generally a scarce commodity in that section of coastal Labrador, was readily procurable in sufficient quantity to satisfy the old "Waterloo," the one-roomed cabin's only stove. Partridge were to be had for the shooting, rabbits wove a fancy pattern on the fresh snow of the clearing. His rifle brought down the occasional deer a day's travel inland; seals learned too late of his keen eye and steady aim, and provided him with most of the few essentials his Spartan life demanded – good solid food for himself and his dogs, harnesses and traces for the team, lash lines for his komatic [sleigh].

Aunt Lottie, a fitting partner for such a man, had learned in childhood to make sealskin boots and mitts, sewn with fine threads of the seal's windpipe which swelled when wet to make a watertight seam; the seal's intestines when dried, stretched and sewn together in strips, made ideal window panes, its fat provided illumination in the long Winter evenings.

I first met this fine couple, well up in years then but still sturdy and self-reliant, one stormy February evening when our [dog] team pulled up the bank from off the bay ice as weary from a day of toiling that they showed no interest in the overtures of Uncle Sam's snarling pack. My driver and I were completely spent after eight hours on snow shoes doing a bare ten miles from the Hudson's Bay Company [HBC] post we had left that morning. The yellow gleam from the cabin's single window seemed almost too good to be true.

DAVID J. CLARKE

Aroused by the outcry of his team, the old Labradorman was out to greet us in a matter of seconds. From then on we were his guests and everything he owned was at our disposal. Ten minutes later our dogs were being fed, our travelling kit had been brushed of snow and carried in, harnesses and traces coiled and hung to dry on the wall, ourselves divested of parkas and outer gear, and everyone once again completely content and at home.

The storm which had overtaken us at noon that day was even worse next morning. Travelling was out of the question and we had no choice but to stay where we were. Conditions in the little twelve by fifteen cabin were somewhat crowded to say the least, for there were six of us, Aunt Lottie and Uncle Sam being the proud foster parents of a young boy and girl orphaned the previous year.

Sleeping accommodations, though somewhat primitive, were quite comfortable. The old man and boy slept in one wooden bunk fastened to the wall, his Wife and the little girl in a similar homemade bed on the same side. The latter was screened with an old blanket as a concession to privacy demanded by our presence. My driver and I, from long habit, saw no reason for complaint that we must sleep in our eiderdowns on the rough floor, and woke each morning as refreshed as if our rest had been taken on the best spring filled mattress.

Seven days the storm continued and yet no one of us found the time long or conditions justifying complaint. We had come to Uncle Sam at a bad time, for his previous Summer had been one of small returns and he was now on the "dole," a form of Government assistance which in the thirties was limited to less than two dollars per head per month. Hunting had been very poor and at our arrival the family had less than two days food on hand.

Our komatic box, provisioned for a week's trip to the south, could not stand up indefinitely under the demands of six hungry mouths, and before the storm had ended we were on short rations indeed. The hardest blow came when tobacco, that wonderful consolation in times of enforced idleness, had dwindled to an insignificant portion of the last remaining plug.

Long before this Uncle Sam had been taking precautionary measures to eke out the supply, perhaps feeling a bit self-conscious that he had none of his own. Filling his pipe was done with extreme care, a little crumbled tobacco, a drop of molasses, more tobacco, then another drop, so on until filled. This, he had found at some earlier time of privation, could provide a man with several smokes before the last whiff was gone. And, as if to make light of the present dearth, he recalled for us the time when some of his companions had cut up their pipe bowls and smoked them until only one pipe remained!

What do you do when you are stormbound under such conditions? You take it and you like it, and you devise ways and means of passing the time. More precious to us than anything else, perhaps, was one lone rabbit which was Wintering near the cabin. Every morning we three men dressed and secured a stock of firewood for the next twenty-four hours. Then we concentrated on that rabbit.

Armed with a breech-loader and twenty-two [types of firearms], we slugged through the snow in the hope of stirring him away from his resting place. As if he entered into the sport, he never failed us. Every day we raised him, and every time one of us took aim as he bounded away, some other of the trio was in the line of fire! Actually I don't think we wanted him dead – he was too much fun alive. He did more to make us healthily tired and ready to face a long night in the sleeping bag than any indoor activity we could have devised.

So passed the days. At night with the seal oil lamp extinguished and the cheery firelight from the old "Waterloo" playing over the smoky walls, we lay awake for a while talking, but mainly listening to Uncle Sam's tales of the past.

Every night provided at least one other break to guard against monotony. The tiny doorless lean-to which served as a porch to the cabin was recognized sleeping quarters for Uncle Sam's huskies, and tight stowing it was at that. Around midnight our eleven would, with one accord, decide to bunk in with them, and a battle royal forthwith ensued. A fight among huskies is something which must be halted with all possible speed, for the husky is a treacherous fighter and will deliberately – and often permanently – lame his opponent by a well directed bite through the joint of a paw.

At the first outcry Uncle Sam would wake from sound sleep and seemingly catapult from his bunk to the door and out into the seething mass. Clad only in his long underwear, but with his dogwhip flailing right and left (from first to last I never saw him take the whip from its peg on the wall) he would have order restored before we were out of our bunk once more. Uncle Sam would have a few more stories to tell before we all settled down again to sleep until daybreak.

Like every other storm this one finally blew itself out and with both teams hitched to one komatic, our host and my driver took off at dawn for the HBC post we had left a week before. Around midnight they were back again with a fine stock of provisions and a generous supply of tobacco. Then, well fed and content, the cozy cabin's walls hardly discernable for smoke from pipe and cigarette, we regaled ourselves with song and story into the small hours of the morning.

Shortly after daybreak we took our leave and continued south, leaving with them sufficient food – and tobacco – for several days, and taking with us enduring memories of a brand of hospitality and cheery comradeship seldom encountered among those more richly blessed in this world's goods.

END

Endnotes

SECTION 1

Notes to Chapter One

1 Recent observations by Newfoundland & Labrador fishers *does* suggest that the stocks are rebuilding, but the full extent of such has yet to be determined.

2 A single wolf, thought to have travelled across the sea ice from Labrador, was killed on the Bonavista Peninsula in 2012, but to date there is no evidence of a breeding population on the Island. Newfoundland's own distinct subspecies, *Canus lupis beothucus*, was officially declared extinct in 1930, with the last known individual being shot in 1911.

Notes to Chapter Two

1 The Maritime Archaic were established at Twillingate from about 3500-3200 BP (Before Present), and a major find of their artifacts occurred at Back Harbour in 1966. Finds of Maritime Archaic materials have also been made at Fogo and Change Islands. See, David J. Clarke, *A History of the Isles. Twillingate, New World Island Fogo Island and Change Islands, Newfoundland & Labrador*, 2nd Edition (Charleston, SC, Createspace, 2014), 21-22, 129.

2 Twillingate was also home to the Dorset people, while an impressive Groswater site was discovered on Fogo Island in 1997. See: Clarke, *A History of the Isles*, 22, 129-30.

3 It is thought by some that Beothuk other than Shanawdithit may have been living in 1829, and considerably later. According to some traditions, members of the group travelled to Labrador and joined the Innu. It is possible that their descendants may be living today, though there can be no doubt that they had vanished as a recognizable cultural group before the middle of the nineteenth century. For a more detailed

treatment of the Beothuk, and their relationship with the Isles, see: Clarke, *A History of the Isles*, 197-221.

Notes to Chapter Three

1 PANL, MG 200, John Guy.

2 *Ibid*.

Notes to Chapter Four

1 A native of Rigolet, John Shiwak travelled to St. John's and enlisted with the Newfoundland Regiment in 1915. He and six comrades were killed by an exploding shell at the Battle of Masnières, 20 November, 1917.

On 8 October, 2014 the renowned sniper was honoured as Newfoundland & Labrador Premier Paul Davis officially dedicated John Shiwak Hall, a new residence at Memorial University.

SECTION 2

Notes to Chapter Five

The items in this section/chapter are culled from a number of sources, including the author's past works, and general histories of the Province of Newfoundland & Labrador (See Bibliography).

SECTION 3*

Notes to Chapter Six

1 "Two Poems," 7 August, 1926, 3. Rev. Thomas Harris was the first Pastor in charge of a new Twillingate and Moreton's Harbour circuit of

the Methodist Church. These poems of his were later reprinted as part of Reverend W. Edgar Mercer's Church history. See: W. Edgar Mercer, *A Century of Methodism in Twillingate and Notre Dame Bay, Newfoundland, 1831-1931* (Twillingate, Twillingate Sun Printers, 1932), 16-17.

John Congrow (or Congdon) Duder (1817-94) was the Brother of St. John's merchant Edwin Duder, Sr. (1822-81), whose business, orignally run in partnership with his Brother-in-law, Robert Livingstone Muir (d.1865), had branches at Twillingate, Herring Neck, Change Islands, Barr'd Islands, Joe Batt's Arm and Fogo. John was the manager of Muir & Duder's Twillingate branch, and according to Cyril Chaulk, spent more time in the community than any other member of his family. Duder moved to Twillingate in the 1850s before relocating to Bett's Cove sometime around 1880 to take up a posting as Sub-collector of HM Customs.

Charles Duder (1818-79) was another Brother of John Congdon and Edwin. He moved to Twillingate in the 1860s, being elected to Represent Twillingate District as an anti-Confederate in 1869. He was later named Chair of the Board of Works, a post he retained until his retirement from politics in 1878.

Dr. Stirling was William M.C. Stirling (1813-91), a Scottish physician who moved to Twillingate sometime after 1842. He was noted as the Father of renowned opera soprano Georgina Stirling (1867-1935).

Mr. Owen is most likely John Woodhouse Owen (c.1831-1902). A native of Devonshire, in the 1860s Owen was the Twillingate agent and attorney for Robert Slade, buying out the Slade holdings at Twillingate and Fogo around 1870 in partnership with Henry J. Earle (1841-1934).

Mr. Blandford may be John Bennett Blandford (c.1815-1908). Like John Owen, Blandford was born in Dorsetshire. He married at Twillingate in 1853, and was appointed Stipendiary Magistrate there around 1906, having previously served at Little Bay.

2 "Autumn," 14 October, 1880, 1.

3 "Original Poetry," 24 March, 1881, 1.

DAVID J. CLARKE

4 "The Fisher Boy," 12 October, 1885, 2.

5 "Poetry," 13 March, 1886, 1.

6 "Liking and Disliking," 11 September, 1886, 2.

7 "Moonbeams," 13 November, 1886, 2.

8 "The Captain of the *Cyprian*," 12 February, 1887, 2.

9 "To the New Year," 31 December, 1887, 4.

10 "Our Native Land," 19 December, 1891, 2.

11 "Wadham's Song," 7 November, 1903, 2.

12 "Berry Song," 28 September, 1929, 4.

13 "Newfoundland," 6 April, 1935, 2.

14 "Beneath the Union Jack," 28 November, 1936, 4.

15 "Come and Join," 19 March, 1938, 3.

16 "Twillingate," 8 December, 1945, 4.

17 "Rhymes on the Bessie," 15 May, 1948, 4.

18 "Old England in Hart's Cove," 29 November, 1951, 4.

Notes to Chapter Seven

1 22 November, 1884, 2.

2 21 May, 1887, 2; 28 May, 1887, 2

3 "Jubilee Year," 30 March, 1935, 4; 6 April, 1935, 4; "A Royal Jubilee," 4 May, 1935, 4; "Celebrating the Twenty-Fifth." 11 May, 1935, 4.

4 25 January, 1936, 1; "The King is Dead, Long Live the King," 25 January, 1936, 4.

5 "The Crisis," 19 December, 1936, 4.

6 27 March, 1937, 4.

7 15 May, 1937, 4.

8 "Health, Joy and Peace to Their Majesties," 17 June, 1939, 4.

9 "A Good Man Dies," 9 February, 1952, 4.

Notes to Chapter Eight

1 As this section is made up of many smaller items, Individual end notes have not been inserted here. Instead, each piece has its date of publication inserted at the front of the article (See, Preface & Acknowledgements).

Notes to Chapter Nine

1 5 May, 1881, 2.

2 10 February, 1882, 2.

3 "Prohibition from a Political, Economic Point of View," 20 January, 1883, 2; 27 January, 1883, 2.

4 "Temperance Meeting," 27 January, 1883, 2.

5 "Prohibition," 3 February, 1883, 3.

6 "Great Temperance Triumph in Twillingate," 2 February, 1883, 2.

7 2 February, 1883, 2.

8 "Recent Correspondence; Dark Spots," 23 February, 1883, 2.

9 March 8, 1883 "Who Paid the Expenses of the Late Temperance Campaign?" 9 March, 1883, 2.

10 "A Brilliant Victory for the Local Option at Fogo," 16 February, 1884, 2.

11 "Poll to be Taken for Local Option at Barr'd Island," 25 October, 1884, 2.

12 "Another Victory for the Temperance Cause," 8 November, 1884, 2.

13 "Prevention" Division Sons of Temperance," 17 March, 1888, 2.

14 "Court News," 7 October, 1880, 3; "Court News," 22 September, 1881, 3; "Court of Quarter Sessions," 27 January, 1882, 3; "Breach of the License Act," 13 February, 1887, 3-4. Captain Richard Wrey and his Wife, Catherine, seem to have established their hotel at Twillingate sometime in the 1870s, if not earlier, and they were certainly resident in the community by the Fall of 1880. As seen in Chapter Nine, Captain Wrey was before the Court on breaches of the various Liquor Acts at least four times from 1880 to 1887, and it appears that his Wife had been charged in this connection on at least one occasion as well.

    The 1880s were a time of sectarian strife in the Colony of Newfoundland, and the Wreys were in the (no doubt) uncomfortable position of being a Roman Catholic family in a community which was, and still is, almost entirely Protestant; this is not to mention their being publicans. Neither of these factors need have caused trouble for the family, but considering that the temperance movement originated largely through the influence of the various Protestant Churches – its siren call had little resonance in Newfoundland's Irish, Catholic communities – a household that was of the "wrong" faith, and purveyors of the "Demon Rum" to boot, was doubly cursed!

In 1884 the family, which made their home on North Side, in the area known (from 1887) as "Jubilee Corner," near where the Anchor Inn Hotel now stands, found themselves at the centre of another controversy, ranged against the Protestant Orange Order. On 26 July of that year the *Twillingate Sun* noted how "...Roman Catholic papers..." had falsely reported that Twillingate Orangemen had fired guns at the Wrey family home a few weeks earlier. According to the Sun, the men were only discharging unloaded muskets in celebration of Queen Victoria's Birthday on 24 May. The paper reported that some members of the family had complained about the noise when the procession passed their house. In the Sun's version of events the Roman Catholic press had blown the trivial incident out of proportion, into an "Orange Outrage" against a law abiding Catholic household. Thompson and his staff retorted that "no Orange outrage has ever taken place here or in any other part of the Colony, and if their rights and privileges as loyal British subjects were not interfered with by prejudiced Roman Catholics, peace, harmony and good will would prevail among all classes." It makes one wonder just who was prejudiced!

The Wreys hung on at Twillingate until at least the beginning of 1887 but by 1893, the year Catherine died, the couple were living at St. John's; I suspect they were glad to have left Twillingate behind! See, "Another Foul Slander Against Orangemen," 26 July, 1886, 4.

My late Grandfather, Leonard C. Clarke (1915-2007), could remember the Wrey's old hotel, which in his youth still stood at North Side, on a parcel of land later owned by two Sisters surnamed Anstey, although by that time it had been closed for many years. It was still known to one and all, as it probably had been in the 1880s, as "Kitty Wrey's Place." It seems that the hotel was finally torn down in the 1920s, when the dwelling house which now occupies the site was towed from its original lot in Back Harbour.

Sergeant Thomas E. Wells of the Newfoundland Constabulary was stationed at Twillingate from at least 1875 until about 1885, when he was succeeded by Sgt. (Later Head Constable) Nathaniel Petten, and Alexander Burt. Burt remained in the community, serving alongside

Petten, until around 1892. Head Constable Petten was stationed at Twillingate until 1915.

15 "Total Prohibition," 26 March, 1887, 2.

16 "Total Prohibition," 21 January, 1888, 2.

17 "The Evil Beast," 28 March , 1896, 1.

18 4 April, 1896, 1.

19 "Prohibition Column," 25 September, 1915, 3; 16 October, 1915, 2.

20 "Great Meeting for Prohibition in Alex. Hall," 16 October, 1915, 3.

21 "Bridgeport (Chance Hr.) in Line," 16 October, 1915, 3.

22 "What's the Verdict,?" 19 November, 1927, 2.

Notes to Chapter Ten

1 24 February, 1881, 2-3. "T" was most likely Rev. Robert Temple (c.1837-1912), incumbent of Twillingate's Anglican parish from 1877 to 1905. During his tenure Temple consecrated a new cemetery at Snellin's Cove and introduced an annual flower service.

In fact, Rev. John Leigh (c.1789-1823) served as Twillingate's Anglican clergyman from 1816 to 1819. A native of Somerset, Leigh was educated at St. Mary Hall, Oxford, and ordained in 1813. During his time at Twillingate Leigh compiled a Beothuk vocabulary of about 200 words from a Native woman named Demasduit. In Leigh's opinion, their tongue was similar to Welsh in its pronunciation. Leigh's stay at Twillingate, with its harsh climate, had a negative effect on his health, and in 1819 he transferred to Harbour Grace. The original St. Peter's Anglican Church was built about the time Leigh arrived, serving until it was replaced by a new St. Peter's in the 1840s.

Thomas Greenshill Laugharne (c.1794-1844) hailed from

Warwickshire. He arrived at Twillingate in the early 1820s, but by 1823 seems to have run afoul of his own congregation, several prominent members of which wrote the Bishop of London to complain that the Reverend was "lacking in morals." Laugharne was removed from the Parish and assigned to other duties. He later returned to England, performing clerical work in the area around Warwick. For a time he served as a chaplain in Honduras, but was forced to return home due to ill health. Broken in mind and body, and in distressed circumstances, Laugharne entered a workhouse, where he later died. The unfortunate clergyman's Wife, Caroline (McKie), died the following year.

2 21 March, 1881, 2-3. John Inglis (1777-1850) was born at New York, the Son of Anglican clergyman Charles Inglis. The family immigrated to England following the British evacuation of New York in 1783, but returned to North America four years later when the elder Inglis was appointed as the first Bishop of Nova Scotia. Educated at King's College, John Inglis became his Father's private secretary in 1798, and was ordained a priest in 1802. For a number of years he continued working for his Father, becoming rector of St. Paul's Church, Halifax in 1816, following Charles' death. He was installed as the third Bishop of Nova Scotia in 1825. His tenure was marked by controversy, as Inglis fought to retain certain Church privileges against other Protestant faiths (For example, he opposed efforts to allow dissenting clergy to perform marriages by license). For the first five years of his episcopate Bishop Inglis travelled extensively through his huge charge, which then included New Brunswick, Prince Edward Island, Newfoundland and Bermuda. Realizing that the task of overseeing such a large area was too much for a single Bishop, he campaigned to have the diocese subdivided, a task completed between 1839 and 1845. Despite having an aristocratic temperament, biographer Judith Fingard notes that his visits to places like Newfoundland greatly moved Inglis, who was saddened by the levels of poverty and lack of education he found. For the remainder of his career Bishop Inglis continued to fight for Church privileges, and resisted cooperation with other denominations. He died in England where he had travelled to seek medical treatment.

  Rev. John C. Chapman was the third Anglican missionary to be stationed at Twillingate, and was its first long-term incumbent, remaining in the community for some twenty years. It was during Chapman's tenure that Bishop Inglis visited Twillingate, and in 1839 Rev. Chapman officiated at the laying of the foundation stone for the new St. Peter's Church. As reported in the diary of Mr. Joseph Pearce, in July, 1844 Chapman and his family returned home to England aboard Mr. Slade's cutter.

John Peyton (1793-1879) hailed from Wimbourne, England, and was schooled at nearby Christchurch. He travelled to Newfoundland in 1812 to assist his Father, John, Sr., in running the family business. Engaged in trapping and other pursuits, Peyton soon expanded his holdings by building shipyards at Exploits and Indian Point. He was named as the area's first Justice of the Peace in 1818. In 1836 Peyton was named Stipendiary Magistrate, relocating with his family to Twillingate. He is best known today for his dealings with the Beothuk, particularly the 1819 capture of the woman Demasduit (Mary March), whose Husband was killed trying to rescue her. John Peyton is also noted as the Maternal Grandfather of opera singer Georgina Stirling.

For a number of years another Beothuk woman, Shanawdithit, was part of Peyton's household at Exploits. She had been found by furriers in 1823, along with her Mother and Sister. The Mother and Sister soon died, but Shanawdithit lived until June of 1829 when she died of tuberculosis at St. John's. With her passing many considered the Beothuk race to have become extinct.

During her time in captivity Shanawdithit provided a certain amount of background on her people's culture and recent history to William Epps Cormack (1796-1868). Cormack was born at St. John's, the Son of a Scottish merchant. Growing up mainly in his native Scotland, he attended the universities of Glasgow and Edinburgh, graduating from the latter with a MA. By 1822 he was back in Newfoundland, and soon became the first European to cross the interior of the Island, accompanied only by Mi,kmaq guide, Joseph Sylvester. Cormack later produced a meticulous, and well-received, account of the journey. He had long taken an interest in the plight of the Beothuk, whom he (justly) felt were being ill-used by Whites, and in serious danger of extinction. In 1827 Cormack founded the "Beothic Institution," with the aim of fostering good relations with the Natives. To this end, in 1827 he once more set off across the interior of the

Island. Though Cormack and his party found the remains of Beothuk villages, no living member of the tribe was encountered. By the 1830s Cormack had left Newfoundland, and after many travels, settled in British Columbia. He died there in 1868.

3 12 May, 1881, 2.

4 26 May, 1881, 3. "Mr. Pearce" may have been Andrew Pearce, Sr. (1772-1841), an agent for Poole merchant Thomas Colbourne and his partners. Pearce spent a considerable amount of time in Newfoundland, and was Fogo's deputy collector of customs for some time. He relocated to Newfoundland permanently in 1834, becoming Twillingate's deputy custom's collector.

The reference might also be to his Son, Joseph James Pearce (1810-81), who went on to serve as Twillingate's collector of customs for over thirty years. Pearce kept a diary which detailed the construction of St. Peter's Church, one of the few records of the building process.

5 9 June, 1881, 2. Aubrey George Spencer (1795-1872) was a Great-Great-Grandson of John Churchill, the first Duke of Marlborough (1650-1722). A graduate of Oxford, he was ordained a priest in 1819. That year he travelled to Ferryland as a Missionary for the Society for the Propagation of the Gospel, and was transferred to Trinity Bay in 1820. By 1821 Spencer was in Bermuda, becoming rector of a church there. In 1825 he was appointed as archdeacon of Bermuda, and in 1839 became the first Bishop of the see of Newfoundland. Under Spencer's leadership missions expanded, and the number of clergy in Newfoundland was increased. As biographer C.E. Thomas notes, the see was "far more progressive" by the time Spencer left in 1843 than it had been upon his assumption of office. From Newfoundland Spencer went to Jamaica, remaining there as Bishop until 1855, when his always frail health completely failed him. Bishop Spencer retired to Torquay, Devonshire, where he passed away some years later.

His successor as Bishop of Newfoundland, Edward Feild (1801-76), was born at Worcester, the Son of a surgeon. Educated at Rugby School and Queen's College, Oxford, Feild became curate of Kidlington, near Oxford. By 1839 he was serving as inspector with the

Anglican National Society, a Church schools organization. He was offered the see of Newfoundland in 1844. Bishop Feild could be as rigid in his beliefs as Bishop Inglis had been, and this created some friction with the Colony's Methodists and Roman Catholics. Still, by 1855 he had had some success in recruiting missionaries for the Island and in the construction of new churches. Each Summer he undertook tours of the outports, as he did in 1845, visiting Twillingate and other locales on the northeast coast in the Church ship *Hawk*. By the 1870s Feild was regarded with genuine affection by his flock, and in 1875 saw his dream of separate Anglican schools realized in Newfoundland. During the Winter of 1876 he took a sabbatical trip to Bermuda, but died there on 8 June. When word of Feild's passing reached St. John's, all the bells in the city were rung in tribute.

* Unless otherwise noted, all references in this section are to the *Twillingate Sun* newspaper.

SECTION FOUR

Notes to Chapter Eleven

1 "Respects to the Deceased," *Twillingate Sun*, 28 January, 1922, 3. See also, *Twillingate Sun*, 4 November, 1911, 2.
    According to Jim Troke, Joey Strickland married his first Wife, Rose, in 1887. She died on 29 October, 1902 at the age of thirty-six. The following year he remarried to the Widow of Simon Legge of Durrell. Joey's second Wife also predeceased him, dying on 30 October, 1911. Anne Strickland had first come to Twillingate as a servant for the Postmaster, John White.
    The Moores residence referred to in the poem still stands on North Side, and is now used as a bed and breakfast. Wells' Lane is near Twillingate's modern Post Office, and Alf Manuel tells me that the well located there was noted for its reliability, not running out of water even in the driest of Summers.
    A "spudgel" or spudgin, was a small wooden bucket with a long handle, most often used for bailing water out of boats.

While Joey Strickland was recorded as a member of the Congregational Church in his earlier life, this religion appears to have died out at Twillingate around the First World War era, and the local congregation did not have a regular clergyman after Rev. J. Jones' tenure from 1902-4. This would explain a Salvation Army Minister conducting Joey's funeral and providing spiritual guidance in his final days.

2 The *Mary Celeste* was a 282 ton, Canadian-built brigantine, registered in New York. She sailed from that port with a cargo of alcohol in November, 1872 under Captain Benjamin Spooner Briggs. On 5 December the *Dei Gratia* spotted the *Mary Celeste* drifting out of control between the Azores and Portugal. Upon boarding the brigantine, members of the *Dei Gratia*'s crew found the vessel to be deserted, and its Captain, Morehouse, felt the crew must have abandoned their craft in a hurry, believing it to be sinking. Though a court of inquiry was called, the fate of the *Mary Celeste*'s crew, like that of the *Mountaineer*, remains a mystery. The vessel was later put back into service, but was considered an unlucky ship, and she was sold a number of times before being wrecked off the coast of Haiti. The brigantine's story was popularized by writer Arthur Conan Doyle (1859-1930), of Sherlock Holmes fame, who, in a fictionalized short story based on the event, called the vessel the *Marie Celeste*.

3 Angus L. Tanner, "*Grace Boehner*," 1974, i-ii.

4 C. William Gillett, "Memories of the Schooner *Grace Boehner*," 1.

5 This would have been in 1894. Rev. Stoney's tenure at Herring Neck began around 1892, and he left the Parish for other duties in 1895. During the years 1898 to 1903 (roughly) the Circuit was known as "Herring Neck and Change Islands."

6 Anon, "A short History of Our Church Life From 1897-1947," 1.

7 *Ibid*, 2

8 *Ibid*, 2

9 *Ibid*, 3.

10 *Ibid*, 4.

11 *Ibid*, 4.

12 One such operation, off New World Island in 1949, resulted in a man being stranded in his boat atop a berg that had flipped over. In reporting on the incident the *Twillingate Sun*'s Editor referred to icebergs as a "...menace to codtraps," and noted that "during the trapping season icebergs in the Bight caused many an anxious moment to crews, and some of them forced the removal of gear from the water either to forestall damage or for repairs after a berg had drifted into a trap or calved [broken up] nearby." *Twillingate Sun*, "On Berg in Boat," 3 September, 1949, 4.

13 Howard T. Barnes, "Some Physical Properties of Icebergs and a Method for Their Destruction," *Proceedings of the Royal Society*, 1 March, 1927, 167 (Cited in: http://rspa.royalsocietypublishing.org).

14 *Ibid*, 168.

15 The Newfoundland Ranger Force was created by Newfoundland's Commission of Government in 1935. Not intended to function simply as a police force, the organization was charged with delivering a wide range of Government services to isolated communities in Newfoundland & Labrador. Some of their tasks included the issuance of relief payments, road building, and the enforcement of game laws. It was likely this wide range of duties which led to the Force being placed under the Department of Natural Resources rather than Justice. By the end of July, 1935 the first class of thirty recruits were training at Ranger Headquarters in Whitbourne. The Rangers were all fit, well-educated young men who could carry out a multitude of tasks with minimal supervision. Once in the field the Rangers were noted for their lengthy patrols, often using boat, dog teams, or on foot. In some communities,

especially in Labrador, the local Ranger was often the only Government representative, performing work for all Government Departments. During World War II the Rangers were given additional responsibilities enforcing regulations on rationing and blackouts, plus patrolling for hostile aircraft or submarines. Following the War the Rangers were asked to gauge public opinion on the Colony's future political prospects, including Confederation with Canada. About a year after this became a reality the new administration of Joseph R. Smallwood disbanded the force as a cost-cutting measure, with most of the serving Rangers joining the RCMP.

By this time Ernest Clarke had already left the Force to take the helm of the *Twillingate Sun* newspaper. Clarke had been a member of the Rangers' second class of recruits, and was assigned Regimental Number fifty-seven. During his tenure with the Force he was stationed at Grand Bank and in various Labrador postings. While serving in Labrador, Clarke was promoted to the rank of (Acting) Inspector, one of only nine men to rise to commissioned rank during the Force's fifteen year history, including its five Chief Rangers.

Photo and Illustration Credits

ARCHIVAL

Libraries and Archives Canada. Archived material.
    nlc-8713   Encounter between John Guy and the Beothuk people in 1612. Engraving by Theodore de Bry or Matthaus Merian, circa 1627-28.

Memorial University of Newfoundland. Centre for Newfoundland Studies. Geography Collection. Coll-137.
02.01.044	Burin Relief.
02.02.006	Presbyterian Kirk, Pre-1892.
03.05.034.	*Florizel*, October, 1914.
03.06.033	S.S. *Caribou* in Dry Dock.
05.01.006	St. John's After the Great Fire, 1892.
05.04.004	Alcock and Brown Depart.
11.03.001	Catalina c.1900.
11.05.001	Trinity, Pre-1892.
13.12.003	Lion's Den.
13.12.007.	Fogo, North Side.
15.01.001	Channel c.1900.
17.03.001	Codroy Valley, Pre-1936.
22.02.001	Moravian Mission at Hopedale.
22.03.001	Okak, Pre-1919.
22.06.001	Schooners at Labrador, pre-1921.
24.02.009.	S.S. *Curlew*.
24.02.019	"On the Banks."
24.02.035	Schooner in Full Sail.
25.01.005	Sealers on the Ice.
26.01.008	Rev. William Pilot and Family.
26.02.023	Inuit Women and Sod House.
28.01.001	Old St. Andrew's, Fogo.
30.02.035	S.S. *Plover* in dry dock.

_____. Maritime History Archive.
    PF-008.028   Schooner *Ariceen*.
    PF-008.046   Schooner *Champion*.
    PF-008.095   Schooner *Sydney Smith*.
    PF-035.004   Eastern Tickle c.1900.
    PF-055.002   S.S. *Virginia Lake* and Other Vessels.

Poole History Centre.
    Schooner *Mountaineer*.

BOOKS

Coaker, William Ford (ed.). *Twenty Years of the Fisherman's Protective Union of Newfoundland*. St. John's: Advocate Publishing, 1930.
    Blandford's Point, Herring Neck (81).
    Captain George Jones (191).
    Herring Neck LOA Lodge (2).
    Home Built by Robert Scott (65).
    Joseph R. Smallwood (392).
    R. Hibbs (191).
    Seldom-Come-By (196).
    William Coaker's Birthplace (182).

Harvey, Moses. *Newfoundland at the Beginning of the Twentieth Century. A treatise of History and Development*. New York: The South Publishing Co., 1902.
    William Whiteway (307).

Holloway, Robert E. *Through Newfoundland With the Camera. London: Sach & Co., 1910.*
    Herring Neck, c.1910 (67).
    The Exploits River (55).

Loveridge, John. *Twillingate. Story in Pictures and Poetry of the 1973 Seal Haul at Twillingate, Newfoundland. Also marking the 85th Year in Business of the Firm of E.J. Linfield.* Grand Falls: Robinson-Blackmore, 1973.
E.J. Linfield (1).
Frederick Linfield (1).

Mercer, W. Edgar. *A Century of Methodism in Twillingate and* Notre Dame Bay. Twillingate: Twillingate Sun Printers, 1932.
Rev. John Reay (Frontispiece).

Mott, Henry Y. *Newfoundland Men. A Collection of Biographical Sketches With Portraits, of Sons and Residents of the Island Who Have Become Known in Commercial and Political Life.* Concord, NH, USA: T.W. & J.F. Cragg, 1894.
Edwin J. Duder (171).
James S. Winter (11).

Prowse, D.W. *A History of Newfoundland. From the English, Colonial and Foreign Records.* London: Macmillan & Co., 1895.
Dorymen fishing the Grand Banks (571).
P.F. Little (404).
Sir Ambrose Shea (500).
Sir George Calvert, First Lord Baltimore (113).
Sir Humphrey Gilbert (72).
Sir John Kent (486).
The Grand Falls (612).
Sebastian Cabot (17).

_____. *A History of the Churches in Newfoundland.* London: Macmillan and Co., 1895.
Bishop Jones (13).
Bishop Spencer (10).
Samuel Codner (7).
Yacht *Lavrock* (16).

Rowley, Owsley Robert. *The Anglican Episcopate of Canada and Newfoundland*. London: A.R. Mowbray & Co., 1928.
    Bishop John Inglis (16).

Townsend, Charles Wendell, MD. (ed.). *Captain Cartwright and His Labrador Journal*. Boston: Dana Estes & Co, 1911.
    George Cartwright (Frontispiece).

PERIODICALS

International Grenfell Association. *Among the Deep Sea Fishers*. April, 1926.
    Doctor Parsons and Hospital Staff (29).

Newfoundland Quarterly. July, 1906.
    Henry J. Earle (17).

Twillingate Sun. 21 July, 1881.
    Francis Berteau Ad (3).

_____. 4 August, 1882.
    Andrew Linfield Ad (3).
    Dr. T. Scott Ad (4).

_____. 6 January, 1883.
    Dr. Stafford Notice (3).

_____. Christmas Special. December, 1915
    Georgina Stirling (8).

_____. 20 January, 1934.
    Edward VIII as Prince of Wales (4).

DAVID J. CLARKE

INTERNET

Barnes, Howard T. "Some Physical Properties of Icebergs and a Method for Their Destruction." *Proceedings of the Royal Society*, 1 March, 1926 (Cited in: http://rspa.royalsocietypublishing.org). Thermite Exploding an Iceberg, Twillingate, 1926.

Wikimedia Commons. www.commons.wikimedia.org

    American Privateer (This media file is in the public domain in the United States. This applies to US works where the copyright has expired, often because its first publication occurred prior to January 1, 1923).

    Anti-Diphtheria Ad (This media file is in the public domain in the United States. This applies to US works where the copyright has expired, often because its first publication occurred prior to January 1, 1923).

    Atlantic Cod (*Gadus Morhua*) (This image is in the public domain because it contains materials that originally came from the US National Oceanic and Atmospheric Administration, taken or made as part of an employee's official duties).

    Beaumont Hamel Stamp (This Canadian stamp is in the public domain because it is more than fifty years old).

    Cabot's *Matthew* (This Canadian stamp is in the public domain because it is more than fifty years old).

    Codfish Stamp (This Canadian stamp is in the public domain because it is more than fifty years old).

    Captain Bartholomew Roberts (This work is in the public domain in the United States because it was published, or registered with the US Copyright Office, before January 1, 1923. This image is in the public domain because its copyright has expired. This applies to Australia, the European Union and those countries with a copyright term of life of the author plus seventy years. PD-1923).

Edward VIII Stamps (This artistic work created by the United Kingdom Government is in the public domain. This is because it is one of the following: It is a photograph created by the United Kingdom Government and taken prior to 1 June, 1957; or It was commercially published prior to 1964; or It is an artistic work other than a photograph or engraving (e.g. a painting) which was created by the United Kingdom Government prior to 1964. HMSO has declared that the expiry of Crown Copyrights applies worldwide).

Frederick B.T. Carter (This work is in the public domain in those countries with a copyright term of life of the author plus seventy-five years or less. PD-1923).

Great Auk (This file is licensed under the Creative Commons Attribution 2.0 Generic license).

Great Eastern at Heart's Content (This image is in the public domain because its copyright has expired. This applies to Australia, the European Union and those countries with a copyright term of life of the author plus seventy years. PD-1923).

HMS *Fantome* and HMS *Opal* (This artistic work created by the United Kingdom Government is in the public domain. This is because it is one of the following: It is a photograph created by the United Kingdom Government and taken prior to 1 June, 1957; or It was commercially published prior to 1964; or It is an artistic work other than a photograph or engraving (e.g. a painting) which was created by the United Kingdom Government prior to 1964. HMSO has declared that the expiry of Crown Copyrights applies worldwide).

Imperial Conference, 1926 (This Canadian work is in the public domain in Canada because its copyright has expired due to one of the following: a. it was subject to Crown copyright and was first published more than fifty years ago, or it was not subject to Crown copyright, and b. it is a photograph that was created prior to January 1, 1949, or c. the creator died more than fifty years ago).

Innu Making Canoes (This Canadian work is in the public domain in Canada because its copyright has expired due to one of the following: a. it was subject to Crown copyright and was first published more than fifty years ago, or it was not subject to Crown copyright, and b. it is a photograph that was created prior to January 1, 1949, or c. the creator died more than fifty years ago. This work is in the public domain in the United States because it was published, or registered with the US Copyright Office, before January 1, 1923).
James Gambier (This work is in the public domain in the United States, and those countries with a copyright term of life of the author plus 100 years or less).
John Peyton (This image is in the public domain because its copyright has expired. This applies to Australia, the European Union and those countries with a copyright term of life of the author plus seventy years. PD-1923).
Joseph R. Smallwood Signs Newfoundland into Confederation (This Canadian work is in the public domain in Canada because its copyright has expired due to one of the following: a. it was subject to Crown copyright and was first published more than fifty years ago, or it was not subject to Crown copyright, and, b. it is a photograph that was created prior to January 1, 1949, or c. the creator died more than fifty years ago).
King George and Queen Elizabeth at Toronto (This Canadian work is in the public domain in Canada because its copyright has expired due to one of the following: a. it was subject to Crown copyright and was first published more than fifty years ago, or it was not subject to Crown copyright, and b. it is a photograph that was created prior to January 1, 1949, or c. the creator died more than fifty years ago. This work is in the public domain in the United States because it meets three requirements: It was first published outside the United States (and not published in the US within thirty days), it was first published before 1978 without complying with US copyright formalities, or after 1978 without copyright notice, it was in the public domain in its home country (Canada) on the URAA date, 1 January, 1996).

Lief Ericsson Discovers North America (This work is in the public domain in its country of origin and other countries and areas where the copyright term is the author's life plus eighty years or less. This work is in the public domain in the United States because it was published, or registered with the US Copyright Office, before January 1, 1923).

Mi'kmaq Camp (This work is in the public domain in the United States because it was published, or registered with the US Copyright Office before January 1, 1923. This image is in the public domain because its copyright has expired. This applies to Australia, the European Union and those countries with a copyright term of life of the author plus seventy years. PD-US).

Newfoundland & Labrador Map (This file is licensed under the Creative Commons Attribution-Share Alike 3.0 Unported license).

Montreal, 1889 (This image is in the public domain because its copyright has expired. This applies to Australia, the European Union and those countries with a copyright term of life of the author plus seventy years. PD-1923).

Pitcher Plant (This work is in the public domain because it was published in the United States between 1923 and 1963, and although there may or may not have been a copyright notice, the copyright was not renewed. The work is in the public domain in Canada because its author has been dead for more than fifty years).

Queen Victoria (This image is in the public domain because its copyright has expired. This applies to Australia, the European Union, and those countries with a copyright term of life of the author plus seventy years. PD-1923).

Sir Richard Squires (This media file is in the public domain in the United States. This applies to US works where the copyright has expired, often because its first publication occurred prior to January 1, 1923).

Southern Cross (This image is of Australian origin and is now in the public domain because its term of copyright has expired. According to the Australian Copyright Council).

DAVID J. CLARKE

Wikipedia. www.wikipedia.org
> Seal of the Society for the Propagation of the Gospel (This work has been released into the public domain by the copyright holder. This applies worldwide. In case this is not legally possible: The copyright holder grants any entity the right to use this work for any purpose, without any conditions, unless such conditions are required by law).

INDIVIDUALS

Anstey, Milt.
> Solomon Roberts.

Ashbourne, Ross.
> Arthur Ashbourne.
> Thomas Ashbourne.

Boyd, Kathleen and Ted.
> Crow Head, 1920s.†
> Durrell Academy School.†
> Hart' Cove.†
> Hodges (Former Waterman's) Premises.††
> Twillingate United (Methodist) Church.†

Clarke, Peter and Ruby.
> Newfoundland Ranger Ernest Clarke.

Forward, Gordena.
> Tizzard's Harbour, early 1900s.

Jennings, Joe.
> Western Head .*

Loveridge, Don.
>Back Harbour, 1921.
>Beaton J. Abbott.
>Captain Alfred Elliott.
>Citizens Gather for King George's Coronation Celebration.
>Crowds Gather at Jubilee Corner.
>Durrell, 1930s.
>G.J. Carter Premises.
>Governor MacDonald Opens the New Tickle Bridge.
>Grenfell Mission Hospital, Battle Harbour.
>Herring Neck, 1950s.
>Loss of the Hospital Cottage.
>Merchant Premises Near Path End, 1930s.
>Moreton's Harbour, 1960s.
>Schooners in Port, Battle Harbour.
>Stage is Set, 1934.
>SUF Hall, 1950.
>SUF Parade at Twillingate, 1926.
>Taking Supplies Over the Ice to *Viking* Survivors From S.S. *Sagona*.
>T.G.W. Ashbourne.
>Twillingate, c.1905.
>Twillingate Schoolboys, Early 1900s.
>Twillingate Salvation Army Barracks.
>Twillingate Residents Parade, 1935.
>Volunteers Cleaning Up After the Twillingate Hospital Fire.
>Wild Cove, 1960s.

Manuel, Eleanor and Alfred.
>Shoal Tickle, Early 1900s.
>Titus Manuel.

Shand, Brenda.
>Change Islands, Early 1900s.

DAVID J. CLARKE

Troke, Jim.
    Nineteenth Century Twillingate.
    Wheelbarrow Man.

Young-Thomas, Pauline.
    Congregational Church Buildings, Twillingate.
    Long Point Lighthouse, Early 1900s.

† From the F.R. Hayward Collection.
†† From the Bill Hayward collection.

* Original photograph by the late Hardy Card.

Bibliography

MANUSCRIPT SOURCES

Provincial Archives of Newfoundland & Labrador, The Rooms, St. John's
  MG 200. John Guy.
  MG 323. Thomas Peyton.

NEWSPAPERS

Twillingate Sun. Various issues.

BOOKS, ARTICLES, THESES

Brent, Peter. *The Viking Saga.* London: George Weidenfeld and Nicolson Limited, 1975,

Butler, Paul. *St. John's City of Fire.* St. John's: Flanker Press, 2007.

_____ and Maura Hanrahan. *Rogues and Heroes of the Island of Newfoundland.* St. John's: Flanker Press, 2005.

Chaulk, Cyril. *Snippets in Time.* St. John's: DRC Publishing, 2009.

Clarke, David. *An Historical Directory of the Isles.* Charleston, SC: Createspace, 2013.
_____. *A History of the Isles.* 2nd Revised Edition. Charleston, SC: Createspace, 2012.

_____. *The Isles Historical Dictionary.* Charleston, SC: Createspace, 2013.

_____. *St. Peter's Anglican Church, Twillingate. A History. From the Nineteenth to the Twenty-first Centuries.* Charleston, SC: Createspace, 2012.

_____. *Sunspots – Best of the Twillingate Sun, 1880-1953.* Vols. I & II. Charleston, SC: Createspace, 2013.

Collins, Michael. *Plants and Wildflowers of Newfoundland.* St. John's: Jesperson Press, 1994.

Coish, Calvin. *Distant Shores. Pages from Newfoundland's Past.* Grand Falls-Windsor: Lifestyle Books, 1994.

____ (ed.). *The Best of the Barrelman. 1938-1940.* St. John's: Creative Publishers, 1998.

Conrad, Margaret R. And James K. Hiller. *Atlantic Canada: A Region in the Making.* Don Mills, ON: Oxford University Press, 2001.

Devine and O'Mara. *Notable Events in the History of Newfoundland. Six Thousand Dates of Historical and Social Happenings.* St. John's: Devine & O'Mara, 1900.

Dixon, James. "Coastal Navigators: The First Americans May have Come by Water." *Discovering Archaeology.* Vol. II. No. 1 (February 2000), 34-35.

English, L.E.F. *Historic Newfoundland & Labrador.* St. John's: Newfoundland Department of Tourism, 1988.

Fitzgerald, Jack. *The Hangman is Never Late. Three Centuries of Newfoundland Justice.* St. John's: Creative Book Publishers, 1999.

_____. *Newfoundland Disasters.* St. John's: Jesperson Publishers, 1984.

_____. *Untold Stories. Mysteries of Newfoundland & Labrador.* St. John's: Creative Book Publishers, 2004.

Fardy, B.D. *Ferryland. The Colony of Avalonia*. St. John's: Flanker Press, 2005.

Guttridge, Roger. "The Mystery Crew of the Mountaineer." *The Downhomer* (September, 1994), 49.

Harrington, Michael. *Goin' to the Ice. Offbeat History of the Newfoundland Sealfishery*. St. John's: Harry Cuff Publications, 1986.

_____. *Prime Ministers of Newfoundland*. St. John's: Harry Cuff Publications, 1991.

Harris, Michael. *Rare Ambition: The Crosbies of Newfoundland*. Toronto, Ontario: Penguin Books, 1993.

Head, C. Grant. *Eighteenth Century Newfoundland*. Toronto: McClelland and Stewart, 1976.

Herman, Arthur. *To Rule the Waves. How the British Navy Shaped the Modern World*. New York: Harper Collins Publishers, 2004.

Hewitt, Benson. "St. Andrew's Anglican Churches, Fogo." *Lewisporte Pilot* (1 October, 2014), B2, B3.

Horwood, Harold. *A History of the Newfoundland Ranger Force*. St. John's: Breakwater Books, 1986.

Howley, James P. *The Beothucks or Red Indians: The Aboriginal Inhabitants of Newfoundland*. Cambridge: Cambridge University Press, 1915.

Hoxie, Frederick E. (ed.). *Encyclopaedia of North American Indians*. New York: Houghton Mifflin Company, 1996.

Hunt, Clayton. "An Historic Signing. New Mi'Kmaq Band by 2010." *Lewisporte Pilot* (17 September, 2008), 7B.

Jackson, Doug. *"On the Country." The Micmac of Newfoundland.* Gerald Penny, ed. St. John's: Harry Cuff Publications, 1993.

Johanson, Michael. "On the Labrador. The Metis Struggle Continues." *The Downhomer.* Vol. XVII. No. 9 (February, 2005), 114-115.

Jones, Edward A. et al (eds.). *Land, Sea & Time. Book Three.* St. John's: Breakwater Books, 2002.

Kenyon, J.P. (ed.). *The Dictionary of British History.* Ware, Hertfordshire, UK: Wordsworth Editions, 1996.

Kielly, Kim. "Cultural Connections. How the Aboriginal Cultures of Central Newfoundland are Influencing the Province." *The Downhomer.* Vol. XVII. No. 10 (March, 2005).

King, Arlène. "Beaumont Hamel, Our Place in the Sun." *Newfoundland Quarterly.* Vol. XCVI. No. 2 (Summer, 2003), 9-15.

Kurlansky, Mark. *Cod.* Canada: Penguin Books, 1998.

Learning, Bonnie. "Labrador Connection. New Hall at Memorial University Named After Inuk WW I Sniper," *The Southern Gazette* (8 October, 2014).

Letto, Doug. *Chocolate Bars & Rubber Boots.* Paradise, NL: Blue Hill Publishing, 1998.

Lewis-Simpson, Shannon (ed.). *Vinland Revisited: the Norse World at the Turn of the First Millennium.* St. John's: Historic Sites Association of Newfoundland & Labrador, Inc., 2003.

Looker, Janet. *Disaster Canada.* Toronto: Lynx Images, 2000.

Macleod, Malcolm (ed.). *Crossroads Country. Memories of Pre-Confederation Newfoundland, at the Intersection of American, British and Canadian Connections.* St. Johns: Breakwater Books, 1999.

McNab, Leslie. "Reviving a Lost Language. Students at St. Anne's School in Conne River are Learning to Speak Mi'Kmaq." *The Downhomer.* Vol. XVI. No. 8 (January, 2004), 72-74.

Magnusson, Magnus (ed.). *Chambers Biographical Dictionary.* Edinburgh: Chambers Harrap Publishers, 1993.

_____, and Hermann Pálsson (trans.) *The Vinland Sagas. The Norse Discovery of America.* Harmondsworth, Middlesex, UK: Penguin Books, 1983.

Major, Kevin. *As Near to Heaven by Sea. A History of Newfoundland & Labrador.* Toronto: Penguin Books, 2001.

Marshall, Ingeborg., *A History and Ethnography of the Beothuk.* Montreal & Kingston: McGill-Queen's University Press, 1996.

_____. *Reports and Letters by George Christopher Pulling Relating to the Beothuk Indians of Newfoundland.* St. John's: Breakwater Books, 1989.

Matthews, Keith. *Lectures on the History of Newfoundland.* St. John's: Breakwater Books, 1988.

Mercer, W. Edgar. *A History of Methodism in Twillingate and Notre Dame Bay, Newfoundland, 1831-1931.* Twillingate: Twillingate Sun Publishing, 1932.

Murphy, Donald L. and Duyane Alexander, "Seek and Destroy? The History of Iceberg Demolition Experiments." USCG Proceedings (Spring, 2005), 50-54.

Murray, Jean M. (ed). *The Newfoundland Journal of Aaron Thomas 1794, Able Seaman in HMS Boston*. Don Mills, Ontario: Longmans Canada, 1968.

Neary, Steve. *The Enemy on our Doorstep. The German Attacks at Bell Island, Newfoundland, 1942*. St. John's: Jesperson Publishing, 1994.

Newfoundland Historical Society. *A Short History of Newfoundland & Labrador*. Portugal Cove-St. Philip's, NL: Boulder Publications, 2008.

Nicholson, G.W.L. *The Fighting Newfoundlander. A History of the Royal Newfoundland Regiment*. Montreal: McGill-Queens, 2006.

____. *More Fighting Newfoundlanders. A History of Newfoundland's Fighting Forces in the Second World War*. St. John's: Government of Newfoundland & Labrador, 1969.

O'Flaherty, Patrick. *Lost Country: The Rise and Fall of Newfoundland 1843-1933*. St. John's: Long Beach Press, 2005.

____. *Old Newfoundland: A History to 1843*. St. John's: Long Beach Press, 1999.

O'Neill, Paul. *Breakers. Stories from Newfoundland & Labrador*. St. John's: Breakwater Books, 1982.

____. *The Oldest City. The Story of St. John's, Newfoundland*. St. Philip's, NL: Boulder Publications, 2003.

Pastore, Ralph T. *Shanawdithit's People. The Archaeology of the Beothuks*. St. John's: Atlantic Archaeology Ltd., 1992.

Pedley, Rev. Charles. *The History of Newfoundland From the Earliest Times to the year 1860*. London: Longman, Green, Longman, Roberts and Green, 1863.

Pope, Peter E. *The Many Landfalls of John Cabot*. Toronto: University of Toronto Press, 1997.

Prowse, D.W. *A History of Newfoundland*. London: Macmillan & Co., 1895.

Rogers, J.D. *A Historical Geography of the British Colonies, Vol. V, Part 5, Newfoundland*. Oxford: The Clarendon Press, 1911.

Rompkey, Bill. *The Story of Labrador*. Montreal: McGill-Queen's University Press, 2003.

_____. "Outpost No More. Who are These Labradorians and Why Aren't They Newfoundlanders?" *Luminus*. Vol. XXX, No. 1 (Spring/Summer, 2005), pp. 6-7.

Rose, George A. "Drilling and Fishing the Grand Bank of Newfoundland." *Newfoundland Quarterly*. Vol. XCVI. No. 1 (Spring, 2003), 28-29.

Rowe, Frederick W. *Extinction: The Beothuks of Newfoundland*. Toronto: McGraw-Hill Ryerson, 1977.

Ryan, Shannon. *Fish Out of Water. The Newfoundland Saltfish Trade 1814-1914*. St. John's: Breakwater Books, 1986.

Smallwood, Joseph R. *Newfoundland Miscellany*, Vol. 1. St. John's: Newfoundland Book Publishers, 1978.

_____. *Newfoundland 1941 Handbook Gazetteer and Almanac*. St. John's: Long Brothers, 1941.

_____ (ed.). *The Book of Newfoundland.* 6 Vols. St. John's: Newfoundland Book Publishers, 1975.

Story, G.M., Kirwin, W.J. and J.D.A. Widdowson. *Dictionary of Newfoundland English.* Toronto: University of Toronto Press, 1982.

Such, Peter. *Vanished Peoples. The Archaic, Dorset & Beothuk People of Newfoundland.* Toronto: NC Press, 1978.

Tankersley, Kenneth B. "The Puzzle of the First Americans." *Discovering Archaeology*, Vol. II. No. 1 (February, 2000), 31-33.

Walls, Martha (ed.). *Newfoundland & Labrador Book of Everything.* Lunenburg, NS: MacIntyre Purcell Publishing, 2006.

Wetzel, Gerry Michael. "Decolonizing Ktaqmkuk History." MLA thesis, Dalhousie University, 1996.

White, Marian Frances. *Discover Canada: Newfoundland & Labrador.* Toronto: Grolier, 1994.

Wilk, Martin B. *Newfoundland & Labrador 400 Years Later. A Statistical Portrait.* St. John's: Publishing information not given, 1983.

Witcher, Eric. *Historic Barr'd Islands. From English Roots.* St. John's: Flanker Press, 2011.

A Year Book & Almanac of Newfoundland. St. John's: J.W. Withers, King's Printer, Various years.

UNPUBLISHED

Anon. "A Short History of Our Church Life from 1897-1947," 1947.

Clarke, Ernest G. "Be it Ever So Humble..." n.d.

Gillett, C. William. "Memories of the Schooner *Grace Boehner*." n.d.

Loveridge, Stephen. "Diaries," Transcribed by Donald Loverridge. Various years.

Tanner, Angus L. "*Grace Boehner*." 1974.

AUDIO-VISUAL

Budgell, Anne and Nigel Markham (directors). *Last Days of Okak*. CBC Newfoundland & Labrador Television, 1985.

Smallwood, Joseph R. and Poole, Cyril F. (editors-in-chief). *The Encyclopedia of Newfoundland & Labrador*. 5 volumes. CD-ROM Edition. Version 1.8. St. John's: Harry Cuff Publications, 1997.

Starowicz, Mark (executive producer). *Canada: A Peoples' History*. Vol. I. Canada: CBC/Radio Canada, 2000.

Wadden, Marie (producer/narrator). "Voyage to the Happy Island." From *East of Canada: The Story of Newfoundland*. St. John's: Fortis, 1997.

Wolochatiuk, Tim (director). *Stealing Mary: Last of the Red Indians*. Windup Filmworks & Firecrown Productions, 2005.

INTERNET

Barnes, Howard T. "Some Physical Properties of Icebergs and a Method for Their Destruction." *Proceedings of the Royal Society* (1 March, 1927). Cited in: http://rspa.royalsocietypublishing.org.

"Bonavista, NL, 'Coyote' Was Really Wolf, Tests Confirm." *CBC News. Newfoundland & Labrador.* 25 May, 2012. http://www.cbc.ca/news/canada/newfoundland-labrador

"A Collection of Newfoundland Wills...Catherine Wrey," *Newfoundland's Grand Banks* website. http://ngb.chebucto.org/Wills/wrey-catherine-6-73.shtml

The Dictionary of Canadian Biography Online. www.biographi.ca

The Internet Archive. www.archive.org

"Jean Baudoin: Priest Missionary at Beaubassin (Chignecto) in Acadia." *Placentia Area Historical Society.* http://collections.ic.gc.ca/placentia/j baudoi.htm

Libarary and Archives Canada. www.collectionscanada.gc.ca

McGill Teaching and Research. http://www.archives.mcgill.ca

The Mary Celeste – *Fact Not Fiction.* www.maryceleste.net

Memorial University of Newfoundland. Digital Archives Initiative (DAI). http://collections.mun.ca/index.php

Newfoundland & Labrador Heritage. www.heritage.nf.ca

Newfoundland Rangers Home Page. http://home.ca.inter.net/~elinorr/ranger-main.html

NL Gen Web. http://nl.canadagenweb.org

Oliver, Jenny. "The Mystery of the *Mountaineer.*" *Poole Museum Society Blog.* http://poolemuseumsociety.wordpress.com

Qalipu Mi'Kmaq First Nations Band. www.qualipu.ca

Stories From These Shores

Shanties & Sea Songs. http://shanty.rendance.org

PERSONAL COMMUNICATION

Anstey, Milt.
Clarke, Leonard.
Linfield, Donald.
Linfield, Peggy.
Manuel, Alfred.
Troke, Jim.

Made in the USA
Charleston, SC
19 July 2016